Television
WHAT'S ON, WHO'S WATCHING, AND WHAT IT MEANS

Television

WHAT'S ON, WHO'S WATCHING, AND WHAT IT MEANS

George Comstock
Syracuse University
Syracuse, New York

Erica Scharrer
State University of New York, Geneseo
Geneseo, New York

ACADEMIC PRESS

San Diego   *London*   *Boston*   *New York*   *Sydney*   *Tokyo*   *Toronto*

Copyright © 1999 by ACADEMIC PRESS

All Rights Reserved.
No part of this publication may be reproduced or transmitted in any form or by any
means, electronic or mechanical, including photocopy, recording, or any information
storage and retrieval system, without permission in writing from the publisher.

Academic Press
a division of Harcourt Brace & Company
525 B Street, Suite 1900, San Diego, California 92101-4495, USA
http://www.apnet.com

Academic Press
24-28 Oval Road, London NW1 7DX, UK
http://www.hbuk.co.uk/ap/

Library of Congress Catalog Card Number: 99-60584

International Standard Book Number: 0-12-183580-4

PRINTED IN THE UNITED STATES OF AMERICA
99 00 01 02 03 04 MM 9 8 7 6 5 4 3 2 1

CONTENTS

PART I

The Industry and the Audience

v

PART **II**

Manufacturing the World

PART **III**

Of Time and Content

PREFACE

We think of our work not only as examining the social and behavioral scientific evidence for the influence and role in society of a mass medium, but also as implicitly advocating certain principles for the aggregation and interpretation of scientific findings. Our five guidelines are:

1. The perfect study is a myth.
2. The fatal flaw is a political expedient.
3. Hypothesis testing is the recourse for dilemmas.
4. The dictates of meta-analysis apply to qualitative reviews.
5. Truth lies in patterns.

No single study will decide any very important question, and few sets of data should be wholly dismissed despite imperfections in their collection or over-interpretation by the investigators. Data provide partial answers that rise or fall in credibility in the context of other data—the "fatal flaw" is a label employed by those with vested interests, who are often in the employ of threatened industries such as advertising, television, and tobacco, to discredit uncongenial data.

When we have been faced with a seeming conflict in outcomes, our preference has been to formulate a hypothesis that could be tested to resolve it. One example is the data on scholastic performance. If we were right that a particular analysis (Gaddy, 1986) so truncated the outcomes for achievement that the influence of television was precluded, we should find that associations with seemingly more formidable predictors similarly are null. Another example is the data on antisocial behavior. If the evidence from the laboratory-type experiments can be applied to everyday life, then we should find associations between exposure to violence in television entertainment and antisocial behavior in school and on the playground. In both cases, additional data governed interpretation of initial evidence.

Meta-analysis advocates the search for an estimate of the average or modal relationship between variables rather than a tally of the number of studies in support or opposition (Hunt, 1997). If this is a sound approach, reveals consistencies in data thought to be in conflict, and sometimes reverses conventional wisdom when applied quantitatively, then logic requires that it guide qualitative assessments. The implication (practically speaking) is that the quantitative tabulation of outcomes is replaced by subjective judgment in making an estimate. The corollary (from a logical perspective) is that such a qualitative assessment will participate in the process of discovery, as does original research, by identifying relationships and recognizing patterns observable only when a literature is examined in the aggregate.

The pattern of findings across bodies of data then becomes the central element in reaching conclusions. We do not expect a study to answer our questions. We expect instead that the answers will come from the clustering of outcomes, whether in the form of an estimate of the relationship between variables in the meta-analytic sense or the convergence of findings of a disparate order that encourage a particular broad interpretation.

ACKNOWLEDGMENTS

Our first debt is to the hundreds of persons who collected the data on which we have drawn. We hope none are disconsolate at our treatment of their work.

We thank David Rubin, Dean, S. I. Newhouse School, for providing a congenial atmosphere, and the S. I. Newhouse chair for financial support. We also thank Kim Bissell, the doctoral candidate who was graduate assistant to the first author, for her help during the unplacid days of final preparation.

We were fortunate that several books that dealt with certain topics we were covering appeared during our writing. We have not always agreed with the interpretations of their authors, but we have found them invaluable. They are:

Dearing, J. W., & Rogers, E. M. (1996). *Agenda-setting*. Thousand Oaks, CA: Sage.

Hamilton, J. T. (1998). *Channeling violence*. Princeton, NJ: Princeton University Press.

McCombs, M. E., Shaw, D. L., & Weaver, D. (1997). *Communication and democracy*. Mahwah, NJ: Erlbaum.

Robinson, J. P., & Godbey, G. (1997). *Time for life: The surprising ways Americans use their time*. University Park: The Pennsylvania State University Press.

Van Evra, J. (1998). *Television and child development*. Mahwah, NJ: Erlbaum.

Webster, J. G., & Phalen, P. F. (1997). *The mass audience. Rediscovering the dominant model*. Mahwah, NJ: Erlbaum.

PART I

The Industry and the Audience

Television is clearly the 800-pound gorilla of free time . . .
        John P. Robinson & Geoffrey Godbey, *Time for Life*

In 1946, two television networks broadcast 11 hours of programming between 7 and 11 P.M. each week. There were only a handful of stations. About 10,000 sets were in use. By 1950, there were about 100 stations, the number of sets had increased to 10.5 million, and four networks—the three that are so familiar, the American Broadcasting Company (ABC), the Columbia Broadcasting System (CBS), and the National Broadcasting Company (NBC), and the short-lived and long unsung DuMont Television Network (DTN)—offered more than 90 hours of programming each week. Today, there are about 1600 stations and more than 224 million sets in use. Over 70% of households have a choice of 10 or more channels, many of them offering programs 24 hours a day.

Television has become a medium of unparalleled reach with a seemingly extraordinary range of choices for the viewer. Its popularity, achieved almost instantly, and consequent growth have significantly changed the environment in which people grow up and live their lives. It has made the pitching of products and the techniques employed in that endeavor a part of everyday life. Its programming peoples the screen with a highly specialized population distinct from the country at large and emphasizes themes more in accord with hopes and fears than with reality. And in response, the viewing public includes television among its priorities for the allocation of time, rejects or embraces programs, and adopts strategies of time use and cognitive processing so that a place can be made for television among the day's other activities, thereby producing the demographics that constitute the currency of economic exchange between television and advertising. We begin with the industry and the audience because they are the foundation for all else. Our topics are the three eras that describe the evolution of the medium; the main means by which television is financially supported, advertising; and the behavior of the vast numbers who assemble to attend to the medium.

Three Eras

The evolution of American television over the five decades since its introduction divides roughly but unambiguously into three eras. We label them the early years, from the late 1940s through the 1950s; equilibrium, from 1960 through the 1970s; and transition, from 1980 to the present.

I. EARLY YEARS

In 1949, the Federal Communications Commission (FCC) imposed a freeze on the granting of licenses for television stations. This remarkable step, which seemingly disrupted the diffusion of a sought-after innovation, remains memorable for three reasons:

1. It represents a paradigm for policy with regard to television that would be repeated, most recently with regard to high-definition television (HDTV).
2. It unintendedly imposed a gigantic experimental design on the nation by which it became possible to assess with confidence some of the effects of the medium.
3. It demonstrated irrefutably the enormous public satisfaction with television.

3

Almost 3 years passed before the license freeze that began late in 1949 ended in mid-1952. Ostensibly, the justification was a review of spectrum problems to avoid interference among signals. However, as observers have pointed out, this could have been accomplished by able engineers within a few months (Winston, 1986). The consequence of this step was to ensure that the oligopoly of CBS and NBC in radio would be transferred to television (Boddy, 1990). These two profited from a monopoly in about 80% of the more than 60 markets with television service and established themselves as preeminent among advertisers and audiences alike.

The industry in fact was not at all frozen. During this period, the number of stations operating on prefreeze licenses doubled to more than 100, sets in use increased 15-fold to more than 15 million, and television came to account for 70% of broadcast advertising revenues. It was a windfall for those in place; in fact, 40 of the 60 markets served by the 108 stations in operation were single-station markets, where the monopoly enriched NBC and CBS. The victory of vested interests was complete when ABC—with the help of a capital-infusing merger with United-Paramount theaters—proved superior to DuMont in vying for third place, while the FCC freeze in effect made any fourth national network impossible.

This step, along with the adoption by the FCC of a Very High Frequency (VHF)-based system that would permit continuing manufacture of sets and their immediate use in preference to an Ultra High Frequency (UHF)-based system that would provide a far better picture but would take several years to develop, represented a persisting FCC disposition. So, too, was its circumscribing of FM radio so that it became an adjunct to the AM band despite being able to deliver superior service to the listener. That disposition is to favor existing economic interests and immediate prosperity over challenges from newcomers and superior technological performance.

Allocating licenses to some areas while denying them to others implemented the quasi-experimental design of Cook and Campbell (1979), a "time series with switching replications." Data comparing trends at (a) the adopting sites, early and late, with those at (b) their nonadopting counterparts (in the first instance, sites without television; in the second, sites that already had television) make possible conclusions about the effects of the introduction of television. Examples include displacement of comic-book buying and library fiction reading (later in this chapter) and increased antisocial behavior (Chapter 8).

The popularity of television was clear enough from the rapid diffusion of sets at early television sites. However, truly remarkable was the even more rapid dissemination at the later sites (Fig. 1.1). At the early sites, it took more than $3\frac{1}{2}$ years for half of households to acquire a set, and 5 years before 75% had one. At the later sites, it took only a year for half the households to acquire a set, and 3 years to reach the 75% mark. This pattern was abetted by greatly increased

Mean household saturation

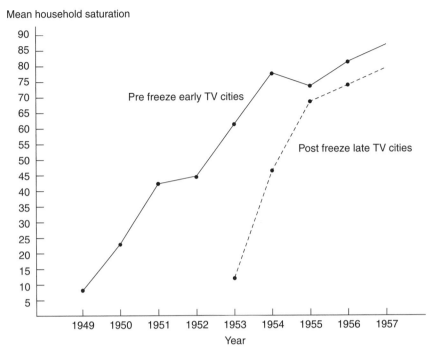

FIGURE 1.1   Rate of television adoption: freeze (no station licenses issued by FCC), prefreeze (stations were licensed in late 1940s), postfreeze (stations were licensed in early 1950s). Adapted from *Quasi-Experimentation: Design and Analysis Issues for Field Settings,* by Thomas Cook and Donald Campbell. Copyright 1979 by Houghton Mifflin Company. Used with permission.

quantities of programming and declining set prices; nevertheless, the more people saw of television, the more they wanted it in their homes.

We are in accord with Winston (1986) that a "supervening necessity" was necessary for television to reach this receptive marketplace, because technologically it was feasible earlier. In this case, the medium provided a new product line for the huge electronics industry created by World War II, thereby protecting corporate fortunes, bolstering employment, and strengthening the economy. As movies earlier had served the growing urban masses, television was an ideal source of diversion for the postwar shift to the suburbs. Television was more compelling to the viewer than radio was to the listener, and the interweaving of advertising with entertainment through visual imagery created a newly powerful means of marketing brand names—one that, with its foundation in the home, fit perfectly the mood of a nation turning away from war and toward home building, childrearing, and everyday jobs.

TABLE 1.1   Selected Trends in Growth of Television

Daily household use of television (five year averages)			
	Hours : Minutes		
	1982–83/ 1986–87	1987–88/ 1991–92	1992–93/ 1996–97
Annual	7:05	6:59	7:14
Fall–Winter	7:41	7:31	7:40

Prime time shares of households using television and sets in use (annual averages)

	Percentages			
	1983–84	1987–88	1992–93	1996–97
Big three (ABC, CBS, NBC)	80	72(67)	63(55)	47(41)
Total broadcast networks (ABC, CBS, NBC, Fox, UPN, WB)			73(64)	67(59)
Independents and PBS[a]	13	23(21)	14(12)	6 (5)
Total broadcast outlets other than big three	13	23(21)	24(21)	26(23)
Basic cable[b]	4	8 (7)	22(19)	35(31)
Premium cable[c]	3	5 (5)	5 (4)	6 (5)

Share, Households Using Television (HUT) $= \dfrac{\text{Rating}}{\text{Total HUT}}$, with HHs in Nielsen calculation able to contribute to more than one source so total shares may exceed 100%.

Share, Sets in Use $= \dfrac{\text{HUT Share}}{\text{Total HUT Shares}}$, our calculation with a 100% base and the assumption that set use is equally distributed across shares.

Number of channels available to viewers

	Percentage U.S. Households			
Channels	1981	1985	1993	1999 (est.)
1–6	25	8	4	1
7–10	22	17	9	6
11–14	40	25	7	5
15–plus	13	50	80	88

(continues)

By the end of the 1950s, television had achieved the majority of its eventual near-universal diffusion (Table 1.1). When the freeze ended, there were 400 applications for station licenses. By the end of the decade, 87% of households—almost 46 million—had one or more television sets. There were 510 commercial stations in operation (433 VHF and 77 UHF) and 35 educational stations

TABLE 1.1 *(continued)*

	Video resources						
	Percentage U.S. Households						
	1950	1960	1970	1980	1990	1993	1999 (est.)
TV Households	10	87	96	98	98	98	98
Multi-set		12	35	50	65	71	75
1 set			65	49	35	31	25
2 sets			29	35	41	37	35
3-plus sets			6	15	24	34	40
Color			34	81	96	97	98
Total Cable			7	20	56	61	68 (75)
Premium Cable					29	29	29 (41)
Remote Control					77	87	95
Videocassette Recorder					66	77	85

	Television stations						
Commercial				Public and Educational			
Year	Total	VHF	UHF	Year	Total	VHF	UHF
1960	533	446	87	1960	44	34	10
1970	677	501	176	1970	184	78	106
1980	734	516	218	1998	367	125	242
1990	1,092	547	545				
1998	1,209	558	651				

[a] Includes local, public, super stations, and other distant broadcast signals.

[b] Includes WTBS.

[c] Subscribers receiving at least one premium channel; excludes satellite Alternate Delivery Service (ADS).

( ) Includes satellite ADS (Alternate Delivery Service).

Adapted from *Broadcasting and Cable,* "People's Choice Nov. 3–9, 1997," "People's Choice Jan. 5–11, 1998," "People's Choice Jan. 26–Feb. 1, 1998," November 17, 1997, January 26, 1998, February 9, 1998; "Public Broadcasting and Federal Policy," by J. Carey, in P. R. Newburg (Ed.), *New Directions in Telecommunications Policy. Vol. 1; Regulatory Policy: Telephony and Mass Media,* Duke University Press; *The Evolution of American Television,* by G. Comstock, 1989, Sage; "Television in America: Success Story," by L. W. Lichty, in P. S. Cook, D. Gomery, and L. W. Lichty (Eds.), *American Media,* 1989, Wilson Center Press; *Report on Television, 1992–1993,* by Nielsen Media Research, 1993; *Trends in Television,* by Television Bureau of Advertising, 1997; *1998 Report on Television* by Nielsen Media Research, 1998.

(28 VHF and 7 UHF) mostly connected with colleges or universities. Daily hours of set use in television households had increased 10% from about $4\frac{1}{2}$ hours in 1950 to about 5 hours in 1960.

The public responded by abandoning to some degree a host of competing activities. Set owners spent less time with other media, such as theater movies, radio, and the reading of comic books, magazines, and books. They also engaged less in social activities outside the home, hobbies, housework, and even sleep (although this might be an artifact of differences in the labeling of the few minutes prior to actual sleep); and spent less time attending religious observances and community events (Parker, 1960; Robinson & Converse, 1972; Szalai, 1972; Williams, 1986). After a few years, some nonmedia activities approached their prior levels but decreased use of other media remained; thus diversity essentially was maintained, with deficits coming from activities engaged in most often (Belson, 1959). Television soon became an activity shared with other activities, including reading, although about three-fourths of the public would consider it at the forefront or the main activity in which they were engaged (Robinson & Godbey, 1997; Szalai, 1972).

The effects on media, entertainment, and sports were dramatic (Bogart, 1972b). Moviegoers stayed home and theaters closed. Comic books lost a large proportion of their readership. National advertisers, seeing that people were spending less time reading, turned away from major magazines and toward television, and the *Saturday Evening Post, Collier's, Life, Look* and others went out of business. Some sports suffered (minor league baseball, local boxing from the competition), whereas others benefited from the attention and techniques of coverage (golf, tennis, professional football).

The pattern that would persist for many years also had been established:

1. The reaching of an audience that amounted to almost the whole country.
2. Dominance by the three networks, with a combined audience share exceeding 90% in prime time (Monday–Saturday, 8–11 P.M. on the East and West Coasts, 7–10 P.M. in the Midwest; Sunday 7–11 P.M.).
3. A pervasive emphasis on entertainment—whether measured by tabulating programs by format; the allocation of time to entertainment, sports, and news; the emphases predominant within the two nonentertainment categories; or the motives of viewers.

The emphasis on entertainment (see Table 2.2) was made inevitable by the paradigm adopted in the United States for the operation of television. The Federal Communications Act of 1932 admonished the licensee that performance must be in "the public interest, convenience, and necessity" without further definition, and the FCC implemented these criteria in a genteel and diffident way (Boddy, 1990; Comstock, 1989). The absence of the paternalism common in many other countries—by which we mean concrete if broad stipulations regarding the cultural, educational, and public service goals of broadcasting—coupled with open competition for survival meant that the main means of financial support was the drawing of large audiences attractive to advertisers. The entertaining of viewers was clearly the best technique for the task.

The same forces brought an end to the so-called Golden Age of television. This was the era of live television productions, generally from New York, that often were controversial, and sometimes compelling and emotionally involving. With surprising frequency, they became Broadway plays or Hollywood movies, such as *Twelve Angry Men, Marty, The Days of Wine and Roses,* and *No Time for Sergeants.* This era began with the *Kraft Television Theater* on May 7, 1947, and ended a decade later with the final presentation of *Playhouse 90* (Brown, 1977). Over these years, there were more than 35 differently titled variants, ranging up to 90 minutes in length. They were replaced by the industrially more efficient series filmed or taped in Hollywood in which a single concept could be embellished and a set of characters intertwined over many programs with far less chance of raising the ire of a sponsor or producing an ambiance discordant with the hawking of brand names (Barnouw, 1978).

Another major shift during the decade was the transfer of program control from the sponsors and their advertising agencies to the networks. The quiz show scandals seemed to be responsible for this shift. Revlon had manipulated the success of contestants on such favorite prime-time programs as *Twenty One, The $64,000 Question,* and *The $64,000 Challenge* to ensure that winners were popular with viewers. There was a congressional investigation, a scattering of criminal charges, a few destroyed and many redirected careers, and the networks assumed responsibility for what would go on the air in the future. However, the networks had long been struggling to gain control of programming (Boddy, 1990). Thus the move was inevitable—as was the change from live drama to filmed or taped series—because it was in the interests of the networks. The networks now would be better able to choose and schedule programming to attract viewers; they could sell programs piecemeal commercial-by-commercial, thereby enlarging the market for advertising; and by controlling program production they would be better positioned to profit from subsequent syndication.

There was much else that would change in the coming years. Television was black and white; screens were comparatively small, typically ranging from 13 to 19 inches; fewer than 1 out of 10 households had more than one set; and the number of channels available was very limited. Nevertheless, the pattern for the next two decades had essentially been cast.

II. EQUILIBRIUM

The next 20 years were marked by a substantial increase in the number of stations, the consolidation of television's initial success with the public, a variety of technological advances, including the advent of color as the industry and household standard, and the creation of public television as it operates today. However, domination by the three networks was the most distinguishing feature.

The slightly more than 500 commercial stations would increase almost 50% to more than 725. The proportion of households with television sets would rise slowly to about 98%. At the beginning of the period, about 7% of households had more than one set. By its end, about half of households had two or more sets. Other, primarily technological innovations included the remote control, which would figure prominently in the use Americans would make of the greater number of channels that would become available in the 1980s and 1990s; larger screens with superior resolution; lowered production costs per set that the competitive marketplace would pass on to consumers, further justifying the acquisition of additional sets; lighter and trimmer sets for which the term portable was far more appropriate than for the bulky items with handles of a few years earlier; and revised spectrum policies that made possible the large increase in the number of stations.

Noncommercial television made enormous strides. By the end of the 1950s, there were only about 35 stations in operation. Many confined their programming to the courses and other offerings of the educational institutions with which they were affiliated. The tripartite public television system of today essentially was created in 1967 by Congress, with the Corporation for Public Broadcasting (CPB) as the policy-making overseer; the Public Broadcasting System (PBS) as the collection of stations by which programs reach the public; and the federal government, the great private foundations, and corporations as major sources of financial support.

When this new era began, there were about 125 noncommercial stations in operation. Some would not participate or would participate only partly in delivering PBS programming because the licenses were held by educational organizations that wished to pursue their own instructional goals. By the end of the 1970s, the number of stations had more than doubled and almost all of the newcomers participated wholly in the CPB–PBS scheme.

The new system in part represented the vision of Newton Minow. The FCC chairman became notorious in the industry shortly after appointment with his speech to the National Association of Broadcasters in 1961. After saying that nothing was better when television was "good," he continued:

> But when television is bad, nothing is worse. I invite you to sit down in front of your television set when your station goes on the air. . . . (Y)ou will observe a vast wasteland. . . . (G)ame shows, violence, audience participation shows, formula comedies . . . blood and thunder, mayhem, violence, sadism, murder . . . private eyes, gangsters, more violence, and cartoons. And, endlessly, commercials. . . . (Minow, 1978).

In his brief two years as FCC Chairman, Minow helped set the stage for the later development of public broadcasting. First, he artfully forced the sale of a

New York channel to the noncommercial sector in a city where there was no public television. Second, he was instrumental in persuading Congress to require that after January 1963 all sets manufactured be capable of receiving both VHF and UHF channels.

The latter was a major advance for public television and competition and diversity in general, for at the time fewer than 10% of households had sets that could receive UHF channels. Now, UHF could be used for public television in the many communities where VHF channels had been fully allocated to commercial interests, and increasingly sizable proportions of the public could be reached by UHF channels whatever their allegiance. The statistics for the end of the decade attest to the success of this step: 60% of public stations and 30% of commercial stations were UHF. Nevertheless, the PBS audience share in prime time where a channel was available was averaging between 3 and 4%, and public television was and would remain a comparatively infrequently used source of programming in the average household.

Cable systems, which had existed before television where radio reception was poor because of distance or terrain, were used for television from almost its first years. These systems were called CATV for "community antennae television." By the mid-1960s, cable systems were used more widely to supply additional television signals to communities with only one or two broadcast stations. Yet, even by the end of the 1970s, after more than 20 years of potential growth, only about one-fifth of the nation's households were subscribers.

By comparison, by 1965 about one of five communities could receive no more than the local affiliates of the three networks. These two decades then were the years of maturity for the initial system by which television was introduced to America, with commercial television, the three networks, and broadcasting at the forefront, and limited choices for viewers the norm.

III. TRANSITION

By the late 1990s, there would be about 1200 commercial and about 365 noncommercial standard-power television stations in operation. These represent vast increases of more than 60% and about 40%, respectively, over the totals at the end of the 1970s. In each case, a majority would be UHF (in 1997, 638 vs 558 and 241 vs 124, respectively). Other statistics would attest to the undiminished prominence of television in the home: the proportion of households with television would slightly outpace the population growth; the proportion of multiset households would increase; and cable subscriptions would rise.

Yet neither fundamental growth, which occurred much earlier, nor the maintenance of the pattern that marked the 1960s and 1970s could be said to characterize the period. Instead, it was the dissolution of that pattern before the twin forces of technology and viewer preferences. We look upon it as an era of transition because the eventual configuration of its elements is uncertain.

The most significant aspect has been the enormous increase in the number of channels offered viewers. This was the result of the further diffusion of television technology—the increase in the number of stations, the rise in cable subscriptions, and the swift adoption of the videocassette recorder (VCR). The seeming implications were that conclusions drawn from decades of data on television would have to be revised and viewing might increase because more people would find what they wanted.

A central factor was the use of satellites and other technological innovations that made it possible to relay a much larger number of signals at a much lower cost per signal. Ironically, Direct Broadcast Satellite (DBS) systems would remain a minor although now growing part of the television marketplace—with alternative delivery systems to broadcast and cable (most of which are DBS) in about 10% of households by 1999 (our estimate, based on Nielsen Media Research data, 1995–1997). The more important role of satellites was to make available to cable operators a great array of signals they could disseminate to the home.

Consumer acquisition of new electronic media technologies—new media or new means of delivering old media—in our view occurs in accord with three laws. We base our model on diffusion of innovation research (Rogers, 1995), the history of media diffusion (Himmelweit, Oppenheim, & Vince, 1958; Lin & Jeffres, 1998; MacBeth, 1996; Schramm, Lyle, & Parker, 1961; Williams, 1986), and various studies of the adoption of and satisfaction with these technologies (Dobrow, 1990; Ducey, Krugman, & Eckrich, 1983; Jacobs, 1995; Levy & Windahl, 1984; Perse, 1990a; Perse & Ferguson, 1993; Williams, Phillips, & Lum, 1985). The first law is that of functional equivalence, which requires that new technologies serve at least most of the functions of established technology. The rapidity of adoption will then be a function of costs and success in this dimension, with greater convenience or superior performance prerequisites. As costs fall, adoption will become more widespread. Technologies that fail this first requirement will be sharply circumscribed in adoption unless costs are trivial or nonexistent or the technology provides novel gratifications. At some point early in the evolution of the media, novel rewards were, conceptually at least, a possibility, but at this point in time it is difficult to imagine what they might be. Even virtual reality in our opinion will be judged on how powerfully it provides gratifications previously sought from other sources. The second law is the Janus-like motives of satisfaction and dissatisfaction. Those viewers particularly pleased by what they are receiving will want the means to receive more of the same. Those not as pleased will be attracted to technology that offers new options. The VCR neatly veered in its main appeal from the first, giving viewers more of the same, to the second in offering an alternative to the dissatisfied, as movie watching replaced off-the-air taping as the major motive for acquisition. Cable benefits by serving both the pleased and the dissatisfied—more of the kind of programming already available as well as options new to the local market—as do Direct Broadcast Satellite (DBS) systems and other alternative means of delivery. The third law is affordability. All technological innovations with costs—in this instance, color, cable, the VCR, DBS, and initially television—are adopted more frequently at first by households of higher socioeconomic status. Among households lower in socioeconomic status, rates of adoption will catch up as costs fall, as was the case with television, color, and, currently, the VCR.

For most of the 20th century, the proportion of the Gross National Product spent on communications media by consumers has been fairly constant across the decades (McCombs, 1972; McCombs & Eyal, 1980), implying that one technology can succeed only at the expense of others. This does not rule out coexistence, as an established technology may stagnate as younger-age cohorts turn to newer technologies. It does mean that costs are a crucial factor. Declining costs for older or newer technologies result in greater survival space for competitors.

More recent data, however, offer a bullish correction (Dupagne, 1994, 1997; Nog & Grant, 1997; Son & McCombs, 1993; Wood & O'Hare, 1991). Apparently, the attractiveness of the new electronic technologies has widened the sphere of alternatives from which financial outlays can be redirected, with the result that the proportion spent on media began to increase in the 1980s. For example, the recent analyses of expenditures between 1978 and 1990 by Glascock (1993) indicate that the newer electronic technologies have converted communications media from a staple drawing a constant expenditure to an expanding sector of the economy. This effect is so culturally robust in the developed world that it has also been observed in Great Britain (Dupagne, 1994) and Belgium (Dupagne, 1997). The proportion of expenditures on communications media by consumers has increased as a consequence of the introduction of cable; interestingly, advertising expenditures have followed a similar trend, probably because many advertisers are fearful of losing market share among those attending to older media while also desiring to reach those using newer technologies. We speculate that as media offer more varied gratifications, as exemplified by encompassing home entertainment centers (Lin, 1993), the earlier long-standing constraint will lift somewhat further as resources are shifted from noncommunication activities, such as vacation travel or automobile replacement. From the perspective of the marketplace, this means a larger share for communications. From the perspective of the consumer, it implies a remapping of the cognitive sphere in which communications become an option among a larger array of leisure choices.

In addition to the increase in choices offered viewers, the principal developments of the period were:

1. The decided failure of three prophecies—the cable-based wiring of America for the delivery of services, the in-home adoption of an electronically delivered newspaper, and the widespread use of interactive television for both leisure and practical applications.
2. The emergence of a competitive fourth network, Fox.
3. The waning of the three pioneering broadcast networks, with their total prime-time share falling below 50%.
4. A new code for labeling entertainment programs in regard to their suitability for young viewers, and a system whereby parents and others will be able to zap signals automatically if a label identifies them as unwanted.

The concepts of the wired city and the wired nation foresaw the linking of almost everyone—to the magnitude of the more than 98% of households reached by television—by cable in an electronic network delivering public and private services such as burglary and fire alarms, medical advice, counseling of various types, adult education, and armchair shopping, banking, and investment. Some of these services are currently available electronically in many homes, but the scale envisioned has not been achieved, with cable subscribers accounting for only about two-thirds of households.

The electronically delivered newspaper was to bypass the printing press, trucks, newsstands, newspaper delivery, and ink-stained hands by transmitting information and features selected by the viewer to the home screen, where it would be converted by an adjunct printer to a custom-tailored newspaper. In communities in all parts of the country, in-home trials consistently have indicated that there is insufficient consumer interest, and a survey of college students reveals that electronic newspapers are viewed as unsatisfactory substitutes for the current medium (Mueller & Kamerer, 1995).

Interactive television is the use of the set's controls to respond reiteratively to signals on the screen. It presumably would have been an accessory of the wired city and wired nation. Interactive television also has been a feature of particular cable systems. Subscribers could vote on public issues, participate in group games and open contests, call up stored information as with the Internet, and submit to the queries of marketing researchers. The most comprehensive consumer test was the QUBE system that began operating in Columbus, Ohio, in 1980; there as elsewhere, viewers persistently displayed little interest in these opportunities, and interactive television has become a technology without significant implementation. In fact, results from a recent national probability sample of over 1800 viewers suggest that interactive television will fail to displace the current technology because viewers are unwilling to invest the necessary effort and would miss the social interaction that often accompanies viewing (Lee & Lee, 1995). On the other hand, many of the features anticipated have become available on the Internet. Television, with the dominant place of entertainment in its appeal and the limited range of interactive options then available, simply was not for most viewers an effective pioneer.

The phenomenon of a fourth competitive network represents a pattern established much earlier. The analogy for Fox (whose prime-time ratings have come to approximate about 75% of the average for ABC, CBS, and NBC) was the calculated appeal of ABC in the 1960s to the weekend sports viewer, mostly males for whom little else was specifically programmed, and to teenagers, who were insightfully recognized as frequently being the family gatekeepers in regard to what the set would be tuned to each evening. By focusing on segments of the audience somewhat under attended to, ABC was able to move from third to first place in popularity and overturn what had seemed a permanent ordering of three networks—CBS, NBC, and ABC. In the case of Fox, the key was appealing to viewers in the 18–34 age category. The basic lesson is that success with audiences lies not in doing what others do better but in doing differently (Lin, 1995)—that is, counterprogramming when there are powerfully successful competitors—and the corollary is that as underserved segments are strategically drawn on by one or another of the networks, their audience shares will change no matter how apparently immutable they are.

The three initial networks and broadcasting nevertheless remain preeminent. The decline in their audience shares is a diminishing and not a dwarfing. In comparison with cable, the three still command substantial shares of the prime-time audience and along with Fox, United Paramount Network (UPN) and the Warner Brothers Network (WB) have access to a much greater number of households; thus, they have the advantage in assembling an audience attractive to advertisers for their programming. Cable is the means by which a large majority of households now receive television. Slightly more than two-thirds are cable system subscribers, and the total receiving equivalent service rises to three-fourths when signal delivery to the household by satellite is included (Alternate Delivery Service, or ADS, in the jargon of Nielsen). Nevertheless, broadcast signals—from the four major networks, the other networked linkages such as UPN and WB with their comparatively small audiences, independent stations, and distant broadcast signals—still constitute the majority of what Americans view.

Ideally, the huge array of new channels becoming more available everywhere would mean a parallel increase in innovative and creative programming. Blumler and Spicer (1990) sought to address this issue by interviewing 150 top executives in all phases of the U.S. television business. What they found was largely in support of the caustic comments of Gerbner, Morgan, and Signorielli (1994):

> Given the convergence of communication technologies, the concentration of
> ownership, and the shrinking of independent creative alternatives, the notion that a
> new abundance of hundreds of channels will provide greater choice is a technocratic
> fantasy. The most profitable programs now being mass-produced for the vast ma-
> jority of viewers will run on more channels more of the time, (whereas) infomercial
> hustle, direct-marketing, and electronically delivered magazines catering to small
> audiences will fill the rest (p. 20).

Blumler and Spicer focused on beliefs and perceptions about professional autonomy and creative freedom. The thrust of what the 150 executives told them
was that there were more opportunities for producing programs because there
were more channels in need of programming, but that there was scant increase
in autonomy and not much of an increase in creative freedom because the basic
constraints of producing to satisfy a mass audience remained. Bielby and Bielby
(1994) further supported the view that the industry relies heavily on tested
formulas in their analysis of the rhetoric announcing new network programs in
which the focus was on the past hits of the producers, the similarity of the
program to previous successes, and the genre ("a cop show from the master of
urban mayhem").

The adoption of a new ratings code in the mid-1990s for entertainment programs was the result of Congress threatening legislation to regulate what
reaches young viewers and the White House asking for action on violence. The
industry initially pledged to fight—armed with the First Amendment and motivated by the fear of reducing audience size and thereby the profitability of
some programs. Soon, with polls showing a majority of Americans favoring
steps to reduce violence, the prospects of public displeasure and the stern regulation that might be the consequence led the industry to agree to devise a code.

The Telecommunications Act of 1996 mandated the installation of a sensor,
called a "V-chip," in newly manufactured sets with screens 13 inches or larger
that would permit parents or anyone else to exclude a program with a particular
label. Despite acceding to warning labels and automated zapping, the industry
nevertheless remained stoutly opposed to giving consumers the ability to block
anything beyond the coded entertainment programs, such as news and sports,
because of the possibility of audience loss (Albiniak & McConnell, 1998). This
was a sign, in our view, of indifference to parental convenience in behalf of
earnings.

The code offered at first resembled that of the Motion Picture Association of
America (MPAA), with only age-graded restrictions and no other explanation.
Critics argued that it would be more informative, and more useful to parents,
to label content specifically in regard to amount and emphasis on violence,
adult situations, adult language, and nudity. They were vigorous, and in some
cases, prestigious enough that the industry augmented the scheme with de-

scriptive labeling, even though its explicitness might cost more in the way of viewers than the vaguer age gradations alone (Hamilton, 1998).

Effective implementation, however, faces some hurdles. In the first large-scale evaluation of the actual operation of the ratings code, Kunkel and colleagues (1998) found in composite weeks covering 2306 programs in 1997 and 1998 on 11 Los Angeles channels that the use of the labels by an industry fearful of losing viewers was so niggardly as to be inaccurate in reflecting the presence of these elements. In addition, technological problems have delayed installation of the V-chip in new sets. As a result, with sets on the average being replaced every 7 years, a decade will pass before the system is fully in place.

When television was introduced in the late 1940s and early 1950s, it was able to adapt for audience measurement the paradigm that had been developed for radio only a few years earlier (Beville, 1988; Webster & Lichty, 1991). Arthur Nielsen, with a degree in electrical engineering from the University of Wisconsin, had introduced the notion of automatically recording the channels an instrument was tuned to and in 1950 initiated the first NTI (Nielsen Television Index) for the new medium. The resulting ratings and shares became the means by which programs are evaluated and discarded as each channel seeks a schedule that maximizes income by offering audiences to advertisers that are optimally attractive in size and composition.[1] February, May, July, and November became "sweeps" months when Neilsen collected data to determine advertising rates within the 250 television markets in the United States (at this writing, 38 major market and 212 small "designated market areas"), and the broadcast networks and their cable competitors drawing income from advertising became eager to schedule particularly attractive programming during these periods to enhance profits.

With the increase in the number of channels, network competition grew more heated in the 1980s and 1990s, and executives became even less inclined to leave a marginally popular program in a time slot to develop a larger audience (Bellamy, McDonald, & Walker, 1990; Blum & Lindheim, 1987). One

---

[1] The two standard measures of program popularity are rating and share. Usually, they are expressed in terms of household but are also used for other demographic categories. Rating = percentage of units with TV sets viewing a channel (R = no. viewing a channel / total with sets). Share = percentage viewing a channel of total units viewing (S = no. viewing a channel / total viewing). Each point = 1% of the possible audience or 994,000 households in the fall of 1998 (Broadcasting and Cable, October 5–11, 1998). The calculation of shares by Nielsen permits a household using television (HUT) to contribute to more than one source of television signals. When channel options were limited, as they were during the 1960s and 1970s that we have labeled the years of equilibrium, the distribution of prime time shares approximated 100 percent, a phenomenon still visible in the data on shares for 1983–84 in Table 1.1. This practice now leads to household shares as reported by Nielsen exceeding 100% (Television Advertising Bureau, 1997; Nielsen Media Research, 1998).

readily observable manifestation of this competition was the adoption in the early 1990s by the four major networks of brisker, visually more fluid transitions at starts, ends, and breaks of prime time programs in an effort to hold viewers, with the two most desperate in their strivings, the network in third place and the fourth-place fledging aiming at a demographically younger adult audience (Fox), adopting this tactic to a more marked degree (Eastman, Neal-Lumsford & Riggs, 1995).

A useful way to conceive of the maneuverings of both national and local channels in search of audiences is the division of a market. Hamilton (1998) makes this irrefutably clear in his analysis of the competitive uses of violent programming. The necessary (but easy to meet) condition is that there are differences among viewers in preferences for a genre or dimension of content. Competitors attempt to attract such viewers up to the point that gains in viewership level out. Competition then centers on other elements of content that differ in their attractiveness to various viewers. This conceptualization vanquishes the question of whether violence, sex, scandal, or situation comedies promise better ratings because it rests on the economic principle of equilibrium in which competitors change their programming emphases in response to whom it is possible to still attract. This conceptualization also admits the possibility that if a major segment of the audience has been captured by a subset of channels, such as young adult males 18 to 34 with an interest in violence by premium cable movies, those remaining might actually decrease their use of that particular program commodity to better attract viewers from other segments.

Ratings and shares have also figured in two other network strategies for developing a popular schedule. One is the spin-off, the transfer of a character from a highly rated program to another, separate program in which he or she is featured. In an analysis of 59 spin-offs over the 33 years between 1956 and 1988, Bellamy, McDonald, and Walker (1990) found that this strategy was consistently successful. It was used less in the later 1980s than earlier because a necessary condition is that the programs be hugely popular. When such successes are not plentiful, the opportunities for spin-offs become more limited. Another strategy has been the extrapolation of present-day ratings to the selection of programs for the future. McDonald and Schecter (1988) examined 2446 programs in the 40 years between 1946 and 1985 and found a strong relationship between the ratings in one season for a category of program and the number of programs of that category in the schedule the subsequent year. Thus, ratings and shares are not only a principal factor in the survival of programs, but they also have a role in the type of program that will be seen in following seasons by their influence on spin-offs and favored program categories.

The most discussed innovation in such industry periodicals as *Broadcasting and Cable* over the past decade has been HDTV (high definition television), a term we will use generically for all variants of markedly improved digital picture and audio quality. This technology will bring the resolution of a 35-mm slide to the home television screen. Its precision almost certainly ensures extensive use in scientific and medical applications, where a better picture will mean that instruction and analysis are more telling and accurate. The widespread prophecy at the beginning of the decade was that HDTV would be well in place in the American home by the year 2000. However, this was another instance of the "technological fallacy" (Comstock, 1989), mistakenly anticipating that what is technically feasible is certain to be achieved.

HDTV in its most perfected state would require new television sets. Station owners would have to invest billions to equip their stations for such broadcasting and eventually would abandon their present equipment. The incentive for consumers to convert to the new technology at first is scant, because there will be only a few programs in the format and HDTV sets would be several times more costly than present-day sets. Broadcasters have almost no incentive at all, because any additions in the aggregate to the size of their audience are likely to be minute as most individuals now spend about as much time as they believe they have available viewing television. Only Zenith still manufactures television sets in the United States, so there is no promising boom for the American appliance industry. Only equipment manufacturers for the television industry would benefit.

Under these circumstances, it is hardly surprising that the FCC and other regulatory bodies that govern national and international standards for communications technology have been very slow to act. The FCC has dictated a measured transition in which broadcasters would remain able to use their old equipment and present-day sets would continue to be able to receive signals. This precludes financial distress and political upheaval among consumers. It also means that even foreign manufacturers will reap no great benefit because television set replacement will continue at the present rate of about 5 to 7 years per household, and some might even be hurt by HDTV if they fail to incorporate newly cost-efficient developments and must sell sets at lowered costs to be competitive. Thus, as it did with setting technical standards at the time of the introduction of television, the FCC adopted a policy favorable to existing economic interests rather than a brute step in favor of superior technological performance.

Broadcasters, meanwhile, are arguing for use of the digital capacity that HDTV would require for additional channels, so they can compete on a broader basis for audience share, rather than improving the image quality of what appears on the screen (Pope, 1998). And successful transmission is in doubt because the signals are very susceptible to multipath interference in which bouncing off objects in their path delivers multiple images that smudge or overlap on the screen (Dickson, 1998). The overall result is that although a few stations are tentatively scheduled to begin some HDTV broadcasting by the beginning of 1999, widespread implementation will be delayed for a number of years well past 2000 (Pope & Robichaux, 1997).

The decade, then, will end with a new pattern of uncertain composition taking shape: more channels offering greater choice, the potential for greatly increased control over what is viewed, a diminished presence for CBS, NBC, and ABC. Yet broadcasting remains at the center of the system. We will seek the answers shortly as to why so much change has left so much close to what it was, and what the future holds, by looking at five decades of data on audience behavior.

The Main Means

The main means by which television financially supports itself is through the sale to advertisers of access to audiences. This has led to the observation that television's product is not programming but the attention of viewers (Brown, 1971; Comstock, 1991b; Owen, Beebe, & Manning, 1974; Phalen, 1996). Much of the statistical trappings of the industry are simply attempts to establish a metric for the pricing of commercials—ratings, shares, demographics. The dramatic "overnights," by which data on program popularity are transmitted within hours to network headquarters in New York, are merely means for the efficient jettisoning of programs insufficient in their appeal to market successfully. Advertising is the economic justification for commercial television. Our examination focuses on four aspects: what sets television advertising apart; commercial design; the public's somewhat pejorative—but not consistently unfavorable—evaluation; and the assessment of effectiveness.

I. SET APART

Paid-for presentations intended to influence the behavior of consumers divide into a number of categories: program-length commercials for one or another personal service, such as hair restoration or real-estate investment strategies; the similar program-length displays of products, involving either a single class such as a floor cleaner or kitchen appliance or a variety of goods, for direct sale by telephone; and the regular commercials that are inserted at the beginnings, endings, and way points of programs. We will focus on the latter—the "commercials" of everyday conversation and occasional vituperation—because they are by far the most frequent of television's appeals to consumers and they have been by far the subject of the greatest amount of empirical inquiry.

Television commercials, as with advertising in all media, represent the vested interest of the party paying for the advertisement. Advertising has no purpose other than to advance the interests of its sponsor. Usually, this interest rests in the purchase of a particular product by the viewer or reader but sometimes lies in elevating the impression of a brand name, company, or genre of goods. The most pervasive and banal feature of display advertising, of which television commercials are essentially a subspecies, is the use of classical conditioning (Harris, 1994; Mullen & Johnson, 1990). The advertised product or brand name is paired with an image that is expected to arouse positive affect, such as a symbol of power and authority, sexual attractiveness, or pleasurable consumption. The response evoked by the latter (in psychological parlance, the "unconditioned response" because it is the product of prior experience unrelated to the current pairing) as a result becomes more likely in response to the product or brand name, enhancing favorability toward it. The success of this psychological truism is not the means by which the effectiveness of a commercial in the specific instance is measured. It is simply a central part of many features that presumably advance favorability toward the product or brand name.

Here, however, resemblances between television commercials and display advertising in other media come to an end. In other media, argumentation in print often plays a major role. Technical details can be explained. Arrows may point to unusual features, such as brass eyelets in a rubberized athletic shoe. The reader may be expected to linger covetously over the portrayed item yet rationally assess its attributes in comparison to alternatives. Even the most advertising-filled magazines and newspapers offer only many dozens of display ads per issue, and frequently in special interest publications the advertised products and brand names are complementary to the editorial content—outdoor sports, home decorating and remodeling, and cooking and wine are examples. It is not uncommon for editorial content to reinforce advertising within the same issue by favorable treatment in features about what's new or how well a product performs—the description of a leisurely drive along the winding roads of a southern coastal state in a luxury sedan also occupying a three-page spread in a fold-out of the front cover is an example. Such advertising has the opportunity to be multidimensional in appeal, touting superior technology, longer life, greater convenience, better price, and wider public acceptance at the same time.

In contrast, television commercials are visual anecdotes enhanced by voice and music. They have become remarkably brief. Argumentation has been largely abandoned in favor of an emotionally satisfying exposure to the product or brand name. Music not only often advances the theme but also has become a cue aiding the viewer in the recall of what is to be presented. This anticipatory aspect is a key element in television advertising not ordinarily present in advertising in other media, and increases the likelihood that viewers will recognize the product or brand name. Commercials are not perused; they are experienced in real time with scant opportunity for reflection or examination.

The more pointed but confined thrust of television commercials compared to other display advertising was documented by Abernethy (1992). Magazine advertisements averaged 1.59 bits of specific information; the score for commercials was 1.06. Slightly more than 33% of magazine ads had three or more bits; the comparable figure for commercials was 9.5%. These are very convincing data because they represent huge samples of 14,554 magazine ads and 1655 television commercials pooled from 11 independent studies published between 1977 and 1990, and the tabulation encompassed 14 different types of information: price, quality, performance, components, availability, special offers, taste, packaging, guarantees or warranties, safety, nutrition, independent research, company-sponsored research, and novel ideas.

We estimate, based on earlier calculations (Comstock, 1991b; Condry & Scheibe, 1989) and adjusting for the proliferation of 15-second spots (Cobb-Walgren, 1990), that the average viewer is exposed to about 60,000 commercials a year. These circumstances invite peripheral processing in which messages with a persuasive element are reacted to emotionally and quickly evaluated in a favorable or unfavorable way. New stimuli briefly become the focus of attention without a great deal of rational consideration, weighing of alternatives, or counterarguments, in the evaluation of an appeal that characterizes what is called central processing. The viewer, exposed to more than 160 commercials a day, has little choice to behave otherwise.

This distinction, drawn from the well-known "elaboration likelihood" model of persuasion developed by Petty and Cacioppo (1980, 1981, 1986, 1990), identifies the central characteristic of television commercials. Many advertisements in other media encourage the elaboration of cognitions as their stimuli elicit memories and knowledge, critical thoughts, and the weighing of the legitimacy of claims. Some commercials make reasoned appeals, such as in behalf of the safety features of an auto; these may well be centrally processed. However, the distinguishing characteristic of television commercials is that their design much more frequently and inevitably elicits peripheral processing. Even persons whose predisposition is to process persuasive appeals centrally typically will process commercials in a peripheral manner. The affect and cognitions engendered by a commercial are processed rapidly; evaluation occurs without further elaboration.

The brand-name household products that constitute such a sizable proportion of television advertising further favor such processing. Involvement in a topic that is the subject of a persuasive appeal favors central processing (Batra & Ray, 1985; Cacioppo & Petty, 1985). However, no matter how favored or consistently purchased a brand may be, it is difficult to imagine a great deal of involvement in household detergents, most sodas and snacks, and brand-name foods and beverages—although for some viewers, certain makes of motor vehicles and some appliances, not perceived as readily fungible, would sometimes be exceptions. Thus, the influence of the design elements on processing are further reinforced by the predominant product categories.

II. COMMERCIAL DESIGN

When we examine the design of commercials, we are looking not only at what people see on the screen but also the way the forces of greed and the fear of propelling the viewer elsewhere have affected their deployment and the beliefs and convictions of those in the advertising industry about what will work. The latter are real enough; for example, Solomon and Greenberg (1993) queried 25 property masters about their choice of three types of props to dress four different commercial sets, each varying by gender and social class, and found almost universal consensus on the chosen props. Design then is a function of informal advertising industry rules and conventions that govern what the viewer will see.

Our survey of the empirical literature divides into three topics: format, or the structure and deployment of commercials; form, or the techniques employed; and content, or subject matter. This conforms to the widely used three-dimensional schema for describing television programming (Huston & Wright, 1989).

A. FORMAT

Our examination of format covers five topics. They are quantity, frequency, and length of commercials; trends; time of day; public service announcements (PSAs); and children's programming.

1. Quantity, Frequency, and Length

This is an area where statistics are stunning because they are so large; similar reactions occur in response to the amount of mayhem in television entertainment and the number of hours per year that children—and everybody else—spend watching television. The most recently available data indicate (Cobb-Walgren, 1990):

- More than 6200 commercials per week appear on ABC, CBS, and NBC alone.
- The comparable figure for all other outlets combined is 100 times greater.
- The average number of commercial minutes per hour per station is about 12, or 20% of all programming, not including the nonprogram material devoted to station breaks, public service announcements, and various transition devices.
- The average number of commercials per hour per station is about 26.
- The typical commercial runs 30 seconds but ABC, CBS, and NBC use many more 15-second spots than other outlets (by the mid-1990s, about 3 out of 10 compared to fewer than 1 out of 10).

2. Trends

There have been three unmistakable trends (Table 2.1):

- Increasing commercialization; the selling of the audience has become more pronounced, so that the Golden Age of television can be recalled not only for its vibrant drama but also for being less base in its profiting from viewer attention.
- Abandonment of small narratives in favor of condensed pitches.
- Evolution of two ideal types of commercials.

Increased commercialization is apparent on three dimensions: time devoted to commercials, number of commercials, and proportion of nonprogram material. Estimates of commercial time per hour have increased from 10.94 in 1982 to 11.61 five years later. Number of commercials per hour over the same period increased from about 22 to about 25. Nonprogram material, which includes public service announcements, promos for coming attractions (in-house commercials), and various drop-ins or other announcements, rose from 12 minutes, 43 seconds to 13 minutes, 19 seconds.

The length of commercials has become drastically shortened. In 1965, about three-fourths of commercials on the three original networks and about two-thirds of those on nonnetwork outlets were 60 seconds in length. Short tales of life enhancement by a product were typical; a consumer hero or heroine encountered a problem, turned to the advertised item, and ended frustration to the frequent applause of spouse and children. In the decade and a half between 1967 and 1981, the average number of commercials per week on the three networks increased from 1856 to 4079 (Bogart & Lehman, 1983) because of the virtual abandonment of the 60-second little story in favor of the 30-second spot.

TABLE 2.1   Network and Nonnetwork Commercials by Length

	Annual percent of all commercials*					
	Length of network commercials (in seconds)			Length of nonnetwork commercials (in seconds)		
Year	15	30	60	15	30	60
1965			76.7		0.8	64.0
1975		79.0	5.6		79.2	10.4
1980		94.6	1.9		85.1	3.9
1985	10.1	83.5	2.2	1.3	88.0	2.7
1990	35.4	60.1	1.7	5.9	84.4	3.7
1995	31.5	64.8	1.2	7.3	84.9	3.3
1996	33.0	63.9	1.2	8.3	83.5	4.0
1997	29.5	67.1	1.5	7.7	85.2	4.0

Year	Avg. no. of network commercials per week	Avg. no. of nonnetwork commercials per week	Avg. no. of commercial minutes per hour	Avg. no. of commercials per hour
1982	4646	416,211	10.94	21.67
1983	4889	448,960	11.16	22.51
1984	5035	472,427	11.35	23.05
1985	5094	512,354	11.53	23.60
1986	5361	525,477	11.58	24.06
1987	6037	576,510	11.61	24.74

*Difference between total for year and 100% is accounted for by the remaining commercials, ranging in length from 10 to 90-plus seconds.

Adapted from "The Changing Commercial Climate," by C. J. Cobb-Walgren, 1990, *Current Issues and Research in Advertising,* 13(1/2), pp. 343–368; and *Trends in Television,* Television Bureau of Advertising, 1997.

This was followed by the beginning of a noticeable trend in the mid-1980s toward again halving the length of commercials (to 15 seconds) with another sizable increase in the average number per week.

These shifts have resulted in two ideal types that account for almost all commercials (Table 2.1): the 15-second spot and the 30-second spot. By the mid-1990s, slightly more than 3 of 10 commercials at the three original networks were 15 seconds in length, whereas at other outlets the 30-second length was used much more frequently, accounting for about 85% of all commercials. This disparity occurs because the three networks deal exclusively with national brands, where maintaining salience among consumers is the major goal. There is a place for 15-second spots because they are almost as effective as 30-second spots and cost less, thereby widening the market for the sale of audience attention. Stations not aligned with ABC, CBS, and NBC sell more commercials locally, and local advertisers must go beyond simply raising consciousness about a brand name and require more time to present their case because they seek to draw consumers to a particular site. The same pattern occurred 20 years earlier, with nonnetwork outlets much slower to abandon the 60-second commercial in favor of the 30-second spot.

3. Time of Day

Commercial placement varies by day-part (Table 2.2), which divides into Saturday mornings (7 A.M.–noon), when children are predominant in the audience; weekday daytime (9 A.M.–3 P.M.), when adult women are much more frequent viewers than adult males; weekend afternoons (noon–6 P.M.), when sports programming attracts a largely male audience; and prime time (8–11 P.M.), when adult males only slightly outnumber adult females (Condry, 1989). Commercials are comparatively infrequent when audiences are very small (such as Sunday mornings); at their most frequent when audiences are moderate in size, which compensates for the necessarily lower prices that can be charged; and somewhat less frequent during prime time when prices are at their peak but television industry angst is high that too many commercials would reduce the audience's incentives for viewing.

TABLE 2.2 Network Television Programming

Distribution of schedule in average broadcast day (percent of hours)		
Entertainment	News and information	Sports
55%	35.5%	9.4%

Average Daypart			
Saturday morning* (7 A.M.–noon)		Weekend afternoon* (noon–6 P.M.)	
Entertainment	92.5%	Sports	68.7%
		Entertainment	19.5
		News and information	4.9
Weekday daytime* (9 A.M.–3 P.M.)		Prime time* (8–11 P.M.)	
Entertainment	73.1%	Entertainment	79.4%
News and information	20.7	News and information	6.2
		Sports	6.0

*6–8% "other" in each day-part. Data from ABC, CBS, NBC.

Adapted from "Nonprogram Content of Television: Mechanisms of Persuasion," by J. Condry and C. Scheibe, 1989, in J. Condry, *The Psychology of Television* (pp. 173–232), Hillsdale, NJ: Erlbaum.

4. Public Service Announcements

There is only about 1 public service announcement (PSA) for every 20 product commercials (Condry & Scheibe, 1989). They resemble product commercials in length. However, they are more frequent Saturday mornings, where they account for more than 20% of nonprogram material compared to 5% overall. This is undoubtedly because, in terms of commercial prices, this is the least valuable of the major day-parts but it also means these messages will reach only a few of the adults to whom they are presumably addressed. Thus, industry estimates of the financial value of the public service contribution represented by PSAs that are based on the average price for all commercials are disingenuous.

5. Children's Programming

It is three decades since the now disbanded but still remembered Action for Children's Television began its campaign to end advertising on programming directed at children. The three arguments offered by the group have all been well established by research and experience (Comstock, 1991a): younger children are unlikely to comprehend the self-interest attached to the persuasive appeal of a commercial, and thereby are exploited; even older children may be harmed by shifting preferences toward unhealthy, highly sugared products; and programs supported by advertising seek large audiences attractive to advertisers rather than serving educational and cultural goals. At the time, children's programming had more minutes of advertising than prime time because it was considered "daytime" when a greater number of advertisements under the then-existing National Association of Broadcasters (NAB) code could be sold to compensate for the lower prices they would bring. The most recent data (Condry & Scheibe, 1989) document that children's programming has about as many minutes and seconds per hour of advertising as prime time and that the total nonprogram material is slightly greater because of the large number of PSAs appearing during these hours. Advertising to children not only continues but remains at about the same level as advertising accompanying general audience evening programming, in accord with recent federal legislation establishing a children's weekend ceiling of 10.5 minutes per hour.

B. FORM

Aspects of form on which there are empirical data are obviously limited to those that have aroused the interest of investigators. This implies that they have some obvious importance. We will at least learn the degree to which these particular elements are thought to be necessary for effectiveness by those in the advertising business. Those that have been given attention include animation, music and humor, pace, and amount and type of information.

Callcott and Lee (1994) examined 2343 commercials representing a composite week of programming by the three original networks, other stations, and cable in regard to animation. Only 15% contained some animation, and only 2% were wholly animated. This is a decline from a similar tabulation of 20% a decade and a half earlier (Bush, Hair, & Bush, 1983). Apparently, animation is thought to be most effective with women and children because it appears most frequently in the mornings, late afternoons, and with children's programming.

Music is frequently part of commercial design. However, it is less frequent than most viewers may think. Stewart and Furse (1986) and Stewart and Koslow (1989) together examined over 2000 commercials and found music present in about 2 of 5. However, only slightly more than 10% of those with music contained lyrics or a jingle carrying the commercial message. Thus, music most often is employed as an executional device to attract attention, maintain interest, create a mood or emotional response, or otherwise act as an accompaniment rather than figure in the foreground. Alden and Hoyer (1993) produced similarly paltry tallies for humor. Only slightly more than about 10% of a 3-day sample of 497 national brand commercials on the three original networks contained humor.

Commercial design employs a very fast pace. The data are clear. Shot length is much briefer than for programs and the pace of commercials (30-second, for this comparison) has become progressively more rapid with total shots increasing from about 8 in 1978 to more than 13 in 1991 (MacLachlan & Logan, 1993).

Stern and Resnik (1991) focused on informational cues, defined as specification of an attribute, such as price, quality, or availability. Almost identical proportions of about 50% from samples of 350 commercials from 1976 and 1986 attest to the stability of advertising design (and thereby professional judgment about what will be effective); the score for a cable sample was 65%. Stayman, Aaker, and Bruzzone (1989) described 855 prime-time commercials broadcast between 1976 and 1986 by the adjectives checked by a sample of 1000 consumers. About one-third were perceived as slightly informative, in contrast to fewer than 2% that were perceived as very informative, and about another third that were described variously as entertaining. The products whose commercials were more frequently informative were consumer nondurables intended to relieve states best avoided, such as headaches, stomach acid, and constipation. Crask and Laskey (1990) found that almost all the commercials in a sample of 767 representing 336 brands of personal, household, and food items contained elements parading as information that would set the item at an advantage when compared to competitors rather than attempting to give the product a distinct personality—illusion as information in the interest of sales. Abernethy and Butler (1992) added a sample of 562 advertisements from 13 newspapers to Abernethy's earlier comparison of television and magazine advertising. Newspaper advertisements far more frequently contained informational elements than those in magazines, which outranked television commercials. Television commercials are thus absolutely and comparatively low in informational elements that could enter into central processing.

Rotfeld, Abernethy, and Parsons (1990) found that more than half of a sample of 426 television stations never asked for advertising claims to be substantiated whereas fewer than 5% asked for substantiation for half or more claims. On the average, substantiation was requested for about 10% of submissions, and about 3% were rejected, with adherence to the code provisions once set forth by the NAB leading to a much higher rejection rate than use of other codes. Thus, the claims of commercials often have undergone little third-party scrutiny. Kolbe and Muehling (1992) found in a sample of 1445 commercials drawn from the three original networks and two cable channels that fully 65% contained disclaimers, warnings, and other printed information, with 40% having fewer than 5 words and an average word count of 7.3. Hoy and Stankey (1993) found in a sample of 1162 commercials shown in February, 1990 on the original three networks that about one-fourth contained disclosures, but among the 157 nonduplicate commercials with disclosures not one fully met the Federal Trade Commission (FTC) "clear and conspicuous" display standards, and only 12% met certain video-specified standards. In effect, commercials invite misapprehension.

C. CONTENT

Our examination of the content of commercials covers three topics. They are the products advertised, the persons who appear, and the themes and values advanced.

1. Products

Products advertised have been quite stable by category over the years. In a 3-year sample in the mid-1980s (Condry & Scheibe, 1989), the top five categories in each of 3 years were the same with the exception of one additional category; that is, the 15 places were occupied by 16 different categories. When examined within each day-part (Saturday morning, 7 A.M.–noon; weekday daytime, 9 A.M.–3 P.M.; weekend afternoon, noon–6 P.M.; and prime time, 8–11 P.M.), the total of 60 places were filled with only 27 categories, or only seven more than if there had been no variation at all. Increases in the number of channels carrying commercials and any growth in the use of 15-second spots with their lower prices would attract new advertisers, but changes in the overall product composition of television advertising are certain to be minor because almost all products suitable for television advertising are well represented and no new categories exist—old categories will simply have some new components.

Retail and home furnishings were the leader, followed by food and beverages, cleaners and paper products, medicine, and soda and snacks. These are all perennials. About 65% are nondurables. All categories of drinks and food total to about a third. Durables (retail and home furnishings, toys, and some unknown but sizable proportion of auto-related commercials) total to slightly more than 20%. The tabulation of advertising industry expenditures by the networks, cable, national spots, and local stations produces similar consistencies across these four categories (Television Bureau of Advertising, 1997). The main point is that the great majority of commercials are for goods that will be regularly replenished, with choices continually made among competing brands or alternative genres (such as a restaurant vs a snack).

2. Persons

The demographic makeup of commercials has long been of interest. Because commercials are designed to evoke a positive response from viewers in regard to the subject or object vended, they represent the perceptions of the advertising industry about acceptability, credibility, and authority. Gender has received the most attention. Data from the 1970s and earlier paint a clear picture: men appeared more often, more frequently had official roles as experts, and more often provided authoritative voice-overs. The most recent data convey a picture that is more similar than different (Bretl & Cantor, 1988; Condry & Scheibe, 1989; Gilly, 1988; Lovdal, 1989):

- Overall, the proportion of male and female characters in commercials is about equal.
- In the mid-1970s, more than four out of five commercials for products to be used in the home had a female product representative. The more recent data put the proportion at just over half. Similarly, the proportions of home settings with females present and proportions of nonhome settings with males present have declined somewhat.
- However, voice-overs remain unchanged across the decades with about 90% male.

Program and product, or the context, make a difference. For example, commercials in pro-football games are more likely to feature males than females and, perhaps surprisingly, scantily clad females are not at all more prominent than they are with soap operas or prime-time television (Riffe, Place, & Mayo,

1993). This is because football games feature commercials for autos, finance, and alcohol, and products where males typically are featured more in commercials (Condry & Scheibe, 1989). Condry and Scheibe's tabulations indicate that most characters in commercials are White (94% at the time) and almost all non-Whites are Black. Furthermore, Blacks tend to be featured as members of larger groups (Bristor, Lee, & Hunt, 1995); this, in fact, is a long-standing means by which television deals with personal attributes perceived by some in the industry as possibly problematic, and was recorded in use for race more than 20 years ago (Comstock, Chaffee, Katzman, McCombs, & Roberts, 1978). The middle and professional classes are overrepresented; blue-collar and clerical workers are underrepresented. Similarly, young adults appearing in television commercials are overrepresented compared to the number in real life by a ratio of 3 to 1, with a sizable majority female; older adults (60-plus years) are underrepresented to a similar degree (Hajjar, 1997); male teenagers are underrepresented by about 3 to 1 and children and adults in their mid-years are only modestly underrepresented.

Physical attractiveness is more emphasized for females than males in commercials, and females are more frequently the receivers of glances from others (Lin, 1997; Signorielli, McLeod, & Healy, 1994). On MTV, women most frequently are presented as sensual and exotic creatures (rather than, say, "cute" or "classic good looks") in a singular example of sex-role specialization (Englis, Solomon, & Ashmore, 1994). Females in general audience commercials are typically slender whereas males are typically muscular. Females generally are more fashionably attired than males, but sexuality and sexual attractiveness in a manner distinct enough to be scored by a viewer for such attributes account for only about 1 in 10 female characters in commercials.

3. Themes and Values

These varying emphases of gender, race, age, and socioeconomic status all represent attempts by advertisers to construct themes and contexts that will please viewers. The biases roughly parallel those for programming except among young adults, where females are more prominent either as instruments in behalf of classical conditioning or as more obviously appropriate for certain products, such as household nondurables. As we will soon see, the data on public opinion about advertising indicate that it is unlikely that any but the most highly involved socially or politically—and then only in regard to the most blatant discriminatory, stereotypic, or offensive portrayals—will complain or threaten to cease purchasing a product because of the portrayal of people in advertising. Most will respond indifferently or even enthusiastically to the way persons like themselves are treated in commercials.

The values advanced by commercials have been most thoroughly investigated by Condry and Scheibe (1989). They used Rokeach's (1979) well-known scheme for categorizing values into those that are a means to a goal (instrumental values) and those that represent the desired outcome (terminal values). In 2135 commercials, the five most frequently occurring instrumental values were capable, helpful, smart, cheerful, and responsible. Fifteen other values had instrumental scores ranging from 2 to 16% of commercials. The five most frequently occurring terminal values were happiness, social recognition, family, accomplishment, and prosperity. However, in this case only 10 other values were recorded with scores between 1 and 11% and happiness was a terminal value in almost 6 of 10 commercials compared to the presence of capability as an instrumental value in only slightly more than 1 of 4 commercials. In sum, a wide range of means to an end are employed in commercials but the overwhelming end-state is pleasure as a result of the advocated consumer decision.

III. PUBLIC OPINION

The public at once is wary and skeptical of the claims and outcomes and is appreciative of the usefulness of advertising. These two veins, less in conflict than in uneasy complementarity toward two distinct aspects of advertising, represent enduring views that have persisted with scant change for at least three decades. Poll data have been collated reflecting national opinion since the mid-1960s through the beginning of the 1990s by Calfee and Ringold (1994). With one exception, the pattern is unchanging.

Only about one-third concur that "most advertising is believable," whereas about one-fifth agree that "ads usually present a true picture." Still, about a half or more agree that, on the whole, ads are at least "fairly believable." More than three-fourths agree that "advertising provides useful information about products and services," whereas about the same proportion agree that "advertising encourages people to use products they don't need" and only somewhat fewer agree with the more stringent charge that "advertising encourages people to use some products that are bad for them."

When asked to choose between informational utility and persuasive perfidy, a majority since 1964 have said they agreed most with the view that advertising "seeks to persuade people to buy things they don't need or can't afford." Here is the exception to the stability of opinion: this majority has increased steadily since 1964 from 54 to 80% 25 years later.

The public supports federal regulation of advertising. In the 1980s, about 70% agreed the government should make at least "some effort" to establish more controls and slightly more than half agreed there was "not enough" regulation, both only slight declines from the 1970s. Calfee and Ringold made the important point that heightened regulation has little effect on public acceptability of advertising because there were no dramatic shifts in opinion during the highly activist 1970s at the Federal Trade Commission.

These views derive from a myriad of experiences of individuals with verifiable and unverifiable claims and satisfactory and unsatisfactory purchases. The public is not thoroughly trusting of advertising, but it is also far from hostile. It is, in fact, quite rational. It acknowledges the usefulness of product information, but believes in advertising's persuasiveness and distrusts the selfish intent of advertisers. We believe it is important to recognize that these public expressions are in response to an amorphous global symbol, "advertising," and more specific stimuli—television commercials, magazine display advertisements, supermodel poses, newspaper classifieds, cosmetic advertisements, or the back pages of a favorite magazine—might draw different, more targeted opinions. Opinion has been largely stable because the mix of experiences, the interests of consumers, the motives of advertisers, and the varied faces of advertising have not changed much. In our view, the exception—the rise in the belief that advertising preys on people by peddling what they don't need or can't afford—most likely represents the increasing exposure in modern life to pitches in all media for durable personal possessions, such as automobiles, appliances, watches, and athletic shoes.

Experience, of course, is not the sole source of the public's opinions about advertising. The news media cover advertising not only in the business pages of newspapers and magazines but also in general news when there is novelty or controversy.

Keenan's (1995) analysis of 24 years of evening news by ABC, CBS, and NBC from 1970 to 1993, using the Vanderbilt Television News Archive, confirmed that advertising indeed is newsworthy, with 1068 stories or only somewhat fewer than one per week. This is a healthy representation in three comparatively brief nightly newscasts that skim the top of the news pyramid with only about 75 stories a week ostensibly representing events of the widest possible interest.

About a third of stories were negative in tone, about four times more than those positive. About a third of stories dealt with regulation, and of these more than half, or more than one out of six of all stories, concerned deception, whereas the rest dealt in some way with some alleged abuse of advertising. More than 40% concerned regularly purchased products or consumer services. In addition to the negative portrait of advertising in general, about one-fourth of the stories displayed some or all of the advertising in question, thus identifying individual advertisers and products for public rebuke when the context was negative. Thus, the treatment of advertising has been consistently negative.

These data refer to advertising in general. We now turn specifically to television, reasons for animosity toward specific commercials, and subliminal advertising.

A. TELEVISION

Television advertising fares much worse in public opinion than advertising in general. Up-to-date data come from a 1990 Chicago sample of more than 200 viewers and a 1991 consumer panel of about 800 matching U.S. Census demographics studied by Alwitt and Prabhaker (1992, 1994), and a consumer panel of about 200 from a southern city studied by Mittal (1994).

The pattern is repeated, although only the large consumer panel produces statistics that can be extrapolated to the population at large. When opinions about television are matched to opinions about advertising in general, television scores dramatically worse in regard to usefulness, entertainment value, and accuracy of product depictions.

In the southern city panel, 48% endorsed "somewhat" or "strongly" disliking television advertising, more than twice the 22% who endorsed comparable degrees of liking. When compared with newspapers, magazines, and radio, newspaper and magazine advertising were decisively perceived as more informative and less deceptive, irritating, and annoying; only radio fared about as badly as television.

These three analyses led to a coherent portrait of the public's disposition toward television advertising. We identified these key elements:

1. Although a negative view is predominant, the public, in fact, is divided in outlook. This division is represented by the differing percentages for approval and disapproval. There are two camps. The predominance of a negative view is represented by the tendency for disapproval to outweigh approval, exemplified by a mean score in the large panel decidedly on the negative side of the scale (Alwitt & Prabhaker, 1994).

2. Demographics are not strong predictors of dispositions toward television advertising, although older and more affluent viewers are somewhat more negative (Alwitt & Prabhaker, 1992).

3. Independent of demographics, beliefs are good predictors (Alwitt & Prabhaker, 1994). In general, those who like television programming also are more likely to like commercials. However, liking and disliking also are functions of specific beliefs about television advertising.

We have constructed a typology from the two analyses that relate specific beliefs to global opinion (Alwitt & Prabhaker, 1994; Mittal, 1994). There are six underlying factors:

Intrusiveness. The more commercials are thought to be repetitive, boring, and excessive in frequency, the more likely television advertising will be disliked.

Marketplace distortion. The more commercials are believed to raise the prices of goods, fail to give information adequate for choosing among products, or lack personal usefulness, the more likely television advertising will be disliked.

Manipulation. The more commercials are believed to be exceedingly persuasive, the more likely television advertising will be disliked.

Exploitation. The more commercials are thought to promote materialistic values, push unneeded products, or take advantage of the naiveté of children, the more likely television advertising will be disliked.

Entertainment. The more commercials are perceived as clever, amusing, and rivaling programs in interest, the more likely television advertising will be liked.

Fair exchange. The more commercials are construed as necessary to pay for television programming, the more likely television advertising will be liked.

Each of these beliefs governs attitudes toward television advertising regardless of other personal attributes. Thus, those who like television programming who also believe commercials distort marketplace decision making become more likely to dislike television advertising. The same holds true for younger or less affluent viewers who, compared with older or more affluent viewers, are less likely to dislike television advertising. The broader conclusion is that liking or disliking commercials is strongly rooted in neither generational nor socioeconomic differences but rather in cognitive beliefs that people have formed about television advertising.

There is no doubt that a substantial number of viewers occasionally or more often attempt to avoid exposure to commercials. Almost 80% in the Mittal panel said they left the room during commercial breaks "sometimes" or more often, and about the same figure was registered for fast-forwarding during VCR replay. There was a big difference attributable to convenience, however. Only 2% said they "always" walked out on commercials whereas almost half said they "always" fast-forwarded. Similarly, a national survey of almost 950 adults comparing media (Speck & Elliott, 1997) found that ad avoidance was more frequent with television and magazines than newspapers or radio and was predicted by attitudes toward advertising in each medium.

Becker and Murphy (1993) ingeniously construe advertisers as supporting programming in order to reward or compensate viewers for watching commercials. The commercials themselves lower the value or utility of the experience, thus the hostile public attitudes. However, they increase the demand for the product, thereby rewarding advertisers. In our view, they do so without providing much information because it is not necessary in the television context. Thus, viewers in fact seek out an unpleasant experience because of the associated rewards.

Our view is that these data as a whole represent a stable accommodation to a practice that disrupts the rewards of watching programming. We certainly do not see the "crisis in advertising" that has been proposed by some (Mittal, 1994; Stipp, 1992). Instead, we see an essentially inevitable irritation on the part of the public that is a long-standing aspect of the "obstinate audience" described by Bauer (1971) three decades ago.

Our reasoning is that there is no evidence that either attitudes toward or avoidance behavior in response to commercials has shifted dramatically. The difference made by fast-forwarding is extremely modest given the small amount of recording in the average household. Avoidance is not always completely successful given the role of the audio in delivering brand names and stimuli that would prompt their recall. The cost to advertisers of reaching viewers is simply higher than audience statistics would indicate.

B. SPECIFIC COMMERCIALS

Obviously, commercials vary in their likeability. *USA Today* presents scores weekly for new commercials from an industry research organization. The empirical data we examine identify three principal elements: creative factors, product categories, and social implications. However, we begin with a paradox.

1. A Paradox

Biel and Bridgwater (1990) queried a representative national sample of about 1000 viewers about 80 prime-time commercials. The average score for disliking them "a lot" was only 3% and only 8% disliked them "somewhat," with the comparable figures for liking 20% ("a lot") and 38% ("somewhat") and the rest neutral. This contrasts sharply with the impression given by the public opinion data about television advertising.

What occurs here is actually commonplace. We will meet the same phenomenon in regard to television violence (Chapter 3). When those sampled are asked to endorse broad statements about the media, large scores are registered for a critical stance. When asked to examine examples more minutely, those expressing disapproval become markedly smaller in number.

In the case of commercials, it is our interpretation that it is the barrier they pose to fuller enjoyment of viewing rather than intrinsic characteristics that is principally responsible for public hostility. Thus, commercials are often rated approvingly when examined on their own terms.

2. Creative Factors and Product Categories

By far, the strongest and most consistent predictor in the Biel and Bridgwater sample of liking a commercial was perceived meaningfulness. Similarly, Hitchon, Duckler, and Thorson (1994) experimentally found that liking for MTV commercials with the same music decreased as ambiguity of visual imagery and narrative increased. In the Biel and Bridgwater sample, meaningfulness was overwhelmingly the best predictor for food and beverages, followed by imputed "energy" and perceived cleverness. It was also first for other products and services, but barely over "rubs the wrong way," a negative predictor. Energy was next. For food and beverages, "rubs the wrong way" was a comparatively minor factor.

Eighty percent of the 20 best-liked commercials in the Biel and Bridgwater sample were for food and beverages; nonfood and beverage commercials similarly dominated the 20 least-liked commercials. Mittal (1994) offers some nonfood and beverage examples on his list of least-liked commercials: hospitals, AIDS, auto manufacturers, car dealers, feminine hygiene. Very similar examples are presented by Biel and Bridgwater: GTE Sprint, Lysol floor cleaner, Anacin, Dodge Lancer, and Arrid. They point to the Sprint commercial as confusing, with a voice-over of "Will you know the future when you see it?" accompanying two children in a space-age setting.

Barnes and Dotson (1990) took a very different approach. They asked about 4200 shoppers at a southeastern mall to rank 21 commercials in regard to offensiveness. Although all the commercials contained content often ranked in surveys as high in offensiveness, there were decided differences. Hygiene products of a comparatively personal nature dominated the most offensive nine, and a factor analysis indicated that scores varied as a function of both product category and execution. Demographics were a comparatively modest predictor, with those older, better-educated, and church-going shoppers somewhat more likely to register offense.

Our conclusion is that likeability rests on two major factors. The first is execution that translates into perceived interpretability and entertainment value. Cognitive satisfaction is foremost; ambiguity is displeasing. It is followed by enjoyment; artfulness draws applause. The second is the degree of offense, irritation, or unpleasant reflection stimulated. This may derive from the content, the treatment, or both, but particularly implicated is product category. Food and beverages are not immune from such stimulation— Mittal's most-disliked list includes beer, cereals, and soft drinks—but they decidedly run less risk of doing so than other products. Thus, after 50 years of refinement the techniques of television advertising still falter when product categories arouse ire.

3. Social Implications

In an attempt to take the social implications of advertising appeals into account, Ford and LaTour (1993) compared responses of small samples of 100–150 drawn from the National Organization of Women (NOW), the League of Women Voters (LWV) and the female population of a mid-Atlantic area. The two activist samples believed they were more sensitive to portrayals of women in advertising and were more likely to perceive advertising as having a conventional or stereotypic slant, such as portraying women as dependent on men, as sex objects, as belonging in the home, and the like. The two interest groups did not differ in any marked way, with the exception that the NOW members believed to a decidedly greater degree that men were accurately portrayed in advertising.

Both activist samples declared to a greater degree that they would take punitive steps if they judged an advertising campaign to be inappropriate. In this instance, they said they would be less likely to buy an attractive new product, more likely to discontinue using a product, and more likely to boycott other products of the company. These views were held more strongly by the NOW members than the LWV members.

We interpret the pattern observable in this seemingly limited sampling as widely applicable. Those who have strong opinions on a topic, represented here by membership in an activist group, are more likely to believe themselves sensitive to pertinent advertising content and more likely to believe they would take punitive steps as consumers if advertising were perceived as inappropriate.

We are skeptical, however, about consequences on the marketplace. The data bear only on expressed opinion, not behavior. The two often do not correspond because the former draws on norms and ideals, or what is perceived to be right, whereas the latter is often driven by convenience and, in this case, product satisfaction. Furthermore, advertisers actively try to avoid serious offense. As a result, much advertising may flirt with inappropriateness from the declared perspective of an activist while being ambiguous enough in that regard and enough in accord with the conventions of media portrayals to escape such classification by most viewers, including activists.

C. SUBLIMINAL ADVERTISING

Subliminal advertising is defined as the transmission of a specific appeal below the threshold of conscious perception, such as by rapidly flashing the message on a theater or television screen. It gained national notoriety in 1957 when a New Jersey market researcher, James Vicary, claimed he had thereby increased movie intermission sales of popcorn and Coca-Cola. Later, he confessed to a hoax (Weir, 1984).

Recently, Rogers and Seiler (1994) found that only 2% of about 250 advertising professionals surveyed said they knew of such a technique being employed, and on closer examination these few all turned out to be referring to the use of symbols and cues rather than explicit subliminal messages. However, the public is bedazzled by the prospect.

The data are highly consistent across 15 years and samples of 200–500 in three cities: Washington, D.C. (Zanot, Pincus, & Lamp, 1983), Honolulu (Synodinos, 1988), and Toledo (Rogers & Smith, 1993). About half had heard of such advertising, a figure that rose to three-fourths or more when a definition was supplied. In the most recent survey (1993), about three-fourths of the post-definition total who had heard of subliminal advertising thought it was successful, and somewhat less than half thought they might not buy a product if they knew the technique had been employed; education was a strong predictor of awareness and a modest predictor of belief in success.

Key (1972, 1976, 1980, 1989) has built a career as a popular author and lecturer on the premise that hidden messages in advertising manipulate consumer desires. Academics and advertising professionals consistently assert that subliminal messages are ineffective (Rogers & Smith, 1993). The contention turns in part on semantics—Key includes all cues and symbols, not only specific messages. Advertising is full of such cues and symbols, both calculatedly and accidentally. Whatever their impact, there is no evidence that specific appeals presented below the threshold of consciousness affect consumers.

Our view is that the data exemplify the suspicion with which people view advertising. They believe that as persuaders advertisers will use whatever works, hidden or not. The data also exemplify the not uncommon phenomenon that education sometimes predicts familiarity with a widely held myth rather than accurate knowledge.

IV. EFFECTIVENESS

The effectiveness of advertising is evaluated by three principal outcomes and television stands them on their head in regard to importance. We begin with this somewhat surprising circumstance, then turn to the role of specific attributes of commercials in regard to format, form, and content, and conclude with the response patterns of the viewers of television advertising.

Each of the three criteria by which the success of commercials is judged is a means of influencing the decisions of consumers about purchases. They are liking for the advertisement, recall of the advertisement, and persuasiveness of the advertising message. The first represents a favorable response to the message itself, which through classical conditioning may result in a more favorable response to the product. The second represents the memorability of the advertisement. The third in effect represents liking for the product or service in contrast to feeling about the advertisement.

We cite these three in the order of importance established, in our interpretation, for the medium of television by the extensive research on each (Blair & Rosenberg, 1994; Dubow, 1994; Leather, McKechnie, & Amirkhanian, 1994; Muehling & McCann, 1993; Walker & Dubitsky, 1994). Our conclusion is sharply at odds with popular opinion about advertising.

Ordinarily, it is the effect of the advertisement on desire for the product that is widely thought to be the key to successful advertising. Persuasiveness is the most important factor (Kuse, 1997). Through the product features emphasized and the means by which they will serve the consumer, followed by recall, which will more readily make these features available to the thought processes of the potential customer, and finally, liking for the advertisement, which will reinforce the favorable impression of the product achieved by the emphasized features, advertising in newspapers and particularly magazines enhances product sales.

Television commercials are different. Persuasiveness was a much more prominent factor in the 1960s and earlier when the 60-second narrative was predominant. Examples abound—such as the dinner saved by a quick-preparation product—in which the story that unfolds is clearly intended to create or increase liking for the product (Rutherford, 1995). As commercials grew shorter, first at 30 seconds, and later at 15 seconds, the opportunity to persuade became diminished. The principal means of affecting consumer decisions, then, becomes liking for the appeal itself and recall, the degree to which the fact of an appeal will be retrieved from memory when some pertinent stimulus or query (such as a question asked by an advertising researcher) is encountered. In this context, with persuasiveness comparatively so impotent, recall in fact will function largely through the degree of favorability toward the advertisement induced by memory of it rather than the evocation of pertinent product features emphasized.

The design of commercials reflects the acknowledgment in the advertising industry that this is how commercials now work. But it really goes much farther than that. Had the 60-second commercials with their much greater opportunity for persuasiveness been more effective in influencing consumers, we would anticipate that they would have been retained to a greater degree. There also would not be the very low rate of repeat commercials tabulated by Condry and

Scheibe (1989). If persuasiveness were the goal, then repetition that would lead the viewer to give greater consideration to product features would be a preferred strategy. Instead, many advertisers use multiple commercials, each of which is seen only once or a few times on the grounds that effects do not increase with repetition. Effects usually occur with the first or second viewing (Longman, 1997)—only with a very complex appeal might a third viewing be necessary for full comprehension (Tellis, 1997)—and are at best merely reinstated at each additional viewing. Boredom (or what in advertising jargon is called "wear-out") then becomes a risk with repetitive exposure. The television commercial has assumed a particular function in the panoply of the advertising of products—one that takes advantage of its capability of offering a visual anecdote with adroit music and cunning language.

The major means by which television commercials sway consumers is by being likable, like Barbie dolls or Winnie-the-Pooh. Concrete product advantages (although not the implication of superiority because of one or another glorified attribute) are immaterial. Thus, there is the small, incidental role for central processing of commercials and the enormous role for peripheral processing that depends not on the rational weighing of alternatives but on an unthinking affective response. Television commercials are not merely advertising in a different medium but are a different means of advertising.

Each of our three criteria have become adopted for measuring the successfulness of commercials because they permit direct measurement of likely success on a commercial-by-commercial basis without taking into account intervening market factors. Each is a correlate of increases in consumer decisions to consider the product, which in turn is a correlate of increased purchases. Thus, liking for the commercial, recall, and persuasiveness each predict increased sales.

It would seem that increased sales by themselves would be the best measure because they are the goal. However, they are awkward and inefficient as measures of commercial effectiveness. When advertising campaigns are examined, it is easy enough to identify those that have been part of a larger marketing effort that has led to a superior or at least largely undiminished position for a product in the marketplace (Jones, 1989). The performance of the company becomes the measure of the campaign. Advertising expenditures are much trickier and often show no relationship to sales (McGuire, 1986). This is partly because they may rise to offset falling sales or remain steady or even increase in opposition to social trends unfavorable to a product, such as has occurred with milk, meat, and hard liquor.

Furthermore, the scheduling of multiple commercials differing in design and the low rates of repeat exposure do not favor trying to trace sales to particular commercials. We acknowledge that scanning technology in store or home and the well-developed electronic measurement of television use permits the linking of exposure to specific commercials with consumer expenditures on a small scale, but we are skeptical that these links will be powerful enough to serve as very meaningful indices. Specific linkages will be largely outweighed by the desirability of a varied campaign. More important, data on sales may tell us what has worked in the past but they are of no help in choosing among the options for future commercials (Poiesz & Robben, 1994), a task for which our three criteria are well suited in the testing of commercials before using them (Chow, Rose, & Clarke, 1992).

Our selection of recall as second in importance will strike some as naive and others as uninformed. We acknowledge that this measure, once accepted widely as the principal indicator of advertising effectiveness in research after World War II, has earned a reputation as an unreliable predictor of consumer decisions on the basis of extensive data collected in the 1970s and 1980s. Once a sturdy variable employed as a proxy for increased sales, it has become every knowledgeable observer's villain of a dependent variable providing uneven, inconsistent, and therefore uninterpretable outcomes. However, the very recent analysis in the mid-1990s of 20 years of data on recall and consumer behavior by Dubow (1994) convinces us otherwise. The problem has not been recall as a dependent variable but the measurement of recall. Dubow demonstrates that the uneven and inconsistent outcomes are entirely the product of a particular means of collecting the data. When all of the data over two decades are sorted into piles representing that questionable means of data collection and different, more recently employed means, the uneven and inconsistent outcomes cluster exclusively in the former. The latter indicate that recall is a sound predictor of advertising influence on consumer behavior. Because we believe the data also indicate it has a more prominent role than persuasiveness in the case of television commercials, we rank it second in importance as a criterion for judging their effectiveness.

Television advertising, then, relies far less on persuasiveness than does advertising in newspapers and magazines. Like all advertising, among its goals is the heightening or maintenance of salience for a product—a specific brand among colas, colas among soft drinks, soft drinks among beverages, beverages among snacks, snacks and beverages among food choices, and the like. However, salience is much more prominently the province of television commercials. The inflow of depictions in real time; the mind-set of the viewer prepared for undemanding entertainment, news, and sports that will provide some escape from the events of his or her day; the short visual, verbal, and musical anecdotes designed so carefully to fit those very circumstances—and because they depend so much on being liked and recalled, at such outstanding expense that the per-minute costs are far greater than the programs they accompany—all make salience the principal intention of television commercials. This role of commercials is exemplified by the power of mere exposure. Those who try to avoid commercials by switching channels or fast-forwarding become especially vulnerable to influence as measured by recall, brand assessment, and purchase intent (Lin, 1990; Zufryden, Pedrick, & Sankaralingam, 1993). This is presumably because these acts heighten attention and so the motive founders in the face of the visual experience, and is particularly so when a commercial need only reinstate an effect it has had at an earlier viewing (Gilmore & Secunda, 1993).

Television commercials do not sell products. They sell a position in the cognitive space of the viewer that will make it more likely that the product in question will fall within the universe of considered options when a purchase is under way, whether it is of a $33,947 sport utility vehicle or a $1.09 bar of soap.

A. FORMAT

Four issues have received attention in regard to format. They are the degree of exposure given prevalent scheduling, commercial length, the role of repetition and risks of clutter, and the program context.

Television audience measurement overestimates the exposure to commercials accompanying programs because viewers are more likely to avoid commercials than ignore program content. Abernethy (1990) examined 6 studies of observed differences between program and ad exposure and 10 studies of self-report differences spanning 20 years, and calculates that the degree of absence totals about 40% of the available audience, with about half that figure actively avoiding commercials only whereas the other half miss the commercials because they are not ardently attending to the screen. About 10% of viewers additionally switch channels when commercials appear. Some are adept enough to switch slightly in advance of commercials, using their knowledge of the conventions of the medium to predict commercial placement (Moriarty & Everett, 1994). Many will not be successful in their attempt at avoidance because commercial presentations typically occur across channels at approximately the same time. Thus, almost a third of viewers actively attempt to avoid exposure to commercials.

The data on 15- vs 30-second commercials indicate that the former may suffer somewhat in effectiveness but not by enough to make the latter the better choice (Patzer, 1991). It is estimated that there is about a 20% deficit in effectiveness. This leads to the rule that if costs are time-based, 15-second commercials are a bargain, and that they remain the better choice until costs equal or exceed 80% of the price for a 30-second spot.

Wear-out and wear-in refer, respectively, to declines and increases in cognitive or affective responses with repetitive exposure to the same commercial (Hughes, 1992). Clutter refers to declines in such responses as a function of quantity of commercials. In our view, the data from the several dozen studies analyzed by Pechmann and Stewart (1988) are quite consistent, and the contributions of others simply elaborate somewhat on the central findings (Brown & Rothschild, 1993; Haugtvedt, Schumann, Schneier, & Warren, 1994; Johnson & Cobb-Walgren, 1994; Kent, 1993; Kent & Allen, 1993; Pieters & Bijmolt, 1997; Singh, Mishra, Bendapudi, & Linville, 1994; Zhao, Shen, & Blake, 1995) that we offer as eight principles:

1. Some commercials never wear out, but continually reinstate the earlier favorable response.
2. Wear-in is not a requisite occurrence, because commercials often perform well with one or two exposures.
3. Commercials that fail to do well early probably will never be very effective.
4. Repetition and variation are both useful strategies; the latter increases knowledge gain whereas the former reinstates initial reactions.
5. Decisive preference for another brand is unlikely to be overcome even by repetitive exposure to a commercial.
6. Forward placement in a pod or grouping of commercials increases effectiveness, but only to a small degree.
7. Inclusion within a program of commercials for competing brands tends to reduce effectiveness—but this knowledge is of no use to advertisers because television channels do not permit advertisers to choose the nearby commercials.
8. Cognitive processing ability increases the effectiveness of commercials when they are grouped together, and thus clutter is a greater problem among older adults than it is among younger adults.

The programming context also has been investigated. Barnouw (1978) long ago argued that television's entire makeup can be attributed to the needs of advertisers, with depressing, challenging, or disturbing content generally avoided as unlikely to be suitable for selling brand products. More narrowly, Hoffman and Batra (1991) empirically identified 39 prime-time programs as high or low in cognitive or affective impact, and argue that viewers are more likely to remain in place for commercials accompanying programs high in cognitive than affective impact because the latter will result in their turning away from the screen at the first opportunity to seek relief from tension. Broach, Page, and Wilson (1995) found that very arousing programs ordinarily led to greater liking for commercials, but that an unpleasant program led to greater liking when it was low in arousal. Mundorf, Zillmann, and Drew (1991) found that an emotionally disturbing news story interfered with the processing of commercials immediately following. Chi, Thorson, and Coyle (1995) found that commercials were more effective when they elicited greater involvement than the accompanying program; a highly involving program was associated with lower effectiveness. Hansen and Krygowski (1994) found that the interpretation of an MTV video could be primed by the content of a video preceding it, an outcome that implies that program content would shape response to a subsequent commercial. Kamins, Marks, and Skinner (1991) found that what they identified as "happy" commercials paired more effectively with "happy" programs and "sad" commercials paired more effectively with "sad" programs. Perry (1997) found in an experiment with a student sample that greater levels of humor when present in commercials were associated with greater recall and purchase intention, whereas program humor detracted from recall of products. These varied studies support the view that programming context makes a difference—context enhances commercial effectiveness when it is pleasant, undisturbing, not highly involving, not particularly affective in impact, and compatible with the content and tone of the commercial. Consistently responsible for enhanced effectiveness is the absence of elements that interfere with the processing of the advertising message.

B. FORM

Our review of the evidence on form elements or techniques of commercial design covers two broad topics: executional style and music. The first divides into three elements—visual and nonverbal content, rhythm, and pacing. The second encompasses the language of music, music as a retrieval cue, and classical conditioning.

The overriding importance of visual elements is clear. A number of experiments support the view that visual displays have at least three effects (Percy & Rossiter, 1992): positive affect that transfers to the brand; implications that emphasize favorable properties of the product; and liking for the advertisement. In television commercials the visual elements take precedence in cognitive processing. This visual precedence occurs even when bunches of commercials are viewed together and persists in recall a week later (Bryce & Yalch, 1993). Commercials take advantage of this phenomenon—visual processing is a correlate of effectiveness (Young & Robinson, 1992). As might be expected, then, forcefulness of a presentation in commercials depends more on nonverbal elements than the stated argument; one reason for this is that viewers perceive spokespersons as hired help and thus discount verbal product advocacy (Thomas & Soldow, 1988). The large role for visual and nonverbal elements is largely attributable to the low involvement of viewers, which makes verbal persuasion and rational decision making comparatively minor. Four of the nonverbal elements that have been demonstrated to affect brand salience are music, paralanguage (pitch, harshness, etc.), the physical attributes of the setting, and the elaborateness of production (Haley, Staffaroni, & Fox, 1994). As the antipathy of viewers toward what is said would predict, paralanguage figures in negative more often than positive reactions.

The rhythm or sequencing of elements in commercial design influences effectiveness. Young and Robinson (1989) on the basis of the aggregated results of 26 studies concluded that a repeated two-step organization of memorable visual elements with increasing emphasis ("rise, pause, rise further, pause") consistently enhanced recall. Alwitt, Benet, and Pitts (1993) found that earlier introduction of the brand, the product package, and the relationships among featured persons led to earlier favorable evaluations that on the whole remained more favorable while watching the commercial—the implication being that commercials should be designed to present their major points during the early part of the initial "rise."

The increased pace of commercials may interfere with their effectiveness. MacLachlan and Logan (1993) found that, as number of shots per commercial increased, both recall and persuasiveness declined, with 30-second commercials with 12 or fewer shots superior in performance and those with 1–5 shots at least as effective as those with a greater number. The intuitively pleasing implication is that the comparative performance of 15-second commercials might be improved by using no more than six and preferably about three shots.

Music is a design element of many commercials (about 2 out of 5) although only a few (slightly more than 10% of those with music) use it as a principal means of delivering the message, such as a jingle. Unlike its role in restaurants and stores where tempo directly influences behavior—such as eating more slowly, drinking more during the long wait for a table, or moving about at a faster pace—music in commercials affects emotions and cognitions as do visual and verbal elements.

A primary mode of influence is through the language of music—strong consistencies exist between judgments about music and its three major dimensions, time and rhythm (tempo and beat), pitch (up, down) and mode (major, minor), and texture (loudness, timbre). Fast tempos are more likely to be perceived as happy, as are bouncy or lightly syncopated tempos (although there is a limit to the linearity of this relationship, with an inverted-U representing a preference for mid-rapid time with both slow and very fast tempos disliked), high pitches as exciting, minor or dissonant modes as sad, loudness as attention getting, and so on. Hitchon and colleagues (1994) found that music is more likely to be associated with commercial effectiveness when the commercial is not too cognitively demanding. They used the same music for each of six product commercials (beer, shampoo, etc.) shown with MTV-type programming in an experiment with college student subjects, and not only liking for the commercial but also favorable evaluation of the brand were greater when the commercial was lower in visual and narrative ambiguity. Similarly, a review of 15 studies of the use of music in commercials by Bruner (1990) concluded that music, whatever its nature in the specific instance, facilitates recall when involvement is low and the response is congruent with the product (which would mostly be upbeat applications). When involvement is high, however, music may distract from processing the message.

Music usually aids recall. In more than 2550 telephone interviews, Stewart, Farmer, and Stannard (1990) found that use of a musical cue increased recall of having seen a commercial from 62% for a verbal cue alone to 83%. Also, the commercial descriptions of those hearing the musical cues far more frequently used words describing action, people, and the setting—that is, memories were more vivid.

Finally, music certainly figures in conditioning. Gorn (1982) seemingly demonstrated classical conditioning when liked music paired with a product (a pen) increased selection over competing brands, but Kellaris and Cox (1987, 1989) failed to replicate this specific outcome. Our view is that music obviously may help to create a favorable affective response to a brand or product, but that a more artful configuration than liked music alone would usually be necessary to influence consumer decision making. Otherwise, advertising would consist solely of pairing liked stimuli with brands and products and the effects of advertising would proliferate to the asymptotes of visual perception and aural reception.

C. CONTENT

Stewart and Furse (1986) examined over 1000 commercials as they were scored by viewers in regard to recall, likeability, and persuasiveness. They identified 159 executional factors that might be present or absent. The element that most consistently predicted high scores on persuasiveness was something that differentiated or set apart the brand. This confirms the wisdom of the practice of designing commercials to emphasize brand features, even if they are double-speak or fragile under analysis ("flavor that is flavor"). Other elements that predicted high scores included humor, memorable auditory cues, brand logos at sign-off, dramatic openings (including early emphasis on the brand, a factor recorded as effective in regard to form), and proportion of time devoted to the brand. These are highly credible findings not only because of the sample size but also because they were replicated 3 years later with another 1000-commercial sample by Stewart and Koslow (1989).

A similar, earlier enterprise by Ogilvy and Raphaelson (1982) that used somewhat different concepts to examine about 800 commercials reached similar conclusions. Their list of effective elements included problem–solution (which could be considered a variant of brand differentiation), humor, convincing characters, realism, newsiness, testimonials, and demonstration of the product (which would imply more time devoted to the brand). Overall, the conclusion of Stewart and Furse seems to hold: elements work when they do not clash with or overwhelm the central message, which is to advance the brand through liking for the commercial, recall, and persuasiveness, which function only through creating some mental link between the commercial and the brand.

The delicate balance that exists is exemplified by the experiment of MacInnis and Stayman (1993). When a commercial specifically depicted competitors as inferior (a negative appeal, in advertising jargon), focus on the brand enhanced effectiveness, but when a commercial in the more common vein was confined to casting the product in a positive light, focus on the brand decreased effectiveness. MacInnis and Stayman concluded that too much focus on the brand inhibited facilitative thoughts and may have made the appeal seem forced or excessive. It is not at all difficult to integrate this with the findings that point to brand emphasis as a condition for effectiveness. The conclusions to be drawn are that the brand should be featured early as well as late but, as one would expect from the paramount importance of liking for the commercial, brand emphasis must occur in the context of other attractive and appealing features.

These data, as representing in part an apparent anomaly, have important implications for interpreting the studies of Stewart and Furse, Stewart and Koslow, and Ogilvy and Raphaelson. When sets of factors survive such multi-commercial analyses, they become identified not only as effective in the past but as conventions of advertising that on the average are executed effectively. Thus, the data do not so much register effectiveness, which in a specific instance might involve any of the elements examined, as the set of elements whose employment effectively has become the standard of professional practice.

Reece, Vanden Bergh, and Li (1994) found that slogans are better associated with a product when they contain the brand name, a practice that came into vogue in the late 1980s (Lipman, 1989), and are more likely to be so identified by those who view more television. Barlow and Wogalter (1993) found that alcohol advisories in commercials were better recalled when they used both visual and auditory modalities than voice only, but print alone was about as effective. These two experiments point to the importance of clearly registering the intended message in the viewer's mind.

D. RESPONSE PATTERNS

Our discussion of viewer response patterns divides into two parts. The first covers the three major formulations of how advertising affects consumers, relates these to the behavior of viewers, and identifies the perspective most applicable to television commercials. The second discusses a highly pertinent population with singular attributes—children.

1. Three Theories

Of the three major theories relating to the effects of persuasive messages, the most applicable and meaningful for understanding the way commercials work is the Elaboration Likelihood Model (Petty & Cacioppo, 1981, 1986, 1990). The Theory of Reasoned Action (Ajzen & Fishbein, 1980) is not at all irrelevant; in fact, we see the important role ascribed to norms as a major background or contingent condition for a genre or brand. Changes of brand are unlikely to occur if alternatives are not socially acceptable; the same holds for trying new categories of product. We see the Hierarchy of Effects (Lavidge & Steiner, 1961) similarly. The theory posits a number of necessary conditions for advertising effects, including those of television commercials. However, we would fault it for the invariant role assigned to recall, the lack of a larger role for affect (although it could easily be incorporated), the omission of the immediate response to a commercial, and the sequential ordering of steps. In the case of commercials, these factors have more limited application than in instances where persuasive argumentation figures more prominently. This is because reactions are so immediate and number of prior exposures for maximum effect at a given time are as few as none.

The Hierarchy of Effects (HoE) places the act of purchase as the final phase in a series of stages of other, less difficult to achieve, phases (Figure 2.1). All outcomes are in ascending order of hypothesized necessity, beginning with the simple cognitive effects that such messages are most likely to achieve (such as the recognition that a commercial features a particular product); then, affective influences, slightly more difficult to attain; and finally, conative effects or purchase decisions, which involve the most complex set of factors and those least likely to be influenced solely by mediated messages. Advertising is assigned several sequential objectives: stimulating awareness of the product, providing knowledge of its attributes, linking the product with the need or desire of the consumer, inspiring a preference for the product over others, and fostering conviction that the product is truly necessary—until, at last, the consumer makes the purchase decision.

The Theory of Reasoned Action (ToRA) posits that an individual's decisions about what to do are determined by his or her intention to perform that behavior, as influenced by both personal evaluation and perceived norms. These are, in turn, the products of previous experience, but particularly important are the consequences perceived as likely to result from adopting the behavior. The receiver of a persuasive message is seen as thoughtful and logical in deciding

FIGURE 2.1   Three theories of advertising influence. Adapted from *Understanding Attitudes and Predicting Social Behavior* by I. Ajzen and M. Fishbein, 1980, Englewood Cliffs, NJ: Prentice-Hall; "A Model for Predictive Measurements of Advertising Effectiveness," by R. J. Lavidge and G. A. Steiner, 1961, *Journal of Marketing, 25*, pp. 59–62; and *The Elaboration Likelihood Model of Persuasion*. In L. Berkowitz (Ed.), Advances in Experimental Social Psychology, Vol. 19 (pp. 123–205). New York: Academic Press.

whether he or she should comply based on favorability toward the specific act in question and perceptions regarding what other people will think about the act. Perceived norms are a function of the beliefs a person ascribes to important others and the motivation of the person to comply with the opinions of those others. Attitudes and norms together will encourage or discourage adoption of a behavior, and individuals will differ as to the weights they assign the two. Positive evaluations may be reinforced or discounted by norms; norms only have an effect among those who consider the practices and opinions of others important. The evaluation of the two determinants may change, as may the weights assigned them, in response to appeals such as those made by advertising. The focus is narrowly on the specific act—in the case of commercials, usually a product or service—rather than the generic class (drinking Corona rather than beer; listening to Art Pepper or Charlie Parker rather than modern jazz; reading the *New York Times* rather than newspaper reading) because this increases the predictability of eventual behavior from the elements of the theory: evaluations, perceived consequences, perceived norms, and the importance attributed to norms.

The Elaboration Likelihood Model (ELM) provides a wide-ranging framework for understanding the way persuasive messages function as well as describing conditions on which compliance will rest, as do the HoE and ToRA. The theory attempts to identify the factors that determine the messages on which an individual will choose to elaborate or focus relatively high levels of cognitive attention. Attitude and behavior change, however, is not exclusive to such central processing. It may occur through one or the other of two routes: the *central,* in which the individual engages in thoughtful reasoning regarding the persuasive arguments used as well as the pros and cons of adopting the suggested change in attitude or behavior, and the *peripheral,* in which the individual responds instead to a cue in the message, which instigates change without requiring focused cognitive consideration.

The process of objectively assessing an argument is influenced by the situational circumstances that affect whether the person has the ability or the inclination to engage in the more cognitively taxing activity of processing arguments centrally. With the increasing clutter from all media of persuasive messages demanding attention, the motivation to centrally process appeals may be decreasing for most individuals. People simply are unable to devote a significant amount of cognitive work to assessing persuasive messages because they are exposed to so many. Peripheral cues then become more important determinants of persuasion. In the case of much advertising (mostly in other media), people may take the time to judge accurately an advertisement's claims. In the case of television commercials, their disposition toward a product or service may change at least briefly because of the pleasing character of the presentation, its memorability, or in a fewer number of cases, the positive attributes claimed.

The ELM reserves central processing for the rational assessment posited by ToRA and HoE and assigns a parallel peripheral processing when primary factors are immediate liking (or disliking), affect, and the source—in this instance, the commercial—rather than the weighing of attributes. The commercial typically positions the product, assigns it positive features, and presents visual, auditory, and musical components intended to hold attention briefly and facilitate favorable recall.

The central element of the ELM, involvement, is a major factor that sets television advertising apart (Krugman, 1965). For most products, involvement is fairly low. Nevertheless, differing levels of involvement are the psychological dynamic through which demographics predict somewhat different responses to product categories. Gender and age each predict differential interest, so that involvement rises and falls. Yet, the overall level remains moderate to low.

In the case of commercials, then, involvement mediates attention. Males are more likely to pay attention to ads for automobile and auto products, where in fact they appear more frequently. Females are more likely to pay attention to ads for cosmetics, feminine hygiene products, and female apparel; here, they are more frequently portrayed. This involvement increases the likelihood of one or the other route of cognitive processing, which facilitates liking for the ad, recall, and persuasion. It typically is at a comparatively low level, so that peripheral processing predominates. When viewers become sufficiently involved, arousal joins pleasantness and these dimensions of affect then facilitate message elaboration (Manno, 1997).

In the ELM, central processing leads to more decisive and lasting persuasion. This is because of the greater degree of review, the rejection of alternatives after they have been weighed, and the reaching of a well-considered decision. Central processing leads to attitudes that are more resistant to change over time, are more durable in the presence of counterpersuasion, and are better indicators of subsequent behavior than are changes in attitudes brought about by peripheral cues. Peripheral processing leads to more transient, less stable effects that derive from affective reactions to the appeal and the source—the commercial. The strategy of major brand advertisers of repeatedly advertising—but with varying messages to minimize boredom, disinterest, or a reaction of dislike—rests on sound principles of persuasion theory. Thus, television repetitiously advertises the same products endlessly to maintain current levels of favorable viewer response. This holds for the great majority of products. The goal is to establish and maintain salience so that the advertised brand will receive equitable consideration when consumers are deciding what they will buy. The message and, in effect, positive salience are continually reinstated.

These circumstances also explain the rather amazing ability of advertising to retain its value to brand marketers despite public opinion that is critical or unfavorable. The less the central processing, the less often these perspectives will be called on in responding to advertising. Thus, the low involvement in advertising generally works to its advantage. Television is the extreme case, with brief exposure and low involvement overriding long-standing critical public opinion.

ELM's peripheral processing not only fits television commercials particularly well, but also its dual pathways are well suited to advertising in general. Its principles account for advertising effectiveness in the context of exposure to huge quantities of such messages in all media and attitudes on the part of many that are hostile to or critical of advertising. It alone accounts for this paradox.

2. Children

Television and trips to the supermarket with a parent introduce children to the vending of brand goods. Children are a distinctly different audience in regard to advertising—as they are in regard to many aspects of the media—because they bring neither the cognitive skills, experience, nor preferences of adults to the exposure. Quantitatively, exposure to commercials is prodigious. Our estimate is that the average child 2 to 11 in age spends enough time with television to see almost as many commercials as the 60,000 seen by the average adult viewer. Even discounting for substantial inattention and the absence of sufficient involvement with a product category for a commercial message to register much of the time, children see at least 12,500 commercials a year that could have some relevance to them: snacks, fast foods, soft drinks, toys, shoes, and clothing. (Comparable figures for teenagers 12 to 17 in age, who watch less but would find far more products relevant, are about 27,000 total and 16,000 relevant commercials). Our analysis covers three topics: comprehension, persuasion, and interaction with parents.

There are three aspects of comprehension that have received empirical attention: recognition and understanding; specific devices, such as disclaimers, separators, and language; and premiums. In each case, the data challenge the propriety of television advertising directed at children.

The data are unambiguous about recognition and understanding. Children of preschool age as young as 3 years can recognize commercials as different somehow from programs and can match characters with the products they advertise (Butter, Popovich, Stackhouse, & Garner, 1981; Levin, Petros, & Petrella, 1982; P. Zuckerman & Gianinno, 1981). However, a majority of children under the age of 8 do not understand that a commercial is a self-interested attempt to gain consumer compliance—that is, a message intended to benefit the advertiser (Davies, 1996). The research of Blosser and Roberts (1985) makes the distinction clear. They exposed 90 children varying in age from preschool to fourth grade to a variety of television messages. When the criterion was recognition that a commercial presented a purchasable item, more than half before the age of 7 could be said to "understand" a commercial. When the criterion was perceiving and articulating persuasive intent, it was not until age 8 that a majority understood a commercial. News was identified earliest; this dramatizes the problematic nature of commercials for children's comprehension because obviously frequency of exposure—which would be greatest for commercials—is not the solution.

The experiment by Gentner (1975) explores the issue further. She examined acquisition of the verbs have, give, take, sell, buy, and spend by asking children varying in age from $3\frac{1}{2}$ to $8\frac{1}{2}$ to dramatize them with two "Sesame Street" puppets. Even the youngest understood give and take, but did not comprehend buy and sell. Comprehension of these two concepts increased with age, reaching 95% for buy and 65% for sell among those $7\frac{1}{2}$ to $8\frac{1}{2}$ in age. The major point is that the transaction of which a commercial is a part is too complex for children to understand fully the position and goal of the advertiser (buy is probably easier than sell because it involves one less step and children participate earlier in the act).

A meta-analysis of 20 studies examining comprehension of persuasive intent and age (Martin, 1997) provides supportive findings. A significant, positive correlation resulted between the two variables ($r = .32$), documenting that the evidence consistently indicates younger children compared to those older have difficulty understanding the persuasive purpose of commercials. The strength of the relationship varied, with younger children showing greater comprehension when nonverbal measures were used and with greater confusion at all ages when ads were shown in isolation rather than embedded in programs.

Our conclusion is that young children do not comprehend the selling intent of commercials. By the standards applied to adults, then, for whom magazines and newspapers label paid-for material that may be mistaken as editorial copy, these children are exploited by television commercials directed at them. An experiment with almost 250 third graders (Austin & Johnson, 1997) found that exposure to media literacy training in the short term increased comprehension of persuasive intent and perceptions of realism in commercials. Thus, even at the age when a majority begin fully to understand commercials, some children will benefit from instruction about their persuasive purpose and techniques.

The data are equally clear that at least those disclaimers and separators—announcements or visual displays that supposedly help children recognize commercials—that have been examined typically have been ineffective (Ballard-Campbell, 1983; Liebert et al., 1977; Palmer & McDowell, 1979; Stutts & Hunnicutt, 1987). The former, although perhaps satisfying to critics and the consciences of advertisers, are largely not understood because they do not use the language of children (for example, by saying "Assembly required" rather than "You have to put it together"). The latter did not register with many children because they were not blunt or sufficiently declamatory. The reason, of course, is that making a pronounced issue of either is not in the interest of the businesses of television and advertising, which wish neither to lessen the effectiveness of a commercial nor to disrupt the attentiveness of the viewer.

In a similar vein, Paget, Kritt, and Bergemann (1984) found that the commonplace techniques of commercial design interfered with their accurate comprehension. They found that the persuasive intent of specific commercials was identified at a somewhat earlier age when it consisted of a spiel directed at the viewer rather than the typical portrayal of persons interacting in connection with a product.

M. L. Geis (1982) presents examples of language (beyond disclaimers) that challenge interpretation. Options or alternatives are often precluded by implication ("_____ is part of a complete breakfast," p. 221) and implied properties may misrepresent the product, as in the describing of artificial flavors as if they were real (. . . "More lemon. More cherry. More lime . . . ," p. 244). He makes the point that children are cognitively unable to evaluate such distinctions in real time (and adults, we would add, are generally disinterested in doing so), so that in effect commercials directed at children often trade in evasion and deception.

Consumer advocates argue that premiums should be secondary to product attributes in purchase intentions; otherwise, product evaluation is distorted (Adler et al., 1980). However, a comparison of first, third, and sixth graders (Rubin, 1972) found that an attractive premium offer inhibited recognition of the product as the major subject of a commercial even among those in the sixth grade. Among those in the first grade the premium was more often perceived as the principal subject of the commercial, and in general, recall of the premium was greater. In our opinion, this is rational behavior given the fungibility of major brands advertised to children, but undeniably the data confirm the ability of advertisers to woo children successfully with toys, logos, and trinkets.

Advertising certainly is effective in directing children's product choices. Endorsements by liked individuals increase product choices (Adler et al., 1980; P. R. Ross et al., 1984). Commercials with characters from other programs are less likely to be recognized as advertisements (Kunkel, 1988); this challenges the FCC policy that host-selling—the use of program characters to vend goods—is permissible when the commercial accompanies another program. Brand selections are readily manipulated by recent exposure to commercials (Galst & White, 1976; Goldberg, Gorn, & Gibson, 1978; Gorn & Goldberg, 1982). Generic choices, however, are comparatively resistant to influence. Thus, commercials advocating fruit and other healthy choices over salty snacks are only marginally effective (Goldberg et al., 1978).

We concur with the conclusion reached by Adler and colleagues (1980), based on the review by Meringoff (1980):

> Empirical evidence attests to the general effectiveness of food advertising to children. Children have been found to learn the information provided in food commercials, believe the product claims about advertised foods, draw inferences about product benefits, and influence the purchase of foods advertised to them. (p. 217)

There has been concern that the advertising of over-the-counter remedies encourages use and abuse among young persons of both legal substances, such as alcohol, and illegal substances, such as marijuana and cocaine—enough so that in 1975 (Bellotti) the attorneys general of 15 states petitioned the FCC to ban all drug commercials between 6 A.M. and 9 P.M. In surveys, very small positive correlations have been recorded among teenage samples between exposure to alcohol advertising in general and alcohol consumption and between exposure to alcoholic beverage commercials and beer consumption (Atkin, Hocking, & Block, 1984; Atkin, Neuendorf, & McDermott, 1983; Strickland, 1983; Tucker, 1985), between exposure to alcohol advertising in general and use of advertised brands (Atkin, Hocking, & Block, 1984), between such exposure and measures of alcohol abuse such as belligerence (Strickland, 1983) and drinking while driving or otherwise in an automobile (Atkin, Neuendorf, & McDermott, 1983), and between a favorable opinion about beer commercials and alcohol consumption (Slater, Rouner, Domenech-Rodriguez, Beavais, Murphy, & Van Leuven, 1997). In all of these instances, the relationships were observable after the control for demographic variables and persisted when various measures of media use (Atkin, Hocking, & Block, 1984; Atkin, Neuendorf, & McDermott, 1983; Strickland, 1983) and such social influences as parental and peer drinking (Atkin, Hocking, & Block, 1984) were taken into account. Experiments with college-age males and females have demonstrated that exposure to alcohol commercials in a context of social drinking may speed up ordering (Kohn & Smart, 1984) or increase consumption (Kohn & Smart, 1987), and those experiments with preteens have demonstrated that exposure to portrayals of drinking in entertainment programming may shift attitudes toward a more favorable appraisal of alcohol (Kotch, Coulter, & Lipsitz, 1986) or increase choice of alcohol as an appropriate drink for adults (Rychtarik, Fairbank, Allen, Foy, & Drabman, 1983). Certainly the use of famous athletes and attractive personages to endorse alcohol in commercials and the fact that much drinking in entertainment programming is done by high-status, favorably portrayed males (Breed & DeFoe, 1981) give some currency to the likelihood of influence. These data together clearly suggest some influence of television on alcohol consumption among the young, although not by the means identified by the 1975 petition to the FCC.

But in the largest, most nationally representative sample of 2000 teenagers (Chirco, 1990), no consistent correlations between amount of exposure to commercials and alcohol or illegal drug use were recorded, with exposure in this case measured by amount of overall viewing. The sole exception was teenage girls, for whom there was a significant correlation between television viewing and wine drinking. This is neatly explained by the data of Frank and Greenberg (1980) in which one audience segment consisted of young women low in socioeconomic status who watched a lot of television and enjoyed indoor games—and while engaging in these activities apparently consumed what we would guess were wine coolers. Almost certainly the alcohol consumption derives from the social setting and not the greater exposure to commercials for alcoholic beverages. In two large samples, no correlations between meticulously measured exposure to over-the-counter drug commercials and use of illicit drugs were recorded either among about 350 teenage boys (Milavsky, Petowsky, & Stipp, 1975–76) or among about 700 preteen boys and girls (Robertson, Rossiter, & Gleason, 1979), although in the same two sets of data small positive correlations between such exposure and use of over-the-counter drugs appeared. Similarly, in another very large sample of 3500 boys and girls 11 to 17 in age, there were no correlations between amount of television viewing and either alcohol- or illegal-drug-related delinquency (Thornton & Voigt, 1984).

The strongest associations in the national sample (Chirco, 1990) for both alcohol consumption and illegal drug use were positive correlations with having friends who use one or another of these substances, and with having friends who have favorable attitudes toward the consumption of these substances, and with the opportunity to drink or use illegal drugs as measured by amount of time spent away from home. This pattern emerged after the control for a wide range of other variables, and the representativeness and size of the sample makes it strong evidence despite the crudity of the exposure measure. Our conclusions are that television drug advertising encourages use of products of the advertised genre among young persons but not alcohol or illegal drug use, and television alcohol commercials and portrayals may have a very small influence on drinking behavior and probably one that is greatest when choices must be made about whether or what to drink. However, there is no evidence of a substantial or widespread (and in the most representative, national sample, even measurable) influence of television on alcohol consumption or illegal drug use, and any contribution is minute compared to the influence of peers and opportunity.

As with adults, repetitive exposure to a commercial ordinarily does not increase persuasiveness beyond the amount necessary to process the stimuli but variation in appeals does inhibit boredom or wear-out. In the one instance when repetition with varied appeals converged toward a deadline, however, Rossiter and Robertson (1974) found that the Christmas toy and game choices of 290 first-, third-, and fifth-grade children were decisively influenced. In early November, those with superior cognitive and affective defenses (such as distrust and indifference, respectively) chose fewer advertised items. By mid-December, defenses ceased to predict choice and those with stronger earlier defenses chose more of the advertised toys and games. Thus, repetitive advertising, in conjunction with comparatively high involvement and the necessity of making a decision, shaped the Christmas wishes of children.

The effectiveness of commercials directed at children also is attested to by the requests for purchase made to parents. Both Galst and White (1976) and Atkin (1978) observed parents and children in supermarket aisles. The former found that amount of prior television viewing was a predictor of frequency of requests, and that the kinds of requested items were those advertised on tele-vision. The latter found that two-thirds of exchanges about products were ini-tiated by children, about three-fourths of these were demands, and parents yielded to about two-thirds of these demands. In fewer than 10%, the parent responded with an alternative; thus, the rejection rate was a compliant 1 of 4. On the other hand, in the one-third of the instances in which the parent initi-ated the choosing of a product, the child in about 1 of 3 instances rejected the parent's choice. Television's child, apparently, is a tough customer.

These data constitute evidence of frequent television-based requests for pur-chases and substantial television-induced conflicts between parents and chil-dren. They also clearly underestimate the role of television in child-related con-sumption because they ignore direct purchases, prior requests, and a parent's regular acquiescence to a child's known preferences.

Assembled to Monitor

Television viewing is a sampling, comprehensive and wide-ranging, of all the ways modern people attend to mass media—browse, momentarily ignore, assemble into a mosaic of contrasting bits, passingly follow, attentively consume. The data of audience measurement mask "a discontinuous, often interrupted, and frequently nonexclusive activity for which a measure in hours and minutes serves only as the outer boundary of possible attention" to the screen (Comstock et al., 1978, pp. 146–147). What makes viewing unique among all modes of media consumption is not a single attribute of attending to the screen but the great amounts of time allocated that bear one or another mark of indifference. This becomes a paradox, given the enormous value that Americans attach to having their television sets on.

Viewers for the most part attend only sufficiently to follow the unfolding narrative, whether drama, comedy, news, sports, or talk shows. This monitoring is a function of the modest demands placed by the content on the cognitive capacities of the viewer. The content, in turn, is a function of the modest degrees of attentiveness that can be given to a medium that many will use for several hours each day. Content and attention function together, with the first maximizing audience size and the second maximizing time that audience members can spend with television.

61

We begin our examination of audience behavior with the empirical documentation of the who and what that are found so attractive on the screen. Next, we advance several psychological and sociological concepts that describe the way the public attends to television. Finally, we assemble a portrait of the audience that is spending time with America's favorite leisure activity.

I. ON THE SCREEN (WHO AND WHAT)

The parameters of television programming consist of conventions that have proved successful in attracting and holding audiences, and they represent the expectations of those turning on their sets at any given time of day. The most prominent characteristic is stability. Genres remain much the same. Innovations, sometimes quite important in terms of presaging trends in programming, are largely confined to the rise or fall of a genre, as exemplified by the demise of the western by the mid-1970s and the recent popularity of adult-oriented situation comedies, or a departure in treatment and style, such as the prime-time soap operas of the 1980s, the social realism of the Steven Bochco law-and-order family, or the melding of science fiction with the law enforcement procedural of the *X-Files*. These innovations typically become the hallmark of new conventions. Yet, the sole clear trends of the past five decades have been toward portrayals of sex that are more explicit and portrayals of violence that are more graphic. Shifts from season to season have been largely minor, except for the abandonment of the live drama at the end of the Golden Age. The quest of television for widespread popularity, like that of theater movies, means that audience expectations must be satisfied. The difference is that in the case of television this quest derives from the marketing of commercials to advertisers and the consequent need for demographics continuously pleasing to them in size and composition, rather than the pursuit of paid admissions, so that the use of formulae of seeming certitude in regard to popularity are even more relied upon. As the patterns of attending to the set will document, these expectations are for programming that is diverting but undemanding in terms of attention or emotional involvement.

The literature representing empirical, quantitative studies of the attributes of television entertainment is enormous. We find, however, that it becomes quite tractable when collated under the topics of people and their attributes, violence, and themes and values.

A. PEOPLE

The two thorough analyses of early 1950s television by Head (1954) and Smythe (1954) provide not only a description of programming in the infancy of the medium but also a benchmark for the detection of major changes. They variously recorded the following:

- Entertainment was the predominant type of programming.
- Within entertainment, drama was predominant, with the most frequent genre that of stories of violence (crime, at the time).
- Males outnumbered females by a substantial margin (at the time, 2 to 1).
- The social hierarchy was topsy-turvy compared to real life, with the professions and middle and upper middle classes outnumbering blue collar workers.
- Young adults at ages of "peak" sexual attractiveness were predominant among characters.
- Females were usually portrayed as housewives; males had more varied roles and more often were portrayed as professionals.
- Four out of five were White Americans; Blacks and other American minorities were almost nonexistent.
- Three fundamental processes of life were ignored: birth, natural death, and failing health.

Head makes the insightful point that certain realities, such as male dominance, in 1950s television were translated into statistically visible misrepresentation. Our interpretation with the benefit of 50 years of hindsight is that these were elements for telling stories that were comprehensible and acceptable to most viewers.

By the calendar, these findings are pathetically out of date. Television is by repute a medium of novelty, with each season bringing new shows with new characters and situations. What makes these and subsequent data so important is that they forcefully challenge such conventional wisdom. In fact, television has been a medium in broad outline frozen in place. The key is "mass entertainment"; this is a commodity that has changed in its essentials only slightly in a half century.

Subsequent analyses document that the predominance of entertainment (Table 2.2)—and within entertainment, violent storytelling— would continue through the late 1990s (Condry & Scheibe, 1989; Television Bureau of Advertising, 1997). What would change is that the western, embraced in the mid-1950s with the appearance of such series as *Cheyenne* (Clint Eastwood) and *Maverick* (James Garner), within two decades would be abandoned with the return to the crime show as the principal vehicle for violent stories.

The dominance of males and the inversion of the social hierarchy would characterize daytime soap operas as well as prime-time entertainment well into the 1980s and 1990s (Gerbner, Gross, Signorielli, & Morgan, 1986). For example, one recent analysis (Greenberg & Collette, 1997) found that in over 27 prime-time seasons ending in 1992–93, males outnumbered females in major new characters introduced in every season, and often by ratios of 2 to 1 or greater; and 1 of 4 occupationally were professionals, such as doctors, lawyers, or accountants. Males would remain preeminent in evening entertainment, although eventually daytime soap operas would offer portrayals somewhat more balanced as to gender (Signorielli, 1989). Greater numbers of cable channels and new broadcast networks (UPN and WB) have accounted for little substantial change in the representation of gender (Eaton, 1997; Kubey, Shifflet, Weerakkody, & Ukeiley, 1995).

Children (Heintz, Delwiche, Lisosky, & Shively, 1996) and the elderly (Cassata & Irwin, 1997) have seldom been seen at any time. With the civil rights movement of the 1960s, Blacks would be allocated a place on television that with some oscillations over subsequent years has approximately matched their presence in the national census; other minorities would remain rare (Comstock et al., 1978; Condry, 1989; Greenberg, 1980). Whites would remain preeminent; so, too, would those in the young adult ages of peak sexual attractiveness and those in the middle and upper middle classes (Bettie, 1995). Women would continue at least in the evenings to have roles largely circumscribed to homemaking or as objects of sexual attraction (Greenberg & Collette, 1997; Signorielli, 1989). The facts of birth, death, and illness would become prominent as medical series, such as *Dr. Kildare* and *Ben Casey*, became a fixture of evening entertainment (Turow, 1989), but the emphasis was on the fortitude of the practitioners rather than the experiences of the patients.

B. VIOLENCE

The most thoroughly examined aspect of television entertainment has been violence. This is partly because of the persisting concern over its effects (Chapter 8), and partly because of the regular and well-publicized "violence profile" tallies undertaken over the past 30 years by Gerbner and colleagues (Gerbner, Morgan, & Signorielli, 1994).

There are four sources of data:

1. The 16 not-quite-annual analyses of physical violence or threat thereof in prime-time and weekend entertainment, each representing a network television season, conducted by Gerbner and colleagues beginning with the 1967–68 season.
2. The similarly representative analyses by Greenberg (1980) and by Potter and Vaughan (1997) that span almost two decades and variously tabulate verbal as well as physical aggression and pro- as well as antisocial behavior.
3. The very recent data from the late 1990s representing violence in cable and broadcast entertainment, whose collection was sponsored by the television industry at enormous expense at the University of California

at Los Angeles (Cole, 1995, 1996, 1997) and the University of California at Santa Barbara (*National Television Violence Study*, 1996a, 1996b, 1997a, 1997b, 1998a, 1998b).

4. A variety of sets of data—including several collected by Potter and colleagues—that focus on various aspects of violence, such as the attributes of those involved or the circumstances of the incident.

The empirical encoding of violence obviously requires a definition. We present two that can be taken as representative of the criteria for physical violence:

> The overt expression of physical force against self or other, compelling action against one's will on pain of being hurt of killed, or actually hurting or killing. (Gerbner, 1972)

> Any overt depiction of a credible threat of physical force or the actual use of such force intended to physically harm an animated being or group of beings. (*National Television Violence Study*, 1996a)

These definitions concur in encompassing credible threats, behavior, and consequences, and the former includes accidents and acts of God and nature. Definitions confined to human malfeasance or criminal acts obviously produce lower frequencies, although when data using such a narrower definition (in the instance, compiled by CBS) were compared with those using a broader compass, trends over time (but not absolute amounts) were the same (Comstock et al., 1978).

Data typically represent a large sample of network offerings—in Gerbner's case, of fall prime-time and daytime weekend programming. Comparisons with larger samples and other time periods within the same season indicate that such samples are adequately representative of these channels and seasons (Signorielli, Gross, & Morgan, 1982).

The data of Gerbner and colleagues present us with a persisting fact and an admonitory pattern. The persisting fact is that children's programming as measured by rate of violence invariably has been much more violent than general audience prime-time programming (Figure 3.1). The admonitory pattern is that across the years the rate of violence has been quite stable in the long term. Large differences occur from season to season and among the networks within a season, but over time violence emerges as a staple. Thus, the data warn against inferring lasting changes or differences from analyses covering only 2 or 3 years, although they may reflect noteworthy temporary shifts in industry practices.

By the Gerbner violence index there nevertheless has been a slight decline in recent years. This becomes clear simply by imagining a (regression) line across the scores since the mid-1980s. Violence in television entertainment has not become an issue because it has been increasing, but has been slightly decreasing possibly because it has become an issue. Across the past three decades,

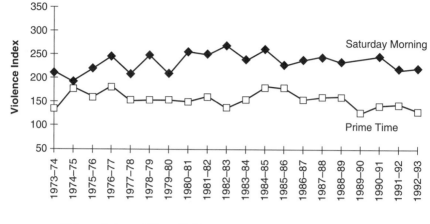

Violence Index = %P + 2(R/P) + 2(R/H) + %V + %K
P = % programs containing any violence
R/P = rate of violent scenes per program
R/H = rate of violent scenes per hour
V = % major characters involved in violence as perpetrators or victims
K = % major characters involved in killing as perpetrators or victims

FIGURE 3.1   Trends in television violence, 1973–1993 (composite weeks of fall programming). Adapted from *Television Violence Profile No. 16,* by G. Gerbner, M. Morgan, and N. Signorielli, 1994, the Annenberg School of Communication, University of Pennsylvania.

violence has ebbed when it has been the focus of public and political pressure (Clark & Blankenburg, 1972); this has been accomplished by the networks through the reduction of proportions of major characters involved in violence, number of violent acts, and frequency of more serious acts (Comstock et al., 1978). Frequency of violence as a central plot element in contrast has remained unchanged. This has allowed violent genres to continue unabated when they were popular at such times.

The data of Greenberg and of Potter and Vaughan, collected about 20 years apart using the same methods, further support the conclusion that violence is a staple. There was little in the way of change across this sweep of time. However, their data make some additionally important points. First, the inclusion of verbal aggression, defined as diminishing or hurtful statements, consistently more than doubles the rate of violent acts. Second, when physical and verbal aggression are summed as a measure the amount of violence in all general audience programs is quite similar, including situation comedies. Third, substantial quantities of verbal and physical prosocial behavior also have consistently been recorded, although at a somewhat lower rate than for antisocial behavior unless the prosocial category is defined very broadly (Potter & Ware, 1987a). These data on the one hand confirm the central role of conflict in popular story-telling and on the other point to the sensitivity of estimates of the frequencies and rates of television violence to the concepts and definitions employed.

The industry-sponsored inquiries each covered a comprehensive range of broadcast, network, cable, and independent channels. The UCLA group essentially followed the model established long ago by the network standards departments that monitored programming for objectionable elements. In this case, coders transcribed every instance of violence, which in turn were reviewed by teams of judges for troubling elements. These included graphicness, gratuitousness to the plot, absence of advisories or warnings to parents, or time periods when children were likely to be in the audience (Cole, 1995, 1996, 1997). The UC-SB group proceeded very differently. They quantitatively recorded the frequency of violence in terms of incidents (ideally including a perpetrator, act, and target), scenes (connected incidents), and programs (*National Television Violence Study*, 1996a, 1996b, 1997a, 1997b, 1998a, 1998b).

Together, these two enterprises cost $4.8 million, an extraordinary sum for analyses of mass media content. The motives of the sponsors were political. Both the cable and broadcast industries wished to placate the White House and Congress to preclude regulatory attempts beyond the V-chip requirement of the 1996 Telecommunications Act (Chapter 1). The cable industry invited the broadcasters to join in their $3.5 million grant to the UC-SB group, but the paranoia over vested interests that characterizes media competition—the belief in this instance that data will hew to the sponsor—led the broadcasters to finance a separate endeavor.

The two studies concur in finding movies, and particularly movies made for initial release in theaters, the most violent of television formats, and therefore the premium movie outlets the most violent of channels. They diverge on trends—the UCLA group discerning some reduction in troublesome violence and the Santa Barbara group finding few signs of meaningful change over the 3 years.

In our judgment, the UC-SB effort is superior conceptually, analytically, and scientifically. One of the purposes of empirical content analysis is to reveal latent characteristics that because of the quantity of data are not apparent (Krippendorf, 1980). The UCLA approach fails to do this. It is scarcely more than a tally anyone might undertake from his or her living room. The UC-SB sample is decidedly larger and more comprehensive, and certainly protects well against anomalies (20 years after the fact, Gerbner is still chided for including in a composite week an episode of a situation comedy that had an atypically high violence count because of a dream sequence). However, we doubt that the sample thereby gains much descriptively other than as a defense against skeptics and critics. Our admiration instead rests on three interrelated qualities: the use of the behavioral research on the effects of television violence (Chapter 8) to construct dimensions for describing programming; the consequent representation of elements documented as influencing behavior in that description; and, by these means, the coherent and artful extension of behavioral research to the description of content.

It is understandable that a television executive or a politician might be content with a survey of worrisome portrayals. The strength of quantification is precision and thoroughness in this respect, and in this instance in validity because the tabulation rests on observed behavioral effects. The result is the most powerful content analysis in the history of mass communication research in identifying latent variables of social as well as scientific importance and meets Merton's criterion of matching empiricism and theory to advance the practice of science (Sztompka, 1996).

The data pinpoint accurately which channels are responsible for the most violence (Table 3.1). The frequent alibis of broadcasters are proved somewhat valid—cable is a source of greater violence, particularly the movie channels. The data also record that television frequently portrays violence in ways that might stimulate aggressive and antisocial behavior (Table 3.2)—in realistic settings, repetitively, often without pain, with infrequent long-term consequences, attractive perpetrators, few penalties, little remorse or criticism, and a display of weapons that could be perceived as tantalizing. These data go beyond the work of Gerbner and colleagues, Greenberg, and Potter and Vaughn in explicitly linking what has been on the screen with what has been discovered to increase the likelihood that portrayals will contribute to aggressive and antisocial behavior.

Other sets of data focus on specific aspects of violent portrayals. Price, Merrill, and Clause (1992) found that over a 2-week period during prime time (8–11 P.M.) on ABC, CBS, Fox, and NBC in 1990, there were 424 instances in which guns were used. In accord with the demography of television entertainment, users were predominantly White males (over 75%), and in accord with violence in general, perpetrators seldom suffered repercussions and suffering on the part of victims, friends, and family largely went unshown. Potter and Ware (1987a), in a 1985 prime-time sampling of ABC, CBS, and NBC, similarly found that most perpetrators and victims were White males in the prime of adulthood whereas females appeared somewhat more often (although still in a decided minority) as perpetrators and receivers of prosocial rather than antisocial acts. Major felonies, the most serious offense recorded, were the province of the youthful White male adult, whereas females became more frequent as perpetrators or victims as seriousness of offense declined, being especially active in leveling insults and telling lies. Potter and colleagues (1995), in an exhaustively detailed examination of manner of portrayal of almost 4000 acts of verbal and physical aggression in 1994 on the four major networks, found that

TABLE 3.1 Violence by Type of Channel

	Overall percentage	Broadcast networks	Public broadcast	Independent broadcast	Basic cable	Premium cable
Percentage of programs with violence	57	F	SF	A	A	SM
Percentage of those programs that contain violence . . .						
with 9 or more interactions	33	F	F	M	A	SM
with advisory or code	15	M	A	A	M	SF
with an antiviolence theme	4	A	F	A	A	A
that show long-term consequences	16	A	A	A	A	F
with violence in realistic settings	51	A	SM	F	A	SM
Percentage of those scenes that contain violence . . .						
with unpunished violence	73	A	A	A	A	A
with blood and gore	15	A	A	A	A	M
with humor	39	A	SF	A	A	A
When a violent interaction occurs, percentage . . .						
that show no pain	58	A	M	A	A	A
that depict unrealistic harm	35	A	SF	A	A	F
with repeated behavioral violence	57	A	A	A	A	A
that appear justified	44	A	A	A	A	A
Of those characters involved in violence, percentage . . .						
of perpetrators who are attractive	37	A	A	A	A	A
of targets who are attractive	43	A	A	A	A	A

SF Substantially fewer than industry average
F Fewer than industry average
A Industry average
M More than industry average
SM Substantially more than industry average

Adapted from Mediascope, *University of California-Santa Barbara National Television Violence Study,* 1996a.

televised life mirrored real life in the preeminence of young males, but failed to do so in the low frequency of Black perpetrators; violence generally was not portrayed in a moralistic framework of harmful consequences and punishments, and the absence of these was particularly frequent for easily copied acts such as lying and insult. Potter and Ware (1987b), in an earlier 1985 three-network prime-time sample of more than 1600 such acts, found that heroes

TABLE 3.2   Overall Industry Averages for Violent Depictions

Depiction	1995	1997
Percentage of programs with violence	58	61
Violent programs		
with an antiviolence theme	4	3
that show long-term consequences	16	16
with "bad" characters who go unpunished	37	37
with violence in realistic settings	51	55
Violent scenes		
with no remorse, criticism, or penalty for violence	73	71
with blood and gore	15	14
with humor	39	42
Violent interactions		
that show no pain	58	51
that depict harm unrealistically	35	34
with use of a gun	25	26
with repeated behavioral violence	58	61
Violent characters		
perpetrators who are attractive	37	39
targets who are attractive	43	45

Adapted from Mediascope, *University of California-Santa Barbara National Television Violence Study*, 1997a.

and villains were about equally likely in the short term to be rewarded or appear to have justification for antisocial acts, which was the case 90% or more of the time. Scharrer (1998), in an analysis of 331 male characters in police and detective series airing between the 1960s and mid-1990s, found that more than three-fourths of "good guys" and "bad guys" were White and that for both groups the committing of violent or aggressive acts was associated with traits of hypermasculinity. For good guys, however, this association decreased with time—serial cops and detectives today are less macho than they once were. Estep and MacDonald (1983) found that network crime shows in the late 1970s and early 1980s consistently underrepresented Blacks, young persons, and those of lower socioeconomic status as both victims and perpetrators of robbery and murder.

The use of violent entertainment varies among national and local channels because it is one of the dimensions of content employed in competing for viewers. As Hamilton (1998) neatly demonstrates in an analysis of all the 2295 movies shown on prime-time broadcast network television over a 6-year period (1987–1993), the networks shift toward or away from violence depending on the makeup of their regular audiences and the "brand image" they seek to present during the sweeps periods when advertising rates for the outlets in each market are established (with ABC and Fox shifting toward and CBS and NBC shifting away in Hamilton's data). Similarly, Hamilton's analysis of 7984 evening movies shown by 22 broadcast and cable channels in 1995–96 shows how violence (and adult language and situations) vary in the establishing of brand identities (with Cinemax, HBO, and The Movie Channel particularly prominent on both dimensions). The nationally representative survey data ($N = 1516$) on which he draws indicate that the audience for violent entertainment disproportionately is younger (19–49), watches a great deal of television, is non-White and male, and has less than a college education. Nielsen data pinpoint males 18–34 as most often represented in the audience for violence, followed by females 18–34, and males 43–49. Genres vary somewhat in appeal, with younger males more often viewing violent movies; women, accounts of family violence; and older viewers and women, mysteries. These are demographics generally sought after by advertisers except for the lower levels of education (which would predict less income), but as one would expect when products vary in demographic appeal, the presence of such viewers in the audience for programs designed to attract them raises the rates for commercials (Hamilton, pp. 68–70).

Overall, the data on the portrayal of violence present three unmistakable patterns. The first is one of great stability across the years and great prominence in all genres of storytelling. The second is that aspects that might deter emulative behavior are often absent, whereas acts easily imitable without requiring much in the way of skill or courage are highly prevalent. The third is that the biases of presentation are those favorable to the relating of stories without undue offense but sufficient glamour to be acceptable to a wide range of viewers.

C. THEMES AND VALUES

We identify five primary themes and values that find expression again and again in a variety of contexts. We do not debate that others when engaged in a similar quest might use somewhat different labels or add or drop one or another. We do argue that these five would be hard to ignore in attempting to describe television entertainment in broad terms. They are:

- The dominance of the White male and the preeminence of the middle and upper middle classes;
- The persisting tide of problems and challenges to success, self-esteem, and often life itself;
- The effectiveness of the remedies offered by society;
- The idealization of the American family; and

- The implicit endorsement of selected categories of behavior that might well have penalties for health.

The dominance of the White male is reflected in the greater frequency of male characters, the greater range and higher status of their occupational roles, and their greater presence among those involved in the dramatically important tasks of perpetrators and victims of crime. However, data also document this emphasis in a variety of other ways, such as the deferent and subservient role in medical series that female nurses play in regard to male physicians (Kalisch & Kalisch, 1984); in MTV, the frequent portrayal of females as sex objects (Sommers-Flanagan, Sommers-Flanagan, & Davis, 1993) or in condescending (Vincent, Davis, & Boruszkowski, 1987) and gender-stereotyped roles (Seidman, 1992); and, in the comparatively few network series with school settings (of which only 40 had been aired prior to 1990), the distribution by gender and race, with the great majority of teachers and students being male (whereas in real life two-thirds of teachers are female), most major characters who were students being male (whereas in real life the gender division is about equal), and Blacks being sharply underrepresented (Mayerle & Rarick, 1989). There is no doubt that the presence of women employed outside the home has increased in prime time, with series featuring such characters rising from as few as 8 in the 1970s to 10–14 in the early 1980s and about 20 by the end of the decade (Atkin, 1991; Atkin, Moorman, & Lin, 1991). However, roles for females have remained somewhat more restricted than for males and, at the most recent tabulation, females compared to males still specialized in interpersonal relations (Vande Berg & Streckfuss, 1992). The preeminence of the middle and upper middle classes is exemplified by the underrepresentation of blue collar males as involved in crime and violence (Estep & MacDonald, 1983; Gerbner et al., 1986) and the pervasive presence among major characters across all types of storytelling during all day-parts of doctors, lawyers, executives, and other professionals (Gerbner et al., 1986; Greenberg & Collette, 1997).

Long ago in his analysis of soap operas, Katzman (1972) observed that the plots largely consisted of dilemmas and threats that the main characters had to resolve to retain their status and meet their responsibilities. He counted 85 in 14 series over 1 week. This seemingly obvious comment in fact cuts to the essence of all of television. This is nowhere better exemplified than by the high and pervasive rates of physical and verbal aggression, each of which is a response to such challenges. Selnow (1986), in an examination of 222 subplots in prime-time fictional programs, found that about 95% introduced a problem, dramatized the conflicts in seeking a solution, and concluded with a resolution—with "honesty as the best policy," "hard work pays off," "ingenuity triumphs," and "good conquers evil" accounting for most resolutions. Potter (1988) found that middle school and high school students overwhelmingly ranked the conflict between good and evil as the most frequent theme, with a large majority perceiving that good usually won. These outcomes clearly support the view that television presents a limited number of themes and values, with confronting tribulations and threats being prominent among them. The construction of storytelling requires conflicts—and of the possibilities, conflicts with others are far preferred for dramatic effectiveness (Baldwin & Lewis, 1972). Conflict within the self or with God are too abstruse; with nature, dramatically too limited. Thus, the world of television entertainment that so many employ as an escape ironically is a world of personal and interpersonal woe.

The effectiveness of remedies is a theme often ascribed to commercials, accompanied by speculation that television endorses quick remedies that could encourage drug or alcohol use or abuse (Comstock et al., 1978). However, the same phenomenon is pervasive in television storytelling. Problems and difficulties are resolved within the 22 minutes of situation comedies (Larson, 1991). Law enforcement personnel and independent operatives in crime dramas consistently have solved cases at a 90% rate that would seem utopian to most police departments (Dominick, 1973; Estep & MacDonald, 1983). Actual officials in "reality-based" programs similarly have succeeded at a 70% rate compared to the 18% for all crimes recorded in the same year by the Federal Bureau of Investigation (Oliver, 1994). And in medical series, diagnoses not only usually are accurate and treatment effective, but also the most modern and expensive of technologies are generally available to alleviate suffering and save lives and limbs (Turow, 1989). This effectiveness again reflects the requirements of format; conflicts must be resolved to the viewer's satisfaction within the framework of each episode.

The idealization of the American family in the domestic situation comedy understandably has been one of the most thoroughly documented aspects of television entertainment. As Cantor (1991) points out in her history of the television family, this places these comedies in contrast to the glorification of the single White male in crime shows and the often dissolute family of the soap opera. Our view is that this is to be expected because the underlying purpose of a variety of genres is to carry somewhat contrasting but similarly widely appealing emphases. We see the treatment of the family in these two other genres as the indirect consequence of achieving their dramatic mission, whereas its treatment in the domestic situation comedy is central to the genre because families are what they are about. The typical family has been middle-class, White, and nuclear, although there have been a variety of types of families, such as one-parent or unmarried, since the early 1950s (Skill & Robinson, 1994). The empirical literature in fact charts several rather clear dimensions (Comstock & Strzyzewski, 1990; Haefner & Comstock, 1990; Larson, 1989, 1993; Perse, Pavitt, & Burggraf, 1990; Skill & Wallace, 1990; Weiss & Wilson, 1996): the nuclear and extended family has been most common; there is generally a positive aura about problem solving and resolving dilemmas; parents are extremely supportive, and are more successful in gaining their children's compliance to their wishes than are children in gaining the compliance of parents. Thus, tradition, success, and authority have been the pillars of the situation-comedy family. Very recent analyses (Douglas, 1996; Douglas & Olson, 1996) point toward a slight increase in the hostility displayed by children and in the conflicts they have with parents and peers, and families are recorded as somewhat less effective at socializing children than in the past, whereas the overall pattern of parental and child roles has remained intact for over 40 years (Skill & Robinson, 1994).

The implicit endorsement of problematic behavior rests on its acceptance by societal norms. The two instances where we find this occurring in television entertainment are sex and alcohol. Sexual relationships or their promise have long been a part of the storyline of daytime television drama (Katzman, 1972), with sexual intimacy in very early soap operas only implied (Greenberg, Abelman, & Neuendorf, 1981). Sexual relationships also have been a consistent element in prime-time entertainment (Sapolsky & Tabarlet, 1991). The data now extend into the early 1990s, but their import in our view is less to describe today's television than to uncover relationships between programming and society. Most sexual intimacy in daytime drama has been occurring among the unmarried (Olson, 1994). It also has become explicit although hardly graphic. Intercourse in prime time, once implied, more recently has been portrayed (Sapolsky & Tabarlet, 1991). Suggestiveness in prime time has been replaced by increased frequencies of portrayals of physical intimacy (Lowry & Shidler, 1993). The most telling aspect is that sexual behavior has been portrayed without any suggestion that it may figure in the transmission of AIDS or other disease (Lowry & Shidler, 1993; Lowry & Towles, 1989). A narrowly focused examination of prime-time drama with incidents of rape found that the presentation of rape myth (in the author's words, "asking for it," "wanting it," "lying about it," and "not being hurt") exceeded countermyth by a ratio of almost 5 to 3 (Brinson, 1992). The appearance for the first time of occasional discussions in soap operas of safe sex (Olson, 1994) in our view reflects the increasing social acceptance of preventive sexual practices, but overall the depictions offer sex, and in the case of rape, male-imposed sex, as without the prospect of serious consequences. Alcohol similarly has been endorsed by television entertainment, with consumption or preparation to consume occurring at about three instances per hour in prime time and somewhat more frequently in daytime soap opera (Diener, 1993; Wallack, Grube, Madden, & Breed, 1990) quite apart from the commercials for alcoholic beverages. These outcomes represent accommodation to and thereby reinforcement of social norms. The medium has signaled that sexual intimacy and alcohol consumption may be indulged in without concern. Our interpretation gains force from the treatment of cigarette smoking within one of these same sets of data (Diener, 1993), where consumption was one-twentieth that of alcohol. Tobacco in the form of cigarettes has lost its social standing.

The who and what of television, then, rests on two basic preoccupations. People, violence, and the themes and values conform to the needs of storytelling and the avoidance of the objectionable, and will change only as the norms of society change.

II. ATTENDING TO THE SET

The measurement of time spent viewing television in recent years has become a controversial topic. There are three reasons. First, as the number of channels increases, audiences grow smaller and harder to measure accurately with the sample sizes and procedures that were once quite adequate for three networks and in major markets a few independent stations. Second, as the diversity of options markedly decreases the audience shares of the original three networks, they become increasingly desperate to leave no viewer uncounted. Third, changes in the technology of measurement have led to changes in audience statistics, raising questions about validity. Huge amounts of money ride on the size and makeup of audiences because they determine the prices for commercial time that advertisers are willing to pay, so these circumstances have made the methods of tabulation become newly subject to suspicion and debate.

Our approach is to begin with the process of viewing, so that time spent viewing can be better assessed as well as its measurement perhaps better evaluated. We cover three topics: purposes and motives, the concept of audience, and modes of response.

A. PURPOSES AND MOTIVES

It is easy to demonstrate active involvement in viewing, such as using a remote control to find greater rewards or choosing the same program again and again when viewing at a particular time. It is also easy to demonstrate passivity, as when people view what others have chosen without concern for what they may be missing or when the audience size for a program is partly predictable by the audience size of the preceding program. We believe, however, that viewing is best described by terms that are more multidimensional and that represent rather complex constructs. Our preference is to build on two concepts introduced by Rubin (1983, 1984)—ritualistic and instrumental viewing.

Ritualistic viewing, in our use of the term, represents giving the medium priority over the specific program. A principal goal is the consumption of time. It is television that motivates viewing, and the particular program is chosen as the most satisfying of those available. This is the well-known two-step viewing decision (Barwise & Ehrenberg, 1988; Barwise, Ehrenberg, & Goodhardt, 1982; Comstock, 1991b), in which the decision to view precedes the choice of program. This is the modal or typical process. It is reflected in the use of television guides to select a program less than half the time, the regular use of such guides by only one-fifth of the audience (Lin, 1990), and the tendency to view television at the same time on various days, regardless of actual content (Rosenstein & Grant, 1997). Viewing typically occurs in blocks of time, and amount of viewing is largely uninfluenced by the programs available. Two correlates of regular ritualistic viewing are higher overall amounts of viewing and a preference for nondemanding content, which leads toward light entertainment and away from news, documentaries, and other informational programming.

Instrumental viewing represents giving priority to the intrinsic merits of content over the rewards of the medium. Often, the program draws the viewer to the set. However, instrumental viewing also can occur within the two-step paradigm when a viewer discovers that the options include a program of high interest. The program is the focus of attention, and thus viewing is more often bounded by the beginnings and endings of specific offerings. Viewing more often involves using television guides to select programs. Correlates of regular instrumental viewing are lower than average amounts of viewing and a comparatively greater preference for interest-based content, such as more serious entertainment, informational programming, and specific sports.

We see these concepts as applicable to individuals, in regard to the predominant kind of viewing, as well as to the process of viewing. Ritualistic and instrumental viewing represent relatively stable patterns of attention to the screen for individuals as well as variability in response to content differing in interest. Almost everyone at one time or another will view instrumentally, exemplified by the Super Bowl. Most who usually view instrumentally occasionally will view ritualistically. The two also may alternate when an option proves especially interesting or interest flags in a choice.

We recognize that these are polar concepts, and that some may have difficulty discerning in a specific instance whether one or the other is operating. The distinguishing element is whether the experience is driven by the program or by the pleasures derived from attending to the medium. Avid transient attention would not by itself disqualify viewing as ritualistic any more than brief inattentiveness would be inconsistent with instrumental viewing. The deciding factor is the underlying motive, not the vagaries that accompany its expression. We also recognize that they have a great deal of surplus meaning, in the sense that they connote as well as denote behavior and describe a broad set of responses that in their composition will vary specifically from time to time and person to person. Nevertheless, we believe they well capture the two essential, contrasting, and concrete manners of viewing.

The majority of viewing and viewers are ritualistic. This is abundantly clear from a variety of findings in numerous sets of data. Forty percent of viewers have been recorded as watching something because it appeared on the channel tuned to or was chosen by someone else (LoSciuto, 1972). In a study of two dozen families (Hopkins & Mullis, 1985), almost half of adult males and about two-thirds of adult females said they did not give full attention to the programs they were recorded as viewing. Time-lapse photography (Allen, 1965) and the videotaping of viewers (Anderson, Lorch, Field, Collins, & Nathan, 1986; Bechtel, Achelpohl, & Akers, 1972) over 20 years consistently have recorded that on average for all types of content about 40% of the time there is no attention to the screen, and about 15–20% of the time there is no one in the room with the operating television set.

These are all outcomes that identify television viewing as an activity attended to passingly. They raise the question of the gratifications that people derive from viewing. These turn out to have been very stable across the decades, at least in terms of how people describe their motivations. This should not be surprising, because television in broad outline has not changed much. The only source of a change in motivation would be greater familiarity with the medium, an accommodation that would have occurred fairly rapidly among its first viewers in the late 1940s and early 1950s. Thus, the one change in cited motivations was a sizable decline in the 1970s in the degree to which television is perceived as a particularly enjoyable way to spend an evening (Bower, 1973). The viewing of television as a special event that might involve a social occasion of some importance (Rothenbuhler, 1988) has become confined to "media events," televised occurrences that take on great importance for vast numbers such as royal weddings, the Olympics, and the Kentucky Derby (Dayan & Katz, 1992; Katz, 1988).

About three-fourths of the public endorse the proposition that they watch to see specific programs that they enjoy, and about half endorse the statement that they view because they feel like watching television (Bower, 1973). It is important to recognize that these figures represent responses to suggested motives. When viewers volunteer their reasons for having watched the night before, almost no one mentions a specific program and a majority cite just the viewing of television (LoSciuto, 1972). Not many find a night's viewing highly pleasurable, memorable, or exciting, and the number who do has been declining since the 1950s (Bower, 1985). The data that put the rate of repeat viewing—the likelihood that someone who sees a particular program scheduled weekly or every weekday also will see the next in the series—at less than 50% further indicate that it is not particularly favored programs that draw viewers to the set. Kubey and Csikszentmihalyi (1990) found that of all activities across the average day, television viewing was rated as among the least rewarding and pleasurable, and although most time with the family was also spent with television this was among the least valued of activities engaged in with family members.

Barwise and Ehrenberg (1988), two British experts on television audiences worldwide, have concluded that people value television highly, but rarely are enthusiastic about programming in general, although they may have one or two particular favorites at various points in time. When Winick (1988) studied families who lost their television sets to the repair shop, he found they often felt deprived or at a loss, but over how to use time or having something to do rather than the unavailability of particular programs. In Sweden, when a telecommunications strike caused lengthier loss of access, Windahl, Hojerback, and Hedinsson (1986) found among a sizable sample of teenagers that almost two-thirds expressed some degree of deprivation. Those who felt especially so were habitual ritualistic viewers whose interest was in passing time rather than viewing programs, and a substantial portion of those who felt deprived turned to other media with similar content so that they might pass time in a familiar way. Viewers in fact watch when they have time available and no other obligations, commitments, or alternative activites that are more attractive. Television viewing is the residual of the use of time for other activities.

Our interpretation of the data on motives (Tables 3.3A and 3.3B) is that people are largely drawn to the set by the opportunity to spend time in a nondemanding, pleasant manner. Entertainment, news (Levy, 1978), and sports viewing derive most of the time from a mixture of the desire to keep up and occupy time, with the latter predominant. We can confidently conclude, contrary to conventional wisdom, that there is no social onus in spending large amounts of time with television because the public tends to overestimate (rather than underestimate, which would be the case for a socially disapproved activity) the actual amounts of time they spend viewing (Comstock, 1991b; Robinson & Godbey, 1997). Thus, we are not at all surprised that only about one of five perceive themselves as "killing time" (LoSciuto, 1972) because this would conflict with the normative judgment that viewing is time passingly well—if not excitingly—spent.

Although it is not realistic to attempt precisely to ascertain motives beyond what viewers can tell us, we believe the varied data identify three broad categories of motive and their ranking in importance. We would label the predominant and pervading motive as escape in one or another of its shadings. Our reasoning is that measures of enjoyment, pleasure, and the passing of time (that

TABLE 3.3A   Deciding to View

Ways of Viewing (percentage answering "often")		Reasons for Viewing (percentage answering "usually")	
"Watch the same shows because you like them and know they're on?"	72	"To see a specific program I enjoy very much"	74
"Make selections from *TV Guide,* or from the weekly guides in weekend newspapers?"	52	"To see a special program I've heard a lot about"	51
"Watch shows picked by other family members?"	31	"Because I feel like watching television"	40
"Read the listings each day in the newspaper?"	23	"Because it's a pleasant way to spend an evening"	35
"Turn dial until you find something interesting?"	20	"Because I think I can learn something"	27
"Look up TV shows several days in advance?"	20	"Because there is nothing else to do at the time"	25
"Select from ads on the radio, in newspapers and in magazines?"	18	"Turn on the set to keep me company when I'm alone"	23
"Follow recommendations given children by their teachers?"	16	"To get away from the ordinary cares and problems of the day"	19
"Watch one program and then just leave the set on?"	13	"Because my husband or wife is or seems to be interested"	16
"Follow recommendations of friends?"	12	"Because I'm afraid I might be missing something good"	13
		"Start on one show and then get stuck for the rest of the evening"	12
		"Mainly to be sociable when others are watching"	10
		"Just for background while I'm doing something else"	10
		"Because everyone I know is and I want to be able to talk about it afterwards"	8
		"Keep watching to put off something else I should do"	5

$N = 2078$

Adapted from *The Changing Television Audience in America,* by R. Bower, 1985, New York: Columbia University Press.

TABLE 3.3B Deciding to View

I watch TV . . .	Whites (N = 414)	Blacks (N = 348)	Hispanics (N = 458)	F Score
To spend time with family.	2.45	2.94	3.30	30.18*
Because it's enjoyable.	3.97	4.14	3.83	18.04*
When there's nothing to do.	3.09	3.58	3.21	15.08*
Because commercials are a fair price for free TV.	3.49	3.38	3.07	14.74*
To learn about myself.	3.05	3.35	3.57	13.15*
Because it gives me something to do.	3.13	3.61	3.35	11.65*
Because it entertains me.	3.96	4.13	3.90	10.33*
Because it helps me unwind.	3.67	3.53	3.67	2.74
Because it keeps me aware.	4.11	4.07	4.20	2.11
Because it relaxes me.	3.54	3.63	3.67	1.24
To learn new things.	3.59	3.69	3.80	0.33

Strongly agree = 5, agree = 4, neutral/not sure = 3, disagree = 2, strongly disagree = 1

* $p < .001$ for row differences with age, education, and income statistically controlled

Adapted from "An Examination of Television Motivations and Program Preferences by Hispanics, Blacks, and Whites," by A. B. Albarran and D. Umphrey, 1993, *Journal of Broadcasting and Electronic Media, 37,* (1), 95–103.

presumably otherwise would be more burdensome) are very frequently the reasons cited for viewing (Tables 3.3A and 3.3B). A key factor in our view is that persons who are under stress, lonely, anxious, in negative mood states, or in conflict with others score higher on amount of viewing or other measures of attraction to television (Anderson et al., 1996; Canary & Spitzberg, 1993; Kubey & Csikszentmihalyi, 1990; Maccoby, 1954; Potts & Sanchez, 1994). Similarly (but inferentially somewhat less significant, in our view), diminished physical, mental, and social well-being are predictors of greater television viewing (Andersen et al., 1998; Dietz, 1990; Sidney et al., 1998; Tucker, 1986, 1987). Xiaoming (1994), in examining many thousands of respondents to the National Opinion Research Center's General Social Survey between the mid-1970s and early 1990s, found not only that those who scored themselves as "not too happy" consistently watched significantly greater amounts of television than those who scored themselves as "pretty happy," but also were among those increasing most in their viewing over the 17 years (ranking third in 22 demographic categories). These data clearly identify television viewing as attractive for psychological or sociological flight.

Barwise and Ehrenberg (1987) found that entertainment programs were cited by half of viewers as helping them relax, whereas only 1 of 10 said the programs made them think, and Hoffman and Batra (1991) found that two-thirds of 36 prime-time network programs were rated as high in affective impact or low in general in impact compared to only one-third said to be high in cognitive impact. Television also has been shown to be used to some extent to manage moods and deflect depression and unhappiness—with women, for example, turning to comedy to counter unpleasant feelings (Bryant & Zillmann, 1984; Zillmann, 1988; Zillmann & Bryant, 1985; Zillmann, Hezel, & Medoff, 1980). A similar pattern has been observed in regard to anger (Zillmann, 1993), although angered males who anticipate an opportunity for retaliation may seek out violent programming, apparently to maintain their levels of hostility, rather than content that might distract from or help dissipate their aroused state (O'Neal & Taylor, 1989).

However, in the particular case of everyday television viewing, escape typically involves a somewhat peculiar mechanism—undemanding attention. This is made plain by the large numbers who rather casually select what they will view (Table 3.3A) or view what others have selected (LoSciuto, 1972) as well as by the typical modes of viewing in regard to attending to the set—monitoring, low involvement, and content indifference. An important datum is the finding by Kubey and Csikszentmihalyi (1990) that viewing is not highly ranked among all activities as rewarding, pleasing, or gratifying, yet people allocate large amounts of time to it. This calls for explanation, and ours is that television is a satisfying way to pass time because it places few demands on viewers. It typically is not escape into but away from. Pleasure, comparatively, has a price; television seemingly does not, although when the total amount of time spent on it—22 hours and 40 minutes per week by the average adult in the fall and winter (Robinson & Godbey, 1997)—is summed it should be thought of as having a high price in foregone activities. This is the predominant pattern, but escape also is achieved when viewers are wholly absorbed by what is on the screen. Thus, it is the single dimension that unites the passing of time undemandingly with the intense focus of some viewers some of the time.

Our second most prominent motive is surveillance, an interpretation for which we are indebted to Harwood (1997). We do not at all intend the long-used and conventional meaning of attending to the news within the context of the upright citizen scrutinizing the horizon for threats (Wright, 1960). Instead, we mean that people follow television to keep abreast but with an emphasis on how they measure up. We admit this appears tenuous, but our interpretation rests on the data: people say they watch to learn or keep up (Tables 3.3A and 3.3B) but do not specifically refer to news or educational programming, and they consistently pay more attention to personages on the screen like themselves, whether the distinguishing characteristic is race (Comstock, 1991b), age (Harwood, 1997), or gender (Maccoby & Wilson, 1957; Maccoby, Wilson, &

Burton, 1958; Sprafkin & Liebert, 1978). Essentially, we propose that a major reason for viewing television is the continuing process of social comparison made prominent in social psychology by Festinger (1954).

These two motives are obviously quite compatible. We strongly favor the first as more pervasive and prominent because there is more evidence on its behalf. We think the second has a strong claim to legitimacy because of the bias of viewers toward personages like themselves. It also fits well with the rise in popularity of the daytime talk shows focused on personal plights.

The third motive we propose is somewhat different in that it is more instrumental. However, the first two could well be served when the third is the governing factor. This is the seeking of information about what is taking place, not for self-reference but for awareness. What we refer to is closer to the initial conceptualization of surveillance but is much more encompassing. We see this motive as having two facets: events and the makeup of television including entertainment. The former is well satisfied by the content of news and informational programming. Typically, as Hamilton (1998) points out in drawing on the analysis by Downs (1957) of the marketplaces for information, this viewing focuses on personalities and dramatic events that leave viewers "rationally ignorant" because of the low incentive to learn about issues they cannot directly affect. In contrast, there are plenty of incentives to collect information about consumer consumption, finance, and entertainment because benefits will accrue only to those paying attention; in Hamilton's phrase, it is "politics as theater and sport" (p. 241). The latter is represented both by news and informational programming and by entertainment. The emphasis here for attending to the medium is not on the what but the how of television's treatment of its subject matter. Our empirical support again is the frequency with which people cite learning or awareness as a reason for watching (Tables 3.3A and 3.3B), the mixture of interest in the presentational aspects of the news with curiosity about events that motivates news viewing (Levy, 1978) and, foremost, the predominance in people's thoughts when viewing of how what they are seeing—regardless of the specific content—measures up as good or bad, well or mediocrely executed by the standards of "good" television (Neuman, 1982).

Our proposed motives, then, are threefold: escape from cares and pressures, evaluate the self, and, keep up with the medium. We would argue that there is wide, stable, and consistent agreement on the rewards of television viewing because similar motives are cited across the decades (Steiner, 1963; Bower, 1973, 1985) and by Whites, Blacks, and Hispanics, who concur as to the top three motives (Table 3.3B). We acknowledge television as serving the social functions of providing a common experience and a reference for conversation. We nevertheless propose—in our view based on the data of several decades—that the foremost function is to serve the individual in seeking to avoid aversive stimuli.

The equilibrium achieved among amount of television use, motives and gratifications, and the design and scheduling of programming is striking. The medium is at its most profitable the larger or more demographically attractive the audience so that substantial prices can be charged for commercial time. The necessary condition is that individuals spend extended lengths of time in the vicinity of operating television sets. This could not be achieved with intellectually demanding or emotionally draining experiences that require close attention during viewing or some relief at its termination. These are characteristics that sometimes apply to theater movies but seldom to television programs. Television programming satisfies popular tastes, is attractive, diverting, and interesting, but not demanding. The viewer, and particularly when the viewing is ritualistic, expends little in terms of involvement emotionally, cognitively, or psychologically, and much only in terms of time.

B. Audience as Concept

The huge numbers of individuals who attend to television exhibit two contradictory traits, depending on the perspective from which they are examined. They are individually heterogeneous in preference and behavior, with unreliable patterns of consumption from day to day. Using their scores on psychological scales measuring needs (such as status enhancement, escape from boredom, or intellectual stimulation) and scores on a battery of 18 interests (such as "investments," "professional sports," and "comprehensive news and information"), Frank and Greenberg (1980) were able to divide the American public into a variety of audience segments with distinctly different preferences for television programs and other media. From this perspective, the audience is an assemblage of individuals somewhat unpredictable in the short run and of segments widely varying in stable preferences.

In the aggregate, however, the audience also behaves very uniformly from day to day, week to week, season to season, and year to year. We agree with Webster and Phalen (1997) that the most sensible way to conceive of viewers is as a mass audience within which there are a variety of "taste publics." These segments differ markedly in preferences and in amount of consumption of the various mass media. However, in the case of television they differ much more in taste and preference than in what they view. The motives and gratifications that find expression in ritualistic viewing make the tastes and preferences of individuals miserly predictors of what they will view. Frank and Greenberg (1980), for example, found that their audience segmentation (which, in the specific instance divided the public into 14 segments each representing 4–10% of the total) could account for only 5% in the variance in the viewing of 19 program categories. In contrast, the audience in aggregate behaves with great predictability in its size and makeup each day and night, in its flow across the year and over the lifespan and in such "laws" or phenomena as duplication, or channel loyalty; lead-in, or the carry-over of viewers from one program to the next; and repeat viewing, or degree of program loyalty. We reject, then, as a conceptual fallacy—that is, a view that hinders more than helps understanding—the revisionist perspective that the television audience should be thought of as an assembly of varied homogeneous segments seeking differing sets of preferred programs in favor of the concept of the mass audience as accurately denoting much of what takes place in television viewing. Our rationale is that the concept embraces the very clear regularities in aggregate viewing that occur, whereas the revisionist view finds no place for these empirical facts.

C. MODES OF RESPONSE

The mode of behavior that most succinctly and thoroughly characterizes the way the television set typically is attended to is monitoring (but except when we want to call particular attention to the process we will use the terms "viewers," "viewing," and "watching" in accord with American English usage). Viewing connotes a theater-like physical disposition in which the screen is watched continuously. Monitoring is defined as paying sufficient attention to three sets of cues—those of the visual and audio elements of the televised presentation and those resident in the behavior of any others in the vicinity who might be viewing—to follow the unfolding narrative (Comstock, 1991b). Visual treatment, sound effects, and the response of other viewers are all employed to gauge the desirability or necessity of paying attention. The underlying principle is that attention rises with the ability and need to assemble a narrative successfully. It falls when elements can be comprehended independently of one another, so there is nothing to assemble, or when missed elements can be supplied by the viewer, so that assembly is unnecessary. Attention is maximal for movies, which are the least episodic, redundant, and stereotypic of television's offerings and for children's programming, which is novel and interesting for its young viewers—so much so that one set of investigators (Argenta, Stoneman, & Brody, 1986) used the term "mesmerized" to describe preschoolers viewing cartoons, the sole type of programming for which they thought the term applied for that audience. Attention is minimal for such episodic constructions as commercials, news, and sports, and such stereotypic fare as daytime and prime-time soap operas. Analogous to the cartoon viewing of children, for most other categories of programming teenagers give more attention to the screen than do younger children (Bechtel, Achelpohl, & Akers, 1972), because they are paying closer attention to understand the content and they are trying to follow more complicated narratives. Comprehension, then, among older children and adults governs attention to the screen. Thus, it is curvilinear as children mature, rises as they progressively attend to more adult-oriented programming, then falls as they become accustomed to the conventions of television storytelling. The low levels of adult attention are the result of the process of learning how to use television efficiently, and the outcome can be called the law of minimum attention.

The corollary is low involvement. People enjoy television as a medium immensely. They find pleasure in having the set turned on, but they do not become deeply involved or intensely interested in specific programs very often (Barwise & Ehrenberg, 1988). Thus, fewer than half of viewers will endorse the statement that a program they saw last night was "really worth watching" (Robinson, 1972a). This is hardly surprising. The many hours registered as viewing television by so many could hardly sustain deep involvement or great interest.

Underlying these two circumstances is a paradoxical indifference to content (Comstock, 1991b). Viewers wish to maximize satisfaction, so they almost always choose the same program among options when viewing at a particular time (Barwise, Ehrenberg, & Goodhardt, 1982). However, they are not drawn to view generally by the particular programs that are scheduled. Instead, the time they have available leads them to incorporate greater or lesser amounts of viewing in their schedules. This is remarkably documented by the similarities among television set owners in the amount of set use around the world, despite vast differences in the amount, variety, and quality of programming available at the various sites and the great social and cultural differences across countries in North and South America, and Western and Eastern Europe (Comstock, 1991b; Robinson & Converse, 1972; Robinson & Godbey, 1997; Szalai, 1972). Differences across countries are modest to minute, with the average deviation in amount of viewing across 15 international locations a mere 4.6% (Robinson & Converse, 1972). Additional testimony to this phenomenon comes from the two-step decision process, in which the decision to view typically precedes the choice among options of what to view; the frequency with which programs not actively chosen are viewed; and the moderate to modest levels of repeat viewing in which majorities of viewers do not return to see the next episode of the option they have indicated they prefer at a given time. The dominance of time is also reflected in the correlations across the years in amount of viewing. The correlations are substantial for adjacent years (about $r = .66$) so that viewing appears as a fairly stable trait but as the time span increases they decline (Feshbach & Singer, 1971). It is the medium and the opportunity to view made possible by available time, not the program, that are paramount.

The data justify some comments about day-parts and demographic segments in regard to monitoring. One would expect monitoring to be at its lowest during prime time, when many employed adults are viewing after work and the most prominent offerings are on. Yet, in a two-week long ethnographic examination of 24 families (Hopkins & Mullis, 1985), fathers reported watching 136 programs but said they gave "complete attention" to only 75, whereas mothers reported watching 143 programs and said they gave complete attention only to 52. The gender difference translates into 45% vs 64% for monitoring, or less than complete attention, and undoubtedly reflects greater female involvement with household tasks and child care. The first conclusion is that monitoring as a mode of viewing is quite frequent even when one would expect it to be at a minimum. The second is that much of the daytime viewing by adult females is made up of monitoring.

This pattern—in which program content plays such a comparatively modest role—strongly encourages the interpretation that there is intrinsic gratification in the use of television. The extraordinary documentation by Plomin and colleagues (Plomin, Corley, DeFries, & Fulker, 1990) that there is a hereditary contribution to amount of time spent with television further supports such an interpretation. The data come from 220 three-, four-, and five-year-olds, their siblings, and natural and adoptive parents in the well-known Colorado Adoption Project (Plomin & DeFries, 1985). Using the recognized methodology for making inferences about genetic and environmental influences, they conclude that in addition to a substantial environmental contribution through parents, peers, siblings, and television availability in the home, there is also a sizable and significant influence of genetic inheritance. This is admittedly somewhat startling but nonetheless a fact and hardly more startling than the earlier documentation that shyness in large part is attributable to heredity. In these data, Plomin and colleagues were able to rule out as an explanation genetic impact on intelligence and temperament. The new data confirm a hint of such a phenomenon a decade and a half earlier, when Loeghlin and Nichols (1976) reported a significantly higher correlation between the television use of identical twins compared to that of fraternal twins. Some (Prescott, Johnson, & McArdle, 1991) have dismissed Plomin and colleagues as an example of atheoretical empiricism—in effect, a meaningless fluke. We think quite differently. There is much in the data on television viewing—including the multination outcomes—that fit an interpretation of intrinsic reward. Our tentative explanation is that the source lies in susceptibility to alpha waves, or right- brain processing, which is generally accepted as representative of the more affective, less critical nonverbal and nonanalytic processing that typifies much television viewing (Krugman, 1971; Rothschild, Thorson, Reeves, Hirsch, & Goldstein, 1986). This affects everyone, hence the similarities in television use across vastly different circumstances. At the same time, we hypothesize that there is a genetically based variability in this trait as reflected in the data of Plomin and colleagues.

The data of Plomin and colleagues also document that there are decided environmental influences. We see the centrality of television as a dimension on which households can be arrayed with important consequences for media use and the rearing of children. Households high in centrality have norms that permit television use at all hours and occasions, television sets operate during most of the waking hours, and adults spend large amounts of time recorded as viewing (Comstock, 1991a; Medrich, Roizen, Rubin, & Buckley, 1982). Such households typically are low in availability of print media—newspapers, magazines, books. Reading is infrequent in many, and when substantial amounts occur it is of escapist material compatible with viewing television at the same time. This latter phenomenon is reflected in the greater than average amounts of reading by teenagers who view greater than average amounts of television (California Assessment Program, 1980; Morgan, 1980).

Households high in television centrality are much more frequent among lower socioeconomic strata but are far from confined to them. Children in these households view particularly large amounts of television. This is a function of the norms, the models provided by parents, and the eternally operating television sets. This household experience will establish for many lifelong commitments to viewing large amounts of television when time to do so is available. The household experience while growing up similarly will influence use of other media over the lifespan. Thus, household television use when growing up predicts amount of viewing by adults (Comstock, 1991a; Schramm, Lyle, & Parker, 1961). This effect is so powerful that it occurs even when possible differences in viewing are constrained by limitations in the time available, as is the case among college students (Kenny, 1985). That is, even when there is little time to view, those who grew up in households where television had a more central place will view more.

The pattern for print use applies much more strongly to White than to Black households. Among Black households scoring high on centrality of television a much greater and substantial proportion are higher in socioeconomic status. Measures of use of other media, such as availability and consumption of print, among these households higher in socioeconomic status conform to the pattern expected for such households—greater availability and higher use. Thus, among Black households socioeconomic status mitigates the negative relationships with print use usually found for television centrality. One result is that among Black households centrality is less strongly predictive of lower levels of scholastic performance (Chapter 7).

In our judgment, this exemption (of households higher in centrality that also are higher in socioeconomic status) applies far less strongly to White households. Our reasoning is that their television use identifies them as deviant from their strata and we would expect them to deviate similarly in use of other media. In contrast, the Black households adhere to the television norms for their strata and so we would expect them to adhere to other media- use norms as well. Their large amount of viewing would not seriously infringe on reading when there is a motive to engage in it, as the data on general recreational activities document (Table 3.4). Thus, the socioeconomic framework within

TABLE 3.4　Changes in Time Use Since 1965—Selected Activities (ages 18–64)

	1965 (N = 1222)	1985 (N = 3704)	Percent Change (shifts of 10 minutes or more)
Nonfree time	Time spent (minutes per day)		
Paid work			
Main job	236	216	−8
Eating	11	8	
Travel to/from work	26	26	
Household work			
Food preparation	44	39	
Cleaning house	33	27	
Clothes care	25	12	−52
Child care			
Baby care	13	7	
Child care	9	8	
Travel/child care	4	5	
Obtaining goods and services			
Everday shopping	28	24	
Travel goods and services	18	19	
Personal services	2	1	
Personal needs and care			
Night sleep	457	463	
Meals at home	58	50	
Washing, etc.	51	53	
Free time			
Education and training			
Homework	4	7	
Students' classes	2	7	
Other classes	3	2	
Organizational activities			
Religious practice	8	7	
Travel/organizations	4	4	
Religious groups	2	2	
Entertainment/social activities			
Visiting	39	29	−26
Travel/events and social	12	16	
Parties	15	6	
Movies	3	2	
Recreation			
Active sports	5	10	
Domestic crafts	7	7	
Games	5	6	

(continues)

TABLE 3.4   (*Continued*)

	1965 (N = 1222)	1985 (N = 3704)	Percent Change (shifts of 10 minutes or more)
Free time	Time spent (minutes per day)		
Communication			
TV	89	129	+45
Conversations	18	24	
Reading newspaper	21	8	−62
Reading magazines/other	8	9	
Think/relax	4	9	
Read books	5	7	
Writing	5	5	
Radio	4	3	
Records/tapes	1	1	
Total travel	82	89	

Adapted from *Time for Life: The Surprising Ways Americans Use Their Time*, by J. P. Robinson and G. Godbey, 1997, University Park, PA: The Pennsylvania State University Press.

which centrality occurs is different among Black households, and the availability and use of print media among households higher in socioeconomic status that are also high in television centrality differs markedly between White and Black households.

III. SPENDING TIME WITH TELEVISION

Our first concern is with the measurement of viewing. We then present our estimates of time spent "viewing." Next, we examine five regularities of mass audience behavior. Finally, we report on the subservience of preference and taste to convenience. We have great confidence in our conclusions because samples typically are large, sometimes numbering in the thousands, often nationally representative, and the same patterns recur consistently.

A. MEASUREMENT

The measurement of viewing, as it has evolved to serve the television industry, has come to rest on three elements (Beville, 1988): a representative sample of the population to be described, the recording of the channels to which the set in question has been tuned, and the identification of the persons who can be said to have been viewing. Despite 50 years of experience, only the second can be said to be well achieved (Comstock, 1991b; Robinson & Godbey, 1997). Samples used by Nielsen Media Research underrepresent the poor and minorities, and probably contain unusual numbers of fans who exaggerate the time they spend viewing or are especially heavy viewers. This is apparent from the smaller estimates produced by more representative samples using similar methods (Robinson, 1977). People meters—devices that are remote-control-like if somewhat larger, by which persons in sampled households record their viewing—have replaced diaries for data on who is viewing but interact with age and gender (Milvasky, 1992). They are less regularly used by children because of indifference, fatigue, or lack of understanding, and by women because they are more often engaged in household tasks.

Our definition assigns the label of viewer to anyone in the vicinity of an operating television set who can be construed as monitoring what is taking place. Because people consistently record themselves as viewing when their attention to the screen is partial, discontinuous, and often interrupted, we believe our view has the sanction of self- or folk-definition; it is a valid representation of what television viewing in our society is construed to be. We would thus include primary viewing, when attending to television is considered the sole or foremost activity (about three-fourths of the total of primary and secondary viewing); secondary viewing, when some other activity is foremost (slightly more than one-fifth of total viewing); and tertiary use, when the operating set is a backdrop to other activities (about 10% of total viewing).

The data from a variety of sources show that estimates of amount of viewing rise and fall as a function of the means of measurement. The less precise the means, the larger the estimate. Thus, an estimate based on a volunteered average day's viewing will be larger than one based on a report of last night's viewing (because people will ignore the days they don't view in offering an average), and both will exceed the results of time-lapse photography or videotaping (Bechtel, Achelpohl, & Akers, 1972). Our preference is for diary rather than people-meter data because the diary figures do not interact with age and gender. We also prefer diary data that represent total time allocation, so that television use must be made compatible with the parameters of other activities. The result in our view is the most accurate estimate possible.

We think the data permit an estimate of the division of time between ritual-istic and instrumental viewing. The amount of inattention establishes a ceiling for instrumental viewing of 60%. If we further assume that about one-third are attending to something they did not choose (and only about 10% of these persons have had their interest aroused) and that half of viewers are only paying partial attention (and we further specify that for the purpose of estimation, full attention is an attribute of instrumental viewing), we conclude that about four-fifths of all viewing is ritualistic and only about one-fifth is instrumental.

The analyses of Hoffman and Batra (1991) offer an alternative approach. They found that prime-time programs rated by viewers as high in cognitive impact were more likely to be watched from beginning to end, conversations during viewing were fewer, and viewers were more likely not to leave the room. These are certainly all expected attributes of instrumental viewing, but they would hardly account for all viewing of programs in this category because of the variability both among the programs and in viewer behavior. They are only correlates of viewer behavior for programs so classified, and the data in fact specify that they are not invariable accompaniments. If we then take the two-thirds of 36 prime-time programs examined by Hoffman and Batra that were rated high in affective impact or generally low in impact of any kind and assigned them a ritualistic rate of 90% and the one-third rated as high in cognitive impact a 50/50 division between ritualistic and instrumental viewing (because of the overall predominance of ritualistic attention), and we assume these two groups of programs are equally attractive to viewers (an assumption favoring instrumental viewing because undemanding programs usually are more popular, Barwise & Ehrenberg, 1988), we arrive at approximately the same four-fifths. Lower ritualistic and higher instrumental rates would produce smaller estimates, but it is hard to conceive of a set of plausible rates using this breakdown of programs that would not leave ritualistic viewing in substantial majority.

B. ESTIMATES

We begin with data reflecting television over the life span. Condry's (1989) averaging of a variety of sets of data records that viewing begins between the ages of $2\frac{1}{2}$ and 3, increases during the elementary school years, decreases during high school and college, and then returns to the higher levels of childhood. It (again) increases as people reach their mid-50s and increasing proportions enter retirement.

Seasonal variations are minor. The annual cycle places summer viewing by households at barely 10% less than in the fall–winter season, based on the averages recorded by Nielsen between the 1992-93 and 1996-97 seasons (Nielsen Media Research, 1998). This is an extraordinarily small deficit, given the frequency of reruns, the lure of superior weather in many parts of the country (although in the South and Southwest air-conditioning draws people indoors), the displacement of people by vacation and leisure travel (transporting some in the sample beyond measurement even though they still may be viewing television), and the greater viewing by children and teenagers (who as a group have a higher than average probability of being missed by people-meter measurement). The latter two make it quite likely that even this small deficit is an overestimate.

The weekly cycle for prime time (Nielsen Media Research, 1998) displays the sensitivity of viewing to valued alternatives. The number of teenagers and men and women 18 and older in the audience on Fridays and Saturdays is 10 to 15% fewer than on other nights, presumably because of entertainment and social activities outside the household. In contrast, the number of children 2–11 increases by almost 20% on Fridays, Saturdays, and Sundays, and although the Sunday prime-time audience overall is the largest of the week (about 12% greater than on other nights) it is on Fridays when, by a small margin over Sundays, the greatest number of children are viewing.

The daily cycle varies by age and gender. Younger and older children and adult men and women present somewhat different patterns, although all peak in viewing in the evening (Figure 3.2). It is the availability of population segments that influences programming; the programming is designed to maximize the likelihood of viewing by those available.

The modest role of initial preferences is exemplified in a number of ways. Audience segmentation produces groups with markedly differing preferences but these preferences only minutely predict what will be viewed. Similarly, exposure to a program of one category only minutely predicts exposure to another of the same category. The reasons are that the exercise of preferences is limited by the governance of viewing by time available and the indifference to content in choosing to view.

We believe that the best data on amount of viewing are those of Robinson and Godbey (1997), who use nationally representative samples of several thousand, diaries that collect data on all time allocation over 24-hour periods, and delve deeply enough so that all three levels of television use are measured.* Our calculations from their data place total use for adults at an average of 3 hours and 16 minutes per day, or about 22 hours and 40 minutes per week.

Demographic patterns are long established and quite stable (Comstock et al., 1978). Older children (6–11 in age) and adults (18–64 in age) are about equal

---

*Whenever possible, we use the Robinson and Godbey (1997) data as the best estimates. They are our fundamental source. For between-group comparisons, we use diary data from either Robinson and Godbey or Nielsen Media Research. Our assumption is that data collected within the same paradigm are comparable in regard to relative differences, although different paradigms may produce different absolute outcomes. We use the Nielsen people-meter data only for long-term household trends (which would be least sensitive to the interaction with age and gender, because the household result would be unaffected by who and how many are viewing). We find no evidence in the most recent 1996 and 1997 Nielsen data (Television Bureau of Advertising, 1997; Nielsen Media Research, 1998) that would lead us to revise the Robinson and Godbey estimates although their data were collected in 1985. Household figures are only slightly higher and show no signs of a decrease. On the other hand, people-meter data that show declines in children's viewing almost certainly are invalid because the allocation of time by children has been highly stable across the decades (Comstock, 1991a) and we see no reason for any changes over the past decade.

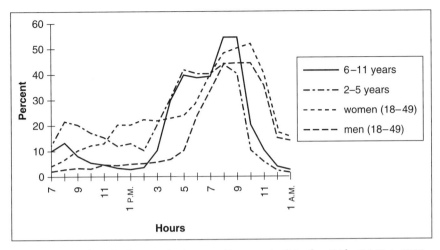

FIGURE 3.2   Daily cycle of viewing by demographic categories (Monday–Friday 7 A.M. to 6 P.M.; Monday–Sunday 6 P.M. to 1 A.M.). Adapted from *Television and Human Behavior* by G. Comstock, S. Chaffee, N. Katzman, M. McCombs, and D. Roberts, 1978, New York: Columbia University Press.

in average amount of viewing, although the average for all children is somewhat less than for adults because of the lower viewing by younger children (Figure 3.4). Teenagers view the least amount of all demographic categories.

Among adults, those older (50-plus) view more than those younger and women view more than men (in the Robinson and Godbey data, primary viewing is slightly higher for males but adjustments for greater amounts of secondary and tertiary viewing by females because of household tasks establish them as higher in total viewing). Blacks view more than Whites (Nielsen estimates household usage at 60% more in daytime and 15% more in prime time; the Robinson and Godbey data estimate 34% more for Black adults 18–64). Among Whites, socioeconomic status is inversely associated with viewing and the most powerful single predictor is education (Figures 3.3 and 3.4). Among Blacks, samples repeatedly record that this inverse relationship that has been pronounced among Whites is truncated, nonexistent, or even occasionally reversed (Bogart, 1972; Bower, 1973; Comstock, 1991b). The data for Hispanics to a less pronounced degree parallel those for Blacks. The differences in average amounts of viewing are often sizable when expressed in deviations from the average (Figure 3.4), but there is great individual variability and substantial portions of the underlying curves overlap. The result is that, although segments noticeably differ on the basis of demographics, they can also be said to be remarkably similar in viewing large amounts of television, so that any set of viewers similar in consumption will be a demographically varied group.

These patterns have changed little over the past five decades with most changes coming from the entry at a particular hour of previous nonviewers into the audience as television use has become increasingly widely accepted as a way to spend time.

Historically, there have been three major trends. The first was an increase of about an hour per day in mass media use with the introduction of the medium (Robinson, 1972b). The second is the progressive rise since then in household viewing—23% over the past 35 years (Figure 3.3). This has been reflected in the behavior of those of all ages, with viewing greater presently by about 3–7 hours a week than it was in 1965 among every age category (Robinson & Godbey, 1997), so that those born later in the century have come to view more television. The third is the narrowing of differences among individuals in amount viewed. Education and income are no longer as strong predictors as they once were, although both higher levels of education and greater income still noticeably predict lower amounts of viewing. What somewhat masks this phenomenon is the shift over the past five decades of increasing proportions into categories higher in education and income, with the result that the few left in the very low strata now view even more than they once did,

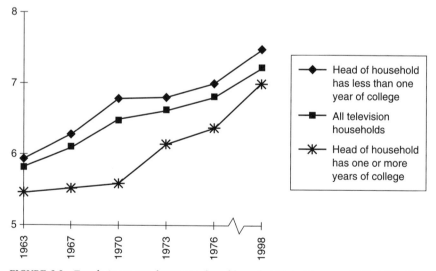

FIGURE 3.3 Trends in average hours per day of household television use, 1963–1998. Constructed from data in *Television and Human Behavior,* by G. Comstock, S. Chaffee, N. Katzman, M. McCombs, and D. Roberts, 1978, New York: Columbia University Press; *Time for Life: The Surprising Ways Americans Use Their Time,* by J. P. Robinson and G. Godbey, 1997, University Park, PA: The Pennsylvania State University Press; and *Trends in Television,* 1997, Television Bureau of Advertising.

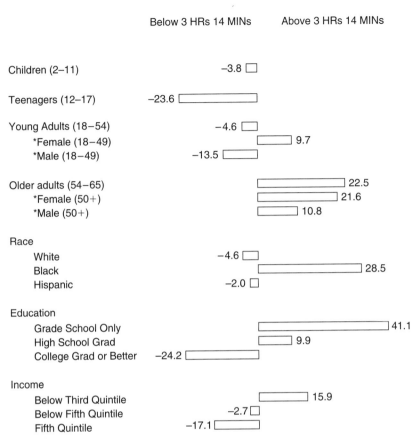

FIGURE 3.4   Amount of viewing by age, gender, race, and socioeconomic status (percent deviation from daily average for adults 18–64). Adapted from *Time for Life: The Surprising Ways Americans Use Their Time,* by J. P. Robinson and G. Godbey, 1997, University Park, PA: The Pennsylvania State University Press, estimates of primary viewing, except (*) based on *Television and Human Behavior,* by G. Comstock, S. Chaffee, N. Katzman, M. McCombs, and D. Roberts, 1978, New York: Columbia University Press.

and this is particularly so for education (Bower, 1985; Robinson & Godbey, 1997; Xiaoming, 1994). Basically, however, distinctions among demographic categories based on age, gender, and ethnicity have changed little over the five decades (Comstock et al., 1978; Xiaoming, 1994).

   The Robinson and Godbey data place viewing as a primary activity in the context of other activities (Table 3.4). It dominates media use and is America's foremost form of leisure. This is partly attributable to convenience and partly to the fact that gains in leisure time have come in daily bits and pieces that can be most efficiently allocated to television rather than in blocks of vacation time that might be spent on grander enterprises. In fact, vacation days see substantial reductions in viewing and increases in sports, attending events, and reading. As Condry (1989) recorded, television viewing stands third behind sleep and school or work across the lifespan as a consumer of time.

In the larger context, Americans have gained significantly in leisure time over the past three decades. The data of Robinson and Godbey (1997) make this irrefutably clear. Data that give the impression that Americans have less time (Schor, 1991) reflect not what they do but what they believe. Americans think they have less leisure time. Robinson and Godbey attribute this paradox to higher expectations about the rewards that generally should accrue to the employed. The irony is that much of the time that has been gained has been allocated to television, an activity not ranked particularly high in pleasure (Kubey & Csikszentmihalyi, 1990; Robinson & Godbey, 1997) although obviously far from unpleasant.

Television is a robust, two-fisted competitor among the media. Reading has decreased over the years, and this decrease is largely attributable to less time spent reading newspapers. Time spent with television, in contrast, has increased, and is about five times greater than the total time spent with all other media.

The data also clearly refute popular speculation that possession of personal computers, access to the Internet, and use of related electronic information and data banks will take significant time away from television viewing. Convincing evidence comes from a recent nationally representative sample of 3600 (Kohut, 1995). There was only a small negative relationship among computer owners (about one-fourth of the sample) between computer use and television viewing, and on closer examination it proved to be an artifact of socioeconomically better-off people using these technologies more frequently (Robinson & Godbey, 1997). Similarly, data from nearly 100 subscribers to an Internet provider in a Virginia community showed use of television and other mass media to be unaffected during the start-up period (Bromley & Bowles, 1995), a time when novelty of the service and the attraction of enthusiasts among early subscribers would predict high use of the new service.

The insightful will not be surprised. Television provides low involvement and easily digested information and requires nondemanding monitoring. These are not the requisite gratifications associated with use of information technology. It is likely that in fact those who most use information technology would be lower than average in use of television and more frequently would be instrumental viewers. This portrait is consistent with much greater viewing by noncomputer owners (almost one-fourth more) and a small positive correlation between computer use and reading and movie viewing. Thus, information technology users—who are disproportionately high in education and income (Katz & Aspden, 1997; Lindstrom, 1997; Nielsen Media Research, 1998)—would not be a population whose decline in television use would much affect overall viewing. Certainly any observable effect in the early and mid-1990s would have been small in any case, with only about 15% of the American population engaging in such activity outside the workplace (Keller & Fay, 1996). However, even with rapid growth in use of such technology we would not expect much time to be taken away from television viewing. The reasons are not that a large proportion of the population will remain nonusers, and that these people in the aggregate account for large amounts of viewing beause they are lower in socioeconomic status and particularly education, although these are factors, but rather because information technology and television are not truly rivals. Viewers would certainly desert television for activities that are more rewarding, but a necessary condition in our view is that they fulfill largely the same function. Information technology fails this condition. The available data are particularly telling because early technology adopters, as enthusiasts, should strongly display any effects on use of other media.

The question of the disruption and suppression of other activities by television viewing has often been raised. Putnam (1995) even assigns it a major role in declines in organizational and civic participation that he asserts harm the effective functioning of American society. We concur that its introduction reduced social interaction and was responsible for a socially important reallocation of time (Chapter 1), and that its role as such dissipated only partially as people became more accustomed to the medium (Belson, 1959; Comstock, 1991; Robinson, 1972a; Szalai, 1972; Williams, 1986). However, this is an issue for which considerable conceptual wiliness and precision in regard to the when, what, who, and how are required to avoid giving an erroneous impression—of the facts and of our interpretation.

When we examine postintroduction data on patterns of time use, we find very little support for any suppressive influence of television among adults with one major exception, and this includes Putnam's decline in organizational and civic participation. Robinson and Godbey (1997) report that over the three decades ending in 1985 the amount of time spent on activities other than the media—*informal* activities, such as socializing, exercise and sports, and hobbies; and *formal* activities, such as religion, organizations, sports and cultural events, and adult education—*increased* slightly. Only time spent on socializing declined markedly (about an hour and a half a week from 8.2 to 6.7 hours). Organizational participation declined only one-tenth of an hour from 1.3 to 1.2 hours per week. Communicating with others directly by telephone and participation in sports and exercise, hobbies, and education all increased. This represents to us, in the first instance, merely the substitution of technology for

face-to-face interaction and, in the remaining, the taking advantage of opportunities for self-improvement (and in the case of education, in a context that
ordinarily would foster informal as well as sometimes formal exchanges—depending on the subject matter—about public affairs and the state of community and society). Liberation from the restrictions of a metaphorical street-cor-
ner society is hardly a basis for the decline of democracy, and any loss in
interaction and participation in our view would be well compensated for by
improvements in individual skills, abilities, and satisfaction.

When we look at the data on general recreation (Table 3.5), we find few
negative relationships with television use except at the extremes. The sole exception is for outdoor activities, where the differences almost certainly reflect
that those preferring the outdoors allot less time to television rather than that
television quashes the desire to camp or hike. The data for cultural recreation
and arts participation certainly display many negative associations but even
here home-based activities are immune. These data again surely should be interpreted as representing differences in tastes and preferences rather than the
suppressive influence of television. People who attend to comparatively little
television attend many cultural and artistic events more frequently than the
average person (and in the case of opera, often watch no television at all). Those
who view a great deal of television attend such events less frequently than the
average. What emerges from the data are taste publics, with one indulging in
the tastes of the mass audience and the others pursuing specialized preferences
and interests.

This is precisely what we would expect if our characterization of television
use—based on data covering five decades and many thousands of persons—is
correct. Viewing for most takes a subsidiary place to a variety of other activities
to which they assign some importance, and for many such activities are numerous and are substantial in the amounts of time they consume. Viewing, then,
does not seriously detract from engaging in other activities; instead, it is the
activity in which people engage in the absence of obligations or preferred
alternatives.

The time logged as viewing obviously could be expended on other activities and those who purposely pursue other activities frequently view less television. Those who sit in judgment of the behavior of society often wish that
people would spend their time in more creative, enriching ways (Kubey &
Csikszentmihalyi, 1990; Putnam, 1995; Robinson & Godbey, 1997), but the
crucial point is that at the threshold of the twenty-first century television
should not be construed as disrupting or suppressing time allocation among
adults—with one major exception—because it largely consumes time otherwise uncommitted or not easily convertible to other uses. The data for general
recreation give strong support for our perspective in the lack of a negative

TABLE 3.5 Participation in General Recreation, Cultural Recreation, and the Arts by Television Viewing

	Daily viewing hours					
	0	1	2	3	4	5+
	N = 130	450	699	516	383	482
General recreation	Percentage of those sampled					
1. Attend movies	51	68	67	66	61	54
2. Attend sports events	44	54	56	50	45	34
3. Visit zoos, parks, etc.	41	37	37	34	32	24
4. Play cards, games	57	64	68	68	67	60
5. Amusement parks	37	51	54	51	48	47
6. Jog, exercise, etc.	52	60	53	55	48	44
7. Play sports	40	47	43	41	36	28
8. Camping, hunting, etc.	40	43	39	36	32	29
9. Read books, magazines	72	85	86	86	86	74
10. Volunteer, charity work	35	36	33	29	25	21
11. Collect stamps, coins, etc.	14	17	15	15	15	13
12. Cook gourmet meals	32	31	32	30	27	23
13. Home improvements	50	66	64	64	60	46
14. Gardening	55	60	60	63	61	51
Cultural recreation						
15. Visit science museum	25	25	25	22	20	13
16. Visit historic areas	43	47	42	39	33	27
17. Poetry reading	35	28	23	19	19	11
18. Visit art-craft fairs	44	46	47	46	38	25
19. Art classes	11	16	12	8	8	7
20. Pottery, etc.	13	14	13	14	10	9
21. Needlework	37	33	32	37	38	34
22. Backstage theatre	5	4	3	1	2	2
23. Backstage music	3	1	1	*	*	*
24. Creative writing	14	8	7	7	4	5
25. Art photography	12	14	13	9	7	8
26. Paint, sculpt, etc.	12	14	11	10	7	8
Arts participation						
27. Attend jazz performances	18	13	8	7	11	9
28. Attend classical music	28	30	15	12	12	5
29. Attend opera	10	1	3	3	2	1
30. Attend musicals	34	33	21	24	22	14
33. Attend ballet	24	20	16	16	12	8
34. Attend art museum	41	43	31	30	23	13
35. Read novel, short story, etc.	47	63	58	55	53	52

Adapted from *Arts Participation in America* by J. Robinson, C. Keegan, M. Karth, T. Triplett, and J. Holland, 1985, University of Maryland, Survey Research Center, College Park, MD.

association between amount of time spent viewing and engaging in most activities except at the extremes (Table 3.5), and these extremes clearly represent two distinct publics: those with a great interest in engaging in certain activities and those with little interest in doing so who turn to the remaining option, television. Similarly, differences in viewing among those who devote greater or lesser time to participating in cultural recreation or the arts represent the expression of tastes and preferences that in contemporary America translate into greater or lesser amounts of time remaining for television viewing.

The major exception is reading. The introduction of television reduced the reading of books and magazines by adults but initially did not affect newspapers (Robinson & Godbey, 1997) because they more centrally served informational needs not as well served by the new medium of television, where television could compete quite effectively with books and magazines for sedentary leisure time (Bogart, 1972b; Comstock et al., 1978). This was, however, not a stable circumstance. By the mid-1960s, newspaper reading too began to decline, with a stunning loss over the next 20 years of more than 60% of the time spent by adults in 1965 (Table 3.4). The exception also applies to children and teenagers (Chapter 7), and in their case television's incursions have implications not only for scholastic achievement but also for the use of leisure time both currently and in later adult life.

The displacement of various activities by the introduction of television (an effect quite apparent in the data in contrast to the contemporary suppression of activities) and the subsequent effects on reading only tell part of the story. The elegant analysis of the time use of several thousand young persons in South Africa over an 8-year period encompassing the introduction of television by Mutz, Roberts, and van Vuuren (1993) indicates that the popularity of the medium not only drew time away from other actitivies but also that the experience with it somewhat changed the priorities governing the allocation of time to other activities. The initial suppression continued stoutly across the 6 years of television's presence and was greatest in this instance for radio listening, movie-going, and to a lesser degree, reading. The change in priorities was manifest in the disinclination of individual viewers to reallocate time to these partly abandoned activities when their viewing declined, although there were no distinctive emphases in the way they did use that time. The interpretation of the authors is that the functions of these various activities were altered by the inclusion of television in the matrix of options, and thus did not consistently recover when an individual's viewing declined. Our opinion is that with television use so governed by time available declines in individual viewing would represent the intrusive demands of other activities—based either on obligation or on interest—and that abandoned media would be unlikely to present such demands (or they would not have been abandoned). These data further support the view of Robinson (1972a, 1990) that the introduction of television led to a reallocation of time on a significant scale.

C. FIVE REGULARITIES

The mass audience is highly predictable. The ebb and flow of television viewers through the day, week, year, and lifespan proceeds uninterrupted by the vagaries of individual behavior or the shifting about of various audience segments in response to fashions and trends in programming or newly popular offerings. The failure of the extensive promos for forthcoming programs that ostensibly justified NBC's financial loss of $30–40 million on the 1992 Summer Olympics unmistakeably to boost their ratings, as recorded by Eastman and Otteson (1994), simply is one example of the implacability of the mass audience in its allocation of time to television. Five day-to-day examples of these regularities have been recorded so consistently that they are sometimes referred to as "laws." These are the phenomena of duplication, lead-in effects, double jeopardy, program disloyalty, and the popularity-weighted heterogeneity of consumption.

Duplication is the behavioral oddity of channel loyalty. There has been a consistent tendency for television sets to be tuned to one or another broadcast channel with greater frequency than one would predict from the ratings of the programs. The arithmetic expression for U.S. audiences has been a ratio of 1.6 times (x) the probability of joint viewing for duplication among programs on the same channel; that is, the estimated likelihood of viewing two programs in the absence of other factors would be the cross product of their ratings (each of which represents the probability of viewing that program) and channel loyalty increases that outcome by 60% (Goodhardt & Ehrenberg, 1969; Goodhardt, Ehrenberg & Collins, 1987).

Our judgment is that although this effect certainly has been somewhat subverted by the increasingly large number of channels available in American homes that give viewers greater choice (Adams, 1998), this subversion in fact is modest. The reason is that viewers concentrate their choices among a very small number of channels (Heeter & Greenberg, 1988; Neuman, 1991)—about six to nine—so that the actual number of options entertained has not changed much. Any subversion would have been largely confined to the mid-1980s as additional broadcast channels became common in most markets while new additions would typically be specialist cable channels that would not be watched as often as mainstream offerings with heterogeneous programming.

Lead-in describes the tendency for viewers of one program to remain tuned to the channel for the subsequent program. It is a specific instance of duplication, but takes its importance from the size of the audience sometimes transferred. Very popular programs contribute sizably to the popularity of subsequent programs, and unlike channel loyalty this is a regularity of mass audience behavior of which those scheduling programs can attempt to take advantage. As the analysis of Webster and Phalen (1997) documents, even when several channels were competing for viewers a program in the 1980s would deliver about half its audience to the next program. In the absence of competition, the delivery rate rose to 70%. The rating for the first program in a pair statistically explained about two-thirds of the variance in the subsequent program's rating. Statistically factor in the flight attributable to competition, and the figure soared to 80%. Only a few additional viewers precede a very popular program by tuning in early, and a similar category of program on competing channels only slightly disrupts and on the same channel only slightly enhances the delivery rate. Television schedules, then, use popularity strategically to guide the linear flow of audience attention from one offering to the next. Of course it should be realized that these statistical explanations represent the relationships as they occur after the painstaking efforts of program scheduling executives to create audience flow across the most attractive programs that could be devised by programming chiefs and television production companies, so that they essentially rest on the acceptability of the offering to which lead-in contributes. They do not occur in a vacuum, and the foundation for the lead-in phenomenon rests as much on the acceptability of the subsequent program as on the popularity of the preceding entry.

Duplication and lead-in are examples of the domination of audience behavior by structural elements. In both cases, the viewing audience is not wholly predictable or attributable to the program being viewed. These are pinpoint examples of the general lack of audience decay. Webster and Phalen (1997) show that about three-fourths of those viewing early in the evening will be viewing an hour later and that about half will be viewing 3 hours later. The mass audience exhibits remarkable constancy in attention. Thus, the viewer who thinks he or she is watching a particularly enjoyed program in fact has often been delivered by inertia or habit.

Double jeopardy is a well-documented mass market phenomenon in which less popular items are sampled less frequently even by those who do occasionally make use of them. In the case of television programs, it means that the small but loyal audience is a rarity (Ehrenberg et al., 1990); more commonly, programs that are less popular are viewed less often by those who do sometimes decide to watch. Thus, less popular offerings face the double threat of small audiences and less frequent viewers. Although some (Webster & Phalen, 1997) puzzle over the explanation, to us it seems simple: mass market standards are widely shared and uniform, so lower popularity signifies an offering with less appeal for almost everyone. As Barwise and Ehrenberg (1988) point out, the sole occasional exception are programs that verge on the unique; the less fungible an offering, the more likely it will deviate from the canon of double jeopardy. The most significant aspect of double jeopardy is the one most likely to be overlooked—that it identifies television programs empirically and unambiguously as part of the universe of mass market products rather than icons of viewers' cultural aspirations.

Program disloyalty is expressed in the repeat viewing rates that are among the strongest evidence that exposure to television is largely a function of time available rather than the attraction of specific programs. Early figures from the 1970s placed repeat viewing at an average of 50% for adults (Barwise et al., 1982; Goodhardt, Ehrenberg, & Collins, 1987; Headen, Klompmaker, & Teel, 1979). A series of recent studies reports an average adult rate of 25% (Ehrenberg & Wakshlag, 1987; Soong, 1988). However, these are people-meter data and may well underestimate the phenomenon because of the unreliable meter use by women. We place much greater credence in the diary data from the same mid-1980s period that offer an adult estimate of about 40% and a substantially lower 30% for children and teenagers (Barwise, 1986). These data also are consistent with the examination of network news (Lichty, 1989) indicating that the viewing of all five of a week's evening broadcasts represented about 1–3% of the Monday audience, a figure compatible with repeat viewing of between 33 and 40%.

People almost always view the same program when viewing at a particular time because it represents the most satisfying choice among options (Barwise et al., 1982). The significance of a repeat viewing rate as low as 40% is that preferred programs are often missed. People are not viewing something else; they have something else to do. The program is discarded rather than the personal schedule bent. Declines in repeat viewing mean that the role of programs has become even less important than it once was.

These same data nevertheless establish that a few programs have extraordinary drawing power. We see this unobscured in the very consistent 65% registered for the repeat viewing of programs with the highest level across the 1980s as well as the 1970s, when repeat viewing in general registered as higher (Barwise, 1986; Barwise et al., 1982; Goodhardt et al., 1987; Headen et al., 1979). These typically have been especially popular situation comedies, soap operas, and news programs—they are the exceptions within each genre. Some viewers apparently reshape their schedules—the times of day are no different than for programs with much lower rates—to see these offerings. Certain programs in these data, as elsewhere, thus play some role in assembling viewers—but here as elsewhere programs are usually subservient to time available.

These various phenomena can be integrated in a single model (Cooper, 1996). Channel loyalty establishes the foundation (duplication) that is enhanced by adjacency (lead-in). These effects are greatest for the more popular programs (double jeopardy). Thus, repeat viewing and repeat exposure to reruns (Litman & Kohl, 1992) are greater for more popular programs. Duplication and lead-in effects decrease slightly as the number of competing channels increases, and are increased slightly when programs on the same channel are compatible—that is, of like category.

The heterogeneity of program consumption reflects the dominance of popularity and the full embrace by the public of television as a mass medium. It would be a very surprising phenomenon outside the context of the mass audience regularities so far observed, which makes it another example of the importance of the structure of programming in what people view. Here, the individual viewer constructs a schedule roughly matching the ratings and shares derived from audience measurement. The average viewer does not concentrate viewing among stated preferences or preferred categories of programs but instead views a balanced selection representing drama and action-adventure, comedy, information and public affairs (including talk shows), news and sports weighted by the popularity of each program and genre. This has been consistently observable across the decades. Better-educated viewers have long been more likely to say there should be more information and news programming, but consistently over the decades, regardless of education, people have allocated their viewing time very similarly (Bower, 1985). The better educated do view somewhat more information and news programming but nowhere near as much as their stated wants would suggest; instead, they, as do the less educated, spend the great majority of their time on entertainment with the most time spent with the most popular program categories (at the time, drama and action-adventure, and comedy). The probability that any given viewer will watch a program is essentially equal to its rating. Viewing a program in a particular category—crime, comedy—is only a scant predictor of being more likely to view another program in the same category than would be expected from its ratings (Goodhardt, Ehrenberg, & Collins, 1987; Headen, Klompmaker, & Rust, 1979; Webster & Phalen, 1997). More popular programs are watched more frequently, and viewers typically distribute their viewing across the varied options to produce a heterogeneous balance representing the various categories in proportion to their popularity (Barwise & Ehrenberg, 1988). Thus, the typical viewer largely allocates time in accord with the behavior of the mass audience.

This authoritarianism of popularity in assembling a mass audience undercuts the notion of homogeneous but diverse segments that happen to be watching at often the same times as adequately descriptive of the television audience. If the latter were the case, we would expect dramatic differences in the demographic makeup of program audiences to be the rule; in fact, it is the exception. The data presented by Hamilton (1998) provide excellent examples. Some programs are wholly egalitarian in drawing similarly from the six major demographic categories of males 18–34, females 18–34, males 35–49, females 35–49, males 50–plus, and females 50–plus (in these data, fictional crime dramas and tabloid news such as *A Current Affair* and *Hard Copy*). Others are somewhat more popular with those in the younger (18–34) or older (35–49, 50–plus) categories (the "reality" shows *Cops* and *Rescue 911*, and news magazines such as *60 Minutes* and *20/20*, respectively). Certainly a few programs are particularly attractive to a single segment (talk shows and *Roseanne* among females 18–34 in this instance). However, even when there is some variation, the appeal to less enamored segments often stands at three-fourths or two-thirds that of the more attracted segments and only occasionally falls below the 50% level. Thus, we see the data as a whole eminently in accord with the concept of a mass audience for television.

These data point to demographic differences as principally responsible for the modest differences among markets in program popularity. For example, a violent police "reality" show is likely to be more popular in markets with a larger number of young adult males (Hamilton, 1998). There is also a hometown favoritism phenomenon reported by Nielsen Media Research (1998). Ratings in the fall of 1997 were higher than the national ratings for 18 of 20 broadcast network series in the locale in which the series is set. Viewers probably enjoy sites they are familiar with, possibly because incorporation in a television plot elevates these rendezvous to a certain notoriety and endorses their possession of character. There is also sometimes a fine fit bweeen the demographics of the market and the content of the program, which in our view accounts partly for a rating 64% higher than the national average for *Frasier* in Seattle, the world capital (except perhaps for Milan) of the coffee bar.

Robinson and Godbey (1997) report on the basis of recent national survey data that the pleasure that the public believes it derives from the medium is at an all-time low. The decline in the rate of repeat viewing testifies that specific programs are less important to viewers than they once were. Other options for spending time in the home that have recently become more widely available, such as video-game playing, personal computer use, and particularly access to the Internet and related information services all have been proposed as conceivably consuming time once spent with the medium. The VCR, although a means for expanding access to programs on broadcast and cable channels, also competes with these channels through prerecorded movies and other specialized videos. It is thus reasonable to ask whether the hold of television on American time use will persist.

We believe the data are quite eloquent. Attitudes toward television historically have been miserable predictors of use of television and this is true generally for the media where norms about use—or attitudes toward media consumption rather than evaluative expressions—and habit play much larger roles (Comstock, 1988). Public endorsements of television—as "interesting," "exciting," "worthwhile," "relaxing," "wonderful"—were in decline for three decades (Bower, 1985) while over the same period amount of time spent viewing was steadily increasing (Comstock, 1991a; Comstock et al., 1978; Robinson & Godbey, 1997). Similarly, the unchanging levels of repeat viewing for programs with the highest levels while averages have declined supports the observation of Bower (1985) about declining attitudes: the public has become more jaded and less enthusiastic in general about television but the loyalty of viewers to the most popular programs has continued undiminished. The unchanging life cycle of viewing, with older adults who already have spent decades using television increasing their viewing, further supports the view that viewing will continue at present or higher levels if time is available.

Programs are the focus of conscious scrutiny. They are what people talk about. They are also what the media cover—mostly with attention to their stars. But time available has been the principal factor governing viewing, with changing norms about the use of television leading to the allocation of additional time to the medium by some population segments.

Fundamentally, viewing will continue much as it has because none of the alternative activities fulfill the essential function of television. Television provides an intellectually and emotionally untaxing but nevertheless passingly absorbing way to spend time. Videos—mostly movies made for theatrical release—are perceived as more exciting, more involving, more demanding of attention; use is thought of as more selective than television in general; and they are more likely to be followed from beginning to end (Cohen, Levy, & Golden, 1988; Kubey & Larson, 1990). They are typically viewed rather than monitored, so although they may deduct small amounts from the time that can be spent with television they cannot substitute to any substantial degree for it. Monitoring, the principal mode of television consumption, is incompatible with the rewards and demands of videos. Furthermore, many people who are newly spending time with personal computers, the Internet, and related information sources are shifting that time from activities other than television viewing. After all, one would hardly expect an untaxing, entertainment-oriented pastime (television) to be replaced by a more taxing information-oriented activity (computer use) unless there were rewards previously unavailable (that books and magazines could not have supplied), and we cannot imagine what they might be.

D. Triumph of Convenience

The evolution of the electronic media over the past five decades has resulted in a sizable to huge increase in the television channels to which households have access, and especially among the two-thirds majority that are cable subscribers.

It has also resulted in a significant increase in the diversity of programming available, again particularly among cable subscribers; the availability of theater movies and other specialized experiences using the VCR; and the possibility of rescheduling programs with the VCR to fit the individual viewer's schedule. The increase in number of options and especially the ability to eliminate the effects of program scheduling have led some (Massey & Baran, 1990) to argue that the end has come for the second role of time available (the first is dictating the amount of time spent with the medium), which is the governance of what people view by what is scheduled during the hours they have available.

The facts so far have proven indifferent to this utopian expectation. Despite the increased options and diversity, most viewers do not consistently make much effort to make careful choices. Only about half "often" used a published television guide 20 years ago (Bower, 1985). The figure seems not to have changed. People still use television guides less than half the time, and only about one of five use them regularly (Lin, 1990). People typically confine themselves to six to nine channels in choosing among options (Neuman, 1991; Heeter & Greenberg, 1988), and seldom sample the remainder. Videos typically are rented at an average rate of about one per household every 3 weeks, and video renting is concentrated among a minority of households so that many hardly ever rent a video (Lin, 1990; Wartella et al., 1990). The promise of program-shifting, once the principal motive for VCR ownership, is redeemed only to a small degree—perhaps about 10% of a week's viewing typically is taped, and half of that will never be viewed if it is not replayed within 24 hours (Lin, 1990). Thus, only about 5% of programs are rescheduled by technology— a significant factor surely for those programs affected and the persons engaging in the practice but hardly the overturning of the disinclination of Americans to pursue television preferences ardently. Instead, the medium continues to be consumed largely on the terms scheduled by programming executives.

This is not to say there have been no changes in the audience or in audience behavior. We see several noteworthy ones within the larger framework of mass audience regularities. They include changes in audience demographics, the spread of cable, the diffusion of the VCR, the ubiquitous remote control, and the fragmentation and polarization attributable to channel diversity.

Since 1970, the average household size has declined noticeably from about 3.1 to 2.6 in the mid-1990s (Nielsen Media Research, 1998). Larger households use television more, which makes the continuing progressive increase in household use of television even more impressive as it points to greater individual viewing (because on the average there are fewer in each household to view). The audience has also become older. Between 1970 and 1998, the proportion of viewers 18–49 has increased from 42.3% to 48.5% and the proportion of viewers 50–plus has increased from 24.5% to 27.3%. This is the oft-commented-on long march of the baby boom generation. Except for possibly a few specialized cable channels and larger audiences for news, this "graying" of the audience will have little effect on programming. The reason is that programming strategies always derive from seeking viewers who might be lost to other channels (Comstock, 1989). Older adults have viewed the most frequently of any demographic age category, and newly customized fare will not be necessary to attract them. Similarly, adults in general have been substantial in amounts of viewing. The competition that will affect programming will be for the viewers most likely to turn to premium movie channels or other cable fare—which means more, not less, programming directed toward very young adults.

It was prophesied in the early 1980s that by the end of the century cable virtually would have replaced the broadcast networks. Almost every household would subscribe and specialized channels would dominate viewing. This has not occurred. The rewards of cable when matched against the monthly fees presently leave subscribing households at about the two-thirds mark, those receiving equivalent service by satellite ADS only advance the figure to three-fourths, and more significantly the mass audience for broadcast television remains substantial and, to many, surprisingly intact—with prime-time shares at almost three-fourths for households using television and almost two-thirds for sets in use (Table 1.1). The reason, essentially, is that cable has proved to be more efficacious in increasing the quantity of sources for the same rewards than in expanding the rewards of television.

Most viewers apparently seek the same gratifications from cable-only channels as they do from broadcast outlets. The most popular channels offer feature films, reruns, sports, and varied entertainment (Waterman, 1986). The premium movie channels have struggled because viewers are not always ready to attend in accord with begin and end times of films or to give them the closer attention required to follow their narratives. They are neither more nor less pleased with cable than with television in general (Perse & Ferguson, 1993). As with television in general, subscribers focus on a repertoire of a few channels (Ferguson & Perse, 1993; Heeter, 1988). Specialized cable channels have miserly audience shares. For example, in a typical fall or winter week the prime-time ratings of the 25 most popular cable programs averaged 2.8 compared to 11.0 for all of the more than 80 programs on ABC, CBS, Fox, and NBC; and the ratings for the venerable CNN, Discovery, and Arts and Entertainment almost always fall below the level for the most popular 25 (McConnell & Albiniak, 1998).

Cable obviously offers an increase in diversity but it is far greater in terms of channel options than genres of material; the great bulk of programming overlaps with the categories scheduled by broadcasters. Cable households (Ducey, Krugman, & Eckrich, 1983) are somewhat higher than average in socioeconomic status because they are better able to afford the subscription costs. They are larger in size than average, possibly because larger numbers of viewers make the cost per viewer more reasonable but more probably because the greater the number of persons the more likely there will be someone for whom the offerings of cable are particularly appealing, such as children. Also, cable households view more television. Cable's diversity would contribute slightly to the latter—perhaps 10% by our estimation (or slightly more than 1 hour per week) whereas the rest would be attributable to cable-subscribing households being greater users of television in general (Jacobs, 1995; Perse, 1990a; Perse & Ferguson, 1993; Williams et al., 1985).

Only about a million households had a VCR at the beginning of the 1980s (Television Bureau of Advertising, 1997). Ten years later, the figure was more than 60 million. In a very few years, the VCR surpassed cable in number of households, and diffusion has been similar to the rapidly adopted color sets. Almost 85% of households currently have a VCR and we expect that figure to rise past 90% in 5 years (Comstock, 1991a).

Although very disappointing as a means of converting the television schedule to a personal menu and not as frequently used for videos as some had expected (Levy & Fink, 1984; Lin, 1990; Wartella, Heinz, Aidman, & Mazzarella, 1990), the VCR has had some important effects. Early purchasers in the mid-1980s sought greater access to television programming, but with the opening of a highly competitive rental market for videos that drove fees down, the viewing of movies became equally important and eventually—as late acquirers turned to VCRs precisely for this access—became predominant (Sims, 1989). One result is an enlarged market for theater films, with rentals supplying half the income of many films, and a market less dominated by teenagers. The VCR, then, has become a major factor in maintaining a diverse and creative motion picture industry with an interest in the tastes and preferences of adults. Another major effect of the VCR has been to greatly increase—by our estimate at least a doubling (Greenberg & Heeter, 1987)—of the viewing of movies by teenagers, including movies with restrictive ratings. Our best estimate of VCR use based on a national sample (Sims, 1989) is $3\frac{1}{2}$ hours per week for teenagers with 90% devoted to movies. Adult females spend about 20% and adult males about 50% less time, with somewhat more than one-half for movie viewing.

The VCR is complementary to television, and is perceived by viewers as more selective and more psychologically and intellectually arousing than television (Cohen, Levy, & Golden, 1988; Kubey & Larson, 1990). It is more likely to substitute for moviegoing or other leisure in an enhanced emphasis on home entertainment, and in contrast to television viewing greater VCR use is not predicted by lower socioeconomic status (Lin, 1993). It permits viewer specialization and selectivity to degrees quite unmatchable through cable or broadcast channels—among subcultures, the viewing of ethnic and foreign language programming, and for a few narrowly focused viewers, one or another genre exclusively. Pay-per-view services will not make much difference in this pattern except for a minute increase in movie viewing if hundreds of titles become available despite the increased convenience. This is because the constraints on attention that now govern movie viewing—as contrasted with television monitoring—will remain, so the main effect will be merely to partially replace one means (the VCR) with another (on-line access). Sociologically and psychologically, then, the VCR is an addition to rather than an extension of the television set.

The remote control became an accepted part of the television environment three decades ago and now is ubiquitous. It was long ago looked on merely as a device to make channel-switching more convenient. With the proliferation of channels, however, the practice of skipping about made easy by the remote control became of interest in itself. Some argued that it constituted a new mode of media consumption—the assembly of pleasurable disconnected incidents (Jensen, 1994). The remote control became the subject of empirical research (Eastman & Newton, 1995; Ferguson, 1994; Walker & Bellamy, 1993). Our initial speculation was that such behavior might further distance viewers from the narratives of specific programs and might help explain the lower rate of repeat viewing. One might also hypothesize that total viewing would increase because the average level of gratification would rise.

The evidence in fact identifies as the sole widespread contribution the fuller exploration of a viewer's limited channel repertoire. Certainly the remote control by the very convenience it affords makes it easier for viewers to counter audience flow programming strategies such as the lead-in (Eastman, Newton, Riggs & Neal-Lumsford, 1997), and this might have figured in the adoption by the networks in the early 1990s of speedier, less measured transitions at the starts, ends, and breaks of prime-time programs (Eastman, Neal-Lumsford & Riggs, 1995). However, to see this as stoutly empowering the viewer vis-á-vis the medium (as Eastman and colleagues, 1997, do) is akin to crediting the electronic auto door opener with vanquishing the perils of parking garages and lonely places. The overall inertia of viewers assigns it a minor role: the parameters of total viewing are set by the time available, the cognitive processing required by channel skipping is no different than that necessary for the browsing of magazines or newspapers, and skipping about extensively would require exactly the degree of attention of which viewers typically deprive their television sets. The major effect of the remote control as one might surmise from these circumstances has been briefly increased satisfaction among those viewers instrumentally seeking excitement at a given moment (Ferguson, 1994).

As Webster and Phalen (1997) observe, the proliferation of channels results in a partial correlation of channels with content. This proliferation leads to some fragmentation of the audience. This is readily observable in the decline of prime-time audience shares of the three initial networks to below 50% from a high in the late 1960s of more than 90%. Each new specialized cable channel usually attracts a smaller audience than those preceding it because the apparently more popular vehicles will be undertaken first—a variant of the law of diminishing returns. Most of their viewers come from other channels but a few, perhaps 10%, will be newly attracted as persons for whom the specialized content constitutes a motive for instrumental viewing. Broadcast channels nevertheless in total still constitute the great majority of viewing, although in a majority of homes (about three-fourths) they are received by cable (or satellite alternate delivery service), and the diminishing audience sizes for new channels means that audience behavior will not be much affected by any one or another of these additions, although cable (and alternate delivery) options in total have a substantial impact. The serious competition for viewers will be among the cable channels that consistently program very popular offerings and the broadcast networks, with the latter having the enormous advantage for the foreseeable future—in terms of the audiences they can offer advertisers and therefore the amounts of money they can pay for programming—of reaching almost every household in the nation.

Meanwhile, the conjunction of channel and content on cable means that a few viewers who have a high interest in specific categories of programming will spend unusual proportions of time with one channel. We think this polarization will be a very minor phenomenon limited sharply by the redundancy and repetition of most specialized channels or, in some cases, by the very variety of what is offered (such as sports with different fan bases). Two exceptions would be Music Television (MTV), which for some might substitute for continuous radio or disc listening, and foreign language stations that have little linguistic competition. (Webster and Phalen, for example, report that a Spanish language channel tuned to by only 16% of the public over a week provided an average of 40% of the viewing of those who did tune in.)

These analyses of the regularities of mass audience behavior and their possible exceptions place us firmly among the many investigators examining different sets of data representing different populations and different time periods who have concluded that the many technological innovations of the past era of transition have become accommodated to the parameters of television viewing in earlier times rather than comprising a revolution in the way television is used (Dorr & Kunkel, 1990; Kubey & Larson, 1990; Levy, 1989; Morgan et al., 1990; Wartella et al., 1990). The framework of stability leads back to the modes of viewing that characterize most of television use: monitoring, low involvement, and a comparative indifference to content except for choosing the most satisfying of available options. Taste publics, or audience segments with different preferences, important though they are in understanding the composition of the mass audience, in effect still assemble willingly in accord with the regimentation of the television schedule. Taste, in this respect, is vanquished by convenience.

PART II

Manufacturing the World

It occurred to her that possibly what was misleading was the
concept of "news" itself, a liberating thought.
Joan Didion, The Last Thing He Wanted

Television news is the product of decision making by key
individuals, expectations of news personnel about audience interest, conventions of format, and public and private events. It is a creative, selective collage decorated by
symbols of authoritativeness. News and politics are intertwined, but there is enough that is separate about television news and enough that is special to the political
messages of television that we begin by treating them independently. We first examine the construction of news,
its makeup, and its audience. We then turn to political coverage, the media strategies of politicians, and polls and
presidential debates. Finally, we treat the two together in
appraising their influence on public thought and action.

CHAPTER 4

Decisions, Stories, and Viewers

I. THE TASK AT HAND

Only selected events of seeming importance and audience interest can be attended to in the 22 minutes alloted to coverage in the typical half-hour newscast, and there will not always be autonomic consensus on which items should be chosen. News personnel must make daily decisions. We divide our discussion of the factors that influence the makeup of newscasts into the norms that govern gatekeeping, the who of decision making, and the application of the gatekeeping norms in national and local news operations.

A. NORMS AND NEWSWORTHINESS

David Manning White (1950) initially examined the process by which news stories were selected by describing the behavior of an editor named Mr. Gates.

Gatekeeping soon became the term for the filtering that advances some stories and bars others from public view. A half century later, the process observed by White remains in place because the need of news personnel for guidelines to choose among potential news stories remains undiminished.

The principal feature of gatekeeping is norms and values that specify newsworthiness. As Breed (1955, 1960) and Fishman (1980) concluded decades apart after observing the behavior of news personnel, most of the time most of these persons will reach the same decision given identical options. As Breed put it, a journalist "internalizes the rights and obligations of his status and its norms and values" (1960, p. 192), so that written rules and spoken admonitions are unnecessary.

Routines similarly help gatekeepers proceed in an orderly manner (Tuchman, 1978). These conventions are to newsroom operation what gears are to an old-fashioned watch. Stories that do not require immediate dissemination are stockpiled for use when needed. The most likely places for stories are canvassed at the expense of occasionally missing something off the beat. "Objectivity" is a ritual upheld in routine ways to protect the newsworker from threats of libel or accusations of unfairness. Clearly attributing quotations, providing multiple points of view, and verifying information do not solely represent lofty ideals but also are concrete means to avoid an appearance of bias that might impugn the popularity of a medium.

Gans (1979) concluded after examining gatekeeping at a television network, a major newspaper, and a news magazine that national news was homogeneous. The most discernible feature was a reliance on people and institutions that were already prominent. For example, almost three-fourths of stories at the network featured public figures, such as the president, presidential candidates, government officials at federal, state, and local levels, and persons prominently accused of breaking the law.

Factors influencing the decision-making process are highly stable (Shoemaker, Danielian, & Brendlinger, 1991). These include timeliness, proximity, importance of event or prominence of person, impact or consequence, interest, conflict or controversy, novelty, and, especially for television, deviance—departures from the ordinary in kind rather than solely in magnitude or severity. Long-standing traditions and strategies largely determine what news personnel will decide to include in the news.

B. THE DECISION MAKERS

Smith (1988, 1989) presents a profile of television decision makers based on a survey of a randomly drawn national sample of hundreds of reporters, photographers, producers, and news directors representing over 150 stations in markets of various sizes. The average age was about 30, compared to 37 for newspaper journalists a few years earlier (Weaver & Wilhoit, 1986). Television reporters also were better educated, with 90% of reporters and 89% of producers with college degrees compared to 74% for newspaper reporters. Just over one-third of newspaper journalists and television news reporters were women; almost one-half of producers were female. Television news directors, on the other hand, were overwhelmingly male (93%). The average age was about 40 years, and they had a median of 14 years of experience.

Empirical support for the view that journalists are largely liberal traces to Lichter, Rothman, and Lichter (1986), who surveyed persons employed in the late 1970s at major media organizations in the Northeast. More recent data (Weaver & Wilhoit, 1992) confirm that the percentages of journalists identifying themselves as Democrats (44%) or Republicans (16%) are 5-10 points higher and lower than for the American public, whereas about the same proportion as the public see themselves as independents (34%). The Democratic plurality has increased and the Republican minority has decreased since the 1970s. The data of Lichter and colleagues suggest that the pattern of political imbalance is exaggerated either among Northeastern elite media or by the use of ideological allegiance; they recorded 54% classifying themselves as liberals compared to 17% as conservatives.

Whether these political and ideological leanings translate into biased reportage is another matter. Our examinations later of data on the political and ideological emphases of news coverage do not turn up consistent or strong patterns of bias.

There are some startling and disturbing results when we look at the representations of women and ethnic minorities. Females have made progress; minorities have taken a step backward.

The most recent data of Stone (1995) record that 32% of television news personnel were women and 18% were members of minorities. The percentage of non-White news directors decreased from 10% in 1990 to 8.5% in 1993 and 7.7% in 1994. In contrast, the proportion of women news directors rose from 16 to 21% between 1990 and 1994. Overall, the television work force had a White male majority (54%), with White women at 28%, minority women at 10%, and minority men at 8%.

Earlier, Stone (1988) had analyzed survey data from 1976 to 1986. White men lost some of their overwhelming majority to White women, with White women increasing from 21 to 27% between 1979 and 1986. In 1976, one of every seven television news workers was a member of a minority; by 1986, the number had dropped to 1 in 8. In 1981, 3.9% of news directors reported being a minority. By 1986, the number was down to 2.6%. These data depict sociological ambivalence (Merton, 1996) in which norms encouraging the inclusion of former outsiders conflict with those entrusting power to familiar figures, so that the medium moves toward and then tentatively shies away from placing members of minorities in positions of authority while their presence overall has been increasing slowly.

Historically, television has employed fewer women than have news magazines and daily and weekly newspapers, while the various media have been similar in the representation of Black males and the same miniscule proportions of Hispanic females, Asians, and Native Americans (Foote, 1993; Weaver & Wilhoit, 1992). However, the average gap between men and women in wages among the news media has narrowed, with female salaries at 81% of males in 1991 compared to 64% 20 years earlier, while among those with 15 or more years of experience the salaries were about the same.

Although women and minorities in the television news work force have increased proportionately, the power represented has been questioned (Johnson, 1991). The 21% of female television news directors in 1994 is a 120% increase over 8 years, but no woman has ever been the head of a national network news operation (Mills, 1993). Blacks comprise about 12% of the population of the United States, but in the mid 1980s 95% of those in top news managerial positions at the three major television networks were White.

One survey of news anchors (Ferri, 1988) found that women perceive gender-specific barriers to advancement—principally, a greater emphasis on appearance and the existence of an old-boys network favoring men. Our belief is that members of minorities would have the same concern about old boys, and we would speculate that such beliefs constrain the exercise of individual vision as threatened personnel attempt to prove they behave no differently than the White males who once would have held the position.

On-air representation also has been examined. Ziegler and White (1990) recently addressed the extent to which network television news includes correspondents who are female or of a racial or ethnic minority. In a content analysis of 45 newscasts airing in three composite weeks on ABC, CBS, and NBC in 1987 and 1989, the authors found a total of 312 stories covered by White and 23 by non-White correspondents and 296 by male and 39 by female correspondents. These appearance rates of 6 and 12% record that actual use of minorities and women on the air nationally lags well behind their workforce representation.

Two issues are involved in the representation of women and minorities. One is diversity of viewpoint. The other is equity of opportunity. The norms of gatekeeping, as well as special pressures perceived by women and members of minorities, in any case would delimit the former. In fact, female and male reporters have been found to exhibit no real differences in selection or presentation of the news (Flanders, 1997; Liebler & Smith, 1997). However, the confinement of women to positions below the top rank and the stunningly small representation for minorities in positions of authority indicates that equity of opportunity is far from achieved.

C. NATIONAL NEWS

The gatekeeping at the news operations of ABC, CBS, and NBC has emphasized deviance from American values, relevance of a country to the United States, and the geographical proximity in the selection of stories about other countries. Shoemaker and colleagues (Chang, Shoemaker, & Brendlinger, 1987; Shoemaker et. al., 1991) matched 400 stories drawn from the three networks and the *New York Times* against Keesing's *Contemporary Archives: Record of World Events*, which attempts to chronicle all noteworthy occurrences. American media coverage was startlingly sparse. Over 355 events were indexed by Keesing over 2 years. The *Times* covered 28%. The three networks covered a meager 12%.

Similar factors predict coverage of earthquakes, other disasters, and health hazards. Gaddy and Tanjong (1986) found that 40% of 110 substantial quakes around the world were not covered by either the *London Times,* the *New York Times,* or one of the three networks, and number dead and extent of damage predicted coverage. Adams (1986) found that network coverage of disasters with 300 or more casualties was predicted by annual influx of American tourists, number of deaths, and geographical proximity to the United States. Singer, Endreny, and Glassman (1991) found that newspaper, news magazine, and network coverage of disasters and health hazards was predicted by continent, with Africa first for all media and Asia a close second for television. Singer and Endreny (1987) found that in covering health hazards the three networks and a variety of print media tend to give priority to novelty—the somewhat serious but rare event—over severity or number of deaths.

When television is compared with newspapers or news magazines, sensationalism, the more readily comprehensible, and the United States as a site are more favored. Deaths become more important than geography for disasters and hazards (Singer, Endreny, & Glassman, 1991), economic disturbances take precedence over political events (Shoemaker et al., 1991), and fewer stories from abroad are covered (Gaddy & Tanjong, 1986; Shoemaker et al., 1991).

Reese, Grant, and Danielian (1994) examined the sources used by *CBS News, Nightline, MacNeil/Lehrer, This Week with David Brinkley, Face the Nation,* and *Meet the Press.* They document a pattern across programs and topics in which officials who are government sources or other insiders played a central role (Table 4.1). Nongovernmental sources typically appeared with sources from

TABLE 4.1   Background of Sources Used by Four Television Newscasts

	Newscast			
Background of source	Nightline	CBS News	MacNeil/ Lehrer News Hour	This Week with David Brinkley
	Each program (percent)			
Insiders[a]	45	60	55	78
Outside analysts[b]	25	22	36	15
Outsiders[c]	30	18	10	7
Number of sources (N)	119	258	162	45

[a] Administration, former administration, military, interest group, political candidate, corporate executive

[b] Think tank, analyst, university expert, journalist

[c] Labor leader, other professional, other worker, local, foreign

Adapted from "The Structure of News Sources on Television: A Network Analysis of *CBS News, Nightline, MacNeil/Lehrer,* and *This Week with David Brinkley,*" by S. D. Reese, A. Grant, and L. Danielian, 1994, *Journal of Communication, 44*(2), pp. 84–107.

the government or were only allowed to speak after the insider had addressed and framed the issue.

The gatekeeping criteria relegate substantive news about most states to the wastebasket. Graber (1989b) found that most stories were about crime, disasters, or entertaining trivia. Political, social, and economic issues were ignored.

These data reflect universal news values. Severity, proximity, and relevance consistently predict coverage. This phenomenon leads to great similarities in television national news—ABC, CBS, NBC, PBS, and CNN. About two-thirds of broadcast stories appear on all three of the major networks, with three-fourths overlapping between any two, and nonduplicated stories are usually features rather than hard news (Lemert, 1974). Even the ranking by amount of coverage intercorrelates highly for the three networks, and although correlations are lower between the networks and PBS (*MacNeil/Lehrer News Hour*) and CNN (*Prime News*) and null between PBS and CNN, the topics covered by CNN and PBS are the same as those covered by the three networks (Stempel, 1988). Thus, PBS and CNN differ somewhat from the three networks in specific stories but in the topics attended to all five outlets are alike.

Our embrace of this concept is only slightly cooled by economic realities. As exemplified by the behavior of the four major networks during sweeps periods, channel operators play to the demographic makeup of their audiences by emphasizing or deemphasizing major dimensions of content, such as violence, that are more or less attractive to various segments in order to ensure that their ratings and shares do not suffer (Hamilton, 1998). We would expect the same in regard to news, but at the national level such maneuvering would be severely tempered by the intrusiveness of major events that essentially demand coverage and by the functioning of the competitors within the same national market. These factors help explain why preferred newscasters are perceived as more in accord with the political outlooks of viewers (Bower, 1985) and the newscasts of ABC, CBS, and NBC as largely different in presentational aspects (Schneider, 1985). Nationally, broadcasters maneuver within limited space as agilely as possible to maximize audience share.

D. The Local Newsroom

Audience relevance and ease of coverage are paramount in gatekeeping at local news operations. News from the town, city, or region predominates (Bernstein, Lacy, Cassara, & Lau, 1990). Stations in small markets where news-gathering resources are limited and little happens nevertheless give comparatively more attention to easy-to-cover nearby occurrences (Carroll, 1988) and larger market stations give comparatively more attention to national and international news (Bernstein et al., 1990). Half of sources are government officials and three-fourths of stories come from routine channels, such as press releases, official proceedings, or press conferences (Berkowitz, 1991). Investigative reporting is rare, aggressive pursuit of stories occurs seldom, and typically the most active news gathering is following police scanners or attending a press conference (Harmon, 1989; McManus, 1992).

Stations in larger markets give more attention to crimes, fires, and accidents, and to civic news, such as candidates for office and local government (Carroll, 1988) and have the resources to engage in more active discovery of the news (Carroll & Tuggle, 1997). About 20% of press releases are carefully considered for inclusion with notices of planned events, local sources, and nonprofit organizations favored (Berkowitz & Adams, 1990). Routine channels (Berkowitz, 1991; Brown, Bybee, Weardon, & Murdock, 1987) are more often used by local television news operations than by local or national newspapers. Universal news values and resources for news gathering are the strongest predictors of coverage (Berkowitz, 1991). The farther the story occurred from the market, the greater the similarity in coverage by local television stations (Carroll et al., 1997), most likely because networks provide similar video to their affiliates (Davie & Lee, 1993). Overall, there has been a trend away from news from the surrounding area, probably as a consequence of technology making the coverage of interesting events far away more feasible.

The data parallel those for national news. Deviant events, geographical proximity, familiar or well-known sources, and routines are at the forefront, with the gatekeeping in this instance more visibly shaped by the lack of news-gathering resources.

These data seemingly again identify the operation of universal news values. However, unlike the situation faced by national networks in which demographic differences can occur only in the audiences typically attracted, the 250 markets staked out by Nielsen can differ considerably demographically and in subtler regional and cultural ways, whereas the latitude is much greater with fewer must-carry stories for stations to position themselves differently both between and within markets. This leads to substantial variation among stations in the exercise of news values.

The phenomenon is well documented in the data of Hamilton (1998), who examined more than 16,000 local news stories in 1993 on 57 stations in 19 markets in his inquiry into crime coverage. Nineteen of 34 news topics registered zero in coverage for at least one station, whereas the maximum coverage accorded these same topics ranged between single digits and the mid-teens (with the exception of "government—other," which had a microscopic maximum of 0.2%). Among these 34 topics, crime received the most frequent coverage with an average of 29% of all stories. However, the per-station range was 18–42%. Similarly, murder accounted for an average of 30% of all crime stories—but the range was an extraordinary 7–70%. Hamilton links the emphasis on crime to newscasts crafted to be entertaining and fast-paced, with shorter but more stories, more visuals, and less government but more accident coverage, and the availability of viewers interested in violent entertainment as evidenced by the ratings for *Cops*. Thus, the regularities observed in the data at the local level mask substantial differences that reveal themselves when topics are examined narrowly and stations compared individually.

II. THE STORIES

We divide our analysis of the makeup of television news into five topics. We begin with the overall composition of network nightly newscasts—format, form features, and content. We then turn to gender and race, four news staples, five themes, and finally the role of technology. Our intent is to describe—within the limits of what has been investigated—the depiction of the world manufactured by news routines.

A. FORMAT, FORM, AND CONTENT

Schneider (1985) examined the format, form features, and content of the evening newscasts at ABC, CBS, and NBC over a 6-month period. He documented the very limited scope of a newscast, in which an average of 16 items was included; the lack of depth in coverage, represented by an average item length of 1 minute, 20 seconds with an average of four or five bits of information; and the limited range of attention, in which most stories pertained to the United States whereas "international news" drew largely from Western Europe and the Middle East. Schneider found an overwhelming consonance among the three networks in both topics represented and the format of newscasts, including the use of devices such as a reporter standing in front of a government building to enhance credibility and the perception of facticity. The networks differed somewhat only in the form features or visual construction of the newscast—pace, shot lengths, cuts to anchors.

B. Gender and Race

Gender and race in television news are attributes that promote the assigning of rather special and sometimes quite delimited social roles. This appears in such disparate facets of the news mosaic as the sources relied on, the depictions of arrested Blacks, coverage of Black politicians, the roles allotted female sources, conflict between Black and Jewish communities, the framing of affirmative action, and athletic coverage.

White males predominate as sources. Ziegler and White (1990) investigated gender and race among television news sources in 45 newscasts representing composite weeks in 1989 on ABC, CBS, and NBC. White males made up the large majority of newsmakers. The major exception was stories featuring a criminal, with 100% non-White male criminals. Non-Whites nevertheless comprised a substantial number—more than a fourth—of the government officials, public figures, criminals, and private individuals in the news.

Rakow and Kranich (1991) analyzed 1 month of newscasts on ABC, CBS, and NBC and found that only about 15% of sources were women. About half were private individuals called on to discuss how they were affected by crime, public policy, or disaster, to refer to members of their family, or to recount victimization. Women thus often have the role of fifth business in regard to topics, as go betweens rather than significant sources.

Liebler and Smith (1997) examined over 150 stories on ABC, CBS, NBC, and CNN that related to the president, the administration, or presidential policies and found that only 16% of sources were female. Male sources were also more often shown in professional settings and female sources more often had nonprofessional titles. The sex of the reporter made no difference in how male and female sources were presented.

Entman (1992) examined the portrayal of African Americans over 3 weeks in 1991 in Chicago nightly news. Blacks accused of crimes were less likely to be named, less likely to be shown in motion, more likely to be poorly dressed, more likely to be shown being physically held or restrained by a police officer, less likely to be spoken on behalf of by a defense lawyer, and more likely to be the focus of stories in which police officers who were minority members also appeared. The largest number of African Americans appeared in political coverage, however one-third discussed ethnic interests and appeared unconcerned with larger issues; only about 5% of White political sources did so.

In a 30-day sample of news on ABC, CBS, and NBC and a 1-year analysis of ABC news transcripts, Entman (1994) found that, as in Chicago, most Blacks shown in network news were involved in crime or politics. The national news, however, also contained a large number of stories in which Blacks were victims of misfortunes such as poverty, fires, or racism. In only a few instances did Blacks appear in non-race-related human interest stories or in the role of expert on non-race-related issues. In the area of crime, 77% of accused Blacks were shown in drug or violent crime situations compared to 42% of Whites, and, as in Chicago, they were more likely to be shown being physically held or restrained by police officers and less likely to have defense lawyers speaking on their behalf. In stories focusing on Black leaders, one-third involved allegations of illegal activity (e.g., Clarence Thomas, Marion Barry) and almost all depicted the leader as critical rather than supportive of governmental policies and actions.

Campbell, Wiggins, and Duhe (1997) analyzed almost 400 stories from four southeastern local television stations and found that Blacks were overrepresented in negative roles; they accounted for 71% of accused suspects and convicted criminals while comprising only 27% of law enforcers. Blacks were also underrepresented overall, appearing in 21% of stories compared to their 32% population in the area.

Rojecki (1996) found no evidence in polls of increases in anti-Semitism among Blacks or high levels of racism among Jews, yet he documents that the media had given considerable attention to Louis Farrakhan and the Nation of Islam despite his continually low ranking by Blacks as the leader best representing them. In effect, Black-Jewish conflict was exaggerated. We recall the same pattern in the coverage of Malcolm X. At the root are the journalistic conventions of focusing on dramatic individuals, reducing events to simplicities, and emphasizing conflict.

Entman (1996) investigated the framing of affirmative action by ABC, CBS, and NBC and the *Chicago Tribune, Chicago Sun Times, Newsweek,* and *Time.* Network and print sources were overwhelmingly split according to race, with 72% of Blacks supporting and 71% of Whites opposing affirmative action. In contrast, Entman reviews data from recent polls documenting public opinion as much more diverse and complex.

Roles also vary by race and gender in sports coverage. The players in televised college basketball games are often predominantly Black whereas the majority of the cheerleaders, fans, coaches, sportscasters, and characters on accompanying commercials are White (Wonsek, 1992). Blacks are performers; Whites comprise the audience. Coverage of women athletes consistently has emphasized gender. In U.S. Open tennis matches and college basketball games, females have been referred to as girls and by first names whereas males have not been called boys and last names have been used (Messner, Duncan, & Jensen, 1993). The 1992 coverage of female athletes by CBS at the Olympic Winter Games was marked by references to attractiveness, skepticism about mental toughness compared to heroic males, allusion to childlike dependency, and emphases on cooperative rather than competitive behavior (Daddario, 1994). The same patterns occurred in coverage of the 1992 "Battle of the Champions" between Martina Navratilova and Jimmy Connors (Halbert & Latimer, 1994).

There is no doubt that television news and sports coverage ascribes different roles on the basis of race and gender. Television, along with other news media, has often been simplistic, stereotypical, and somewhat divisive on race-related topics, as exemplified by coverage of criminal suspects, Black politicians, Jewish–Black relations, and affirmative action. Television has assigned women a distinctly minor and supporting role and one that emphasizes stereotypically feminine attributes, as illustrated by their rate of on-air appearance as reporters, their role as sources, and the attributes ascribed to female athletes.

C. FOUR STAPLES

The four staples of national television news are dispatches from other countries; crime, terrorism, and justice; the economy; and hazards and disasters. The data identify remarkable consistencies. Events enter and leave the newscasts, but their composition is eternal.

The proportion of stories from abroad has remained constant, although there has been some shifting about in regions covered (Graber, 1996; Hester, 1978; Weaver, Porter, & Evans, 1984). Television news in the United States, as in most large nations where much that is newsworthy occurs, gives much more attention to domestic than international coverage (Kitagawa, Salwen, & Driscoll, 1994; Sreberny-Mohammadi, 1984); only in very small entities such as Jamaica, where events meriting prominent coverage are comparatively rare, has international rivalled domestic in amount of coverage (Chen, 1989).

Television news stories are often framed in accord with national interests. The Soviet downing of a Korean airliner was presented as murder and an outrage; the U.S. downing of an Iranian passenger plane was a mishap attributable to technological error (Entman, 1991). Coverage of the 1988 launch of the

Soviet *Cosmos* unmanned satellite placed the United States at the forefront of technology, while the Soviet Union was portrayed as backward (Campbell & Reeves, 1989).

On average, about 30–40% of the evening network newscasts is devoted to international coverage (Gozenbach, Arant, & Stevenson, 1992; Weaver, Porter, & Evans, 1984). Recent estimates are that four out of five stories cover internal politics or military topics and that two of five are explicitly linked to U.S. goals or interests (Graber, 1996). The Middle East has received the most attention (Graber, 1996; Hester, 1978; Weaver et al., 1984). The two other regions usually among the top three have been Western Europe and Asia (Gozenbach, Arant, & Stevenson, 1992). In the most recent data from an analysis of 1049 stories from 61 countries on ABC between March 1993 and February 1994, Eastern Europe received the most attention because of the ongoing armed strife (Graber, 1996). Latin America and Africa typically generate the fewest stories, although Africa led in one study of the coverage of disasters and health hazards (Singer, Endreny, & Glassman, 1991). The emphasis on the Middle East, Western Europe, and Asia spans almost three decades. Areas rise and fall depending on events, but the fundamental framework remains unchanged in which U.S. interests—social, economic, and political—and deviance lead to coverage.

CNN's *World News,* to which foreign media submit stories, emphasizes foreign relations and internal politics, as do the U.S. networks, and also gives more attention to Western Europe, Asia, and the Middle East (Ganzert & Flournoy, 1992). However, *World News* does give comparatively greater attention to the arts and culture and to economic development than do the networks (Dilawari, Stewart, & Flournoy, 1991; Ganzert & Flournoy, 1992).

Crime is covered on most newscasts, with an average of about 60 seconds for crime stories per news broadcast and no significant differences among ABC, CBS, and NBC over a 13-year period (Randall, Lee-Sammons, & Hagner, 1988). Crime is the subject of almost half of all items covered in tabloid news magazines such as *A Current Affair, Inside Edition,* and *Hard Copy* and one of four items on network news magazines such as *Dateline NBC, Primetime Live, 60 Minutes,* and *20/20* (Graber, 1996). The emphases are invariant: common crimes like burglary and homicide (in contrast to elite crimes, such as price fixing or tax evasion), crimes against people rather than property, and the stage of accusation rather than of prosecution or sentencing.

The exception to the latter is the notorious crime in which investigative occurrences and judicial events continually provoke coverage followed attentively by the public. For example, the O.J. Simpson criminal trial received more coverage over its course from day to day than any other domestic or international story (Tyndall, 1998).

Again, no real differences appeared among the three networks in the rate of coverage of 1093 stories of corporate crime over a decade ending in the mid-1980s, with 40% of newscasts containing at least one corporate crime story (Randall, 1987). The topic usually was violation of manufacturing regulations or financial skullduggery and discovery of the crime or the verdict typically were the focus.

The oil industry represents a similar pattern (Randall & DeFillippi, 1987). The same stories were covered by ABC, CBS, and NBC, the news magazines, and the *Wall Street Journal*. Seriousness of the charge was a strong predictor of coverage and the emphasis was on financial wrongdoings rather than environmental allegations. Larger proportions of oil industry coverage by the networks dealt with crime, because the industry ordinarily is not a topic of interest to the television news audience (except for gasoline prices).

Similar consistencies among media appear in Supreme Court coverage. In a content analysis of ABC, CBS, and NBC, news magazines, the *New York Times,* the *Los Angeles Times,* and the *Chicago Tribune* from 1986 to 1987, all media made similar decisions about what to cover (O'Callaghan & Dukes, 1992). Civil rights issues and criminal law led, with First Amendment and economic issues also receiving a fair amount of coverage.

Terrorism likewise conforms to universal news values across media. Deviance and identifiability of culprits consistently predicted coverage by ABC, CBS, and NBC and nine newspapers from different countries (Weimann & Brosius, 1991). More specifically, coverage was a function of the magnitude and severity of terrorist act, the possibility of attributing responsibility, and the notoriety of the perpetrators.

ABC, CBS, and NBC have been quite similar in production practices, allotment of time, type of story, and sources consulted in covering terrorist actions (Atwater, 1989). For example, in an analysis of 790 soundbites from coverage of the 1985 TWA hostage incident (Atwater & Green, 1988), the three networks preferred domestic sources at a rate of about 5 to 1 and about half the time used the hostages or friends and relatives as sources.

Crime is a consistent and homogeneous entity varying little in substance or quantity among the three network nightly newscasts. Accusation is more consistently the focus than are other aspects of a criminal investigation. Topics of emotional interest, such as financial manipulations, take precedence in coverage of corporate crime. Rarely, a notorious crime will hold the attention of media and public over a long period.

A sampling of 739 newscasts from ABC, CBS, and NBC over the decade ending in 1983 indicates that there were an average of about 3.25 economic stories per newscast (Reese, Daly, & Hardy, 1987). Amount of coverage and division among topics were highly stable. Only about 1 of 10 stories dealt with the state of the economy. Private sector and government stories each totaled slightly more than a third; the former emphasized labor disputes and plant closings, the latter the federal budget, defense spending, social security, and welfare.

When bad economic news is available, it usually will get more television coverage than good news (Harrington, 1989). The unemployment rate, inflation, consumer price index, and gross national product are all top stories. For example, one-third of unemployment rate stories opened their newscasts. In non-presidential-election years, increases in unemployment or inflation and decreases in the gross national product were more often the lead story and were of greater average length than favorable shifts. For example, the probability of leading the newscast was three times greater for an increase in the unemployment rate than for a decrease. In presidential election years, the emphasis on bad news diminished. However, it is impossible to tell whether this is a function of the scruples of news personnel over possibly influencing the standing of the incumbent candidate or party or the product of economic upturns that often occur during election years.

The economy is a major source of news. Coverage is stable and consistent across years. Bad news is paramount. The pattern is only disrupted by the diminishing of bad news in presidential election years.

Patterson (1984) examined coverage of the Vietnam War on ABC, CBS, and NBC from 1968 to 1973. Almost one-quarter of all items concerned Vietnam, a proportion that was quite stable over the 5 years, was the same for all three networks, and represents the armed conflict pattern in which war-related stories dominate the news. A large majority of reports from Vietnam appeared to be sanitized, with only about 3% including visuals of combat and even fewer pictures of dead or wounded persons. The "body count" typically was announced without visuals only once per week. The on-camera assassination of a prisoner by a South Vietnamese officer was the exception rather than the rule although it remains prominent in the memory of many, perhaps because of the attention given to the network decision to use the footage (Bailey & Lichty, 1972). Any influence of television coverage on public support for the war apparently was attributable as much or more to its regularity and unavoidability than—as conventional wisdom holds—to its graphic attention to casualties.

One important issue is constraints on the freedom of the media. Newhagen (1994a) analyzed 424 news stories originating from the Persian Gulf from January 31, 1991 to March 3, 1991 on ABC, CBS, NBC, CNN, and PBS. Over twice as many U.S. sources than Iraqi sources were used, and 31% of the stories contained either audio or video disclaimers in which the audience was informed that some censoring had taken place. Censored stories were significantly more likely to be negative in tone, more likely to be intense in nature, and more likely to be critical of the source. We are not surprised because the very features that would attract the censor are unlikely to be fully eradicable;

we label this the residue explanation. The "flag-waving hypothesis" was supported with stories based on U.S. sources less critical than those from Iraqi-based sources. The United States also received more positive and less intense news scrutiny.

Peer and Chestnut (1995) studied 2 weeks of coverage of the Bush administration's decision to respond to Iraq's invasion of Kuwait by ABC, the *New York Times,* and the *Washington Post,* and concluded that television news was more "supportive of the official government line" and, on the whole, less independent of government influence than the two elite newspapers, with the ratio of supportive to critical assertions about 4 to 1 for ABC and about 1 to 3 for the newspapers. Reese and Buckalew (1995) similarly concluded that local television news largely acted as a support system for official policy in the Gulf, with information framed so that those against the war were unpatriotic and protest was a threat to order. Similarly, Gottschalk (1992) accuses the media of providing "jingoistic, misleading coverage" and laments the demise of the "crusading press" as the news media parroted the administration and censored themselves (p. 449).

Protests and demonstrations also have been examined. McCarthy, McPhail, and Smith (1996) compared police records of applications for protest permits with the corresponding stories on ABC, CBS, and NBC and in the *New York Times* and the *Washington Post* in 1982 and 1991. Those demonstrations in which large numbers were expected to protest as well as those concerned with issues high in media attention were more likely to receive coverage. Size of protest was a less strong predictor of television coverage, probably because the medium can compensate for magnitude by interesting video footage. We are reminded of the famous Lang and Lang (1968) study of MacArthur Day in Chicago in which by adroit camera work television displayed the public enthusiasm and ideological support that had been anticipated but was in fact not observed by those stationed by the investigators to describe what occurred.

Hazards, risks, and disasters regularly receive coverage by television and other news media (Adams, 1986; Gaddy & Tanjong, 1986; Singer & Endreny, 1987; Singer, Endreny, & Glassman, 1991). Deaths, geographical proximity, and novelty of the event predict coverage. These disruptive occurrences are of general interest, but in some instances will bear directly on the welfare of audience members. Coverage of disasters by the networks has also been associated with greater aggregate donations to relief efforts by private citizens in the United States (Simon, 1997).

The media, including television, tend to emphasize possible harm rather than risk (Singer & Endreny, 1987). That is, the focus often is on the severity of the threat rather than on the likelihood of becoming a victim. Risks from everyday threats, such as traffic accidents or common illness, in effect become underrepresented by the emphasis on potential if unlikely disaster. The news relishes the scary. Long-term threats fail to sustain media attention unless specific events occur to trigger renewed interest (Kitzinger & Reilly, 1997). Again, official spokespersons and elected officials were frequent as sources in hurricane and earthquake coverage, although in these circumstances they were second to those with direct experience—victims and witnesses (Walters & Hornig, 1993).

Because the environment ordinarily does not supply the required news values of death, severe threat, or novelty, coverage rests on the substitution for the chronic condition of a sudden threat (Greenberg, Sachsman, Sandman, & Salomone, 1989) or a newsworthy intrusion, such as the pending policy decision or White House conference that were connected with coverage of the old growth forest and the spotted owl (Liebler & Bendix, 1996).

Sensational visuals and alarming statements were absent from television coverage of the Chernobyl nuclear incident, but there was much dramatic terminology, such as "horror" or "nightmare" (Gorney, 1992). Neither television nor newspapers dealt much with risk levels for radiation or details that would have enhanced public understanding of what was taking place (Friedman, Gorney, & Egolf, 1987). Reassuring outnumbered alarming statements in television and print coverage of the accident at Three Mile Island on all topics except the chance of meltdown (Stephens & Edison, 1982). Harm thus takes precedence over causation (Singer & Endreny, 1987) and risk whereas the context— that might give the public a more complete and accurate picture and thereby sometimes alleviate anxieties (Graber, 1996)— is frequently absent.

Television implicitly recognizes the possibility of alarming the public exemplified by the famous Orson Welles radio dramatization of *War of the Worlds* (Cantril, 1940) while still favoring attention-getting elements, such as threat, harm, or amount of destructiveness and affect-laden descriptions. In the case of this news staple, universal news values stand between the public and accurate information about life's risks.

D. Five Themes

We identify five themes. Two are identical to those for entertainment—the dominance of the White male and the pervasiveness of conflict and threat. The former is exemplified by the frequency of White males as sources and reporters and by the different roles allotted on the basis of race and gender in news coverage. The second is represented by the emphases on death, strife, and political conflict in news from abroad; the role of crime as a staple and particularly the focus on crimes against persons; the nonelection year prominence of bad news in economic coverage that often has consequences for personal employment and income; and the continuing attention to hazards and disasters.

We also see three others. The emphasis on bad news is so pervasive we think it merits treatment on its own. In addition, trends in soft vs hard news and the phenomenon of the overarching story are prominent enough in our view to receive explicit attention.

A survey of a nationally representative sample of more than 100 news directors (Galician & Pasternack, 1987) informs us that more than two-thirds thought good news was "fluff," a ratio of 2 to 1 believed that bad news rather than good news matched news values best, 6 of 10 agreed that bad news was more effective than good news in attracting an audience, and television was preceived as having the most bad news among all the media. Thus, the priorities of gatekeepers favor bad news.

Analyses of news content confirm that these opinions operate forcefully in the selection of stories. Stone and Grusin (1984) analyzed a constructed week of ABC, CBS, and NBC newscasts in 1983 resulting in 238 stories that were coded as being either good news ("positive and upbeat") or bad ("negative and downbeat") (Table 4.2). Almost half (47%) were bad news compared to about one-fourth each for good news (25%) or "indeterminable" (28%). For

TABLE 4.2   Good vs Bad News in Network News

| | Newscasts by network | | | |
	ABC $(N = 78)$	CBS $(N = 79)$	NBC $(N = 81)$	Total $(N = 238)$
Content of story	Each network (percent)			
Good news	28	23	25	25
Bad news	57	44	39	47
Indeterminable	15	33	36	28
	Story content (percent)		
	Good news	Bad news	Indeterminable
Among first five stories in newscast			
ABC $(N = 25)$	24	56	20
CBS $(N = 25)$	16	56	28
NBC $(N = 25)$	20	28	52
Stories more than 30 seconds in length			
ABC $(N = 36)$	31	64	6
CBS $(N = 41)$	22	54	24
NBC $(N = 45)$	16	49	36
Stories having video clips			
ABC $(N = 47)$	32	62	6
CBS $(N = 54)$	22	56	22
NBC $(N = 54)$	15	46	39

Adapted from "Network TV as the Bad News Bearer," by G. C. Stone and E. Grusin, 1984, *Journalism Quarterly, 61*(3), pp. 517–523, 592.

all three networks, bad news stories were about twice as likely to appear in the first five stories, to be more than 30 seconds long, and to have an accompanying video clip.

Earlier data indicate that this is a long-standing pattern. Lowry (1971) found not only more bad than good news on all three networks, but also bad news was more likely to be placed at or near the beginning of the newscast and was more likely to be accompanied by visuals. Singer (1972) recorded that CBS evening news carried more stories of war, protest, and violence than the national news of the Canadian Broadcasting Company.

These emphases are repeated at the local level. Stone, Hartung, and Jensen (1987) applied the procedures of Stone and Grusin to the local news in Memphis, San Diego, and Syracuse. Local news was only minutely lower in bad news (43%) and only slightly higher in good news (33%) than national news, and as at the networks, bad news was largely located in the first third of the newcast.

Nevertheless, there has been an observable trend toward a greater emphasis on soft news and features. The Scott and Gobetz (1992) analysis of ABC, CBS, and NBC spans 15 years from 1972 to 1987 and includes 558 newscasts. The average time devoted to soft news increased over the period. All networks most of the time placed soft items in the last third of the newscast.

Again, data indicate that somewhat similar trends are occurring at the local level. Slattery and Hakanen (1994) collected data from a sampling of Pennsylvania markets in 1992 and compared the outcomes with 1976 data (Adams, 1978) from the same areas. The percentage of items classified as either sensationalistic or human interest in early evening news increased from an average of 12% in 1976 to 41% in 1992, largely at the expense of stories regarding government, politics, or education, which fell from 64% in 1976 to 19% in 1992. Results became less dramatic but the trends remained when Pittsburgh stations with extended and late evening newscasts were included.

Finally, there is the overarching story that dominates or is consistently present in the news for an extended period. Such stories have two dimensions, the frequency with which they are covered and the length of time during which they receive coverage. The most obvious example is armed conflict, as exemplified by the Vietnam War, which beginning in mid-1964 received extensive coverage in all media and on the network news was given more attention than any other topic for 5 years beginning in 1968 (Funkhouser, 1973a, 1973b; Patterson, 1984), and the Gulf War, which dominated television news in 1990 (Tyndall, 1998). Most of our four staples appear sporadically although with regularity, but occasionally a story will pierce the usual boundaries, such as the O.J. Simpson criminal trial that received more attention than any other story on television for 9 months (Tyndall, 1998). Between 1985 and 1992, AIDS was a top story repeatedly for several weeks at a time as a series of media and sports celebrities either died of the illness, announced they had contracted it, or revealed they had tested positive to HIV—Rock Hudson, Liberace, Arthur Ashe, and Magic Johnson. The Ethiopian famine was the recipient for all of 1984 (Rogers & Chang, 1991) as was the war on drugs between mid-1988 and the beginning of 1991 (Dearing & Rogers, 1996). These stories made a large claim on public attention and their media prominence rested on the interest of the news media in appealing to the public, whereas the fickleness of the process is demonstrated by the failure of the Brazilian drought, ranked as an equally vicious and massive threat to human life and occurring at the same time as the Ethiopian famine, to become an overarching news story.

Critics (Altheide, 1976; Comstock, 1989; Real, 1996; Ryu, 1982) have long and consistently argued that the pursuit of ratings leads to emphases on the dramatic, the entertaining, and the visual. The data are in accord with these views. Bad news is paramount, there has been an increasing place for stories that are entertaining and amusing, and stories that seize the public imagination get inordinate attention whereas others of similar import are largely ignored.

E. TECHNOLOGY

Technology is the invisible backbone of television news. The story lies in events, but the way events can be covered is a function of the electronic tools available. Graphics, once rare, have become ubiquitous (Foote & Saunders, 1991). Portable cameras and news vans with microwave capacity made on-site coverage common in the 1970s, and satellites in the 1980s extended this ability to distant places (Lacy, Atwater, & Powers, 1988).

These capabilities, although extending enormously the range of coverage for a local news operation, have not resulted in the reduced reliance of affiliates on the network. Instead, they continue to use the coverage the network supplies and become an occasional supplier when newsworthy events occur in the local market. Thus, technology enhances the capability to "go live" but supplements rather than supplants reliance on the network (Lacy, Atwater, & Powers, 1988).

Technology has led to the globalization of the news market. About 200 countries receive news from global networks (Foote, 1995). Near-instant access to events in distant places is becoming available to all audiences. Especially in times of crisis, these networks become a source of centralized information.

So far, only tiny audiences use such linkages between television and computers as Microsoft and NBC's MSNBC (Newhagen, Cordes, & Levy, 1995). However, it does make the network one of the many suppliers among information sources available to computer users, and over the next decade it is possible that more television screens will become capable of receiving information from the Internet and other electronic sources through such now-fledgling services as Microsoft's Web TV.

Surveys of news directors indicate that stations in larger markets adopt new technologies earlier because they have the resources to do so. The news directors largely agree that the technologies provide a competitive edge and that they affect the content of the news (Broholm, 1985; Lacy et al., 1988; Smith, 1984). They do so by influencing the way stories are covered and by making some stories more attractive because of the visuals or live coverage now available. In fact, particularly savvy organizations send video news releases (VNRs) to increase their chances of gaining coverage by providing the necessary video (Cameron & Blount, 1996). Thus, technological advances can be expected to increase what has been a long-standing influence on what television chooses to report (Epstein, 1973; Lang & Lang, 1953)—interesting camera coverage. The implication is that more stories will compete for the 15 or 16 slots in the average half-hour newscast, and those without camera coverage will be even less likely to receive attention.

III. THE VIEWERS

We now turn to the audience for news. The data overturn four myths of conventional wisdom: that there are two large audiences for news, one that relies on television and another that relies on newspapers and magazines; that sizable proportions of the public never miss the network evening news; that children and teenagers are infrequent in the audience for television news; and that network evening news is America's most turned to news source. We cover three topics: the characteristics of those who view, public opinion about television news, and why people view.

A. Who Views

There are several striking aspects about the demographics of the audience for evening network news. The first is that it is singularly older than the audience for most evening entertainment programs (Comstock, 1989; Comstock et al., 1978; Israel & Robinson, 1972). The second is that it is much smaller than the audience for those entertainment programs (Comstock et al., 1978). The third is that, among adults, females outnumber males in the audience (Fishman, 1998). Television is perceived by females as a particularly important news medium for they describe themselves more often than do males as relying primarily on television for news (Smith, Lichter, & Harris, 1997). Their current presence in the audience represents a significant change from the pattern of the late 1960s when males were more prominent (Israel & Robinson, 1972; Robinson,

1971) and is the product of a rise in viewership and the greater proportion of adult females in the total population. Males are more likely to tell opinion pollsters that they regularly watch the news (Hamilton, 1998), perhaps because it seems a responsible civic activity for a man. The fourth is that college-educated Blacks, who are part of a demographic segment that overall views more television than do Whites (Nielsen Media Research, 1998), are much more likely than the college-educated in general to be in the audience for national television news (Comstock et al., 1978; Israel & Robinson, 1972).

Those who watch television news regularly typically also seek news from other media. Patterson (1980), in two very large samples from an eastern and a West coast city, found that those who regularly read newspapers often also watched national television news regularly, with television only expanding the total news audience by about one-fourth over what it was for newspapers alone. He also found that when regular and nonregular viewers of national news were compared, the groups did not differ as would have been expected from the demographic patterns of television viewing in education and income. One reason is that news viewing is curvilinearly associated with education (Israel & Robinson, 1972; Robinson, 1971), so that the category "regular viewer" will contain a counterbalance of those higher and lower in education (and in income, too, because education is a predictor of average earnings). Another, and more important for understanding the dynamics of television use, is that total amount of television viewing—where undemanding distraction is a major motive—is a poor predictor of news viewing. Information seeking for awareness figures more prominently for news viewing. The news viewer, then, is representative of the large regular audience for news that to some degree follows events in several media rather than of the huge audience for television in general.

Within this news audience, reliance on one or another medium varies enough that it is possible to identify many individuals as either more television oriented or more print oriented (Neuman, Just, & Crigler, 1992). The greater the degree of education, the more likely a print orientation except among Blacks where socioeconomic status generally fails to predict less use of television by those with more education (Comstock et al., 1978). McDonald and Reese (1987) found some evidence of a qualitative difference in other types of news programs sought, with television-reliant subjects more often watching a television news magazine and newspaper-reliant subjects more often watching PBS's *MacNeil/Lehrer News Hour*.

Among the fairly large number who pay only passing attention to events of the day there is a disproportionate representation of people low in education and income. When an event—war, assassination, health hazard—leads them to seek out the news, they are more likely to choose television over other media.

There also is a much smaller group high in average level of education that regularly seeks news primarily from print media and pays little attention to news programming on television.

It is a myth, then, that there are two large, distinct news audiences relying on different media. Instead, there is an audience for news from a diversity of sources.

The dominance of time available in governing viewing means that only a steadfast few nightly attend to network evening news, and the stability of preferences among available options ensures that when a newscast is viewed it will be the same one viewed previously. An average repeat viewing rate of 40% or less matches the actual percent of the news audience who see all five of a week's network evening newscasts—1–3% (Lichty, 1982). Fewer than 1.5 million persons—a hefty enough figure but a very small share of the weekly audience—will view five newscasts in a row. It is a myth that a substantial proportion of viewers never misses a newcast.

However, there are two circumstances in which the ordinary patterns of news viewing are altered in the direction of greater and more consistent attention. One are crises that embody a threat to personal tranquility and the status quo. The Gulf War was an example. Events of this kind soar beyond ordinary levels of public interest because of their implications for the way lives may be led or lost. News consumption in general increases and audiences for specialized channels such as CNN rival those of the networks in size, with several times more viewers than ordinarily the case. Observers frequently predict that the enhanced attention to news will lead to permanent increases in the consumption of news in general and use of CNN specifically. So far, they have been wrong. When the crisis has ended, viewing invariably has returned to its earlier pattern. The other are "media events" where coverage commands unusually high levels of interest and attention (Dayan & Katz, 1992). Royal weddings are an example. There is often a confluence of ritual and ceremony with the participation of individuals of great renown. These occasions take on the aura in many households of the early days of television when viewing was something special around which timetables would be arranged and social events scheduled (Rothenbuhler, 1988).

News ranks among the least favorite programs of children (Lyle & Hoffman, 1972). Nevertheless, children and teenagers are surprisingly prominent in the audience. More than 40% of those 9 and older reported they watched news daily in a national survey of 100,000 (Anderson, Mead, & Sullivan, 1986) and the average ratings in diary data for network evening news among those 2–11 and 12–17 in age are about three-fourths and one-half of those for adults 18–55, with the numbers slightly greater for local news (Comstock, 1991a). The explanation for children is that they are in the vicinity when parents have the set turned to the news. The Nielsen estimates for children are particularly impressive because news is a category of programming that parents often might neglect to record their children as viewing in diaries even when they are in the room when the news is on (and children are among those least likely to record themselves as viewing with people meters). Thus, news ratings for children are very likely to be underestimates of their presence in the audience. Teenagers also sometimes are simply viewing with the family but often have become motivated to follow the news (Chaffee, Ward, & Tipton, 1970) and their freedom to do otherwise is the explanation for the lower ratings despite greater likelihood of a motive to view. Thus, it is another myth that children and teenagers are not much exposed to the news.

B. WHAT THEY THINK

Our examination of public opinion about television news discloses an extraordinary contrast between what people say and what people do, a lively oscillation between the popularity of the president and the confidence of the public in the media, and the development of a political climate in which ideology newly predicts the perception of the news media as hostile. We also inquire into the factors behind the high opinion the public has of television news, the criteria on which perceptions of credibility are based, and the circumstances in which the public would infringe on the First Amendment rights of the media.

Forty years of public opinion data document that in the mind of the American public television has become the nation's number one news source. Roper has been collecting data since the 1950s, and the most recent poll (Roper Starch, 1995) reports that television continues to gain ground against its nearest competitor, daily newspapers. Almost three-fourths counted television among their primary sources of news compared to 38% for newspapers (multiple responses were permitted). The 34-point gap represents an 8-percentage-point increase since 1992. Majorities or pluralities have long cited television as the most credible or believable if information conflicted, the most rapid disseminator, and the most complete and comprehensive of all media (Bower, 1973, 1985; Steiner, 1963) but the most recent rankings on these dimensions are higher than at any time in the past. This is a thoroughly national and socially pervasive phenomenon, although television is somewhat more favored by those with lower levels of income and education and those residing in rural areas (Bower, 1973, 1985).

The behavior of the public, however, has ignored for decades the declared reliance on television in regard to its best known national offering—network evening news. Long ago, analysis of about 2000 media-use diaries from a national sample by Robinson (1971) revealed that although a majority of the public at the time ranked television as their primary news source, more than half of the adults in the sample did not report seeing any portion of a network evening newscast during the 2 weeks covered by the data. On a typical day, three times as many read some part of a daily newspaper than saw any portion of the evening news. This pattern had not changed by the late 1980s when the daily readership was more than 100 million for newspapers, the weekly circulation was about 50 million for the three major news magazines, and fewer than 40 million nightly were in the audience for network evening news (Comstock, 1989).

This paradox has not been eliminated by the increases in time spent viewing television and the decreases in time spent reading newspapers over the past three decades. This is because the disparity rests on two factors that have not changed. The first factor is the large difference in the magnitude of the audiences for the media. The second is an anomaly in the interpretation of the term "news" by many individuals. Quick inspection of audience size is sufficient to realize that it would be unlikely that people would have more contact with the evening news than with newspapers. More telling is that the term news connotes the important national and international events typical of television coverage so that, without additional qualification, people readily name television as their primary source. When the query is qualified by local or regional news, city or congressional rather than presidential elections, or specific topics not prominent in television coverage (such as changes in building codes), the rankings of newspapers rise and those of television decline (Carter & Greenberg, 1965; Comstock et al., 1978; Levy, 1978; Roper, 1973, 1975).

The addition of local news and the weekday morning magazine formats would not change the pattern. This is because their audiences to a great extent overlap with those for the network evening news (Webster & Phalen, 1997) and the ratings for the morning programs are modest, so that the total audience for evening news, local news, and the magazine formats would still not exceed use of daily newspapers.

Television becomes associated with certain stories and features, particularly those that use dramatic visual imagery, are highly memorable, or particularly useful. Thus, it is said to be best by the public for national politics, international events, disasters, advances in space technology, science, and the weather (Bogart, 1989). These are what "the news" connotes, and so it is television that is said to be the primary news source.

There is no doubt that the public will endorse statements highly critical of the news media, including television (Gaziano, 1988; Immerwhar & Doble, 1982; Smith et al., 1997). Large proportions agree that the media are at least somewhat biased politically and that there should be laws requiring fairness in coverage for both television and print media. Our view is that these seemingly threatening data (in terms of the welfare and independence of the media) are best interpreted in terms of four additional factors: confidence gap trends, contrary public opinion, the salience of media performance as an issue, and the hostile media phenomenon.

Lipset and Schneider (1983) examined "confidence gap" data from national surveys on the ratings of major institutions. These amount to precise estimates in response to vague stimuli that often encompass an enormous variety of entities ("media" and "business" are two examples). Yet, because the stimuli remain the same, the data do provide some sense of patterns and trends. Confidence ratings, including those for the media, had declined over the past few decades. Yet the ranking of the media had never been high and comparatively remained about the same. An inverse relationship between expressed confidence in the media and the popularity of the president was observable. The sometimes adversarial role of the news media leads the public to be more displeased with the media when it is pleased with the president. Thus, confidence in the media oscillates a few percentage points around a modest figure, which in turn gives an exaggerated impression of the importance of these shifts. Given these circumstances, a prolonged series of rankings lower than historically usual would be required to infer a loss of confidence.

Our skepticism over deep, broad public dissatisfaction with the media is strengthened by two other bodies of data. One is the evidence on elicited vs volunteered opinion (Comstock, 1989). As exemplified by the data on public opinion about television violence (Chapter 3), statements critical of the media are willingly endorsed, and often by substantial majorities, whereas such views are not held strongly enough for them to be volunteered by more than a very few. The other is the readiness with which people endorse contrary statements. For example, large majorities agree it would be dangerous to limit press freedoms (Freedom Forum, 1997) and endorse statements praising the performance of the news media (Gaziano, 1988).

We also think that the great increase in news outlets across the mass media since the introduction of television makes some decline in declared confidence inevitable. After all, with more outlets comes a greater likelihood of a breech on the part of one or another of a standard, ethic, or criterion honored by a member of the news audience or a conflict in coverage, and the inevitable intensified competition would only exacerbate what greater numbers have already brought about. Thus, the registering of slightly enhanced disenchantment over the performance of the news media would only reflect a realistic perception of a more crowded marketplace.

The concept of the hostile-media phenomenon first surfaced in an experiment by Vallone, Ross, and Lepper (1985) in which pro-Arab and pro-Israeli groups were shown the same ABC, CBS, and NBC news coverage of the Middle East. Each side perceived the other as receiving decidedly more favorable treatment. Contrary to the wishful thinking of news personnel, more informed persons were not less likely to perceive bias. The opposite occurred. The higher the viewers scored on factual knowledge of the conflict, the greater the degree to which they judged the news accounts to be biased against their side. Perloff (1989) similarly found that pro-Israeli and pro-Palestinian subjects seeing the same coverage were convinced that their side had received less favorable treatment. Thus, the media will be seen by partisans as hostile to their interests.

We think the hostile-media phenomenon explains current patterns in public perceptions of the political outlook of news personnel. The recent survey by Smith, Lichter, and Harris (1997) of a nationally representative sample of more than 3000 adults records that about twice as many perceive the media as politically liberal than as conservative. Forty-three percent said they thought the media were liberal compared to 19% who said they were conservative, with 33% saying they thought the media were middle of the road (Table 4.3). This contrasts with similar national survey data from 1970 and 1980 in which the division between perceptions of liberal and conservative leanings were much more equal and the middle of the road response was much more frequent (Bower, 1973, 1985).

The explanation in our view lies in the changed political posture of those who describe themselves as conservative. Inspection of the data makes it clear that those who perceive themselves as liberal or middle of the road perceive the media to be much like themselves; this is strikingly evident in the 47% of middle of the roaders who perceive the media as middle of the road. Among

TABLE 4.3   Perceived Views of Media by Political Orientation

How would you describe the views of the media on most matters having to do with politics?	Political philosophy of respondent			
	Total	Liberal	Middle of the road	Conservative
Sample size (N)	3004	760	1008	1173
Respondent said	Number of respondents (percent)			
Liberal	43	40	30	57
Middle of the road	33	34	47	19
Conservative	19	21	16	21
Don't know	5	6	6	3
Refused to say	—	—	—	1

Adapted from *What the People Want from the Press,* by T. J. Smith, S. R. Lichter, and L. Harris and Associates, 1997, Washington, DC: Center for Media and Public Affairs.

those who perceive themselves as conservative, there is no matching perception of similarity and far higher proportions perceive the media as liberal.

We interpret this as representing the enhanced degree to which conservatives presently think of themselves as advancing an agenda and functioning as partisans. In contrast, the fist of the liberal today is not raised in support of social reform. The label no longer stands for the impassioned advocacy of specific issues (such as civil rights and opposition to the Vietnam War), and instead refers to the endorsement of the various legacies of Roosevelt's New Deal, Truman's Fair Deal, and Johnson's War on Poverty that in fact is shared by substantial proportions of the public. Thus, the conservatives, as more partisan, are more likely to perceive the media as hostile. These data do not represent either the degree of liberal influence—other than the acceptance of those past reforms—or general public dissatisfaction with the media.

Television has long been named by more individuals as most credible when media differ (Bower, 1973, 1985; Roper, 1973, 1975) and in the most recent survey it outpolls newspapers in this regard, 51–31% (Roper Starch, 1995). This derives partly from the way television represents the news, including the seeming authenticity of visuals (Carter & Greenberg, 1965; Graber, 1990), the use of personable newscasters that make the newscast seem less cold and distant than a newspaper (Newhagen & Nass, 1989), and the symbols of facticity that are so regularly employed (Tuchman, 1973, 1978), and partly from the structure and immediacy of television news in which story brevity precludes much in the way of error and there is no publication lag during which things might have changed as there is for newspapers (Comstock, 1989).

These factors shield television from the skepticism to which newspapers are vulnerable, and the standing of television is not dependent on some connotative bias as was the case for it being named primary source (Carter & Greenberg, 1965). However, the public may well become dissatisfied with coverage in a specific instance— such as the aggressiveness of an interviewer—so imputed credibility will certainly vary by story with television typically having an advantage.

Viewers, in fact, do not seem to approach television news critically. Hacker and colleagues (Hacker, Coste, Kamm, & Bybee, 1991) found that viewers were more likely to criticize content or technique of production than to perceive some role for ideology or bias. Even manipulation by announcing the use of staged footage does not diminish credibility if it is not repeatedly used (Slattery & Tiedge, 1992). Viewers, however, are somewhat more trusting of persons they perceive as like themselves or those who present themselves well and are articulate (Johnson, 1984; Thayer & Pasternack, 1992).

Local and national news are about equal in public esteem. Similar proportions (between 50 and 60%) say they regularly watch one or the other and agree that one or the other is very or extremely important to them, with national news leading in viewing and local news in importance.

The public does perceive television news as guilty of presenting too much bad news. The Smith, Lichter, and Harris data (1997) recorded that about 6 of 10 Americans who say they rely primarily on television for news believe it is too negative. Similarly, Galician (1986) found that 3 of 4 of about 250 viewers in the Phoenix area agreed that television newscasts report too much bad news and not enough good news. Three of 5 agreed that TV news tends to make things seem worse than they are. Large majorities advocated such counterpractices as having more "positive and bright" stories and including more "information to help you cope with bad news."

Immerwahr and Doble (1982) collected data from a representative national sample on beliefs about the rights and obligations of the media. When asked to choose among stated options, overwhelming majorities agreed that the media have obligations to be impartial in covering politics and controversial issues, including giving major presidential candidates equal coverage. Eighty percent favored a law requiring equal coverage. Twenty-five percent endorsed a law that would prohibit the media from embarrassing the president, government, or country. About one-fifth agreed that the government has a right to arrest an errant reporter and that the president has the right to close down a newspaper. A substantial proportion, and in the case of equal coverage a majority, would prohibit activities protected at present by the First Amendment.

The findings seemingly suggest that the rights of the media are in peril. We argue otherwise. The data demonstrate exceptionally well the problematic aspects of eliciting opinion. Pro-First Amendment views could and have been as readily elicited (Freedom Forum, 1997). Volunteered opinion in response to open-ended queries consistently has indicated that media performance is not a salient or important concern to most of the public, as exemplified by the failure of enough people to name the media as the "most important problem" facing the country in more than 200 Gallup polls since World War II to register above a scant few percentage points (Comstock, 1989; Dearing & Rogers, 1996; Funkhouser, 1973a, 1973b).

Concerns about the news media revolve around the issue of truth. We see three distinct dimensions. The first is adherence to factual elements, which means reporting what is verifiably known, avoiding unreliable sources, and labeling uncertainties and speculation—necessary if the media are to be at the edge of events—as such. The second is inclusiveness, in that all known elements favorable or unfavorable to a perspective are included. The third is balance, which requires presenting a variety of viewpoints and roughly equal proportions for opposing sides. We label these accuracy, completeness, and fairness.

The performance of the media remains difficult to assess because they are typically the sole source of information for the occurrences they cover. Fairness is easily measured and accuracy and completeness, although open to argument, can be empirically assessed. The media may meet these criteria in their coverage, but the fact of coverage often remains open to challenge. Truth becomes hard to discern when it is a function of news values. Thus, the fundamental truthfulness of the news media remains elusive.

C. WHY THEY WATCH

As Webster and Phalen (1997) point out, the two principal perspectives in explaining exposure to the news have been the seeking of particular gratifications that derive from the internal motives of viewers and structural factors in which regularities of viewing predict the size of the audience. They see some difficulty in reconciling the two, but we find none. Gratifications represent the preferences of individual viewers. Structural factors represent the options for their expression. The proper analogy is a motor trip in which the preferences of the occupants of a BMW 3 are limited by the road map; a detour for dim sum at L.A.'s Empress Pavillion will remain the lust of a Chinese food freak if the drive is taking place in upstate New York.

The most prominent motive behind choosing to view the news is that of surveillance with an emphasis on events (Chapter 3). This is joined by a variety of other gratifications as demonstrated by the data of Levy (1978) and McDonald (1990) collected from samples of several hundred in urban Northeast sites. Major motives included the desire to be diverted by the peculiar and unusual events that make up the news, the opportunity for passing emotional involvement through excitement and identification, the pleasures of seeing favorite news personnel, and the obtaining of topics to converse about with others. Thus, keeping up with events, the obvious motive, is abetted by the desire to be entertained, and keeping up extends well beyond the acquisition of information. This fits well with the data on motives in general (Chapter 3) and with the recent national survey (Roper Starch, 1995) in which the two most cited reasons for watching television were to keep up with what's happening and to be entertained.

There is a linkage between gratification seeking and choice of newscasts by viewers. Palmgreen, Wenner, and Rayburn (1981) found that the perception that the newscasts of one or another of the three original networks better served such gratifications as being entertained or keeping up with events predicted viewing of those newscasts. Bower (1985) found that Americans who labeled themselves conservative, liberal, or middle of the road in political perspective perceived their preferred newscaster as closer than other newscasters to their own political outlook. Babrow and Swanson (1988) found that the gratifications sought predicted attitudes toward different news programs, whereas "expectancy value"—beliefs about whether and what sorts of gratification actually will flow from viewing—more clearly predicted exposure to particular news programs. Thus, perceptions and beliefs about news programs do play some role in the decisions viewers make about which newscasts to watch as would be expected.

A good, recent example of the investigation of individual preferences is the survey by Lin (1992) of about 260 news viewers in the Midwest. Quality of local coverage and weather reports and on-air personalities were all cited by substantial proportions as reasons for choosing a particular newscast. The weather person typically was judged as being "important" or "very important" and news reporters as "somewhat important" in choosing a program. In response to an open-ended query, only about 5% mentioned carry-over effects from a previous program. Similar results were found in a study of San Diego viewers (Wulfemeyer, 1983) in which 30% said they chose a local newscast due to its quality, 28% due to the newscasters, and 12% out of habit.

The viewer thinks and acts on the premise of personal latitude. In fact, the mass audience regularities that exist for news viewing make motive only a modest factor in explaining the popularity of different newscasts. Much larger forces are at work. The analyses of audience flow by Webster and Newton (1988) and Webster and Phalen (1997) document that the ratings of local newscasts are largely a function of three factors: size of the available audience (operationally defined as the proportion viewing television at the time), ratings of the lead-in show prior to the news, and, for the affiliates, the ratings for the network news. These three account for 80% of the variance in ratings. Audience size was negatively correlated with amount of competition or number of other commercial stations; with inconvenience of access or higher channel numbers; and with the opportunity for flight or the number of channels offering entertainment.

The publicity goes to network news, but it is local news that is stronger in influencing audience loyalty. Local news contributes more to network ratings than the reverse—and this is true both for lead-in effects (Webster & Phalen, 1997) and channel loyalty (Wakshlag, Agostino, Terry, Driscoll, & Ramsey, 1983).

Further evidence of an audience for news and the power of mass audience popularity to predict attention are found in two recent surveys of several hundred Northeast viewers. News viewers were also likely to be newspaper readers (McDonald, 1990), and CNN and national broadcast news viewers did not differ demographically (except that the CNN viewers were somewhat younger and therefore had less channel loyalty) and even those citing the superiority of CNN watched broadcast news more frequently (Baldwin, Barrett, & Bates, 1992).

The Political Medium

Television became a factor in national politics in the United States in the 1952 presidential election. Only a very few homes had television at the time of the previous election. In 1952, nearly 1 of every 3 had a set. Huge audiences were able to watch party conventions and see political commercials (Cranston, 1960). Candidates certainly were concerned with their images before television, but the medium advanced the construction of images as goal and practice (Chester, 1969; Hiebert, 1971; Mendelsohn & Crespi, 1970; Nimmo, 1970; Rubin, 1967).

The average American citizen assigns to politics a relatively low level of salience. Low voter turnout rates, the dominance of two broad political parties rather than several markedly different and differently labeled factions, and the distaste with which many people view displays of extreme political views are all indicators that in America politics typically does not arouse great fervor (Comstock et. al., 1978; Neuman, 1986; Neuman et al., 1992).

The well-known, major pretelevision voting studies—Erie County, 1940 (Lazarsfeld, Berelson, & Gaudet, 1948) and Elmira, New York, 1948 (Berelson, Lazarsfeld, & McPhee, 1954)—recorded scant if any signs of media influence on voter behavior. In our judgment, data collected over the past five decades, and particularly since 1970, point to a much larger role for the media. They continue to alert, arouse, reinforce, and channel opinion—outcomes generally construed as dependent on previously held beliefs (Klapper, 1960)—but these more recent data in fact assign the media a very influential role in elections. The most recent research indicates that the media affect opinions about parties, policies, and candidates as well as what people think about and debate.

We cover three topics: the coverage of political events, the strategies and successes and failures of politicians, and the role of polls and debates.

I. NEWS COVERAGE

Favorable news coverage is the goal of every political candidate. Certainly, politicians can be confident that missteps, conflicts with the law or propriety, or unusual behavior will receive attention from the media, and that the higher their status the greater and more assertive such scrutiny will be (Patterson, 1993). Baring the life of the well known is the business of the late 20th-century press in America, and prominent politicians are even more vulnerable to it than entertainers or athletes because integrity is seen as central to their professional competence. Newscasters demonstrably bias impressions of candidates and events by facial and verbal mannerisms (Skinner & Mullen, 1991); this is simply an example of the general phenomenon by which people intuitively quickly form impressions from brief moments of observed behavior that are largely in agreement and are accurate (Ambady & Rosenthal, 1992). However, the several empirical analyses of television news content do not provide much support for systematic partisan bias, either throughout the ordinary year or during election campaigns.

In the 1970s, data from representative national samples repeatedly confirmed that a sizable proportion perceived television news as politically biased, that the proportions perceiving news persons as liberal or conservative were about equal, and that those who described themselves as liberal or conservative were surprisingly alike in the frequency with which they perceived news personnel as middle of the road or opposite in political ideology (Bower, 1973, 1985; Hickey, 1972). Recent national survey data (Smith et al., 1997) disclose a different pattern. Substantial proportions still perceive the media as biased, but many more perceive the media as liberal than as conservative and conservatives are particularly likely to do so. We have interpreted this as an example of the hostile media phenomenon at work among conservatives who presently are partisans with an agenda, whereas liberal has become a label for broad tolerance and an acceptance that much of the public shares for the reforms of past Democratic administrations (such as Social Security, Medicare, and welfare). Thus, we do not think the data point as much toward a public perception of a biased press as to the sensitivity of those who label themselves as conservatives.

Examinations of the network coverage of the 1968, 1972, 1980, 1984, and

1996 presidential campaigns disclosed no persisting partisan bias with one major exception (Domke et al., 1997; Hofstetter, 1976; Robinson & Sheehan, 1983; Smith & Roden, 1988; Stevenson, Eisinger, Feinberg, & Kotok, 1973). The majority of coverage typically was neutral; opponents usually were about equal in negative and positive emphases. One (Hofstetter, 1976) covered 27 variables for the coverage of ABC, CBS, and NBC throughout the campaign where bias might occur and found no consistent partisan favoritism. The one exception is third-party candidates, who historically have received somewhat less favorable coverage than those candidates of the two major parties (Nimmo, 1989).

One of the most comprehensive studies is also of particular interest because it covers the 1996 campaign. Domke and colleagues (Domke et al., 1997) examined over 12,000 stories between March 10 and November 6 from transcripts of television newscasts and newspapers. Both Clinton and Dole received somewhat more favorable than unfavorable paragraphs and had almost identical ratios of favorable and unfavorable paragraphs. Domke and colleagues conclude that coverage was "remarkably balanced." However, Clinton received 27% more coverage than Dole (or slightly more than 56% of total coverage) so that in our view his apparently greater newsworthiness gave him the advantage not only in attention but also in net amount of favorable coverage.

A recent analysis of statements made by news reporters on ABC, CBS, and NBC regarding Democrats and Republicans uncovered no consistent pattern of bias, although the three did vary in their treatment of the two parties (Semetko, Blumler, Gurevitch, & Weaver, 1991). CBS seemed to favor Republicans, with more reinforcing remarks and fewer deflating statements; NBC carried about equal numbers of reinforcing remarks about the two political parties but slightly more deflating remarks about Republicans than Democrats; ABC carried higher numbers of both deflating and reinforcing remarks about the same party, the Democrats.

There are three major conclusions. First, a substantial proportion of the public for 30 years has perceived some bias. Second, the shift toward the perception of partisan imbalance reflects changes in the political meaning of the labels conservative and liberal. Third, there is no empirical documentation of overall, consistent partisan bias. However, in any given election the coverage may favor one or another candidate—in quantity, in favorability, or both—and outlets may differ in their emphases in coverage and attention to the candidates as a consequence of the perceived newsworthiness of what transpires in a campaign.

The media have the power to establish the viability of contenders. Status is a function of nonnegative news attention. As Johnson (1993, p. 313) explains, "Past studies suggest that the media will rank the candidates as front-runners, plausibles, and hopeless cases and dole out amount of coverage based on these rankings."

We subscribe to the "focus and discard" primary process (Patterson, 1993). The media focus on the anticipated front-runner and challenger. Journalists strive to find flaws, defects, and transgressions; their motive is the big story. The decisions of voters or party caucuses then guide coverage, which correlates with expected success. The intense scrutiny shifts to any additional face who becomes a front-runner or challenger. This scrutiny—which may uncover dishonesty, lying, plagiarism, adultery, lack of frankness under pressure, emotionality, or the violation long ago of current norms (legalization of marijuana was once the sure wave of the future)—may lead to voter rejection of a candidate. Thus the front-runner is in the enviable position of receiving the most coverage, and thus being likely to be considered by the most voters, but runs an inevitably greater risk of receiving damaging coverage. The same phenomenon occurs in the general election. Robinson and Sheehan (1983) call it the "front-runner effect." The media are enchanted with popularity and obsessed with unearthing the uncomplimentary.

Dark-horse candidates are shunned; front-runners and major challengers get more coverage and, if negative items do not surface, more favorable coverage (Halpern, 1996; Nimmo, 1989; Patterson, 1993, 1980; Ross, 1992). The analysis of 1000 stories on ABC, CBS, and NBC is typical (Ross, 1992): the front-runner got the most attention. In one examination of a New Hampshire television forum (Halpern, 1996), less regarded candidates received less time and were more often questioned about their prospects.

What if there is no clear-cut front-runner? Johnson (1993) examined 1988 Democratic primary stories on ABC, CBS, and NBC as well as those in the *Chicago Tribune* and the *New York Times* before Dukakis became the favorite. All active campaigners received approximately equal coverage. In the absence of a front-runner, the media focus equally on all contenders for fear of ignoring the person who will receive the nomination.

Television has insinuated itself more centrally in the electoral process and increasingly emphasizes the dramatic in using techniques of the medium more fully. Presidential candidates are given less opportunity to speak to the public, with sound bites decreasing in length from about 43 seconds in 1968 to about 9 seconds in 1992, whereas the time allotted to television commentators has increased (Hallin, 1992; Lowry & Shidler, 1995; Steele & Barnhurst, 1996). Events, speculation about winners, and assessments of likely success or failure dominate coverage (Graber, 1971; McCombs & Shaw, 1972; Patterson & McClure, 1976). Only half of stories in the 10 days prior to the election in 1984 on ABC, CBS, NBC, CNN's *Prime News*, and PBS's *MacNeil/Lehrer News Hour* that dealt with issues identified the positions of the opposing candidates (Rudd & Fish, 1989). With *MacNeil/Lehrer* eliminated from these data, only slightly more than 1 of 10 stories on issues provided a rationale for or background information on candidate positions; about 6 of 10 stories overall involved attacks on a candidate; and an amazing 1% of issue-based stories on ABC, CBS, and NBC merited a check mark for providing some background for both candidates on their positions.

Between 1965 and 1988, the length of questions and comments by reporters at presidential news conferences lengthened, although so too did replies by the president (Burriss, 1989a). In coverage of speeches during the 1992 presidential primaries on ABC, CBS, and NBC reporters generally spoke longer than the candidates, often provided summaries, and even showed the candidate's lips moving while failing to include the audio portion to hear what he was saying (Kendall, 1993). CNN, ABC, CBS, and NBC evening news coverage of the 1996 Clinton–Dole debates focused on whether the debates created a change in the polls, emphasized candidates' images rather than their ideas, and gave journalists a prominent role (Kendall, 1997). News stories about political commercials have become more common, with about 80 tabulated in 1988, mostly about negative ads, compared to an average of 13 in the preceding four campaigns (Kaid, Gobetz, Garner, Leland, & Scott, 1993). During the 1992 presidential election there were almost 450 stories about how the media cover politics on ABC, CBS, NBC, the *New York Times,* and *Chicago Tribune,* with more stories and a more positive tone in newspaper coverage compared to television coverage (Johnson, Boudreau, & Glowacki, 1996).

Cinematic depiction also has increased. Comparisons of presidential debates in 1976 and 1984 show an increase in the attention to questioners and the audience and a reduction in the average length of camera shots of speakers (Morello, 1988a). In the 1988 debates, only about half of 97 verbal clashes were depicted in a way that clarified or emphasized the exchange (Morello, 1988b). Production techniques in covering speeches often elevate drama over substance, with audience shots prevalent and speakers given brief, fragmentary attention (Tiemens, Sillars, Alexander, & Werling, 1988). Visual coverage of the 1996 presidential election on ABC, CBS, and NBC relied heavily on hype and hoopla, featuring photo opportunities, motorcades, and handshaking with members of crowds (Fox & Goble, 1997).

Television in broad terms does not differ too much from newspapers. Both emphasize horse-race aspects, although television typically does so to a greater degree and gives more attention to readily understood polls and endorsements rather than to financial and organizational aspects of the campaign that receive newspaper coverage (Graber, 1971; Johnson, 1993). About half of stories on polls appear as the lead or second item in the newscast (Keenan, 1986). Similarly, in a comparison of two major activities of a sitting president, a proposed tax cut and a trip to Europe, the emphasis on personal aspects ranged from 3 to 10% for the newscasts of a network, the *New York Times,* and a daily newspaper in a small city (Paletz & Guthrie, 1987). The data again support the concept of universal news values.

The context for campaign coverage unsurprisingly is the bad news that predominates generally. Graber (1987) coded all introductory headline statements on ABC, CBS, and NBC between Labor Day and election day in 1984 and found that half of stories about foreign or domestic events were bad news compared to only 17% that were good news. Campaign coverage by the news media in general has itself grown progressively more negative. Patterson (1993) records that since World War II positive coverage of the candidates, once in the majority, has declined whereas negative coverage has increased and has come to represent an increasing majority of coverage.

A president and others associated with the White House, of course, are always under attack and in television news those who attack are most often other politicans. Almost a third of negative statements on one network between 1969 and 1985 were by senators and representatives (Smoller, 1988).

The prominence of the office ensures television coverage for presidential candidates. Coverage of members of the House and Senate depends on established routines of news gathering, the prominence of the figure, and the utility of utterances for composing a newscast. Examinations of news stories from ABC, CBS, and NBC over the last three decades identify a stable pattern (Havick, 1997; Hess, 1986; Kuklinski & Sigelman, 1992; Smoller, 1988; Squire, 1988; Wafai, 1989; Wilhoit & Sherrill, 1968). Key predictors are being a past or potential presidential candidate, figuring in a scandal, holding an influential committee post, representing a large state, or being able to articulate a clear position forcefully, and particularly one favored by the political climate such as a pro-Israel, anti-Arab stance. The concept of an inner circle that has occurred so often recurs—the same faces appear again and again, with one famous personage accounting for one-fourth of over 400 mentions of all senators (Kuklinski & Sigelman, 1992) and 14 persons providing half of favorable and unfavorable comments about the White House in the stories analyzed across two decades (Smoller, 1988).

Local television news coverage of political contests is comparatively modest. Gubernatorial races occupy only small portions of local newscasts (Ostroff & Sandell, 1989). Candidates for House and Senate seldom receive coverage unless there is a well-orchestrated series of public appearances, a visit by the president or other political celebrity, or an unusual event (Goldenberg & Traugott, 1987; Katz, 1985). In contrast, daily newspapers regularly devote extensive coverage to these contests.

Television coverage of presidential politics has increasingly emphasized the role of the media at the expense of the role of the politicians and their platforms. The focus on the horse race rather than on campaign issues, the decreasing length of the sound bite, the focus on events rather than issues, the proliferation of "experts"—often the television journalists themselves—to analyze the campaign, and the scrutiny with which journalists treat many candidates characterize political coverage by the networks. An analogous pattern can be discerned in other media—newspapers and newsmagazines—but, on the whole, has been much more striking and bold among the television networks.

II. STRATEGIES

Television is a particularly important medium for politicians. Paid campaign announcements and news coverage permit a candidate to electronically address a large audience that is heterogeneous demographically and ideologically. It has enormous reach and can overcome self-selective avoidance. It also has characteristics that make it highly serviceable as a vehicle for political persuasion. It presents candidates multidimensionally—the person as well as the figure— and its depictions can readily arouse emotions.

Image management of political candidates can conservatively be said to be a multi-million dollar industry, and politicians essentially are "political brands" marketed as if they were legal or medical services (Newman, 1993). Political advertising is a direct form of image management, whereas positive news coverage is an indirect route (Axford, Madgwick, & Turner, 1992). Image or identity is particularly important when party loyalty is low and the race is close. Image making is a necessary strategy so that candidates control the way they are perceived rather than being at the mercy of their opponents.

Our review of the principal strategies by which politicians attempt to make use of the media, and particularly television, begins with news coverage and then turns to advertising. We then examine the craft of image making, with attention to nontraditional media outlets, the role of image in campaigns, and candidate gender.

A. NEWS

The conventions of television news production, such as lighting, editing, and shot selection, can create a favorable or unfavorable image of the same set of events. There are also demand characteristics by which a medium depicts events to take advantage of the features that give it an advantage over competitors. These are analogous to the characteristics of experiments that elicit behavior external to the treatment under study (Rosenthal, 1966); in this case, media differentially cover events even though the news personnel are all trying to cover the same story.

The Lang and Lang (1968) study of MacArthur Day in Chicago is an historic example. The general was on his way to Washington to deliver his "Old soldiers never die. They just fade away" speech to a joint session of Congress after his dismissal by President Truman as commander-in-chief in Korea; some newspapers were trumpeting him as a conservative presidential prospect. The televised coverage portrayed huge crowds excitedly welcoming the general. Eyewitness testimony differed substantially. Those on the scene reported modest to sparse crowds largely motivated by curiosity.

Lang and Lang labeled this phenomenon technological bias because the medium used the flexibility of its visual resources to tell the story that had been expected to unfold. We see this as one of three distinct types of bias that might occur in news coverage. The other two are partisan bias, in which one or another party or candidate is purposefully favored, and ideological bias, in which the media of a society treat various topics very similarly because of consensus on predominant values as exemplified in the United States by flag waving and the comparative disinterest in white collar crime.

The media undeniably differ in their essential characteristics, and as a result often will deliver somewhat different impressions to their audiences. Thus, universal news values are somewhat undermined by the attributes that lead media to cover the same events differently. Television typically delivers bits of information accompanied by interesting film or interviews with an authority or interested party; it personalizes and dramatizes events. Newspapers can relay complex and detailed information, such as an economic platform, and their readers typically are more politically motivated and involved. News magazines reach a similar audience with a longer perspective, adding background and focusing on the linkages between events.

One reason television figures so largely in the media strategies of politicians is its ability to overcome selective exposure. Partisan audience members can more readily ignore messages in other media that are contrary to their views, and those with little or no interest in politics can ignore the topic entirely. However, because televised commercials and political news accounts are embedded in programs with vast and diverse audiences, political messages are less easy to avoid (Mendelsohn & O'Keefe, 1976), although admittedly newspaper front pages function similarly. We concur with Weiss (1969) that the balanced nature of political coverage in the United States makes it difficult for audience members to avoid political messages that run counter to their own views, but television is the medium in which this task is most difficult. Selective exposure to favored political commercials or congenial television news stories is difficult to achieve.

Sigelman and Bullock (1991) examined presidential campaign coverage in the *Atlanta Constitution, Chicago Tribune, New York Times, San Francisco Chronicle,* and *Washington Post* during two randomly selected weeks across 101 years from 1888 to 1988 to determine whether newspapers had changed in competition with television. There was a decline instead of an increase in em-

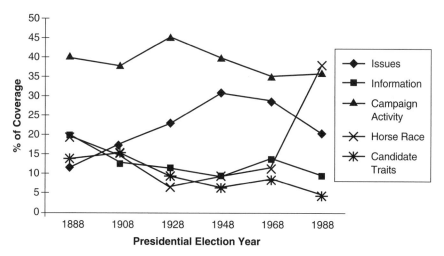

FIGURE 5.1 Presidential election coverage in newspapers, 1888–1988. Adapted from "Candidates, Issues, Horse Races, and Hoopla: Presidential Campaign Coverage, 1888–1988," by L. Sigelman and D. Bullock, 1991, *American Politics Quarterly, 19*(1), pp. 5–32.

phasis on the personal attributes and traits of candidates (Figure 5.1). Policy issues comprised the second most frequent type of coverage but amount of coverage had decidedly declined since 1968. Attention to who stands the best chance of being elected has increased since the introduction of television, slowly at first and then quite dramatically since 1968. Major daily newspapers thus have accommodated to the competition of television by decreased attention to issues and a sharp increase in attention to the likely outcome and thus the use of polls to identify who is winning and losing. These represent real changes in news values, although in the latter case one facilitated by the increasing frequency with which there have been polls to cover (sponsored by the media to create stories, by pollsters to sell to the media and other clients, and by politicians for their own use and for public release when advantageous) and by the enormously enhanced capability of computers to process poll data.

After examining the interplay between candidates, audiences, and media in the process of political opinion formation, we conclude that the evidence identifies four broad patterns. These represent different strategies on the part of incumbents and nonincumbents, matches between the attributes of audience members and characteristics of media chosen, a slight instructional superiority for more fundamental political knowledge of newspapers over television, and consistent influence of television on the evaluation and ranking of candidates.

The behavior of voters in response to 272 candidates for Congress indicates that news coverage has different meanings for incumbents and nonincumbents (Weaver-Lariscy & Tinkham, 1991). For incumbents, it is bad news; for nonincumbents, it is good news. Incumbents play to their strengths, which are name recognition, reputation, and achievements. Coverage implies something uncomplimentary because successes of the past are not newsworthy. Coverage, then, predicts lower levels of support from voters. Nonincumbents require coverage to reach the electorate and their proportion of the vote rises with endorsements from community leaders, often televised, and supportive newspaper editorials, both of which signify a viable candidacy.

Cognitive skills, expected utility, and interests combine to predict media use for political information by individuals. Those in the news audience with lower cognitive skills will use television more than print (Neuman, Just, & Crigler, 1992). The oft-recorded pattern in which expected utility influences media consumption leads to greater use early in a campaign by those particularly interested who anticipate conversations and perhaps persuasive attempts (which include the strongly partisan) and those seeking information on which to base a choice (Atkin, 1972; Chaffee & McLeod, 1973; Kraus & Davis, 1976; Weaver, 1977). The viewing of national television news during a presidential campaign, however, powerfully advances the decision-making process as do personal conversations about the candidates (Lucas & Adams, 1978). Voters seemingly are able to make up their minds sooner because of the impressions only television can widely convey about the candidates as individuals. Similarly, discussions with others about the candidates enhance voter confidence in their judgments, presumably because most such discussions take place with those leaning in the same direction (Kraus & Davis, 1976).

When a decision has been reached, the likelihood increases that a voter will follow the campaign in a newspaper. Those who remain uncertain become particularly likely to pay attention to direct mail because they are still collecting information on which to base an opinion (Strand, Dozier, Hofstetter, & Ledingham, 1983). Those particularly interested in issues more frequently read newspapers, whereas those attracted by the personal attributes of the candidates will use television more (Lowden, Andersen, Dozier, & Lauzen, 1994).

The evidence on behalf of the influence of television news, however, is pervasive. It appears in study after study, despite variations in method, time, and facet of coverage. It has grown increasingly influential and become much more prominent among the media in shaping political outcomes with the steady decline in newspaper reading among young adults (Bogart, 1989), among whom media influence is less likely to be constrained by party allegiance. The major questions are the form and degree of influence.

We begin with experimental demonstrations of the matter-of-fact ways the differences in treatment and editing that are always part of television production can have an effect. Our first two examples concern on-the-air demeanor, the first of candidates and the second of news anchors. Then we turn to content.

Sullivan and Masters (1988) exposed subjects to television news stories containing the actual, naturally occurring facial expressions of presidential candidates that differed in the display of anger and threat, fear and evasion, and happiness and reassurance. Happy and reassuring expressions increased positive emotional responses among viewers that, in turn, enhanced favorability toward the candidates (smile, it may help). The meta-analysis by Skinner and Mullen (1991) of the influence of facial expressions leads to the conclusion that the opinions of viewers about candidates would shift in accord with the seemingly positive or negative expressions and verbal nuances of anchorpersons reporting about them. In regard to content, Iyengar and Kinder (1987a) repeatedly have demonstrated experimentally that differences in the subject matter and emphases of newscasts affect the importance that viewers assign to topics, and as a consequence their evaluations of political figures associated with those topics (with opinions rising or falling, depending on whether the topic for a particular individual connotes success and competence or failure and ineptitude).

Coverage is important not only for presidential hopefuls. Goldenberg and Traugott (1987) found that local television news exposure resulted in greater recognition of some congressional candidates. In an analysis of the 1984 and 1986 campaigns, local television news viewing of politics was associated with slightly increased recognition rates for Senate candidates, especially challengers who were less likely to be well known beforehand. However, the relationship did not hold for those running for the House, and newspaper reading about politics consistently resulted in recognition rates that were higher than those for local television news viewing.

Bowler, Donovan, and Snipp (1993), in an analysis of the 1990 California state elections, found that the greater the distance between the media market of a voter and the candidate, the less knowledge and greater uncertainty the voter had about the candidate, with uncertainty a predictor of lower likelihood of voting for a candidate. Thus, state candidates are highly dependent on local coverage and regionalism is a factor in what the media convey.

Kaid, Downs, and Ragan (1990) focused on a clash between Dan Rather and President Bush on CBS *Evening News*. The lesson is that a reporter who is perceived as inappropriately aggressive will draw public ire. A minidocumentary of Bush's role in the Iran–Contra affair was shown prior to an interview, resulting in an on-air argument between the two. The investigators showed neither, both, only the documentary, or only the interview to groups of about 40 subjects. The documentary alone led to lower evaluations of Bush and the interview alone led to lower evaluations of Rather, and the two together led to lower scores for Rather and higher scores for Bush. Viewers who indicated having feelings of discomfort, sympathy, and embarassment lowered their evaluations of Rather, whereas those sympathetic to the president and who were surprised increased their evaluations of Bush. Thus, viewers find antagonistic tactics reprehensible even when in possession of information that the subject merits criticism.

Television helped to transform the nominating conventions from deliberative bodies to celebratory spectacles. It was joined by reforms that led to delegates becoming committed to candidates in advance through primaries and caucuses, thereby leaving the public with little to wonder about that it was interested in. With the opening of the conventions to the viewing public in 1952, they soon were packaged to place the parties in a favorable light. Suspense diminished even apart from the presidential nominee as the hundreds of journalists arrayed by the networks tallied every vote in advance. These factors led the networks in 1988 to abandon gavel-to-gavel coverage in favor of selectively presenting the events thought to hold the most public interest—major speeches, confetti and flag-filled demonstrations in behalf of nominated candidates, tart and stark statements from warring advocates, and the acceptance addresses. Only two conventions, both Democratic, have violated the rule of pleasing spectacle—1968 in Chicago, with clashes between police and Vietnam protestors, and 1972 in Miami, where George McGovern was too lackadaisical to insist on giving his acceptance speech in prime time—with both elections won by Republicans.

This search for favor has worked well. Across the eight elections between 1964 and 1992, 14 of the 16 conventions have been accompanied by an increase in the polls in the proportion favoring the party's ticket, with the greatest rise usually occurring for the first convention (Campbell, Cherry, & Wink, 1992; Holbrook, 1996). We see two principal explanations. First, the conventions present the candidates in a positive aura of success, and their voices briefly dominate the news. Second, the conventions provide new information, so that more voters are at least temporarily ready to make a decision. The information factor underlying these two undoubtedly also enters into the success of the first convention, which will have a greater opportunity to provide new information, and which is usually held by the challenging party, where less typically will be known beforehand about the nominee. The two conventions that failed to produce what has been called a public opinion "bump" were those of the Democrats in 1968 (Chicago) and in 1964, when the well-known Adlai Stevenson was running for the second time against the very popular Dwight Eisenhower and the convention would have given little justification for an increase in public enthusiasm.

Simon and Ostrum (1989) examined 35 years of televised presidential speeches and found that those in prime time on average were followed by increases in approval ratings. They also found that when a positive or negative event occurred close to a televised speech or major announcement of foreign travel, approval ratings rose or fell. Particularly prominent speeches help, then, whereas speeches and travel—and presumably other prominent activities that are not in themselves highly favorable or unfavorable—are subordinate to events that elicit an immediate evaluative reaction although they may help to draw attention to those events.

West (1991) matched approval ratings of Carter and Reagan against the emphases of CBS news. In half of six comparisons, viewing of the news when coverage was negative predicted lower approval ratings after controlling for party identification, ideology, and education. More than half the stories about each president were critical in tone, so the phenomenon occurs quite regularly.

Mughan (1995) found that the esteem accorded Reagan was more strongly correlated with use of television than with use of newspapers for political information. However, the data are moot on whether this reflects the effects of the medium or the media preferences of those favorably disposed toward that particular president.

Ross (1992) tracked horse-race stories on network news and the rise and decline in the polls of contenders for the 1984 Democratic nomination. Stories of success typically were followed by surges in support. So, too, were greater amounts of coverage except for signs of the "front-runner effect" (Robinson & Sheehan, 1983) when heightened but negative coverage was sometimes followed by dips in support.

Media use is clearly predictive of greater knowledge about the campaign in progress, and the varying nature of each campaign makes some contribution by the media the most plausible explanation. The data of Chaffee, Zhao, and Leshner (1994) and Zhao and Chaffee (1995) covering six national campaigns make the case very strongly. Exposure to television news and newspaper reading consistently predicted greater knowledge. Reading the newspaper was more strongly predictive of knowledge of the parties, whereas television viewing was more predictive of knowledge about candidates and their stands on issues. On the whole, newspaper reading was associated more with "enduring knowledge," such as background and history, and television news viewing was more associated with "transitory knowledge" about the issues and candidates of the specific campaign. Similarly, Hollander (1993) examined the ability to discriminate between the views of presidential candidates in 1988 and 1992 of persons oriented more toward television or newspapers for political information—and in 4 of 7 instances newspaper use predicted greater knowledge.

The three analyses of presidential election dynamics and media use by Bartels (1993), Domke and colleagues (1997), and Holbrook (1996) are complementary and depict a clear and coherent picture. They cover the five elections of 1980, 1984, 1988, 1992, and 1996 and match measures of media coverage against shifts in standings in the polls during the campaign or the vote on election day (Table 5.1). One (Holbrook) tabulates the favorability of events that could only be known to the public through the media, including

TABLE 5.1   Influence of Media Coverage in Five Presidential Elections

Data source	Election(s)	Sample	Independent variables	
			Campaign events	Composite newspaper/TV coverage
Bartels, 1993	1980	NES panel[a]		
Holbrook, 1996	1984 1988 1992	Polls, 4 months[b]	X	
Domke et al., 1997	1996	Polls, 8 months[c]		X

[a] National Election Study, with interviews of same 758 respondents in Jan.–Feb., June, and Sept., 1980 (Institute for Social Research, University of Michigan).

[b] Published polls, June 1–Nov. 5, and CBS/New York Times pre- and postdebate polls, 1984, 1988, 1992.

[c] Roper Center POLL archive entries, Mar. 10–Nov. 6, 1996.

Adapted from "Message Received: The Political Impact of Media Exposure," by L. M. Bartels, 1993, American Political Science Review, 87(2), pp. 267–285; "New Media, Candidates and Issues, and Public Opinion in the 1996 Presidential Campaign," by D. Domke, D. P. Fan, M. Fibison, D. V. Shah, S. S. Smith, and M. D. Watts, 1997, Journalism and Mass Communication Quarterly, 74(4) pp. 718–737; and Do Campaigns Matter? by T. M. Holbrook, 1996, Thousand Oaks, CA: Sage.

conventions and debates. Another (Bartels) measures exposure of individuals to television news and newspapers with regard to shifts in opinion. The third (Domke and colleagues) employs a composite measure of television and newspaper coverage to predict shifts in voter opinion and the vote on election day. Variously, they examine (in our terminology) public opinion in regard to issues, images, support for the candidates, and the vote. Two match aggregate data (Holbrook and Domke and colleagues); one, individual exposure and response (Bartels).

These constitute a remarkable body of evidence. The picture that develops is consistently one in which the media have highly variable but often very strong effects. This variation should be expected, because circumstances always will differ somewhat. The framework for the likely variability of voter support is established by public approval of the candidates early in the election year (positive), the state of the economy (positive), and the duration of the party in the White House (negative), which together consistently predict the vote

Independent variables		Dependent variables			
Media exposure					
Newspaper	TV news	Issues	Image	Support	Vote
X	X	X	X		
		X	X	X	
		X	X		X

☐ = Positive association with independent variable

■ = Relationship stronger for TV news than for newspapers

within one or two percentage points for the 12 elections between 1948 and 1992 (Abramowitz, 1996; Campbell, 1996). Party allegiance and opinion prior to the campaign thus suppress effects of media coverage (Bartels, 1993). Possibilities for effects are greatest when standings diverge from projections, thereby creating an opportunity—in the form of an improbable and unstable gap between the statistically established pattern and the standings of the candidates in the current campaign that is likely to vanish as voters become better informed—for media influence (Holbrook, 1996).

Favorability of coverage during the campaign nevertheless is associated with shifts in voter opinion about image, issues, and voter support (Bartels, 1993; Domke et al., 1997; Holbrook, 1996). These shifts are not simply a product of a positive depiction but rather the association of a positive depiction with an issue or image wherein public interest or concern resides (Domke et al., 1997; Holbrook, 1996). Candidates gain when portrayed as advocating positions or presenting an image that speaks to current public anxieties. Thus, the rise and

fall in the favorability of the coverage of Clinton in 1996 was a stronger predictor of public favorability because he addressed issues of public concern,
whereas the favorable coverage of Dole had much less effect. Candidates may
be marooned by positions not new or compellingly articulated, as would seem
to have been the predicament of Dole.

Media coverage is most likely to make a difference when it stands out in
some way, and as a result the direct comparisons of newspapers and television
news show much stronger effects for television (Bartels, 1993). The reason is
that in the current matrix of media availability television is best able to present
the kind of coverage that functions as a spotlight in the face of party allegiance,
the state of the economy, and already formed opinions about the candidates
and the incumbent party.

We found these data surprising in their sweep. The samples in total exceed
150,000 by our estimates, the measures focus on the relationship between media exposure and voter response using a variety of independent and dependent
variables, and the findings arrange themselves in a coherent mosaic of media
influence led over the past decade and a half by television. As conservative
analysts, we caution that the data do not unequivocally demonstrate media effects. Only one study (Bartels) links individual response with individual media
exposure, although it does so convincingly. The other two (Holbrook, Domke
et al.) develop statistical models that display associations between aggregate
media behavior and voter response that are consistent with media influence.
Nevertheless, these three analyses as a body of evidence covering five presidential elections are convincing with regard to a major role for newspapers and
particularly for television.

B. ADVERTISING

The enormous amount of data on advertising in political contests divides into
three distinct topics. The first is the strategic use of advertising. The second is
the effectiveness of political advertising in increasing political knowledge. The
third is the effects of various features of political commercials, such as negative
advertising, on viewers.

Candidates buy time on television as an integral part of campaign strategy.
Sheer quantity and placement of political commercials are widely thought to be
crucial to the success of the modern campaign.

Devlin (1989) attempted to identify the strengths and weaknesses of the
1988 Dukakis and Bush campaigns. He attributed the Bush victory in part to
the way in which his commercials redefined him. Characterized as cold and
unresponsive, the campaign portrayed him as warm and caring and often pic-
tured him with wife and grandchildren. Dukakis commercials were mainly informative. His strategy also was less focused, and one series of commercials

intended to portray Bush as hyped by media techniques was misinterpreted by some viewers as pro-Bush. A substantial proportion of commercials were negative. There were attacks in 14 of the 37 Bush and 23 of the 47 Dukakis commercials. Opinion polls at the time showed public awareness that the campaign was harsh. Although Dukakis was on the attack more frequently, Devlin concludes he did so at ill-advised times and less effectively.

Devlin (1993) undertook a similar analysis of the three-way 1992 presidential race that recorded an unprecedented amount of money spent on media, a combined $133 million by Bush, Clinton, and Perot. Another noteworthy aspect was the local ad-buying strategy of Clinton in which particular states were targeted. It paralleled the key-state approach of John F. Kennedy in 1960, and was in contrast to the concentration of Bush and Perot on network buying. The scheme proved successful once again; Clinton won 19 of the 20 states he had targeted.

To give an impression of substance, the Clinton campaign used 60-second ads that included details and specific information. To undermine Bush, Clinton ads juxtaposed the infamous "No new taxes" quote with information about tax increases under Bush. The Perot campaign employed several innovations. One was 30-minute segments explaining with graphs and charts why the proposals of his opponents would fail. Perot was not considered particularly likeable by the public, so early paid-for announcements focused on ideas rather than on the candidate. Later, they were supplemented by $2\frac{1}{2}$ hours of biographical reminiscences to build rapport with the public. The long messages had surprisingly high viewership with about 17 million in the audience for the first 30-minute program; the average rating was 9.4, about twice that for the Kentucky Derby.

Despite the wide variety in length of paid-for presentations, the majority was 30-second spots, although Perot had more that were 60- than 30-second. A new high was set for proportion of negative advertising by two of the candidates, with Clinton and Bush both airing half positive and half negative ads.

West, Kern, Alger, and Goggin (1995) compared advertising strategies of the 1992 Presidential candidates by examining both nationally aired spots and local ads seen in four areas of the country between July 1 and November 2. Behind these commercials lie decisions about national vs local, themes and issues, placement and repetition, and use of negative appeals. Perot purchased the largest number of national spots (205), followed by Bush (189) and Clinton (143). Perot made a strong late effort, using three times as many commercials as Bush and one and a half times as many as Clinton in the last week. The Perot campaign was diversified (29 different ads) compared to that of Clinton (17) and the narrow focus of Bush (9). The comparatively small number of national spots for Clinton reflected his state-based strategy. No candidate bought time in all four areas, and the enormous differences in amounts spent indicate that expectations of benefits varied greatly.

The most frequently aired spot for Bush ran 64 times nationally and was a positive message about his economic agenda. His second and third most frequent spots were negative attacks on Clinton. Perhaps as a response, Clinton's most commonly run ad, aired 41 times nationally, was an attack on Bush's economic record. His second most visible ad, aired 23 times, was positive in appeal. Perot's most frequently used ad was broadcast 23 times and portrayed him positively as having solutions to the nation's problems.

Devlin (1997) also analyzed the 1996 presidential campaign. The successful Clinton campaign featured comparative rather than purely negative commercials and operated under a coherent strategy in which commercials used at various times in the campaign were linked conceptually and thematically. Clinton was able to spend $20 million more than Dole, which provided a huge advertising advantage. The Dole campaign—relying largely on biographical and negative commercials—was marked by inconsistency and confusion after changing creative directors midway through the race. Perot received far fewer federal funds and was forced to rely on a smattering of expensive infomercials and less expensive 15-second commercials. The 1996 campaign was the most expensive and the most negative to date and featured a large number of commercials that used the tools of audio and video editing to distort the image of an opponent (Kaid, 1997).

These data correct conventional wisdom and contribute to a legend. The conventional wisdom is that presidential campaigns are largely alike except for charges, slogans, and themes. The legend is the audacious power of the market-based strategy introduced by Kennedy.

Shyles (1984) coded 140 commercials from the 1980 presidential primaries for emphasis on image versus issues and method of presentation using 22 different indicators, including format, visuals, and use of graphics. Seven image categories emerged: altruism, competence, experience, honesty, leadership, personal characteristics, and strength. Nine types of issues were identified: record in office, domestic, economy, energy, federalism, foreign policy, government management, national security/military strength, and national well-being. Image and issue commercials were different in design. Image ads more often featured citizens or endorsements by famous people, still shots of the candidate, fast transitions, music, and oblique camera angles. Issue ads more often used direct shots, with the candidate in formal attire speaking directly to the camera the most common technique. These data indicate that campaign strategists, as do those who design product commercials, adhere to widely accepted conventions and perceive issues as the property of the candidate, whereas image is a function of social approval.

Tinkham and Weaver-Lariscy (1990, 1995) collected data from nearly 600 candidates for the House in 1982 and 1990 on media and advertising strategies. Incumbents emphasized voting record, service to constituents, and accomplishments. Challengers gave more attention to issues and the personal attributes of opponents. Campaigns were particularly issue oriented when there was greater financial support, interest group involvement, and strong party support, all of which were associated with greater press coverage. These are the crusades. Few commercials were impersonal or purely negative; instead, commercials were about equally divided between comparative and positive appeals. Incumbents were much more successful in vote getting. Candidates in open races (without an incumbent), which were usually quite close, on the average received many more votes than those challenging incumbents. As a result, successful campaigns generally emphasized the merits of the candidate and positive rather than negative appeals.

The broad pattern is one in which incumbents play to their strengths and challengers attempt to overcome their weaknesses. The former, with greater voter awareness, emphasize the positive and in particular their merit. The latter attack, raising issues and challenging the personal characteristics of incumbents. The closer the race, the more prevalent the negativity in campaigning (Hernson, 1995).

Of the hundreds of thousands typically spent on a congressional race, remarkable proportions are reserved for advertising and particularly for electronic media where television is overwhelmingly used most often. Between the mid-1980s and early 1990s (Goldenberg & Traugott, 1987; Morris & Gamache, 1994), the proportions of total monies spent by candidates during a race that were allocated to the media summed to about a third for the House and more than 40% for the Senate. Expenditures devoted specifically to campaign activities—media, brochures, direct mail, travel, campaign workers—accounted for slightly more than half of all monies spent. Media were predominant among these campaign expenditures, accounting for about 60% in the House races and about 85% in Senate races. Electronic media were at the forefront of media spending: 90% in House races and 98% in Senate races. Three distinctive features of modern congressional elections, then, are that media dominate campaign spending, electronic media and primarily television are at the forefront of media use, and the predominance of media but particularly electronic media increases the larger the territory to be covered and the greater the population to be reached.

Strategic heuristics guide advertising timing (Goldenberg, Traugott, & Baumgartner, 1986). Some candidates attempt "preemptive spending" very early as a demonstration of power not only to the public but also to the challenger. Others use "reactive spending" in which they create and place commercials in response to the actions of their opponent. The factors that enter into product advertising—size of audience, size of the media market, demographics of the audience, and whether the cost is deemed worthwhile for the number of people reached—similarly affect political advertising decisions (Goldenberg & Traugott, 1987).

A common marketing strategy of candidates is to align themselves with successful political figures. Smith and Golden (1988) point to the successful 1984 campaign of Jesse Helms as an example. Helms portrayed himself as a supporting character, whereas President Reagan was featured as the starring hero. Helms benefited from the popularity of the president and became less vulnerable to attack.

There is very convincing evidence that political commercials can influence knowledge about and evaluations of candidates. They may sometimes be more instructionally effective than news coverage, but that depends on the specifics of the commercial and the coverage.

Patterson and McClure (1976), in a well-known analysis of a Syracuse sample in the 1972 election, found that exposure to paid-for television political announcements but not television news was predictive of knowledge about the positions of presidential candidates. Similarly, Zhao and Bleske (1995) found among over 300 randomly selected North Carolina residents that when attention—rather than exposure—was measured and multiple controls used, commercials fared better than television news in predicting both accuracy and confidence in knowledge, whereas when exposure only was the measure commercials were equal to news in predicting confidence and superior to news in predicting accuracy of knowledge. In apparent contrast, Zhao and Chaffee (1995), with national samples from six campaigns, found that viewing the news was a more consistent predictor of such knowledge and there was only one campaign where a correlation between a measure of advertising exposure and knowledge remained when news exposure was controlled.

These data leave us with a decisive impression. Commercials can influence knowledge, but more recent comparisons between exposure to commercials and news favor the instructional influence of television news. The data are consistent with two obvious explanations. The first is attention, which more often than not would favor commercials because news stories are part of a familiar format frequently less likely to receive full attention. The second is similarly obvious—not all commercials are particularly instructive, so that the outcomes of comparisons between news and political advertising rest on specific attributes of the commercials. We also suspect that as television becomes even more central in the dissemination of political information and more relied on by voters, and especially younger adults, the attention given to television's political coverage rises as it becomes more pronouncedly the medium of choice among those interested in politics and public affairs.

Just, Crigler, and Wallach (1990) dramatically demonstrated the instructional zing of a focused, single-issue commercial when compared to the more complex stimulus of a debate. Eighty percent of the subjects who saw a commercial from a congressional campaign recalled the position of the candidate on the issue, whereas recall after viewing a debate ranged from about 30 to 50% for different issues.

Opinion has been divided on the effectiveness of negative ads in political campaigns. Some suggest that negative ads may be counterproductive with the attacker viewed harshly (Garramone, 1984; Jamieson, 1992). Others suggest that negative political ads can win support because they are easily recalled and increase interest in the contest (Kern, 1989; Newhagen & Reeves, 1991). The evidence is not at all mixed. Instead, the data on influence and public opinion go in opposite directions. The trend toward negative commercials has considerable empirical evidence in its behalf in regard to influencing viewers, but there also is no doubt that the public believes that some topics are inappropriate as the subject of attack and in general often will express dislike or disapproval for commercials that impugn the opponent.

Johnson-Cartee and Copeland (1989) surveyed over 1900 respondents on what was "fair" for a candidate to attack (Table 5.2). There was specific dislike for negative ads, with almost two-thirds reporting some degree of dislike. Most respondents deemed fair attacks on issues, criminal activities, voting records, and political record. Personal lives, sex lives, and marriages were largely considered off-limits. About two-thirds reported recalling a negative ad and could describe the ad. Those with higher income and education were more likely to view negative ads about issues as acceptable; males thought them more acceptable than did females.

TABLE 5.2   Public Beliefs about Fairness of
Political Attacks

"Do you believe it is fair or unfair for an opponent to attack a candidate's. . . ."

Topic	Think it is fair (percent)
Stand on issues	93
Criminal activities	88
Voting record	84
Political record	83
Medical history	36
Personal life	21
Religion	17
Sex life	16
Family members	14
Current or past marriage	10

Sample size (N) = 1900

Adpated from "Southern Voters' Reaction to Negative Political Advertisements in the 1986 Election," by K. S. Johnson-Cartee and G. Copeland, 1989, *Journalism Quarterly, 66*(4), pp. 888–893.

In his analysis of the 1988 Bush-Dukakis election in which negative commercials became so noticeable, Gronbeck (1992) observed that the focus shifted from issues to more personal attacks. He concluded that negative commercials are most likely to be used by a trailing candidate to undermine the opponent's apparent success, and that a spiral of heightening bitterness is possible if he or she is not successful.

Kaid, Leland, and Whitney (1992) experimentally compared free recall of issues and images for positive and negative advertisements, using commercials from the 1988 presidential election (Table 5.3). The positive ads proved superior on average by 3 to 1 for issues and 2 to 1 for images.

Tinkham and Weaver-Lariscy (1993) exposed about 200 students to positive and negative political advertisements. Negative ads increased confidence about judgments, enhanced evaluations of the attacking candidate, and diminished evaluations of the target, whereas positive ads only increased evaluations of the subject of the ad. In a similar experiment, Pinkleton (1997) found that exposure to negative comparative advertising—in which the benefits of the sponsor are contrasted with the alleged deficiencies of the target—lowered evaluations of the target without lowering evaluations of the sponsor.

Roddy and Garramone (1988) simulated a campaign clash among more than

TABLE 5.3 Free Recall of Images and Issues After Exposure to Presidential Campaign Commercials

	Candidate		
	Dukakis ($N = 38$)	Bush ($N = 31$)	Average ($N = 69$)
Type of appeal	Number recalled—issues vs images		
Issues	148	128	138
Images	134	133	133.5
Valence of appeal	Percent recalled—positive vs negative		
Issues			
Positive	82	73	78
Negative	18	27	22
Images			
Positive	52	87	70
Negative	48	13	30

Adapted from "The Impact of Televised Political Advertisements: Evoking Viewer Response in the 1988 Presidential Campaign," by L. L. Kaid, C. M. Leland, and S. Whitney, 1992, *Southern Communication Journal*, 57(4), pp. 285–295.

270 subjects. Issue attacks were much more successful than image or personal attacks, in accord with public opinion. A positive commercial in reply was evaluated more favorably, but only the negative comeback lowered the likelihood of voting for the initial attacker. Similarly, Pfau and Burgoon (1989) asked more than 730 subjects verbally committed to the opposing Senate candidate to read the scripts for issue- and image-based negative commercials. Issue scripts were more effective in increasing evaluations of the attacker and support for the advocated position.

Garramone, Atkin, Pinkleton, and Cole (1990) compared the reactions of 372 students to negative and positive commercials. Exposure to a single positive commercial had no effect on the perceived strengths of the two candidates, whereas exposure to a single negative commercial led to a dramatic difference in favor of the sponsoring candidate. Negative commercials had greater influence on liking for candidates, perceived strengths, and knowledge. Effects were confined to the candidates, with no differences in election involvement, communication about the election, and likelihood of turnout.

Thorson, Christ, and Caywood (1991) evoked a more complex pattern of responses in their experimental comparison of the effectiveness of issue and image and positive and negative political commercials among 160 students. Issue ads were more effective. Positive commercials generally scored better. Visuals with family members increased character ratings but decreased competence ratings. Recall was better for positive appeals and visuals with a family setting than ones with a professional setting. Music interfered with recall for issue and negative commercials.

Faber, Tims, and Schmitt (1993) surveyed 286 voters in Minnesota during a Senate race. Reports of being influenced by negative ads were associated with an interest in politics, involvement in the election, and television news viewing for political information. Bowen (1994), in a sample of 414 Washington voters, found that late-deciders—who relied more on advertisements in making up their minds—most frequently recalled negative ads. Wanta, Lemert, and Lee (1997) found among a randomly drawn sample of over 300 Oregon voters that those who had seen negative Senate campaign commercials did not score higher on issue knowledge, reported concern for issues, or an index measuring political alienation.

Christ, Thorson, and Caywood (1994) and Tinkham and Weaver-Lariscy (1994) also explored the acceptability of negative commercials. The former found that negative appeals become more effective as attitudes toward such tactics became more favorable. The latter similarly found that those scoring higher on ethical concerns in regard to political ads were more approving of messages stressing issues than those emphasizing candidate attributes, and that generally ads stressing issues scored higher in ethicality than comparative or attack ads.

Issue commercials and commercials positive in appeal have been associated fairly consistently with more favorable evaluations and greater recall. However, evaluation of the candidate has been a different matter. In the three instances in which candidate evaluation was specifically measured (Garramone et al., 1990; Pfau & Burgoon, 1989; Tinkham & Weaver-Lariscy, 1993), negative ads were superior. Those most likely to be influenced are those who use television for political information, those involved in the election, and those interested in politics—that is, those favorable to the medium and those interested enough to pay attention. Because of the certainty of uncontrolled-for factors among the commercials whose effects have been examined, the consistent support for the effectiveness of those with a negative cast is impressive.

The data on behalf of negative commercials in our view are compelling. The fundamental question is the relative advantage of different stimuli, and experimental design specifically addresses that. However, experimental outcomes become more sobering in the context of practical application. The surveys by Tinkham and Weaver-Lariscy (1990, 1995) of nearly 600 candidates for the House indicate that prominent use of negative appeals consistently predicted a lower proportion of the vote. This was true for incumbents, challengers, and those in open races. In our view, these data do not contradict the evidence that negative appeals can be effective but instead reflect the fact that in practice they are used more often by those with least chance of election so that their concrete effectiveness is masked by the record of failed campaigns.

The hostile media phenomenon leads partisans to perceive coverage as biased against their point of view. An analogous phenomenon occurs with commercials. Cohen and Davis (1991) showed 95 students actual negative campaign commercials attacking Bush and Dukakis. Subjects who supported the attacked candidate demonstrated the third-person effect—they thought themselves not susceptible but assumed other people would be influenced.

Kaid, Chanslor, and Hovind (1992) and Ansolabehere and Iyengar (1994) investigated context effects, with the former examining program types and the latter the symmetry between topic and advocate. The former found that commercials were more effective when they were perceived as compatible with the accompanying program. In general, the matches most likely to be effective were negative ads with news programs, image ads with situation comedies, and issue ads with dramas. The latter found two instances of the influence of symmetry. Appeals by a member of a political party known to have a deep and long-standing commitment to the issue were more effective, and news programs containing a story related to such issues enhanced support for those with such commitments; the authors label this phenomenon "issue ownership."

The role of advertising in voter decision making increases dramatically during a campaign. Bowen (1994) interviewed 414 voters in Washington and found that among early deciders news coverage was paramount, with only a few naming advertising as an influence. As the campaign progressed, news declined and advertising rose, with advertising particularly named by late deciders, who also more often recalled ads and particularly negative ads.

Pfau and colleagues have investigated a variety of ways in which the effects of political commercials might be mitigated. Pfau and Burgoon (1988) found that among about 700 voters advance exposure to inoculation messages—essentially, warnings about and refutation of claims—reduced the effectiveness of a subsequent negative appeal in accord with the well-known experimentation in the late 1940s by Hovland (Hovland, Lumsdaine, & Sheffield, 1949) in which among the better educated the acknowledgment of counterclaims reduced their effectiveness. Later, Pfau and colleagues (1997) found that the receipt of inoculatory messages enhanced both the sense of involvement with the campaign and the perception of a threat to the hoped-for outcome, thereby heightening resistance to the claims of commercials. Pfau and Louden (1994) found that some commercials remain effective even when viewers watch them in the "adwatch" context of critical comment by a newsperson, and that this is particularly so when the commercial is simply shown full screen without graphically framing it as the subject of criticism. This confirms earlier data (Jamieson, 1992) indicating that critical analyses by newscasters sometimes boomerang and legitimate or simply give additional exposure to a commercial.

Adwatches can be useful in making viewers more wary of claims, however. A field experiment with 165 subjects found exposure to an adwatch during the Michigan presidential primary affected the perceived fairness of the ad but only affected attitudes toward the source on one of three measures (Cappella & Jamieson, 1994). Bennett (1997) documented a 68% decrease in the use of adwatches by ABC, CBS, and NBC between the 1992 and 1996 presidential elections, suggesting that network gatekeepers have become skeptical either of their effectiveness or of viewer interest.

Kern and Just (1995) had focus groups view television news coverage and commercials in the order they appeared in a Senate campaign and asked the participants to react as if they were deciding on how to vote. About 2 of 5 explicitly referred to the media as an influence, with most emphasizing character. However, the majority drew primarily on already held options, values, and beliefs, underscoring the obvious—that campaigns function within boundaries set by existing views.

Negative commercials can be successful, but they are more often used by those whose campaigns are failing. Inoculation has limited practical application because no politician would confess to a weakness, so that the technique only applies after an attack has begun. Criticism of campaign commercials by television commentators may backfire. Television advertising fairly consistently increases knowledge but in general is not as effective in that regard as television news. Campaigns occur within a context in which an incumbent has a large advantage and previously held views delimit what a campaign can achieve.

C. IMAGE MAKING

The media are the means by which politicians give shape to the way the public perceives them. This image making has long been one of the goals assigned by candidates and their strategists to news coverage and political advertising. Television is at the forefront of this process because it stands apart from other media in combining what may be an emotionally arousing presentation with a depiction of the person. Formats that are nontraditional for political appeals became very prominent in the 1992 presidential election, with the candidates appearing on late-night television, talk shows, and *Larry King Live*. This apparent trend further advances the exploitation of the properties of television to affect the public's impression of a candidate.

The importance of these properties is well represented by the data of Lucas and Adams (1978). They surveyed several thousand Pennsylvania voters during the Ford–Carter election of 1976. The election was marked by a great degree of uncertainty, with as much as half of the electorate at least somewhat undecided a few weeks before election day. The data indicate that early decision making was positively correlated with two communication variables—watching network news and having interpersonal conversations about the candidates. Other media use was uncorrelated with decision making. We concur with the interpretation of the authors that the two served the same function of giving voters confidence about their leanings thereby assisting them in making a choice. Television alone among the media could convey that telling an impression.

Our review of the empirical evidence begins with nontraditional media. We then turn to comparisons of issue and image appeals. Finally, we examine the special case of gender as a factor in creating a successful political image.

1. Nontraditional Outlets

Samuel L. Popkin, a professor of political science at the University of California, San Diego, had no doubt that the use of media outlets not traditionally part of presidential campaigns produced Clinton's 1992 victory:

> Clinton's comeback would not have been possible 10 years earlier because it depended on new television networks, such as MTV, Fox, and CNN, and on specific types of programs and formats, particularly viewer call-in shows . . .
>
> [A]fter he had secured the nomination, Clinton began to make guest appear-

ances . . . on entertainment outlets. He appeared on the late-night *Arsenio Hall Show* wearing sunglasses and playing the saxophone and he appeared on the *NBC Today* show and *CBS This Morning* answering hours of questions called in by viewers. He appeared on CNN's *Larry King Live* and on an MTV "Rock the Vote" special. . . . (Popkin, 1997)

He attributes shifts in public opinion over a 3-week period regarding which candidate was saying enough about his plans—Bush, Clinton, or Perot—to the longer statements afforded Clinton by these formats.

The data we introduce match exposure to various nontraditional outlets in 1992 with viewers' knowledge about or evaluation of the candidates. Such data are inferentially superior to historical accounts or anecdotal analyses of the sources of apparent shifts in voter support because they focus on whether exposure was associated with a difference. They nevertheless are somewhat problematic. First, the highly variable exposition of these outlets does not ensure that any effects could be expected, so that null instances could mask real outcomes and generalizations to a genre are risky. Second, these outlets, generally trumpeted in advance over the appearance of a candidate, might well attract those particularly informed or favorable.

The most convincing sets of data in terms of some influence are those of Chaffee et al. (1994) and Pfau and Eveland (1996). After controlling for exposure and attention to traditional outlets, viewing of the nominating conventions, viewing of debates, candidate preference, intention to vote, and demographics—which together represent a comprehensive range of artifacts—Chaffee and Zhao found that exposure to talk shows was a positive predictor of knowledge of the stands of candidates on issues. Pfau and Eveland found that among those who particularly valued the nontraditional outlets, viewing predicted impressions of the communicatory styles of the candidates and enhanced judgments of their competence.

Elliott and Wickert (1993) found use of nontraditional media associated with more favorable images of Clinton and Perot but inversely associated with reported likelihood of voting for Clinton. McLeod and colleagues (McLeod et al., 1993) found a significant, positive relationship between exposure to talk shows and increased affect ratings only for Perot, but there was no evidence of any influence on voting intentions for any of the three candidates. In a national sample of over 2000, Simon (1996) found that though messages in nontraditional outlets reached segments of the audience who would not otherwise have followed the campaign, those exposed were not more likely to vote. After controlling for numerous other variables, Weaver and Drew (1995) found only small, insignificant associations between exposure to four categories of nontraditional outlets and issue knowledge, a positive significant relationship only for news viewing, and no relationships with intention to vote. In a similar analysis of the 1996 Clinton–Dole election, Drew and Weaver (1998) found that interest in the campaign was associated with giving attention to coverage in newspapers, on radio, and by television talk shows; issue knowledge was not predicted by any media variable (a result they attribute to unusually low interest in the campaign); and only attention to newspaper coverage predicted greater likelihood of voting.

These data do not support the huge effects that have been claimed for nontraditional outlets. The implausibility of such assertions becomes even more apparent when one considers the comparatively small audiences for most of these formats. However, the data do point to small effects at least for talk shows. In this regard, the survival of a relationship after the control for so many artifacts by Chaffee and colleagues, the confinement of effects to those who value these formats in the Pfau and Eveland data, and the greater frequency of effects for the least-familiar candidate (Perot) constitute a plausible and convincing pattern of nontraditional media effects—talk shows, interested viewers, and less familiar candidates. However, the isolated nature of any effects is underscored by talk shows being the only one of several formats examined by Chaffee and colleagues associated with greater viewer knowledge. We concur with Barnett (1997), who predicts that "traditional mass media will continue to dominate the discourse and conduct of politics" (p. 217).

The motive for participating in political call-in television shows apparently rests on the self-confidence of the caller rather than on dissatisfaction with society. This follows from the data of Newhagen (1994b) from a Washington, D.C. sample in which calling in was predicted by scores on self-efficacy (in this case, feeling qualified to make political judgments) but not by scores for belief in the efficacy of the political system or trust in leaders. This is a surprise, for we would have thought that the generally anti-establishment contents of these shows would attract mostly the unhappy and suspicious. However, those who feel they won't make a difference most likely simply won't call.

2. In the Campaign

Some components of image in the course of a campaign may translate into issues—honesty, competence, consistency, integrity. It is sometimes difficult to separate image from issues. Nevertheless, the underlying referents remain distinct, with image equaling personal attributes and issue equaling acknowledged advocacy.

The three instances in which the examination of negative appeals included comparisons between issue and image commercials (Pfau & Burgoon, 1989; Roddy & Garramone, 1988; Thorson et al., 1991) on the whole favored issues in effectiveness. They either were more acceptable when the subject of attack or were more persuasive, although image appeals scored better in recall.

Cundy in two experiments (1989, 1994) demonstrated that image is affected by television portrayals. In each case, about 400 subjects were exposed to favorable news stories or editorials about a fictional politician, who appeared on camera. These portrayals consistently increased liking and the attribution of favorable traits, such as honesty, fair-mindedness, and dependability, whereas a still picture accompanied merely by a description of the person as a politician led to a decrease in favorable attributions. In addition, the on-camera portrayals increased scores for traits tangential to the accounts, such as intelligence and strength under pressure.

Pfau, Diedrich, Larson, and Van Winkle (1993) examined the role of images over the course of a presidential campaign. They interviewed about 200 South Dakota voters at the time of the New Hampshire primary and 2 weeks later after their own primary. In the first interview, manner of communicating was a strong predictor of favorability and issues had no role, whereas by the second interview perceived competence was the only substantial predictor. Thus, image was consistently a predictor of favorability but its locus shifted from style to ability.

Roberts, Anderson, and McCombs (1994) found among a panel of more than 200 voters in the Texas gubernatorial campaign in 1990 that 2 weeks before the election image was a much stronger predictor of voter decisions than were issues. Images were fairly stable in components, but developed persuasive strength so that although earlier images were correlated with images 2 weeks before the election, they were less powerful in predicting election-day behavior.

Johnston (1989) asked more than 100 subjects to list thoughts after viewing commercials for Senate candidates and found that some responded mostly with image thoughts and others with issue thoughts, with more than three-fourths consistently making the same category of response to both ads. Image-oriented respondents rated such information as more important, whereas those younger and higher in income gave more emphasis to issues.

Harrison, Stephen, Husson, and Fehr (1991) explored whether males and females differ in the importance they attach to image vs issue. The authors surveyed more than 300 students of voting age during the last week of the 1984 presidential campaign. For males, perceptions of Reagan's and Mondale's communication styles centered on fairness, humor, and dominance. For females, the top three were made up of sensitivity and thoughtfulness along with humor. For females, image but not issue perceptions were significant predictors of candidate preference. For males, issue but not image perceptions were significant predictors of candidate preference.

Gregg (1994) analyzed the role of the single issue of abortion among nationally representative samples in the 1992 presidential campaign. About one-fourth deemed it important and among them it outweighed all variables except party identification in influencing voter choice. When issues are assigned high importance, they will be strong predictors of the vote.

There is no doubt that image is affected by news exposure, campaign coverage, and political advertising. So, too, is knowledge about issues. Image, however, takes precedence over issues in early decision making. Although aspects of image that are important change as a campaign develops, this predominance continues except when particular issues are assigned high importance by voters. The superiority of issues is confined to negative appeals because they thereby elude imputations of bad behavior on the part of the sponsoring candidate. A thorough review of recent studies (King, 1997) concludes that candidate image is "a significant, if not the best, predictor of voting decisions" (p. 30).

3. Candidate Gender

There has been speculation that female candidates who use negative appeals may be perceived as "unfeminine, shrill, vicious, nagging" (Procter, Schenck-Hamlin, & Haase, 1994, p. 5) and risk losing favor among voters (Jamieson, 1986). The data, which can be construed as reflecting the gender-specific norms perceived by candidates, identify only one clear gender-based difference in campaign strategies and no penalties for negative appeals.

Benze and Declercq (1985), Procter et al., (1994), Kahn (1993), and Johnston and White (1994) focused on the types of appeals used. Benze and Declercq looked at 113 commercials in House, Senate, and state races in 1982, Procter and colleagues analyzed 99 negative appeals in state and federal mixed-gender elections in 1990, Kahn examined 405 commercials used by Senate candidates in 1984 and 1986, and Johnston and White coded 39 commercials used by female candidates in 1986 Senate campaigns. Most of the females were challengers and most of the males were incumbents, and in accord with the established pattern the challengers much more often used negative appeals than did the incumbents. In open races males and females were almost identical in using negative more often than positive appeals. Both genders stressed stereotypically male traits such as leadership more than stereotypically female traits such as compassion, although females did emphasize social issues whereas males emphasized economic concerns. There was no striking difference based on gender except for a greater disinclination on the part of males to use negative appeals when their opponent was female.

Procter, Aden, and Japp (1988), Pfau and Kenski (1990), and Sheckels (1994) analyzed television advertising in two 1986 campaigns between women candidates. Procter and colleagues examined the Nebraska gubernatorial race in which Republican Kay Orr defeated Democrat Helen Boosalis. Pfau and Kenski and Sheckels focused on the Maryland Senate contest in which Democrat Barbara Mikulski defeated Republican Linda Chavez. In both instances, negative appeals seemingly were effective. In the case of the victorious Orr, the appeals by Orr went unanswered on television and the authors judge this a key factor. In the case of the defeated Chavez, whose negative appeals, similarly, went unanswered, support for her opponent was reduced but her own support did not increase. The lesson from Orr is that negative appeals can win, although the investigators note that they were placed within a carefully modulated campaign emphasizing the positive attributes of leadership and compassion, and the lesson from Chavez is that negative appeals may have an effect but may not be sufficient to overcome an opponent's advantage.

Hitchon and Chang (1995), Wadsworth and colleagues (Wadsworth et al., 1987), and Hitchon, Chang, and Harris (1997) investigated the use of gender schema in processing political commercials. In the first instance, recall was greater for male than for female candidates, for the physical appearance of females than that of males, for females rather than males when a family theme was used, when males attacked females than when females attacked males, and in general males drew more negative affect ratings. In the second, females consistently were higher rated when they used stereotypically masculine appeals as to qualifications, experience, intelligence, and effectiveness, although they also were more often rated as bossy, less cooperative, less feminine, and aggressive. Career appeals led to higher ratings than did family appeals. In the last, neutral commercials—rather than positively or negatively toned emotional commercials—when used by female candidates were associated with more favorable responses. Thus, gender of candidate affects processing but females on the whole benefit from an aggressive approach.

The empirical literature strongly suggests that female candidates can use negative appeals without suffering major consequences. Female candidates sometimes select seemingly gender-relevant strategies and emphases in their campaigns (Trent & Sabourin, 1993) and gender-specific norms sometimes are adhered to by males and females, but these differences are subordinate to the goal of a successful campaign in which aggressiveness is prominent. For the most part, female and male candidates behave much alike. The data support the sociological axiom that role is a major determinant of behavior.

III. POLLS AND DEBATES

Polls and debates play a large role in the media strategies of politicians and they are a major focus of attention by television and other news media. Our emphasis is on the presidency. However, the model established by this office for polls and debates has made them part of office seeking from sheriff, school board, and city council to House, Senate, and governor's mansion.

A. POLLS

Polls fulfill a myriad of political functions. They affect the behavior of candidates and the way campaigns are waged and under certain circumstances the outcomes of elections. They also sometimes provide misleading information about likely winners.

They are used by candidates to better understand public mood and opinion and for feedback on commercials and the campaign. Polls were used to determine the "winner" of the televised debates in the 1988 presidential election and have been used in the same capacity since, and are an easy way for newscasters to analyze the race (Fallows, 1992). When one network or a major newspaper uses a poll, competitors are quick to follow to maintain equity in what they offer the public.

There has been speculation that polls influence the outcomes of elections by making widely known the greater popularity of one or another candidate. This certainly occurs (Lavrakas, Holley, & Miller, 1991), but not in the manner generally suggested. Bandwagon effects do not ordinarily occur or elections would be predicted regularly by early polls. However, when voters are unfamiliar with the candidates, a common occurrence at local and state levels, polls may figure importantly in decision making. Thus, polls are most likely to affect the decision making of voters who are ambivalent (Glynn & McLeod, 1992), lack fundamental knowledge (Gawiser & Witt, 1994), or are without information (Cotter & Stovall, 1994). They provide social confirmation or disconfirmation of tentative choices. The basis of influence is not popularity but knowledge of how others are behaving. Polls also may warn of emerging consensus on controversial issues, possibly leading to a "spiral of silence" (Noelle-Neuman, 1984) in which those in the minority become increasingly less ready to express their views. This is most likely when prominent sources of support are absent or social or economic sanctions are imposed. In the case of third-party presidential candidates, polls may play a role in declining support by recording publicly the initial waning of early enthusiasm. A recent meta-analysis (Glynn, Hayes, & Shanahan, 1997) supported the spiral of silence in that a very small but statistically significant relationship resulted between perceptions of support for opinions and willingness to express them.

The use of polls by presidential candidates is long-standing (Mendelsohn & Crespi, 1970). From the beginning of the primaries, weekly sweeps chart popularity and public opinion on issues. The pollsters sometimes become newsworthy themselves and, when their interpretation of data leads to victory, occasionally heroes. Gary Hart, for example, who helped the underdog George McGovern win the Democratic nomination in 1972, became a U.S. Senator and briefly was the front-runner for the presidential nomination before media disclosure of adulterous behavior.

However, candidates for lesser office also often use polls. For example, the Tinkham and Weaver-Lariscy (1996) survey of nearly 600 candidates for the House in 1982 and 1990 recorded extensive use. About two-thirds of incumbents used polls in both election years, and they increased in their use of them to plan image making. In 1990, 9 of 10 in open races used polls. Only challengers declined in frequency of use, almost certainly because of the increasing cost of polls.

Polls are central to American politics. The concept of the "new politics" devised 20 years ago by Mendelsohn and Crespi (1970) as the triumvirate of the long-established technique of polling, the then-new power of computers to analyze data quickly, and the use of the media and especially television to woo voters using the resulting information has become traditional politics.

The poll as a strategic tool in a presidential election traces to the Kennedy campaign of 1960 (Ratzan, 1989). Polls were used to allocate resources to states where the race was close and to identify issues that could be profitably addressed. Johnson and Nixon further popularized the strategic use of polling data in the 1960s and early 1970s until the practice became central in the White House. Polls now provide feedback on anything from a position on an issue to the hairstyle of the president or first lady.

The modern, publicized poll—as distinct from the private poll used for campaign planning—is used both to describe current opinion and to predict election outcomes. This raises the twin issues of accuracy in prognosticating and potential consequences of identifying the likely winner. Polls can be wrong.

There has been considerable controversy over the possibility that television coverage of election day affects the vote by telegraphing likely winners before voting has concluded. The principal villains have been exit polls and projections that predict winners, and the principal allegation has been that turnout decreases disproportionately with greater numbers of supporters for the losing candidate deciding not to vote. The result would be increased losses among candidates of the same party for other offices.

Most of the attention has been on the presidential race, but the same effect could occur at the state or district level. The concern has been so great that national television no longer uses exit polls for this purpose and avoids projections until polls in a state are closed.

Data on the effects of television coverage of exit polls, projections, and early results on later voters in presidential races point to little if any influence (Fuchs, 1966; Lang & Lang, 1968; Mendelsohn, 1966; Tuchman & Coffin, 1971). Only between 6 and 12% of those yet to vote were exposed to such coverage. Consistently, those voting early and those voting in the East and Midwest, who would not have access to such coverage, were very similar to those voting later or in the West in turnout and switching among candidates. The strongest possible magnitude of effect would be up to 1%.

We are not surprised. Effects are limited by the small proportions exposed. Furthermore, the two key assumptions of no interest in other contests and disproportionate effects are unlikely to be met (Tannenbaum & Kostrick, 1983). The net outcomes of new confidence and disappointment are hard to gauge.

Numerous pre-election-day polls and prognostications usually will have long conveyed the trends apparent on election day so that they have been incorporated already in decision making. Polls play their greatest role in shaping expectations and any influence this may have on turnout and choice is likely to occur before election day.

In our view, however, the use of exit polls on election day to predict outcomes is journalistically untenable. Their purpose has changed from tracking public opinion to scoring a scoop. Unhappily, polls have both quantifiable and unquantifiable degrees of error and certainly sometimes will be wrong. Thus, they place the journalist in the role of using a source occasionally known to lie.

In regard to public perceptions of viability, polls are crucial to third-party candidates. Early favorable results extend credibility. A candidate who registers 20% early becomes a contender. Any subsequent decline then marks a loss of momentum, and remaining supporters become more likely to reconsider their options. Thus, third-party candidates whose early support registers in the high teens or low 20s typically get less than 5% of the votes on election day; Perot's 19% in 1992 was an extraordinary exception.

Two related phenomena in which television figures prominently because of its role in disseminating the major stories of the day are the overestimates of support for highly qualified minority candidates and for pre-election favorites. Repeatedly (but hardly invariably), polls have indicated greater support for minority candidates than the votes they have received on election day (Kaplan, 1989; Lake, 1989). A similar overestimation occurs for candidates that are thought to be certain winners when they are losing support as election day approaches. The source, in our view, is social norms. In each case, enough people are giving what they think is the proper answer to bias the outcome.

Shelley and Hwang (1991) examined the accuracy of polling in the 1988 presidential election. All poll stories by the *Wall Street Journal*/NBC News, *New York Times*/CBS News, *Washington Post*/ABC News, *Newsweek*/Gallup, and *Time*/Yankelovich Clancy Shulman regarding the Bush vs Dukakis election were analyzed. Most poll results were similar, but some discrepancies occurred regarding who was leading at what time. In determining accuracy, the authors measured the difference between the predicted outcome and actual percentage of the vote. Final polls by these five sources were consistent and accurate within one or two percentage points after undecideds (not a voting booth option) were eliminated. Agreement among the polls was lowest when opinion was shifting, and at such times differences in the day of data collection can have large consequences for the standings of the candidates. These 1988 data are in accord with other estimates of accuracy (Holbrook, 1996). We have compiled similar statistics for the 1996 election (Table 5.4) for six polls conducted at approximately the same time late in the campaign. Results were uniformly accurate in

TABLE 5.4 Accuracy of Final Presidential Polls, 1996

Polling Organization	Date	Who would you vote for if the election were held today?			Deviations from election results*		
		Clinton	Dole	Perot	Clinton	Dole	Perot
Wall Street Journal/NBC	9/17	51%	38%	5%	+2	−3	−5
New York Times/CBS	9/4	50%	35%	5%	+1	−6	−5
Washington Post/ABC	9/5	51%	37%	8%	+2	−4	−2
Time/CNN	9/6	52%	38%	6%	+3	−3	−4
Gallup England	9/5	55%	34%	6%	+6	−7	−4
Newsweek	9/21	51%	35%	5%	+2	−6	−5

*Undecided, don't know, and no response were eliminated; poll estimate—actual vote

Adapted from Polling the Nations (CD-ROM), 1997, Bethesda, MD: ORS Publishing, Inc. and U.S. Bureau of the Census, *Statistical Abstract of the United States: 1997.* (117th edition), Washington, D.C., 1997.

predicting the outcome. However, consistent with the "expected winner" bias, the number of votes Clinton would receive was consistently overestimated, whereas the number that Dole and Perot would receive were consistently underestimated. This suggests that in a closer race when there nevertheless was widespread confidence about the victory of the apparently leading candidate, the polls very well could be wrong.

B. DEBATES

The first televised presidential debates between John F. Kennedy and Richard Nixon in 1960 became the subject of extensive research (Kraus, 1962). The second debates 16 years later between Jimmy Carter and Gerald Ford received similar attention (Kraus, 1979). The data from these two initial series reveal patterns that continue to mark the debate process, but our knowledge has increased with the evidence from subsequent encounters.

Debates have become a tradition because no candidate dares to refuse to participate. This came about because of the insecurities of Carter and Ford. Between 1960 and 1976, the candidate with the apparent advantage took Nixon's experience as a lesson and avoided a debate. But in 1976 the incumbent, Ford, was perilously behind in the polls and Carter, the challenger, had promised during the primaries to debate. The consequence was that when Carter ran for reelection, he could hardly refuse to debate Reagan. Debates are extremely popular with the public (Comstock, 1991b; Kraus, 1988), and the risk of public disapproval for refusing to participate is now perceived as riskier than any advantage an opponent might achieve.

The candidates, however, remain highly risk-aversive. Debates well in advance of election day are preferred so that any misstep can be overcome. Endless negotiations lead to the format, with the underdog typically seeking more debates, longer debates, and a less restrictive schema. The higher the stakes, the stricter the rules. Thus, debates during the primaries or among candidates for lesser office typically are free-wheeling, whereas those between presidential candidates are far more structured (Comstock, 1991b).

The debates have also become the subject of a number of myths. The first, most enduring, and widely believed is that Kennedy surged to victory by his performance in the first 1960 debate. The second, and a point in which the data are surprising, is that debates have their greatest effects on image and not on substance. The third is that there are usually decisively perceived winners. The fourth is that successful debate performance translates into substantial numbers of votes on election day.

In the Nixon–Kennedy debate of 1960, a review of 31 individual studies by Katz and Feldman (1962) found little evidence of change in attitude or opinion on issues but that public evaluations of the candidates had been affected. This is the source of the belief that debates affect image but not issues. Democrats reported improvement in their evaluations of Kennedy more often than Republicans reported improvement in their views of Nixon; more Republicans became more favorable to Kennedy than did Democrats to Nixon; and independents became more favorable toward Kennedy than toward Nixon. Overall, cognitions related to a favorable image of Kennedy crystallized and were reinforced more often than for Nixon. However, voting intentions displayed remarkable resilience—there was no evidence of a net gain for Kennedy in the proportion that expected to vote for him.

We believe that the persuasive role of the first debate is best assessed by examining the surrounding polls (Table 5.5). There was a steady trend toward the Democrats with the exception of the poll on the eve of the first debate, September 25. There was a shift favoring Kennedy–Johnson in the first post-debate poll (October 12) but the advantage had disappeared 2 weeks later when the two tickets were even. These data are wholly inconsistent with a deciding role for the first debate and better fit a picture of early Democrat gains that were not sustained after the first debate when the final stage of the campaign began. This interpretation is in accord with the conclusion of Katz and Feldman that the data they examined did not identify changes among debate viewers in the candidate for whom they intended to vote.

The data on the 1976 debates between Jimmy Carter and Gerald Ford put greater emphasis on the process of voter decision making (Kraus, 1979). The

TABLE 5.5 Trend of Political Support in 1960.

| Gallup poll release date | Percent saying how they would vote "If the election were held today . . ." | | |
	Kennedy	Nixon	Undecided
August 17	44	50	6
August 31	47	47	6
September 14	48	47	5
September 25	46	47	7
October 12	49	46	5
October 26	48	48	4
November 4	51	45	4
November 7	49	48	3
Actual vote	50.1	49.9	

The results include those registered and intending to vote. Sample size (N) varied from 1500 to 8000.
Adapted from "The Debates in the Light of Research: A Survey of Surveys," by E. Katz and J. J. Feldman, 1962, in S. Kraus (Ed.), *The Great Debates,* Bloomington: Indiana University Press.

picture that emerges, based on more than a half dozen samples typically numbering in the low hundreds that roughly represent the voting public, confounds both those who accord a decisive influence to debates and those who would assign them a redundant, trivial role. The anticipation of some effect heightened the likelihood that viewers would express a shift in outlook (O'Keefe & Mendelsohn, 1979), although such a response to the hoopla preceding the debates probably has decreased as they have become an accepted part of presidential politics. There was not much effect on the agenda of issues and topics that voters thought were important (Becker, Weaver, Graber, & McCombs, 1979), except for usually transient attention to one or another comment or exchange. Image changes were small but generally continual over the course of the debates (Simons & Leibowitz, 1979). Regular viewers of the debates relied markedly more on what they learned about the positions of the candidates on issues than did those who were occasional or nonviewers, whereas the latter two groups relied much more on images than on issues in arriving at a decision about the candidate for whom they would vote (Dennis, Chaffee, & Choe, 1979). The debates clearly stimulated thought and discussion about the candidates and to a small degree heightened interest in the campaign, and generally narrowed the disparity in acceptance between a favored candidate and his opponent (Atkin, Hocking, & McDermott, 1979; Becker, Pepper, Wenner, & Kim, 1979). Image and issue effects favoring one candidate over another often were offsetting or self-cancelling, and as time passed influence of the debates became difficult to isolate from the influence of exposure to other political communication through and outside of the mass media (Becker, Pepper, Wenner, & Kim, 1979; Davis, 1979; McLeod, Durall, Ziemke, & Bybee, 1979). The role of the debates in actively contributing to the decision making of voters was most conspicuous in its effects on issue-based decisions among regular viewers, whereas a secondary role was served for occasional viewers by providing an opportunity to confirm choices largely governed by issues (Dennis, Chaffee, & Choe, 1979). Shifts between the candidates were quite rare, however. For example, in one panel in which more than 160 voters were interviewed four times over the course of the debates and the election, there was only one instance of a switch from one candidate to the other (Dennis, Chaffee, & Choe, 1979). Thus, the debates figured prominently for many viewers in their decision making without being themselves decisive.

The key thread in these data is the functions served by the debates. Regular viewers were actively searching for information that would help them reach a decision, which they found in issue information. Occasional viewers sought reassurance that their party had nominated a worthy candidate, which they found in impressions confirmed by viewing. Nonviewers typically needed neither because they had made up their minds (Dennis, Chaffee, & Choe, 1979). Studies of the role of mass media have usually found that persons most likely to pay attention to campaign events are also most partisan and therefore least likely to be influenced by the media (Comstock et al., 1978; Kraus & Davis, 1976; Neuman, 1986). These 1976 data suggest that presidential debates had become an important exception.

The data document that televised debates facilitated thought and communication about a presidential election and served many voters in their decision making. National polls (Robinson, 1979) and the various smaller-scale surveys we have just examined lead to an estimate of slightly more than a third of voters as regular viewers (Sears & Chaffee, 1979), many of whom found the debates central to their deliberations, whereas about half were occasional viewers, many of whom gained impressions that enhanced their confidence in their tentative choice. Thus, contributions of the debates among voters to the process of deciding firmly on a candidate were widespread. Another 40% were occasional viewers and can be said to have had their choice confirmed or disconfirmed. These are substantial contributions to the process of decision making, although not contributions that would necessarily favor one or another of the debate participants.

The audiences for the 1960 and 1976 debates were huge, rivaling the Super Bowl. The first Kennedy–Nixon debate, for instance, drew the largest television audience ever up to that time—more than 80 million—of which about one-sixth were young people not old enough to vote (Katz & Feldman, 1962). The audience for the first Carter–Ford debate in 1976 was comparable in size although represented a somewhat smaller proportion of the voting public, whereas the single Carter–Reagan encounter in 1980 approached the ratings for the Kennedy–Nixon debates, attracting more than 80 million (Nielsen Media Research, 1993). Typically, audience size decreases with subsequent debates in a series.

The audience for contemporary televised presidential debates is comparatively modest. Estimates range only as high as 41 million for 1996 and 67 million for 1988 (Dean & Weaver, 1998; Lowry, 1996; Sharbutt, 1988). These are remarkable declines in public attention given the growth in the population of voting age between 1960 and 1996 of about 66% and between 1976 and 1996 of about 36%. The 1992 debates were an exception with the novel presence of a third candidate, Perot, resulting in a record high of an estimated 90 million viewers for the first encounter (Kamber, 1993). The reasons for the general decrease in audience size are twofold. First, televised debates have become a matter of course, rather than an extraordinary occurrence, and have proved less resilient to familiarity than the Super Bowl. Second, the channels that air the debates now face vastly greater competition. In 1960 and 1976, the near monopoly of the three networks meant that there was little else to choose from. Today, even without a subscription to cable, most households will have access to several broadcast channels offering hit movies (a favorite tactic) or other entertainment during the debates.

Early debates certainly reached some who were not typical consumers of political information, but they now do so to a far lesser degree because of the increased viewing options. Viewing always has been greater among the better educated and those with an interest in politics, and this is now so to a more pronounced degree. Audience size, in any case, gives an inflated impression of attention. We would expect that the format and viewer expectations and interest would result in greater than ordinary degrees of attentiveness, yet we would not expect suspension for all viewers of the low involvement and monitoring that typically characterize viewing. It has been estimated (Comstock, 1989; Sears & Chaffee, 1979) that no more than between one-fourth and one-half of those in the audience give close attention to any one debate, and that no more than a fourth of the electorate attends to a series with fairly consistent attention.

The data since 1960 identify a pattern that makes it important to distinguish between ceremonial exchanges that fulfill public expectations about what ought to take place and those in which the public perceives something of great importance at stake for the candidates or the nation. The early debates of 1960 and 1976 by their novelty eluded the ceremonial category, as did Carter and Reagan in 1980 by engaging in only one late encounter, whereas the very recent example of Bush–Clinton–Perot exemplifies the latent power of the debate format to engage the attention and interest of a wide portion of the voting public. However, the role of presidential debates in widening the public base of attentiveness to political figures and issues by attracting viewers who otherwise would ignore political information has been greatly abridged—by the diminished audiences and by the accompanying lowered likelihood that those with little interest will be in the audience for ceremonial exchanges.

The public evaluates debates very favorably. Majorities believe they are worthwhile and figure in their voting decisions (Comstock, 1989). Nine of 10 say they watch to learn about issues compared to three-fourths who say they want to evaluate the candidates as individuals.

In an analysis of the 1988 vice presidential debate between Dan Quayle and Lloyd Bentsen, Clayman (1995) identifies the role of "quotability" in determining news coverage. The media search the debate for a "defining moment" that will serve as a symbol of the event. In this particular debate, it came when Bentsen ended an exchange by declaring, "Senator, you're no Jack Kennedy." Extensive examination of media coverage of presidential debates confirms this observation (Kraus, 1979; Sears & Chaffee, 1979). Except for the *New York Times* and a few other major dailies that publish the transcripts, media coverage focuses on dramatic exchanges, gaffes, physical demeanor, and elements of human performance (confidence, nervousness, alacrity, displays of temper) rather than on issues or substance. In effect, the entertainment medium delivers information that is reinterpreted as entertainment by the information media.

Shields and MacDowell (1987) focused on emotion in postdebate instant analysis of the 1984 vice presidential encounter between Geraldine Ferraro and George Bush on the three major networks and PBS's MacNeil–Lehrer show. Two-thirds of the nearly 40 people making comments referred to emotion, with the female candidate mentioned more often in this regard. Whether the imputed emotion was positive or negative depended, of course, on the party affiliation of the commentator. Thus, gender again—as it does so often in television coverage—figured prominently in the treatment given those in the news.

About two-thirds of the public will encounter some form of news coverage or commentary after a debate (Atkin, Hocking, & McDermott, 1979), and these will not only affect the impressions of nonviewers but also may change what viewers have concluded. Even initial perceptions are shaped by the comments of the political experts and veteran journalists that immediately follow a debate on television. Very similar findings come from the data of Lowry, Bridges, and Barefield (1990) and Elliott and Sothirajah (1993) that compare those who saw the postdebate analysis following the September 25, 1988 debate between Bush and Dukakis. The candidate favored in these comments (Dukakis generally, but Bush on one channel) was more likely to be perceived as winning.

The public, in fact, comes to misjudge its own perceptions in concluding who has won a presidential or vice presidential debate (Comstock, 1989, 1991b; Sears & Chaffee, 1979). Typically, national polls record fairly close proportions separated by about five to seven percentage points. There have been clear, repetitive patterns of selective perceptions, with supporters more likely to see their preferred candidate as having won. Usually, about one-fourth to one-third are undecided, don't know, or judge the outcome as even. Independents (and undecideds) contribute the major portion of the margin of perceived victory, which usually could shift the other way with a change of merely two and a half to three and a half percentage points. The winner becomes a story covered by all the news media beginning with television's instant analyses following each debate. The leader in the polls is declared the winner. The proportion of the public who perceive this candidate as having won then rises from a modest advantage in the mid-30s to a substantial majority during the days following a debate as the identity of the winner is more thoroughly disseminated by the media. Unlike in sports, the winner is entered in the record without the qualification of the score.

There has been evidence of the influence of the debates on public beliefs about issues since 1960 and 1976. Surveys frequently registered increases in knowledge about the stands of the candidates on issues and changes in the salience of issues, particularly with regard to the evaluation of one or another candidate (Carter, 1962; Katz & Feldman, 1962; Sears & Chaffee, 1979). These effects often were modest in size and the level of abstraction at which issues were defined quite broad. Nevertheless, they stand as clear signs of influence on knowledge and are striking because they advance issues as affected even at the time of the first debate, where image received so much attention.

More recent data are highly supportive of the influence of debates. Drew and Weaver (1991) found in a sample of more than 250 Bloomington adults that viewing the Bush–Dukakis debate in 1988 was unassociated with image scores, whereas viewing positively predicted knowledge about issues after controlling for demographics, campaign interest, and use of mass media. Lemert (1993) found in a large sample of voters from the East, Midwest, and Pacific Coast that viewing of those same debates was associated with greater issue knowledge after controlling for demographics, political predisposition, and mass media use. Lanoue (1991) found among a sample of 250 Illinois students that viewing the second debate in that series increased issue knowledge. Zhu, Milavsky, and Biswas (1994) in a New York student sample found that viewing of the 1992 debates changed image perceptions on only a few dimensions for Perot and none for Bush and Clinton, whereas issue knowledge for all three was increased. Similarly, Powell and Wanzenreid (1993) found various ratings of the competence, sincerity, and boldness of the three 1992 candidates little affected by viewing the debates except for a very few measures for Perot and Clinton. These outcomes across several elections, different samples, using somewhat different measures, and with major sources of artifactual relationship removed make a strong case for influence on issue knowledge.

The sole exception appears to occur through impressions formed about the manner in which the candidates communicate. Thus, Pfau and Kang (1991) found that the scoring of the candidates on these dimensions by viewers of the 1988 debates predicted favorability, competence, and vote intention. This is consistent with earlier evidence that impressions of communicatory style affect impressions voter favorability (Pfau et al., 1993).

Our interpretation is that image advanced to the front of the stage with regard to the debates because of the particular drama associated with the performances of Kennedy and Nixon in 1960. The ironic truth is that debates expand and sharpen knowledge about issues. A review of political debates from 1960 to 1996 (Friedenberg, 1997) comes to the same conclusion we have: though debates educate citizens and legitimize the transfer of power, their principal effect is to reinforce rather than shift attitudes of voters. As with all political communication, debates crystallize already held beliefs and perceptions more than they persuade or convert but this is to be expected—those typically are the roles of the media (Sears & Chaffee, 1979). The limitation of debates with regard to image is that images largely develop before voters attend to the debates, because they are the first factor about which political impressions form. Issues, however, are less clear and well known, and particularly so for those with an interest in the election and an intention to vote who have not followed the campaign with great attention, for they have been at the mercy of television and other news media in their emphases on the horse race, campaign activities, and occurrences unrelated to stands of the candidates on issues. The exception is communicatory style, about which impressions for many voters would depend on precisely the kind of experience provided by a debate, whereas impressions of such attributes as integrity, competence, and leadership would have already been developed.

The vice presidential debates play a distinctly minor—and mostly mute—role. This is because voters long ago will have taken the vice presidential choice into account, and most will have cast it aside as irrelevant (Comstock, 1989). This was well illustrated by the Bentsen–Quayle debate that was perceived as won by Bentsen by an extraordinary two-to-one margin without any subsequent change in the standings of the two tickets in the polls. Thus, we dismiss as civic-minded self-delusion Holbrook's (1994) data from the 1984 and 1988 CBS News/ New York Times polls in which viewers said they were influenced.

In fact, the seven series of debates so far (1960, 1976, 1980, 1984, 1988, 1992, 1996) provide only modest evidence of effects of debates on standings in the polls even for presidential candidates. The trend for Kennedy was under way before the first debate. Ford regained the support of Republicans before the first debate. A performance in the first debate rated poorly by analysts on the part of Reagan did not affect his lead over Mondale. Dukakis was behind before and remained behind Bush after the first debate. Holbrook (1996) examined shifts in public opinion polls during the debates in 1984, 1988, and 1992 and found only very small if discernible changes related to perceived performance or superiority of the participants. Neither we nor the author would claim that votes on election day were affected, but favorability and support at the time surely were to a small degree.

The particular authority of television in public impressions of the debates also has been documented in instances in which viewers reach somewhat different conclusions from the audio than from the complete video (Kraus, 1996). The most famous example is a rumored comparison between several hundred polled by a commercial firm after the first Kennedy–Nixon debate. Some saw the debate; others heard it on radio. Those who saw it responded as did viewers in other surveys: they were more favorably impressed with Kennedy. Those who heard the encounter were more favorably impressed with Nixon. Again, these are a matter of pluralities, not consensus. The difference presumably would be attributable to Nixon's somewhat haggard appearance, his scruffy makeup, and now notorious unshaven jaws. Unfortunately, although these data are in perfect accord with the popular understanding of the influence of television in this instance more than 35 years after their ostensible collection, this evidence was never published and exists in no archive. The original pollster claims it is true; others question its veracity. Kraus (1996) investigated and concluded that probably there were such data. We recall the New Jersey subliminal advertising hoax (Chapter 1). In any case, the belief that Nixon was essentially undone by deep facial shadow will persist, and the essential point that hearing is not seeing is valid.

The debates typically broaden support for their participants (Sears & Chaffee, 1979). This is reflected in generally enhanced rankings on one or another dimension of the candidates. This is the consequence of the usually good performances that these professionals at public appearance deliver and their adherence to the example of Kennedy in offering goals and paths that most can respect and many at least can partially endorse. The debates have been criticized for being press conferences and for obscuring differences, and these depictions are accurate. However, such criticisms ignore their function in the American system, which is to accent differences that matter to voters rather than identify irreconcilable disagreements. Thus, the candidates emerge from the debates with a wider base of acceptance than otherwise would be the case, thereby contributing to continuity and stability. Partisanship is mitigated but not abandoned.

We have not been able to find an instance in which a debate dramatically altered the apparent outcome of an election or even the course of a campaign. They are not decisive encounters from which a candidate emerges with certainty of election-day victory, and they do not establish the issues and topics that will figure importantly as the campaign proceeds. Instead, they are symbols of the electoral process that further rouse the majority, they reflect rather than determine the central issues and topics of a campaign, and their locus of influence lies in assisting voters—who for the most part would not have complete knowledge or fully developed impressions of the candidates—in reaching a decision.

There is no instance in which an advantage on election day has been clearly traceable to debate performance. The data go no further than identifying small shifts at the time of a debate, mostly in degree of support for rather than choice among the candidates. They are certainly redundant with much else that occurs in a campaign, and this circumstance along with their clear failure to have established a presence in the voting booth raises the question of their contribution. Our view is that they are one of the most successful educational undertakings of television. They advance the decision-making process among the electorate, and we cannot imagine an estimate of the more than 30 million who now view who acquire knowledge or an impression that otherwise would be absent that would be small enough to dismiss them as unimportant. They are instructionally superior to the news and advertising in regard to issues because attention is motivated and focused, however diluted by the low involvement and monitoring so ingrained as a response to television. They serve the specific purpose of providing information about the candidates that becomes larger and more influential the less certain voters are about their choice and accomplish what the news media otherwise do not so clearly do by identifying candidates with stands on issues.

Public Thought and Action

We end our examination of news and politics by assessing at a broad level the contribution of television to public thought and action. Our conclusions rest firmly on empirical evidence, although we would not deny that there are occasional findings contrary to the patterns we discern. We begin with two contrasting views of information—civic knowledge and public understanding. We then turn to the construction of the importance imputed to issues, people, and events and its role in shaping opinions about them. We conclude with the function of the mass media in the democratic process, with an emphasis on the particular place occupied by television.

I. CIVIC KNOWLEDGE VS PUBLIC UNDERSTANDING

The measurement of the public's civic knowledge—about political figures, the operation of government, pending legislation, and events in general—has disclosed a disappointing pattern that has persisted for decades (Neuman, 1976; Neuman et al., 1992). There are three components. First, public knowledge scores typically are low. Often, fewer than 50% can name their congressman or senator, describe major pending legislation, or identify recent events surrounding a world leader. Second, media exposure has not been a very strong predictor of knowledge, and although exposure more often than not has been associated with greater knowledge, there are instances in which no association was recorded (Patterson & McClure, 1976). Third, television viewing has been less predictive of knowledge than newspaper reading or print use (Clark & Fredin, 1978), and television news viewing has been less strongly associated with knowledge than has newspaper reading (Martinelli & Chaffee, 1995; Patterson, 1980; Robinson & Levy, 1986a; Stamm, Johnson, & Martin, 1997; Vincent & Basil, 1997), whereas overall amount of television viewing—entertainment and news—has sometimes been found to be associated with lower levels of knowledge (Chaffee et al., 1970).

A great amount of data document that television news is instructionally ineffective. Television news viewers do not remember much of what they hear and see (Gunter, 1987; Katz, Adonni, & Parness, 1977; Neuman, 1976; Wilson, 1974). The design of the news would appear to favor a different outcome. Items are brief, simplistic, sometimes dramatic, accompanied by attention-getting visuals, selected and shaped to fit the public's interests, and there are not many of them—only 15 or 16 per half hour of newscast. They should achieve for events what commercials attempt for products—a memory trace. Yet, studies repeatedly show that, on average, fewer than one-fourth of all items in a newscast can be accurately recalled (Comstock, 1991b). This is so minutes after viewing and does not improve dramatically when viewers are asked to pay close attention or are warned they will be tested later.

The civic knowledge record is dismal on all counts—knowledge, media, and in particular television. Public understanding gives a very different impression. This is the measurement of what the public thinks and believes about the events of the day and the people who figure in them. The emphasis is on response to the news rather than on acquisition of facts. This perspective is consistent with the conclusion of a recent analysis of the evidence on what voters learn from the mass media by Weaver (1996) that awareness and concern about issues and people are typically what is acquired from attending to the news.

Neuman et al. (1992) have labeled these outcomes "common knowledge"—the understandings that people develop. An identicality of belief across millions is not implied; the term denotes broadly termed topics—Watergate, Woodstock, or Whitewater—about which knowledge can be described at the aggregate or at the individual level.

Despite the low levels of civic knowledge and poor recall of the news, there is extensive learning from the mass media, including television. However, what is learned is not a factual almanac; instead, it is an increasing apprehension of unfolding events that will differ somewhat in its composition from individual to individual. Neuman et al. (1992) describe the process. Cognitive schema are crucial. The pictures—or lack thereof—that people have in their minds are the foundation. Prior knowledge leads to incorporating additional information more readily. Understanding builds incrementally. Recall of facts or specific features often remains low. What transpires is the continuing elaboration and accenting of comprehension. Comprehension and recall are most likely when an element of the presentation activates cognitive schema so that new information can be incorporated with prior knowledge and translated into understanding. News facilitates this process by the regular use of labels and terms that signify the nature of the story, but sometimes interferes with it when stories that call for different schema are treated similarly. Repeated exposure and additional coverage then slowly advance individual understanding as the consumer incorporates new elements.

Viewers and readers in their understandings focus on right and wrong, success and failure, justice and tragedy. The media emphasize novelty and conflict. Viewers and readers attempt to assemble a narrative. The media typically draw on recent events. Thus, the values that govern the assembly of the news are ignored by consumers in favor of morality tales where deviance becomes a question of deserved or undeserved outcomes following from the disregard of ethics. Viewers and readers seek truth, and tests of the possession of information inaccurately reflect the instructional role of the news media.

There is abundant evidence that television news viewing is associated with lower recall of information about public events than is the reading of newspapers (Chaffee et al., 1970; Martinelli & Chaffee, 1995; Patterson, 1980; Robinson & Levy, 1986a; Stamm et al., 1997; Vincent & Basil, 1997). However, there is also good evidence that a stronger orientation toward television as a news source is a correlate of lesser cognitive skills and that the inverse relationship between use of television news and information levels is explained by the attributes of those who use television rather than by the properties of the medium (Neuman et al., 1992). When this factor is taken into account, television and print media become similar in potential influence.

For some stories, television may be superior. These are stories of some complexity in regard to the connections among their constituent parts—for example, science, economics, and international strife-—that benefit hugely in public understanding from the visual means by which television can draw attention, encourage involvement, and create interest, and the personalization of anchors and correspondents of which television is so capable. For example, the factors perceived as responsible for terrorism and poverty have been demonstrated to be influenced by the treatment given such stories on television news (Iyengar, 1987). In short, the simplicity—visualization, dramatization, simplification—of which television has often been accused can be an advantage.

Neuman and colleagues see television, newspapers, and news magazines as complementary media. This is in accord with the concept of a news audience, for if the media each functioned identically there would be no motive to attend to more than one. The more cognitively skilled, they argue, are better able to invest newspaper accounts of daily events with drama, thereby compensating for the properties of television that are absent. News magazines specialize in context and background. Thus, they are especially important to the development of cognitive schema. The visual emphases, the brevity of stories, and the mixing of disparate elements that have been said to reduce the instructional effectiveness of television news (Robinson & Sheehan, 1983) probably do have a toll, but the major weakness of television for those who rely on it primarily is that repetition becomes the major means for the formation of schema on unfamiliar topics, and the concentration of the medium on topics of proven interest restricts the development of new schema.

News is more quickly and easily incorporated with prior knowledge when there is a framework of understanding. Attention and interest are necessary conditions; without an existing schema, they are likely to be absent. Television is especially effective at drawing attention to and creating interest in complex stories that in print might prove daunting, and this would be especially so for those of lower cognitive abilities. The weather is an excellent example: television personalizes and dramatizes the topic and makes the white swirls of conflicting pressure and animated raindrops pleasing to the eye and attractive to the mind. As a consequence, news viewers are more likely than those more oriented toward print sources to know that the weather in the United States moves from west to east (Robinson, 1972a).

Three major factors on which comprehension and recall of television news are contingent are personal attributes, such as the abilities, interests, and needs of the viewer; format and form features of the telecast; and the content. These function in concert, but because the available studies focus on one or another we give them separate treatment.

A. PERSONAL ATTRIBUTES

Cognitive skills are a major factor (Neuman et al., 1992). Television's mode of presentation makes it a more instructionally effective medium for those lower in such skills, as well as a more preferred medium. Nevertheless, what is learned from any of the news media will rise and fall with the cognitive ability of the individual. Rhee and Cappella (1997), for example, found those higher in political sophistication—consisting of both knowledge and ideology—learned more from both broadcast and print news.

Interest, involvement, and emotional arousal all facilitate learning from the news (Gurevitch & Levy, 1986; Neuman et al., 1992; Patterson & McClure, 1976), as will the motive to gain information and reflection later on what has been viewed (Perse, 1990b). These factors, in turn, will be influenced by beliefs about the degree of attention required to understand television news, with most believing little attention is required (Salomon, 1984), and the perceptions that others are paying attention, either in the same room or among the public at large as in the case of the O.J. Simpson criminal trial, thereby endorsing attention as normative.

B. FORMAT AND FORMAL FEATURES

Three distinct aspects of format and form have been investigated. They are sequencing, visuals, and visual and verbal relationships.

Complexity of story construction, such as number of shots or bits of information, decreases learning (Burriss, 1989b) as does the invitation to confusion that occurs when stories are grouped under a common topic, such as economics, news from Asia, or politics (Robinson & Levy, 1986a). In contrast, aids to thoughtful processing, such as pauses, are helpful as is the repetition of stories (Perloff, Wartella, & Becker, 1982). This cluster of outcomes advocates simplicity, clear identification of individual stories, and pacing that invites reflection. These are somewhat counter to the conventions of newscast organization, but the justification is that they assist viewers in assigning the story to the correct schema and reduce the confusing of places, events, and occurrences. Television's visual storytelling nevertheless is superior to the audio only of radio (Graber, 1990; Katz et al., 1971), an effect attributable to the interest aroused and information provided by the visual properties of television rather than to differences in the skills of their audiences.

When the preceding program is very exciting, memory will be clouded for the first half of a subsequent newscast (Scott & Goff, 1988), whereas in the short term an exciting or arousing news item may interfere with recall of the preceding item but heighten the memorability of one that follows (Newhagen & Reeves, 1992). However, teasers that advertise upcoming stories ("Gunfire at the border. News at 11.") increase story recall if the item is prominent (such as early) in the newscast (Cameron, Schleuder, & Thorson, 1991). Images that evoke anger or fear are better recalled than those that result in disgust (Newhagen, 1998), which explains why displays of violence and risk may be remembered while those of the dying are forgotten unless they are part of extended, dramatic coverage that cannot be ignored as in the case of a report on a famine (Dearing & Rogers, 1996). Memory is also increased by a pleasing presentation (in this case, a set of commercials) that follows news items, presumably because it associates them with a reward (Reeves, Lang, Thorson, &

Rothschild, 1989). However, commercials, whether humorous or not, ordinarily do not interfere with memory, probably because viewers long ago became accustomed to their presence (Biocca et al., 1992).

The data identifying television as instructionally superior to radio are reinforced by evidence that the visuals generally enhance recall and comprehension. In one experiment, twice as many visual as verbal elements of a news story were recalled (Graber, 1990). Visuals other than talking heads enhance interest and emotional arousal, which in turn promote recall. People are particularly effective as subjects in this regard, but people-based stories are sometimes more difficult for viewers to assimilate than are event-based stories (Brosius, 1989) because they require the integration of persons and events, and useful schema may be difficult to apply when persons are unfamiliar in identity or attributes. Impersonal images of places or locations must contain something visually exciting or unusual to achieve recall. Recall was better not only for visual themes, but among the better remembered verbal elements were anchor-read synopses of the story. This hints that viewers learn better when less effort is required. Visuals can improve learning and recall over talking heads for the same story, but a newscast alternating the two is more effective than visuals used exclusively (Brosius, 1991). Redundancy of visuals increases overall understanding but may decrease recall of one or another through confusion (Drew & Grimes, 1987).

The fit between visual and verbal elements, or content and illustration, is very important. There are two related aspects—redundancy and conflict or irrelevancy. Experimentally, recall of news has been found to be more complete and accurate when pictorial and audio elements reinforce one another (Reese, 1984). It is a specific application of the more general principle that except when it introduces some confusion, redundancy generally enhances understanding and recall (Drew & Grimes, 1987; Findahl, 1981; Nugent, 1982; Robinson & Levy, 1986b).

One noteworthy pattern is the curvilinear relationship between redundancy and attention. Grimes (1991), for example, varied the redundancy of audio and video elements of news stories. Subjects in the medium-redundancy condition, in which only some visual images did not correspond with the text, paid comparatively more attention to the audio. Those in high and low redundancy conditions paid more attention to the visuals. News viewers thus employed the least cognitively taxing strategy. This meant focusing on the visual element except when there was a modest amount of conflict resolvable by the audio portion. The significance is that viewers are unlikely to sort out marked discrepancies between the two and in those cases learning and recall will be less accurate.

Errors in recall sometimes are attributable to visual elements, such as the translation phenomenon when facts presented in narration are later attributed to a visual source (Grimes, 1990). Thus, an interpretation offered by the narrative might be recalled as an impression formed from and seemingly verified by video footage.

Errors are more likely when there is a discrepancy between story content and illustration. In these cases, reliance on visuals in accord with the principle of minimum effort in processing, along with their role in drawing attention and arousing interest and thereby activating schema, is very likely to lead to misunderstanding (Robinson & Levy, 1986a). Two examples are a story on peace negotiations accompanied by footage of armed fighting and a story on presidential politics using photos of dead presidents. Highly emotional visuals (Brosius, 1993) and visuals that distract when a narrative is complex (Housel, 1984) lower learning and recall. For example, scenes depicting pain and suffering will be recalled more for screams and noises than for the verbal narration (Newhagen & Reeves, 1992).

However, there is no convincing case for the argument of some (Gibbons, Anderson, Smith, Field, & Fischer, 1986) that there is persistent interference with learning and recall from the conflict between the visual and audio portions of television news. The data clearly document that under some conditions visuals enhance such outcomes. The relationship, like that between redundancy and attention, is probably best conceived of as curvilinear, with effectiveness tapering off when too many or the wrong types of visuals are used.

In our judgment, the visual elements of television news generally increase learning. Graber (1990) points out that visual depictions are more unique than verbal descriptions, so are probably harder to assimilate to existing schema. On the other hand, so many are redundant with one another—the correspondent on the steps of the Supreme Court, the stretch limos as diplomats gather for a meeting, the jeering and rock throwing of protesters—that they are probably quickly and easily incorporated into an existing framework. In general, television's visual element probably serves learning fairly well by arousing interest, generating an emotional response that will make a report more memorable, and encouraging easy incorporation with prior knowledge. Sometimes, it will trigger such an intense response that it will be mostly what the viewer recalls. Occasionally, it will conflict with the content of the story and hamper the application of schema. In general, audiovisual processing—as contrasted with that confined to verbal exposition—leads to more comprehensive and accurate recall and greater emotional involvement (Graber, 1996).

We largely agree with the hypothesis of Neuman, Just, and Crigler (1992) that visuals, like symbols in general, prove most useful in the initial stage of comprehension in which the information is decoded—the point of attention and schema selection—rather than in subsequent elements, such as reasoning or making inferences. We also agree with Rolandelli (1989) that a visual element may take precedence in recall when it is more concrete than the narration.

In our view, the key variable is attention. Viewers typically give greater attention to visual elements because they are more concrete and less taxing to interpret. When attention to the audio portion of a newscast is triggered, recall will equal that for visual elements. Thus, it is not inherent properties but the attention they elicit that gives depictions the advantage over descriptions.

C. CONTENT

Graphics increase understanding of statistics and quantitative relationships, and they can help viewers trace out multistage processes, such as money transfers and financial relationships (Robinson & Levy, 1986a). Surprise and bad news, if not too horrific, increase memory (Katz et al., 1977). Attitudes and emotions elicited by a story decay slower than recall of facts (Graber, 1988). Some violent visuals are particularly memorable (Mundorf, Drew, Zillmann, & Weaver, 1990). Emotion-arousing visuals, however, are not always better recalled (Brosius, 1993; Furnham & Gunter, 1985; Mundorf et al., 1990), but close-ups of people, which often have that quality, have been well recalled (Graber, 1990; Heuer & Reisberg, 1990). High credibility increases memory (Drew & Reese, 1984). Acronyms and jargon may not be recognized by many viewers (Robinson & Levy, 1986a); they assume far too much prior knowledge.

Robinson and Levy (1986a) proposed reforms in the format and form features of television news to improve instructional effectiveness. They argue for more effort to make themes and interpretations of events explicit, the avoidance of jargon, the use of graphics, the disaggregation of stories that later might be confused with one another, and a focus on everyday implications and the human element that would enhance interest and involvement. Gunter (1987), however, contends that news personnel have little interest in altering the ways they present information because they adhere to journalistic values and conventions that define public service rather than measures of public recall and understanding. Thus, the goal of improving instructional effectiveness has become the victim of the sociology of the news business as well as subject to the very real uncertainties of designing newscasts that would enhance the cognitive processing of viewers.

II. THE IMPUTATION OF IMPORTANCE

Agenda setting is a label that has become widely used for the study of the relationship between the emphases of the news media and the imputed importance or salience the public assigns to issues, topics, events, people, and their attributes (McCombs & Shaw, 1993). It has its contemporary origin in Cohen's (1963) comment that if the media fail in telling people "what to think"—a broad conclusion that for many summed up research on political communication from the late 1940s through the 1960s (Klapper, 1960; Neuman, Just, & Crigler, 1992)—they certainly succeed in telling them "what to think about." Data specifically intended to examine such relationships were first collected by McCombs and Shaw (1972) in Chapel Hill during the 1968 presidential campaign. They analyzed the coverage of issues by nine newspapers, the three television networks, and the three major newsmagazines and found that the amount of attention devoted to issues was highly correlated with the ranking of the importance of these issues by the public. The data themselves of course did not permit causally attributing the views of the public to the influence of the media (Comstock et al., 1978; Neuman, 1990), although the authors stoutly argued in behalf of such an interpretation. In this initial instance, the evidence in behalf of agenda setting was confined to no more than an association between public rankings and amounts of media coverage at one point in time.

Since then, the original agenda-setting hypothesis has been expanded and elaborated. The presentation of data displaying parallels between media attention and public interest in topics has become common (Figure 6.1). Frequently, media attention has preceded the enhanced imputation of importance. Often, too, the two have been parallel, and in retrospect (and in accord with Occam's razor) the original argument of McCombs and Shaw attains considerable credence because it would require uncanny sensitivity to public nuance for the media to follow opinion to such a degree, whereas the likelihood that media attention would guide opinion requires no such miraculous intervention.

The concept has been taken beyond politics to include personal agendas, of which the political is often only a small part (Weaver, Graber, McCombs, & Eyal, 1981); the way the media affect the prominence the public gives to selected dimensions of a topic, or "framing" (Iyengar, 1991); how subsequent judgments of political figures are shaped by the emphases of media, or "priming" (Fiske & Taylor, 1984; Iyengar & Kinder, 1987a); and the factors that influence the shifting emphases of the media (McCombs, 1992).

Our treatment of agenda setting will employ three dimensions (Table 6.1). They are the research questions addressed, the processes by which media coverage and public outlook are linked, and the attributes of the phenomenon (Dearing & Rogers, 1996; McCombs & Shaw, 1993; Neuman, 1990).

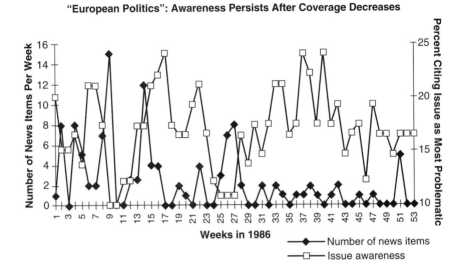

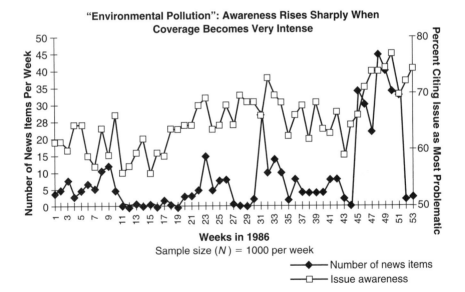

FIGURE 6.1 Public identification of two issues as politically most problematic and television news coverage. (Adapted from "The Agenda-Setting Function of Television News," by H. B. Brosius and H. M. Kepplinger, 1990, *Communication Research, 17*(2), pp. 183–211.)

TABLE 6.1 Public Imputation of Importance to Issues and Topics—Three Dimensions
of Agenda Setting

Questions	Process	Attributes
Are associations observable between media attention and the importance assigned by the public to issues and topics? Do shifts in media attention precede changes in the salience of issues and topics? Do changes in the public salience of issues and topics precede media attention? What personal attributes predict a correlation between media attention and the importance assigned to an issue or topic? Do issues and topics differ in the likelihood of an association between media attention and public salience? Do the media differ in the associations observed between attention given an issue or topic and the importance assigned them by the public? What is the particular role of television in the associations observed between media attention and the importance assigned issues and topics by the public? What factors influence the attention given issues and topics by the media?	Changes in emphases of media are followed by shifts in the public's imputation of importance to issues and topics. Importance of a topic and its attributes are both affected, with the latter often constituting the basis for evaluative judgment. Public interest sometimes precedes coverage, with the media agenda set by the public. Crises (such as war) dictate media attention and are assured of salience. Always available dislocations (political scandals, health risks, environmental threats, international strife) depend on media attention for salience. What the public finds interesting guides the media in issue and topic selection. Obtrusive topics are more affected by personal experience than by media attention. Some topics are resistant to influence because they are perceived as fixtures. Topics vary in amount of media coverage required, with shifts in salience sometimes dependent on exceeding a threshold.	Mostly same issues and topics are covered by different media. Media attention is often independent of statistical indices of topic importance. Topics rise and fall on public agenda as a consequence of media attention. Salience is a social construction; individuals variously combine personal experience, the impressions of others, and media coverage. Increased salience is most likely when the White House is involved, there is *New York Times* coverage, or there is a highly prominent event. Certain issues and topics seldom receive extensive media attention and are rarely prominent on the public agenda.

Based on *Agenda Setting,* by J. W. Dearing and E. M. Rogers, 1996, Thousand Oaks, CA: Sage; "The Evolution of Agenda-Setting Research: Twenty-Five Years in the Marketplace of Ideas," by M. E. McCombs and D. L. Shaw, 1993, *Journal of Communication, 43*(2), pp. 58–67; and "The Threshold of Public Attention," by W. R. Neuman, 1990, *Public Opinion Quarterly, 54,* pp. 159–176.

A. Research Questions

Our first concern is whether the hypothesized influence of media attention on public salience occurs. Three admittedly overlapping bodies of evidence leave no doubt that it does. First, there is a large social science literature of more than 200 items (Rogers, Dearing, & Bregman, 1993), and although there are various qualifications that can be made regarding the type of issue, time span, kind of media, or attributes of affected individuals, there is no pattern that discredits the hypothesis. Second, the empirical data include not only many associations between media attention and public salience that are difficult to explain in the absence of media influence, but also experimental designs—including both laboratory-type and quasi-experimentation (Cook & Campbell, 1979)—that permit or encourage causal inference. Third, Dearing and Rogers recently (1996) examined 112 studies, each based on empirical data, and concluded that 60% supported agenda setting of some sort—an extraordinary record given the expectation that in many circumstances the phenomenon might not occur. (In our view, 10% in support would be compelling if those cases could be conceptually distinguished from the others.)

The objects affected by agenda setting include issues, topics, events, persons, and their attributes. With the latter, an evaluative element enters; the importance of an issue, topic, event, or person is supplemented by characteristics that are likely to affect favorability toward the object. The evaluation of a financier will vary with the salience of his successful shopping malls or failed savings and loans; or that of a horse breeder when the mysterious death of a heavily insured champion is mentioned instead of his Triple Crown contenders; or that of a president when his worst fiasco rather than his greatest success is brought to mind. We see the focus as anything subject to changes in public salience. In this context, we use issue and topic as essentially synonymous and encompassing persons—unless we wish to make a point applying only to one or another. Issues are not only topics on which people may differ and with varying degrees of intensity, but they also extend to thematic concerns about which public enthusiasm may gather or remain dormant, such as the ecology, nuclear power, and the politically incorrect-isms, ageism, racism, and sexism.

Analysis has shifted from looking at a single point in time to searching for trends in media coverage and public opinion. The data suggest there often is a lag between the time at which a topic is given emphasis by the media and an increase in public perception of its importance (Weaver, Graber, McCombs, & Eyal, 1981). Brosius and Kepplinger (1990) and Neuman (1990) suggest that the time it takes for an agenda-setting influence to occur depends on the topic. General ideas or perspectives may take years to achieve increased public awareness (Funkhouser, 1973a). Issues in election campaigns that take place within several months have generally shown a 4- to 6-week time lag (Wanta,

1997a; Winter & Eyal, 1981). Perceived importance of issues that are topical, congenial to current fashion, or represented by an event attracting immense coverage, such as a huge oil spill, can change within days or a very few weeks (Atwater, Salwen, & Anderson, 1985).

When events accumulate gradually before becoming identified with a topic of significance, as was the case with the Vietnam War, coverage will have to cross thresholds of frequency and prominence before the topic is assigned particular importance by the public (Neuman, 1990). This frequent dependence of public salience on a certain minimum of media attention has been called the requirement for a critical mass (Dearing & Rogers, 1996). Generally, media attention will rise with the risk to well-being, the offense to public ideals, and the departure of circumstances from the ordinary.

A major individual attribute on which influence depends is a person's need for orientation (Weaver, 1977, 1984). Those with high interest or high uncertainty—or the two in combination—are particularly likely to be influenced (Blood, 1989). Important issue factors include prominence to the individual, intrusiveness or nonintrusiveness, and sensitivity to public response (Neuman, 1990; Zhu & Boroson, 1997). Demographics and other individual differences generally do not make much difference in agenda setting (Miller & Wanta, 1996; Wanta, 1997b; Zhu & Boroson, 1997). High salience and obtrusiveness are inversely associated with agenda setting; the media are less likely to influence the standing of topics about which the viewer has strong opinions or has had or is having personal experience (Eyal, 1980). A premium example of the latter is a gasoline shortage, where the media may be wholly responsible for public concern in areas where gasoline is plentiful but in areas of scarcity salience will be a function of the inconvenience of long lines and disruption of personal plans. The media have their greatest authority over the salience of topics that do not intrude on or affect directly the lives of individuals. Then there are issues such as crime, which receive continuing media coverage that sometimes escalates greatly—O.J. Simpson, a serial killer—without affecting imputed importance (Neuman, 1990).

Amount of media attention often diverges from the statistical trends of real-world occurrences (Funkhouser, 1973a, 1973b). Three examples have been crime, drug abuse, and the American military commitment in Vietnam (Figure 6.2). For example, Hamilton (1998), in his analysis of crime coverage in local news by 57 stations in 19 different markets in the fall of 1993, found no relationship between number of stories about aggravated assaults, murders, or rapes and the frequency of these crimes, and no relationship between total number of crime stories and a general index of the frequency of crime. The media adopt their own agenda in accord with what is judged newsworthy, and these decisions then influence public perceptions of national problems. The major factor is the vulnerability of the public to take an interest in an issue,

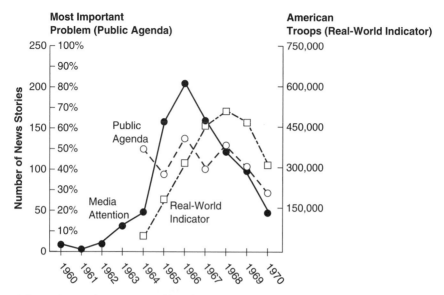

FIGURE 6.2   Media attention, public salience, and a real-world indicator for the Vietnam War. (Adapted from *Agenda Setting,* by J. W. Dearing and E. M. Rogers, 1996, Thousand Oaks, CA: Sage; "The Issues of the Sixties: An Exploratory Study in the Dynamics of Public Opinion," by G. R. Funkhouser, 1973, *Public Opinion Quarterly,* 37(1), pp. 62–75; and "Trends in Media Coverage of the Issues of the Sixties," by G. R. Funkhouser, 1973, *Journalism Quarterly, 50,* pp. 533–538.)

which then will rise on the public agenda as a consequence of increased coverage.

Agenda setting also has varied with the medium. Data consistently indicate that on the whole newspapers were more likely to have an influence than television news (Comstock et. al., 1978; McCombs, 1981). McCombs (1976), in a study of the 1972 presidential election in Charlotte, North Carolina, found that television news did not predict voters' agendas until the end of the campaign when a slight association was found. At about the same time, Benton and Frazier (1976) divided topics into three levels: broad issues, subissues including specific problems or solutions, and specific information. For each level, correlations between television coverage and the public agenda were not only small but much smaller than those for newspaper coverage. Other findings suggest television is more influential in "spotlighting" high-profile issues that are then covered with greater depth by print media, thereby intensifying the public's perceptions of their importance (Schoenbach, 1991). Results of Trumbo's (1995) analysis of coverage of the global warming issue are consistent with the notion of prolonged newspaper coverage leading to an influence on public opinion that is boosted by intense television attention to the same issue.

Nevertheless, the many experiments—at least 14 by one recent count (Dearing & Rogers, 1996)—of Iyengar and colleagues (Iyengar & Kinder, 1987a, 1987b; Iyengar, Peters, & Kinder, 1982) repeatedly have demonstrated salience effects of television news. For example, importance of defense, pollution, civil rights, arms control, and unemployment were rated higher after subjects saw newscasts in which these topics were emphasized, whereas no effect was found for inflation, which the investigators attributed to its already high salience.

Television effects are most likely to occur when the topic is prominent (Weaver, Graber, McCombs, & Eyal, 1981) or intensely reported. In an extensive examination of television news in West Germany, Brosius and Kepplinger (1990) found that coverage influenced public awareness on some topics, such as energy supply, defense, environmental issues, and politics, but not others, including pensions, the debt, and public security. The authors attribute the differences to the way in which the topics were covered rather than to their substance. They present two examples (Figure 6.1): a rise in public awareness following fairly intense coverage that would persist for many weeks after coverage ceased, and substantial awareness during sporadic coverage that would rise suddenly after coverage became very intense. When the coverage was heavy—including more than 30 news stories per month—and increased suddenly, television news was particularly likely to help set the public agenda. Wanta (1997) found that agenda-setting effects from broadcast both occur and decay more quickly than agenda-setting effects from print. This again identifies television's unusual capability to draw high attention rapidly but sometimes sporadically to a topic. Television's influence is further strengthened by being the medium considered to be the most credible, which increases the likelihood that viewers will consider its coverage accurate and its emphases meaningful (Wanta & Hu, 1994).

B. Process and Attributes

There are several possible explanations for the often-recorded superiority in the past of newspapers for agenda setting (Comstock et. al., 1978). The graphic makeup of newspapers may well make differing emphases clearer to the reader than the sequencing of items similar in length on television news. Degree of attention paid to the news may contribute (Wanta & Hu, 1994), with viewers typically more passive cognitively than readers. The lower cognitive skills of those more oriented toward television as a news source implies that they would be less apt at discerning differences in emphases. Specific elite newspapers such as the *New York Times, Wall Street Journal,* and *Washington Post,* the first of which especially has often served as the independent variable in agenda-setting studies, may have an advantage over television in perceived authoritativeness that would lead news consumers to take their coverage more seriously. Readers may mull, selectively attend, and set their own pace; viewers must accept the dictates of the newscast. Certainly when television influences the agenda it is precisely when it overcomes these factors by the extensiveness and intensity of coverage.

Recently, attention has turned to the influences on media coverage, or how the media's agenda is set, and intermedia agenda setting in which consonance across media leads exposure to varied news outlets collectively to influence judgments of salience (Dearing & Rogers, 1996). Data increasingly point to "a high degree of similarity" among different media (p. 33). There are four distinct factors. There are the real-world events and clues to which the media and consumers of the news both respond. They do so differentially, however, because media have wide nets and many indirect sources that will converge toward a common vision much as the means produced by repeated sampling cluster closely about a central tendency, whereas direct personal experience is comparatively very limited and impressions more idiosyncratic. These are assessed similarly by all news media using universal news values. Those that involve very prominent institutions and entities, such as the White House or the government of Israel, are assured of coverage in all media. Competition leads the media to match coverage on less prominent issues to preclude one or another outlet gaining greater favor or repute among consumers. Certain elite media, such as the *New York Times,* serve as guides for other media; the major television news organizations function similarly when they break a story. Lesser media will play the same role when the story is big; everybody in Los Angeles at one time or another was the media leader in setting their agenda during the O.J. Simpson criminal trial.

For example, Neuman (1990) examined coverage of 10 topics for periods ranging from 5 to 27 years, with 7 topics in the 13- to 27-year range, in the *New York Times, Reader's Guide to Periodical Literature* (representing all magazines), and the three networks (ABC, CBS, and NBC). Amount of coverage for all three types of media was quite similar; so much so that discrepancies between the two print sources did not receive even a passing comment and for the years (on the average, about 8) for which television data were available "the TV agenda generally corresponded quite closely with the other media" (p. 166) with only an occasional divergence.

Williams, Shapiro, and Cutbirth (1983) examined newscasts of the three major networks and front-page stories and editorials in a central Illinois daily newspaper for 47 days during the 1980 presidential election campaign. They also surveyed a random sample of 356 local respondents who were asked, "When talking to others, what is the most important presidential campaign issue?" News items were divided into "campaign agendas" in which a link was made between issues and one of the two major candidates, Reagan or Carter, and "noncampaign agendas" in which no such link occurred.

Campaign and noncampaign coverage on ABC, NBC, and CBS were much the same. Network and newspaper coverage overlapped about half the time. For each of the three networks, amount of coverage was significantly associated with public assessment of importance of issues, and for campaign agendas the relationship held for both candidates. In this instance, the associations were stronger for television than for the newspaper, probably because the networks were more in accord with other prominent media nationally as well as being more prestigious and interesting than a modest circulation central Illinois daily.

Despite the high similarity among media in coverage, we nevertheless would expect some differences in the saliences assigned by those who attend primarily to one medium or outlet rather than another. This is because the very process by which importance is imputed to an issue or topic by media coverage designates the emphases of the media as influencing the impressions of readers and viewers, and media (with their differing essential characteristics) and outlets (with news policies intended to satisfy their particular audiences) will not always be the same in these emphases.

The interplay among the president, the media, and the public has become the focus of recent attention. Wanta (1992; Wanta & Foote, 1994) investigated the impact of the president on the agenda of both the media and the public. Wanta collated data from 34 polls from 1970 to 1988 that asked nationally representative samples to name the number one problem facing the country. Policy statements and speeches made by the president in the 4 weeks before each poll and 4 weeks after were analyzed. The authors also examined the coverage of *CBS Evening News* and front page stories from the *New York Times* during the same period. The principle measure was the lagged correlation between a prior and subsequent agenda—that is, the predictability of a later agenda by another entity's prior emphases.

Results show the relationship between the presidential agenda and the media agenda fluctuates wildly, with correlation coefficients ranging from .02 to .95 (Table 6.2). No substantial differences emerged regarding the influence of the president's agenda on each medium. Nor was there a resounding result favoring one institution's influence on the other. The evidence for presidential influence on the *New York Times* was equal to that for the influence of the *New York Times* on the president's agenda. Although the president appeared slightly more likely to influence CBS news than to have CBS news influence him, the difference was quite small. No clear direction emerged when comparing the public agenda directly to the president's agenda, with 62% of the measures suggesting presidential influence on the public and 65% suggesting public influence on the president. Similar results emerged from the comparison of the influence of the

TABLE 6.2   Presidential, News Media, and Public Agendas

Percent correlations significant at $p < .05$ when prior agenda of one source
is used to predict subsequent agenda of second party

President	President → *New York Times*	*New York Times* → President	President → CBS	CBS → President
Nixon	50	63	25	0
Ford	80	100	80	80
Carter	50	25	38	13
Reagan	77	77	69	54
Overall	65	65	60	40

President	President → Public	Public → President	*New York Times* → Public	Public → *New York Times*
Nixon	50	75	75	75
Ford	40	40	100	60
Carter	63	50	88	100
Reagan	77	77	100	69
Overall	62	65		76

President	CBS → Public	Public → CBS
Nixon	50	75
Ford	100	80
Carter	88	100
Reagan	69	54
Overall	83	83

Statistical control for association with other party: President as control*

President	*New York Times* → Public	Public → *New York Times*	CBS → Public	Public → CBS	Earlier Coverage as Control	
					Public → *New York Times*	Public → CBS
Nixon	63	75	50	50	25	50
Ford	60	20	60	40	0	0
Carter	50	25	50	88	13	25
Reagan	15	8	23	23	8	8
Overall	41	29	47	53	12	23

* Contribution of President or earlier coverage by same media statistically eliminated.

Adapted from "The Influence of the President on the News Media and Public Agendas," by W. Wanta, 1992, *Mass Communication Review, 19*(1/2), pp. 14–21.

media on public opinion and the influence of public opinion on the media; there was modest evidence that the public exerted less influence on the *New York Times* than on *CBS News.*

The media, public, and presidential agendas on the whole were very much intertwined. A topic that receives attention by one of these is likely to be adopted by the other two as well. Lang and Lang (1983) coined the term "agenda-building" to describe the cycle in which the president, media, and public jointly develop what becomes a common agenda. Coverage of an issue by the media or public concern can lead to the president responding. That, in turn, receives media attention, and thus reinforces the public agenda. The president similarly may initiate the sequence. Current issues are eventually replaced by new ones, which begins the cycle again.

Wanta and Foote (1994) investigated the issues through which presidents are most likely to have an impact on media coverage. The authors analyzed ABC, CBS, and NBC news stories in the first 80 days of the Bush administration. Significant associations emerged between the topics addressed by the president and topics covered in network news for international issues, social problems (including education, the environment, poverty, and crime), and social issues (such as abortion, gun control, patriotism/flag burning, and censorship). There was no such association on the topic of the economy, perhaps because there are several other major factors—the stock market, inflation, trade balances, federal economic indices, the Federal Reserve Board—that influence coverage. Changes in the presidential agenda and television news agenda often occurred simultaneously, documenting immediate responsiveness by the networks to the stressing of an issue by the president. For international crises and patriotism/flag burning, two issues emphasized by the president, results indicate President Bush influenced television coverage. For social issues, such as crime, results suggest the president may have allowed news coverage to influence him. These data hint at a role for issue seizure—the president had the greatest influence for topics otherwise less covered by the media. Both the president and the media—television in this instance, but the sameness of presidential coverage across media implies that newspapers would register similarly—initiated the process by which issues were placed on the public's agenda.

Influences on the evaluative beliefs or attitudes of news audience members, or "what to think" in Cohen's (1963) terms, have been recorded regularly and often, although less frequently and therefore are less likely than the imputation of importance. For instance, in addition to enhancing the standing of nuclear issues, Robinson and colleagues (Robinson, Chivian, & Tudge, 1989) found news exposure was associated with worry or concern in surveys of large probability samples of adolescents in both the United States and the former Soviet Union. Similarly, exposure to local television news stories regarding crime was associated with greater support for punitive crime policies in a Madison, Wisconsin probability sample (McLeod et al., 1996).

There is increasing evidence that confining the effects of news media to telling the public "what to think about" underestimates their power. Page and Shapiro (1992) concluded that television coverage of foreign policy issues over a 15-year period had effects that went well beyond their importance rankings, with the emphases of coverage consistently preceding shifts toward greater or lesser support for policies. Jordan and Page (1992) recorded foreign policy preferences of a representative national sample that drew not only on the remarks in newscasts of a popular president and an opposition party spokesman but also on the statements of television commentators. Similarly, Iyengar and Simon (1993) found that the attention of the big three networks to the Gulf War was correlated with the proportion in representative national samples naming the conflict as the nation's most important problem and the weight respondents placed on the conflict when evaluating President Bush. Furthermore, those reporting higher levels of exposure to television news, which emphasized military options, scored higher in support for military rather than diplomatic solutions.

Galician and Vestre (1987) present data indicating that bad news in local television newscasts may increase negative perceptions of the community among viewers. This is an example of the emphases of the media elevating a mood and shaping opinion without giving direction or focus to these responses.

Iyengar and colleagues (Iyengar, 1991; Iyengar & Kinder, 1987a, 1987b) have contributed the concept of priming. In the context of public affairs, priming refers to the introduction of topics or issues in connection with political figures, such as a president, that then serve as bases for their evaluation. For any one figure, there will be several and possibly many such topics and issues. All are unlikely to lead to equally favorable evaluations. There will have been successes and failures, and positions that draw greater or lesser degrees of approval. Priming, in agenda-setting terms, makes salient one or another of a range of issues and topics that affect the evaluation of the political figure—and, by analogy, of parties, countries, and other entities. This phenomenon, in which evaluation varies in accord with the context in which a person or other entity is placed by the media (because of the referents primed or brought to mind by that context), has been repeatedly demonstrated in experiments and confirmed in surveys; the weight given to the Gulf Crisis in evaluating Bush in the Iyengar and Simon (1994) survey is an example. Pan and Kosicki (1997) found that President Bush's approval ratings were closely tied to changes in the salience of two issues, the Gulf War and economic recession. Education, political interest, and political participation are three other personal attributes identified in Willnat's (1997) recent review as increasing the likelihood that evaluations will shift in response to such contextual factors, so that it is among the politically active and informed that priming effects most often occur. This is because it is precisely such persons who will have the background information from which the necessary connections and inferences will derive.

The related concept of framing (Gitlin, 1980) operates analogously. Framing refers to the angle, theme, or justification for coverage—the verbal and visual cast that gives a topic or event its predominant character. Frames may vary for the same subject matter. In agenda-setting terms, framing makes a particular perspective or interpretation more salient. These then play a role in shaping evaluative opinion; the public acceptance of a military response in the same Iyengar and Simon survey is an example. Framing has been combined with the imputation of importance to form what has been termed "second-level agenda setting" in which specific attributes of an issue become more salient to the public through the emphases found in news frames (Ghanem, 1997; Rhee, 1997; Takeshita, 1997).

Conceptually, priming and framing are subspecies of agenda-setting effects that influence public evaluation and interpretation beyond the imputation of importance. They coexist despite their similar function in providing cues for opinion formation because each was developed in different scholarly contexts—the former, in the investigation of how television news influences evaluations of politicians (Iyengar & Kinder, 1987a); the latter, in the study of news media portrayal of radical political dissent (Gitlin, 1980).

In addition to effects on salience generally and specifically on attributes that affect evaluative opinions, Shaw and Martin (1992) point to a third, more indirect media effect. The authors found, in a survey of North Carolina residents, that greater exposure to television news also was associated with heightened group consensus on public concerns so that distinctions based on gender, race, age, and level of education are reduced. This is similar to the findings of Gerbner and colleagues (Gerbner, Gross, Morgan, & Signorielli, 1980, 1984) that differences in political opinions associated with these same demographic variables are reduced among those who view more television. Whether one wishes to attribute this outcome to agenda setting or "cultivation" (Gerbner's preferred concept for the homogenizing—or in his terms "mainstreaming"— influence of exposure to a common set of mass media symbols) is moot; so, too, is whether it should be construed as conformity, social integration, or consensus.

These effects of the media on salience, on priming, and in framing unobtrusively influence the evaluations of politicians, parties, and policies and are concretely expressed in electoral outcomes. They affect the formulation and shape of public opinion not only in the imputation of importance but also in regard to what should be thought about important things (McCombs & Shaw, 1993). The latter prospers through priming, framing, and the salience accorded attributes of topics, issues, and persons that govern their evaluation.

However, it would be naive to expect that news coverage will invariably affect behavior even when it may appear obvious that a story has implications for the welfare of audience members. For example, Wei (1993) found that although audience members were persuaded to view an impending earthquake as dangerous and potentially harmful after news exposure, neither exposure to local television news nor to local newspapers was associated with an increase in the purchase of earthquake insurance. In a somewhat similar circumstance, Spencer and colleagues (Spencer, Seydlitz, Laska, & Triche, 1992) in contrast found a marked increase in bottled water sales after both television and newspaper exposure to stories regarding health hazards from intruding salt water along the New Orleans coastal area. Television exposure was associated with a more immediate result (again, the spotlight effect), whereas newspaper reading was linked with a slower reaction.

We believe the barriers between the content of the news and its behavioral influence are better understood with an explication of the properties of the news. We see two dimensions—relevance to the consumer and magnitude of the occurrence that impact whether behavioral effects will occur.

1. *Distant events*—news that implies no specific behavior, such as foreign wars, Peruvian earthquakes, or a schoolyard shooting in another community. Such reports nevertheless may alter impressions of the goodness or meanness, dangers or security, or rate of change of contemporary life, and will be subject to the moral interpretations imposed by consumers of the news.

2. *Proximate opportunities and threats*—news that could translate into specific actions, such as the lowering of mortgage rates, flu epidemics, or a rash of gold chain snatchings on the New York subway. These reports often will be ignored as in the case of earthquake insurance in the Wei study, sometimes because of external barriers, such as cost, inconvenience, ignorance of sources, or unavailability of options. They also may be ignored to some degree because of denial (Rodin, 1985), possibly attributable in part to the very vividness and force of coverage—and especially television coverage—as well as the difficulty of overcoming such barriers.

3. *Genuine risks*—clear warnings about immediate dangers: hurricanes, blizzards, supermarket and pharmacy recalls. Bottled water purchase in the study of Spencer and colleagues is an example, and one for which external barriers would be largely absent. However, even here risks that are not imminent and specific probably will be ignored (a serial killer is heinous and frightening, and the phenomenon is unnerving, but for most readers and viewers will not be conceived of as a threat).

4. *Public affairs*—social and political information that will translate for some into shifts in opinion and voting intentions. Salience heightens the degree

to which an issue is viewed as requiring resolution, and as options are reviewed the salience attached to them in turn will affect their likelihood of adoption. Voting is the concrete expression of public opinion and, outside of violent protests, its most dramatic and visible expression. Nevertheless, public opinion alone sets priorities for and limitations on political figures who are unlikely to ignore apparent public mandates or adopt options that fall outside the boundaries of public acceptance. In these respects, opinion formation is an important behavioral consequence. For example, the president sometimes adjusts his agenda to fit that of the public with the media closely following.

Except occasionally for (2) and (3), effects generally will be modest because the benefit to the viewer or reader for reaching a decision on what might be done will be minute. In the cases of both (1) and (4), coverage is likely to emphasize personalities and the dramatic, which provides an immediate benefit in entertaining the audience, with the result being that understanding of the larger social context will be minimal so that information necessary for effective action will be absent (Downs, 1957; Hamilton, 1998). Even in the cases of (2) and (3), threats that are acute may be ignored because of the psychological discomforts or material difficulties of taking effective action.

We identify six principal attributes of agenda setting (Table 6.1). The first is the considerable consonance among the media in what is covered. The second is the fundamental role of audience interest, which leads the media to depart from real-world indicators of the significance of an issue or topic in catering to that interest. The third is the rise and fall of issues on the public agenda as a consequence of media attention rather than real-world indicators of urgency or importance. The fourth is the construction by individuals of salience based on what is reported and what was experienced, with the result that firsthand knowledge plays only a partial and usually small role. The fifth is the occasional intrusive role of a triggering occurrence, such as attention by the White House, coverage by the *New York Times,* or an event that moves a topic into the spotlight (such as the death of Rock Hudson in the case of AIDS). Finally, there is the generic exclusion of certain topics from extended coverage and thereby from the public agenda, such as the environment and science, unless they become the beneficiary of a triggering event like the Exxon *Valdez* oil spill in Alaska's Price William Sound in 1989.

We conclude that decisions of news personnel about coverage have the capability to affect not only the importance assigned to topics but also the disposition—attitude and judgment—of topics, issues, and persons. The way in which media assemble an agenda, frame information, and induce priming in the words of McCombs and Shaw (1993) "not only tell us what to think about, but also how to think about it, and consequently, what to think" (p. 65).

III. DEMOCRACY AND THE MEDIA

We conclude on a more speculative note, because we look to the future as well as draw on past data. The American political system is stratified with intense participation by a few and passing interest by the great majority (Almond & Verba, 1989a, 1989b; Berelson et al., 1954; Neuman, 1986). There is passive delegation to a select few of the responsibility to engage in continuing active conflict, and thereby to advance the resolution of political issues. The majority takes active part only when it is time to vote. Despite occasional bitter rhetoric, this system results in comparative tranquility, facilitates cooperation, and enhances tolerance because it is not marked by persisting, deep ideological divisions. However, it assigns a huge role to the mass media by which the great majority is mobilized to participate at election time and provided with sufficient knowledge to do so to their satisfaction. We focus on three social processes— citizen participation, political socialization, and the unobtrusive but concrete influence of the media in the resolution of political controversies and conflicts.

A. CITIZEN PARTICIPATION

Fewer than 50% of those eligible have voted in several recent presidential elections, with the turnout of 50.8% in the 1992 Bush–Clinton–Perot race (*Statistical Abstracts,* 1997) the first sizable disruption of the trend toward declining participation since 1960. This is the lowest rate of turnout among 28 countries that regularly hold elections. Gerbner and colleagues (Gerbner et al., 1984) observe that "the mass media have usually been blamed for the apparently increasing 'rootlessness' of the electorate and its abandonment of traditional voting patterns" (p. 283). Certainly the balanced emphases of the media, and particularly television, often give the impression that the two major party contenders are in many ways fairly similar and equally reputable. We have seen that this is one of the functions of televised presidential debates. Scandals and questionable maneuverings that become embedded in social memory with such labels as Watergate and Iran-gate conceivably have left some disenchanted (Schudson, 1992), whereas the continual portrayal on television of politics as usual involving the self-interests of parties and politicians may contribute to cynicism (Cappella & Jamieson, 1997). The increasing emphasis by the media on the negative in presidential campaign coverage may have contributed to skepticism about the integrity, honesty, and sincerity of politicians (Patterson, 1993). Self-descriptive labels such as liberal, moderate, and conservative have remained fairly stable in use (Bower, 1973, 1985; Smith et al., 1997), whereas party identification and satisfaction with the parties have declined (Holbrook, 1996; Nie, Verba & Petrocik, 1976). Television not only has become a major

factor in presidential campaigns at all levels through both paid-for announcements and news coverage, but the role of the medium in presidential contests
compared to that of the candidates and parties has grown more prominent.
These are all factors that might adversely affect participation.

We are certainly not impressed with the usual interpretation—exemplified
in *Television and Human Behavior* (Comstock et al., 1978)—given to the well-
known pretelevision-era election data of Berelson and colleagues (1954). They
measured interest and support for the presidential candidates before and after
the campaign, and because greater media use during the campaign was associated with higher levels of interest and support at the end of the campaign, concluded that the media facilitated interest and support. Our problem is not with
the likely truth of this opinion, but with the paradigm. It treats the variables of
interest and support as if they were experimental manipulations imposed on
otherwise alike populations. In fact, we can think of no reason for lower media
use during the campaign other than prior declines in interest and support.

Bédy (1996) found that total amount of television viewing was associated
with a diminished tendency to vote in presidential elections. In an analysis of
nationally representative data from 1976 through 1984, a significant, negative
correlation emerged among data pooled for the three elections between amount
of television viewing and whether respondents voted. When the data were analyzed by election, the relationship remained significant for two of the three and
approached significance in the third (1976 and 1984 elections, $p < .05$; 1980
election, $p < .10$) when controlling for numerous variables including demographics, membership in organizations, newspaper exposure, confidence in
public institutions such as business and government, anomie, and perceived
political efficacy.

The robustness of the relationship to the control of so many variables—
demographics as major predictors of viewing by themselves would have been
impressive, but this set also includes social contact with others and various
beliefs that might affect both viewing and voting—makes it clear that it is no
artifact. We do not see television as the cause in a villainous sense; our interpretation is that television as one of three major components of time use after
sleep and work or school (Chapter 3) is what people do when time is not otherwise occupied. In this case, apathetic nonvoters apparently have plenty of
time available.

Putnam (1995), of course, holds television responsible for a decline in civic
and organizational participation at all levels of American life. A famous precursor was the "narcoticizing dysfunction" proposed several decades earlier by
Lazarsfeld and Merton (1971) in which public absorption in the news and
entertainment offered by the mass media substituted for and essentially suppressed constructive thought and action in regard to social issues.

Our perspective is quite different, although we agree that more than 50 years of empirical examination of the relationships between use of the mass media and political participation present a number of puzzles (Kinder & Sears, 1985; Kraus & Davis, 1976). The biggest in the eyes of many is the failure of the data in the past to point consistently toward the building of interest and support that translates into voter turnout on election day. This would seem an at least likely and possibly inevitable consequence of attention to the media. However, the sole consistent predictor of voting and other measures of participation in the nine presidential contests beginning with the 1940 election encompassed by the analyses of Kraus and Davis (1976) has been socioeconomic status, with education the most important component.

An extraordinary number of discussions of this question have been of the walk-in-the-garden variety, with the guide identifying this theory, that concept, or these findings before awkwardly halting before the precipice of a conclusion. We diligently have sought a discernible pattern, and we believe that a coherent one based on empirical evidence emerges when three major factors are given sufficient weight. These are differences in the characteristics of those drawn to the various mass media, differences in the role of the media at different times and various levels of the electoral process, and changes over time in the use of the media.

Our principal measure of participation is voting, but we include interest in the campaign, support for a candidate, and intention to vote because they are predictors of voting (Patterson & McClure, 1976). We also include more personally demanding activities such as circulating a petition, attending a meeting, or contributing money because those who engage in them also are likely to vote.

Our principal sources of data are large-scale television-era voting studies of six presidential elections with samples representing many thousands that match media exposure against participation. The earliest represented is the 1972 contest between McGovern and Nixon (Mendelsohn & O'Keefe, 1976); the most recent is the Clinton–Dole 1996 race (Domke et al., 1997). In between are the elections of 1976 (Lucas & Adams, 1977; Patterson, 1980) and 1984, 1988, and 1992 (Holbrook, 1996). We will also draw on data from samples of several hundred from the primaries (Kennamer, 1990; Smith & Ferguson, 1990), other elections (Kennamer, 1987), and between elections (Boyd, 1996), as well as our earlier analyses of the effects of political advertising and news coverage.

Those who are alienated—in the anomic sense of feeling out of place, uncared for, and skeptical of the altruism of officials and trustworthiness of others—are particularly likely to use the media (Kraus & Davis, 1976). However, they focus particularly on entertainment and undemanding content and are principally users of television and television-like print media (McLeod, Ward, & Tancill, 1965). They are largely uninterested in the everyday politics of the major parties and the electoral process, although they may be drawn to candidates or movements representing dissatisfaction with political institutions (Altemeyer, 1998; Kinder & Sears, 1985; Kraus & Davis, 1976). These persons are not ordinarily part of the news audience, but their extensive consumption of television sometimes will place them among viewers of the news and political coverage and invariably will expose them to political commercials. They are not narcoticized by the media but motivated by a search for narcoticization, and their inferential role is to confound attempts to relate media use to participation by a correlation between use and alienation.

Others suggest that, rather than narcoticizing the public, the media contribute to cynicism or distrust. Cappella and Jamieson (1997) proposed that news frames focusing on political strategies and the use of issues to gain public support imply self-interest rather than public service, and thereby promote cynicism that may affect a wide range of public attitudes. They suggest that although cynicism about the government used to be associated with the belief that the media were sources of truth in political affairs (Sniderman, 1972), "the public now tends to see the media as part of the problem, not part of the solution" (p. 227). Chan (1997), using National Election Study data, provides some empirical support by showing that attention to television campaign coverage was associated with a diminished trust in government.

The mass media also do not function alike, and their functioning differs by electoral level and stage of the campaign. Newspapers are the primary sources of information about local and state politics and elections, and their use is a predictor of participation in those contests (Kennamer, 1987). Local television stations often do not give extensive attention to these races, so not much should be expected from viewing their newscasts. Television is conceived of by the public as a major source of national news (Bogart, 1989), and as early as 1972 was named by a majority of voters as their major source of information about the presidential campaign (Mendelsohn & O'Keefe, 1976). In the subsequent 1976 election, use of network news was recorded as having a small effect on knowledge and support but less than that of newspaper reading (Patterson, 1980). We also find that television's influence is greatest during the primaries when images begin to form, during the conventions when the candidates appear on the screen cloaked in victory, and during the first debate (Holbrook, 1996; Patterson, 1980) when new knowledge about issues joins the formation of images (Hollander, 1993; Sears & Chaffee, 1979), although political commercials may have a strong influence in the final stages of a campaign on the undecided and uncertain (Bowen, 1994).

The characteristics of viewers enter again. Those with greater initial interest pay more attention to the media and this leads to greater knowledge acquisition. However, a paradox occurs in the coverage of presidential debates, with interest inversely associated with learning (Patterson, 1980). Although at first ominously puzzling, this is almost certainly explained by interest itself. Those with greater interest attend to the debates with greater prior knowledge, so there is less possibility for learning.

Use of mass media also has changed dramatically. The thinking about media and voting has been strongly influenced by the so-called "classic" studies (Kraus & Davis, 1976) of the elections of 1940, 1944, and 1952 (Berelson et al., 1954; Campbell, Gurin, & Miller, 1954) before television became common as a household appliance. These are now out of date (Graber, 1989a) because the real-world equivalents of so many key concepts have changed in frequency or attributes—undecided and leaning voters, party allegiance, use of mass media. Time spent reading newspapers has declined significantly and television has become increasingly prominent as a source of news. In terms of frequency of use, newspapers remain predominant, but the fact that the term news connotes television because of its focus on big events implies that its role in covering national politics is underrepresented by measures of frequency of exposure. This has been accompanied by a more forceful intrusion of the television medium in the coverage of political campaigns (Patterson, 1996), as exemplified by the diminution of sound bites.

The consequence has been that television has brought about a slight but important reduction in the role of motive in access to political information (Chaffee & Frank, 1996). People are much more likely to become accidental viewers of political television coverage and commercials than to accidentally encounter such material in newspapers or magazines. Exposure to news coverage has come to predict knowledge of candidates and issues during the campaign (Chaffee et al., 1994; Zhao & Chaffee, 1995), so that this accidental viewing implies a wider dissemination of political information although the knowledge gains of such viewers would be much less than the gains for those attending with interest and cognitive schema well attuned to the political events.

Nevertheless, motive remains the key concept. We construe it as broadly embodying political efficacy, or the belief that participation and voting matter; prior knowledge, which denotes schema by which political information can be processed; and interest, which would heighten attention to political news. Motive is the prerequisite to media use for political information, and the specific motive for using the media to this end, such as guidance about whom to vote for or following an exciting campaign, are stronger predictors of such outcomes as knowledge, participation, and continuing interest than is media exposure (McLeod & Becker, 1974).

In our judgment, data collected over six decades beginning with the classic election studies consistently support such a view. We think the expectation that such media use would importantly enhance motive is not insightful. We believe media should be construed as serving motive, as exemplified by the clear-cut evidence on public understanding (knowledge acquisition), agenda setting (imputed importance), and evaluative opinions (what to think).

We reject the view that mass media—and for the moment suspend consideration of differences among the media—suppress political participation. If so, we should find negative associations between use of news media in election campaigns and participation. We do not.

The recent data from the five presidential contests we examined in fact support the view that the news media facilitate participation. The model of Domke and colleagues (1997) indicates that voter support for both Clinton and Dole fluctuated with media coverage, with Clinton benefiting to a much greater degree. Similarly, the three-election data (1984, 1988, 1992) of Holbrook (1996) indicate that shifts in support followed the favorability of events conveyed to the public by the media. In the 1972 election data of Mendelsohn and O'Keefe (1976), substantial proportions of voters thought the media figured in their decisions, and participation in the campaign was a correlate of both attention to the news generally and dependence on television for political information. Bartels (1993) confined his analysis of the 1980 campaign to outcomes on public understanding (as measured by image and issues) but he did record relationships indicating that both newspapers and particularly television contributed to beliefs and perceptions of voters that plausibly would enter into decisions about whether and for whom to vote.

As for differences among the media, we do find in the past that newspapers consistently have been a superior predictor of participation at both the local and national levels (Kennamer, 1987; Kraus & Davis, 1976; Patterson, 1980). However, the role of television in national campaigns has grown larger, and the evidence in regard to issue knowledge for the debates is convincing that television makes a substantial contribution. The most recent data from the elections of 1980, 1984, 1988, 1992, and 1996 identify considerable learning from the mass media coverage, where television has become increasingly prominent, about the campaign in progress (Bartels, 1993; Chaffee & Frank, 1996; Domke et al., 1997; Holbrook, 1996).

Six additional sets of data have been particularly helpful. Television was in almost every home and well into its transitional stage when these data were collected so they represent contemporary circumstances, samples are sizable (between about 350 and 600), and they encompass a wide variety of electoral situations. Pinkleton, Austin, and Fortman (1998) found that among about 600 Washington voters just before the November 1996 presidential election, negativism toward media coverage was associated with *lower* use of the media for political information, whereas use of the media for such information was associated with both *higher* levels of perceived personal political efficacy and a greater likelihood of voting. Smith and Ferguson (1990) found that among about 400 Toledo voters before the Iowa caucus those more *partisan* paid greater attention to television coverage and independents with high interest became *particularly likely* to vote if they followed the campaign on television. Kennamer (1990) similarly found that among about 450 Richmond, Virginia voters independents were more likely to vote in the general election if they had followed the campaign *on television,* although for voters generally newspaper reading was a more consistent predictor of voting. Earlier, Kennamer (1987) had found that among about 350 voters following the coverage of a Virginia gubernatorial race on television *increased* the likelihood of voting. Drew and Weaver (1998) found that among about 550 Indiana voters in the 1996 presidential election *interest* was associated with following the campaign in the newspapers, by radio, and on television talk shows, although in these data there was no association between any media variable and intention to vote. (A possible explanation is the unusually low levels of public interest in the campaign recorded by the authors, which would have made the act of voting less open to influence by exciting and arousing campaign events and their media coverage than by commitment to taking part in the political process).

These data are clearly supportive of our two major conclusions that neither television news viewing nor newspaper reading are inversely associated with political participation and that the news media serve positively the motives of interested voters. They also point to those without party allegiance, independents, as likely to find the news media most useful. Boyd (1996) extends these conclusions to more demanding forms of participation such as attending meetings and contributing money. Among about 460 Dane County, Wisconsin adults, the viewing of both local and national public affairs coverage was associated with such participation and for a wider range of activities for local than for national news (probably because the additional activities, circulating petitions and working with others, are more readily available and more efficacious in regard to local politics). Thus, the data across a wide range of outcomes fail to support the dire speculations about the suppressive role of the mass media.

B. POLITICAL SOCIALIZATION

Political socialization is the process by which people learn about the political system and the possibilities for participation. It encompasses thoughts, attitudes, and behavior (Atkin, 1981). The decline in party allegiance has greatly enlarged the role of the mass media in this form of socialization (Devries & Tarrance, 1972; Nie, Petrocik, & Verba, 1976). One consequence of this decline has been the volatility of the electorate so recently exemplified by the showing of Perot in 1992, the frequent party division between occupancy of the White House and dominance in Congress, and the reelection of Bill Clinton in 1996 after precampaign analyses (Roberts, 1995) concluded he had scant hope. An equally important consequence has been the sharp diminishment of what was once one of the principal roles of the family—the inculcation of strong political preferences for one or another party (Kraus & Davis, 1976).

We begin with the exposure of children and teenagers to public affairs coverage. Then we turn to the role of parents, and finally to the contributions of the media.

We saw that exposure of children and teenagers to television news is surprisingly substantial (Chapter 3). In a gigantic national sample (Anderson, Mead, & Sullivan, 1986) of 100,000 (Table 6.3), 41% of 4th graders, 45% of 8th graders, and 49% of 11th graders said they viewed daily, whereas Nielsen estimates that the ratings for national news among children 2–11 and teenagers 12–17 in age are fully three-fourths and one-half, respectively, of those for adults (Comstock, 1991a).

Television is overwhelmingly the medium preferred by young persons for following public affairs (Simon & Merrill, 1997) and the majority of children and teenagers believe they get most of their news from television (Hollander, 1971; Tolley, 1973). They are probably correct in the latter perception, for unlike adults they do not read newspapers with anywhere near the frequency with which they are exposed to television news (Meadowcroft, 1986) and interpersonal conversations about political events, a major source for adults (Robinson & Levy, 1986a), would be less frequent among young persons.

The viewing environment established by parents makes a great difference. Parents provide the model for the use of news media. Children and teenagers often follow the example of their parents in the use of newspapers and television news (Comstock, 1991a; Schramm et al., 1961). For children, and especially young children, news exposure is largely the consequence of their being in the room where the parents have the set tuned to the news. The high percentages-for viewing by 8th and 11th graders become very impressive when the absence of this accidental exposure is acknowledged and the figures are placed in the

TABLE 6.3   Survey of News Viewing by Children and Teenagers

Grade	Frequency of viewing by those who say they view (percent)			
	Daily	Weekly	Monthly or less	Never
4	41	25	11	24
8	45	34	11	10
11	49	33	13	5

Sample size (N) = 100,000

Adapted from "Television: What Do National Assessment Tests Tell Us?" by B. Anderson, N. Mead, and S. Sullivan, 1986, Princeton, NJ: Educational Testing Service.

context of generally lower consumption of television. Many of these young viewers have become motivated consumers of television news. Television will be a particularly important source of political information for them because newspaper readership has decreased not only among the young but also among the younger adults who are their parents (Bogart, 1989; Robinson & Godbey, 1996). Thus, newspaper use will be inhibited by both the norms of their cohort and the example of their parents.

Parents also influence attention to the coverage of public affairs by the climate of expression they create, both generically and topically. When the expression of opinion and exchange of viewpoints rather than harmony and the avoidance of controversy are the operating motif of family interchange, the viewing of news and the reading of newspapers by young persons is greater (Chaffee, McLeod, & Wackman, 1973). In those circumstances, civic concerns come to occupy a more prominent place and young persons spend comparatively less time viewing television entertainment. When parents express interest in a specific topic in the news, young persons become more likely to pay attention to its coverage (Tolley, 1973).

Historically, one of the major effects of television has been to make the events of the day more prominent to young persons. What might have been ignored in a world of print and radio becomes inescapable. The data of Cairns, Hunter, and Herring (1980) present a telling example. When asked to make up stories, young persons age 10–13 whose news programming included reports from Northern Ireland included many more incidents with bombs. Similarly, Reitzes and White (1982) found that 6th and 8th graders twice as frequently concocted negative outcomes when inventing endings for news stories than when inventing them for entertainment programs. Thus, television often makes the news a particularly malevolent mirror of life for the young.

A subtle rivalry transpires between parents and the mass media. When parents express an opinion clearly on a controversial topic, their children are more likely to agree with them than with the position they perceive is taken by a prominent television news personality (Tolley, 1973). However, many topics are not particularly controversial and opinions are not always clearly voiced. More than 30 years ago, Jennings and Niemi (1968) found in a sample of more than 1500 high school seniors that media exposure was a stronger predictor of a variety of later political beliefs than parental views, with the sole instance of a reversal party allegiance—an issue akin to an ongoing controversy. Twenty years later, with party allegiance declining, Dennis (1986) found that the only predictors of describing oneself as an independent among several hundred 10- to 17-year-olds was exposure to television news and newspapers and whether their parents labeled themselves as independents. The pattern observable for more than three decades, then, is one of considerable influence for television except for views deeply held and clearly voiced by parents.

TABLE 6.4   Media Exposure and Political Knowledge and Behavior among
7th and 10th Graders

	Correlation coefficients				
	Knowledge			Behavior	
Media exposure	Overall	Current events	Fundamental	Interpersonal discussion	Anticipated participation
Broadcast	.52[c]	.53[a]	.35[a]	.54[b]	.46[b]
Print	.43[c]	.36	.36	.52[d]	.65[d]

Sample size (N) = 280
Coefficients with common subscripts differ at $p < .05$
 Adapted from "Mass Communication and Political Socialization: Specifying the Effects," by
G. M. Garramone and C. K. Atkin, 1986, *Public Opinion Quarterly, 50*(1), pp. 76–86.

Comprehensive contemporary evidence is provided by Garramone and
Atkin (1986). They examined television, radio, newspapers, and news magazines as sources of political information among public school students in seventh and tenth grades in two Midwestern cities. Television and print functioned
somewhat differently (Table 6.4). Television news exposure was correlated with
both knowledge of current events and fundamental knowledge, involving ideology, philosophy, and history of politics, but the association with current
events knowledge was significantly larger. Correlations for news magazines and
newspapers were similar in size, suggesting a consistent impact of print. Overall, the association with knowledge was significantly greater for television because of the strong influence on current events, and among the younger respondents only television news exposure remained a significant predictor of
knowledge after controlling for socioeconomic status, gender, grade level, and
scholarly orientation.
    The motivated use of the mass media for political information emerges in
the early teenage years, as exemplified by increased use of news media and the
appearance of gender differences (Owen & Dennis, 1992). Males come to use
news media somewhat earlier and more frequently, including various forms of
televised public affairs programming, and interest and knowledge become more
highly correlated with media use; females come to attend more to television for
political information. This parallels the adult pattern in which males use news
media more but females express a greater preference for television as a news
source.
    Television is at the forefront in a number of respects. However, newspapers
reflect more thoughtful involvement, with their use predicting anticipated later
participation in the political process, whereas following politics on television
finds immediate gratification in conversations (Garramone & Atkin, 1986), and

the use of newspapers is more open to an increase by classroom interventions (Chaffee, Moon, & McDevitt, 1996), presumably because television habits are more firmly established.

We see television's accessibility as the foundation of its importance in political socialization. When the civil rights movement increased the electoral participation of Blacks in the 1950s and 1960s, Blacks turned to television to follow politics at a rate almost double that for newspapers (McCombs, 1968). The reason is that use of the medium for a new purpose requires neither additional expenditures nor changes in major norms about media, whereas newly turning to newspapers requires both. Thus, television typically stands as the entry medium for children and teenagers in any involvement in public affairs and in this process has become much more prominent than print.

In conclusion, we offer a paradox. The media, and especially television, have become more important in political socialization. Correlations with knowledge and opinion, as well as interpersonal conversation, are consistently positive; print is somewhat more consistently important for participation. Young people, however, on the whole are less informed and interested in public affairs than they were several decades ago (Comstock, 1991a)—the exceptions are particularly violent events, sports, and social issues that directly affect them by the media. This pattern is plausibly attributed to the large role of television in the news consumption of the young—only very prominent items gain attention, and this derives either from striking properties or entertaining elements (violence, sports) or self-interest.

C. Unobtrusive Role

The news media by their very nature are participants and not spectators when they report on political events. They have an obtrusive role when the investigative pursuit of a particular story or an interview with a presidential candidate has large consequences. This obtrusive role is echoed when attention from the media is a goal in the hijacking of an airplane or the seizure of hostages. In these instances, the media play a strong part in the events they cover.

Less remarked upon but also pervasive is unobtrusive participation by the media. This role is the inevitable result of the application of universal news values. Partisan or ideological bias is often set forth as the necessary condition for the media to influence the events on which it reports. The assumption is that the distortions of coverage will affect what the public thinks and does. The media must favor the Democrats or the Republicans, conservatives or liberals. The evidence on the role of the media in the public's imputation of importance to issues and topics and in political campaigns clearly attests to the power of bias to have such effects, although they are somewhat circumscribed by the critical lens through which some occasionally filter what reaches them in the media, the more frequent discount of the allegations exchanged during a political campaign because of the context of competitive tumult and outcry in which they occur, and the frequent presence of already-held beliefs and opinions that sometimes will be resistant to change.

The flaw in this perspective is not that it proposes media influence but that it posits bias as a necessary condition. More than a half century of empirical inquiry and critical commentary on the performance of the news media assert otherwise. The pursuit of universal news values in the application of gate-keeping is sufficient. The result is a selection of geographical areas, social issues, and political disputes, along with portraits of the participants, and it is this selectivity that establishes the pictures of the world in the minds of people that are the basis for thought and action.

We also believe that the evidence points to dramatic emerging changes. As newspaper readership declines, television becomes more prominent in the agenda-setting process. However, television is a different medium than newspapers. Emphases are somewhat more difficult to discern and the data are clear that effects follow more dramatically from barrages of coverage, spotlighting, and forceful depictions. These effects occur comparatively rapidly; salience will be strongly influenced by television news but the difficulty of discerning emphases means that only a few issues can be affected. The neat ordering of issues in accord with the emphases of the media, and primarily newspapers, as observed in early agenda-setting research (Funkhouser, 1973a, 1973b; McCombs & Shaw, 1972), is likely to become a museum piece. The result will be a two-tier composition—a very few topics to which the public imputes great importance and a brickyard of odd shapes and sizes on which there is little aggregate agreement. Hierarchy will have given way to oligarchy. The limited attention span of television will mean considerable volatility among the handful receiving attention, and the agendas of both the public and politicians will then shift more swiftly as well. Already, there is clear evidence that the length of time that an issue remains prominent on the public agenda is diminishing (McCombs & Zhu, 1995). Issues will take shape at the center of the screen, and whirl away. Politicians will be less bound by public opinion because its fickleness will leave accountability unrewarded. The world will become more exciting, but less manageable.

PART III

Of Time and Content

Proverbs for Paranoids, 3: If they can get you asking the wrong questions, they don't have to worry about answers.
                                        Thomas Pynchon, *Gravity's Rainbow*

We conclude with analyses of the very extensive data on two major questions that have persistently been asked about the effects of television on children and teenagers. Does television have an influence on scholastic achievement? Does the violence in television entertainment affect behavior? Both have been the subject of controversy. Both remain so. In our view, in both cases sufficient evidence has accrued to reach definitive conclusions unlikely to be altered with the passing of time. In one case, we are led to open a Pandora's box that many have thought was well and thoroughly closed. In the other case, quite recent data lead us beyond conclusions that at one time seemed forceful.

CHAPTER 7

Scholastic Performance

I. **Favorable Expectations**
 A. Vocabulary
 B. Interests
 C. Visual Skills
 D. Televised Interventions
II. **Additional Relationships**
 A. Tolerance for Schooling
 B. Imaginative Play and Daydreaming
 C. Creativity
 D. Mental Ability
III. **Viewing and Achievement**
 A. The Relationship
 B. Television Use
IV. **Interpretation**
 A. Interference
 B. Displacement
 C. Three Clusters

The effects of television on scholastic performance and cognitive activity continue to be debated. Several specific outcomes have been hypothesized that would mediate performance, some positively, some negatively (Comstock, 1991a). With regard to the relationship between viewing and achievement, some (Gaddy, 1986; Gortmaker, Salter, Walker, & Dietz, 1990) have concluded that when confounding variables are properly controlled there is no evidence of any association. Others have concluded that achievement declines as viewing increases, but there is disagreement on the causal contribution of viewing (Comstock, 1991a; S. Neuman, 1988). We begin with four topics on which the expectations have been that television would enhance achievement. We then turn to a variety of other relationships where expectations have been less favorable or more mixed and ambiguous. Next we specify the relationship between viewing and achievement, and finally offer our interpretation of the role of television in scholastic performance.

I. FAVORABLE EXPECTATIONS

Our review of specific outcomes that might contribute positively covers vocabulary, interests, visual skills, and televised interventions.

A. VOCABULARY

The contribution of television to the vocabularies of young viewers rests on a paradox. Viewing at the present time does not matter but the existence of television probably does; the role of television is greatest for the words and phrases in which television specializes—brand names, jargon, and references to entertainment—and decays as children grow older. There is also a role for research history: early findings of a large contribution to general vocabulary attributable to viewing have proved invalid because two key points—the emphasis of television on media-related vocabulary and the role of social interaction in the diffusion of any vocabulary presented—went unnoticed.

Schramm, Lyle, and Parker (1961) unambiguously found that the introduction of television increased vocabularies. When they compared children in communities with and without television on a test of general vocabulary, they found that children with television entered the first grade about a year ahead of the others. The results were similar for "timely and topical" terms ("enduring" would have been more prophetic) such as satellite, war, and cancer. Such outcomes were clearer for those high or low in mental ability than for those average. Among 6th and 10th graders, the only evidence of a contribution by television to miscellaneous knowledge was for information about entertainment figures. By the sixth grade, any general vocabulary advantage had disappeared. Yet there is ample evidence that today's children and teenagers learn brand names from television (Adler et al., 1980).

As a consequence, T. M. Williams (1986) and colleagues hypothesized in their three-community natural experiment that the vocabularies of young persons would increase in the community newly receiving television. They employed three widely used measures: the Stanford–Binet (S-B) vocabulary subtest, the vocabulary subscale of the Wechsler Intelligence Scale for Children (WISC), and the Peabody Picture Vocabulary Test (PPVT). Their disappointment was complete. At no grade level and on none of the tests did the data support the hypothesized effect.

A series of studies, including several by Rice and colleagues, introduces program character and quality as factors. One demonstrated that children can acquire new words representing objects and their attributes from a television sequence (Rice & Woodsmall, 1988). This is hardly surprising because children acquire language by listening to others. Other studies suggested that the content of children's programming (Rice, 1983, 1984), which contains words of interest to children, and the verbal interplay that occurs when parents and children view together (Lemish & Rice, 1986) would make television a modern factor in language acquisition and vocabulary building. Another study (Csapo-Sweet, 1997) found that exposure of Hungarian children to *Sesame Street* was associated with significant gains in English vocabulary. The three-community data, however, make it clear that any direct contribution is minute at best. It is no surprise that more recent data examining several hundred children over a period of several years (Anderson et al., 1996; Clifford, Gunter, & McAleer, 1997; Rice et al., 1990; Wright & Huston, 1995) confirm that any contribution of television is confined to educational programming, such as *Sesame Street* or science programs. Viewing of such programming at ages 3 to 5 predicted better performance on the Peabody Picture Vocabulary Test—Revised (PPVT-R). Viewing of animated cartoons did not. Similarly, Selnow and Bettinghaus (1982) report a small negative correlation among preschool children between total amount of viewing and language competency and a positive association between language ability and quality of language in programs viewed.

A little perspective assigns an educationally insignificant role to television viewing. Children acquired language and developed vocabularies before the existence of television. They would do so today in its absence. Educational programming may accelerate the process slightly. There is no reason to believe that viewing in general directly raises the asymptote of eventual performance; that is, greater viewing does not lend itself to superior levels of linguistic ability or larger vocabularies.

Harrison and Williams (1986) point out that the issue is not what television does but how it compares to other alternatives:

> It is possible that television has the potential to have a positive impact. . . . Whether this occurs, however, probably depends on what the child would be doing if she or he were not watching TV. If older children spend some of that time reading, or if younger children are read to (by siblings, parents, baby-sitters), then it becomes a question of which activity is most effective for teaching vocabulary knowledge. (p. 114)

In support of the view that alternative linguistic experiences might be more beneficial, they cite the finding of Meringoff and colleagues (1983) that fanciful language was better recalled by children of preschool age when a story was read from a picture book than when presented in a televised dramatization.

Our conclusions are severalfold. First, television viewing does not contribute to general vocabulary except possibly for the viewing of educational programs. Children's entertainment, such as animated cartoons, has no benefit. Second, children of greater mental ability who would have a better command of language are more likely to choose programs with a higher quality of language, so that although educational programming may teach vocabulary, any positive association between viewing and vocabulary is surely partly and possibly wholly explained by the programs chosen by those of superior skill. Third, any effects of overall viewing are limited to jargon, brands, and entertainment figures (and such specialized vocabulary eludes the scope of tests of general vocabulary). Fourth, the absence of observable effects is attributable to the ubiquity of television, which leads to the diffusion of what television presents through social interaction. These last two are almost certainly the explanation for the failed hypothesis in the three-community experiment. Television almost certainly has increased the vocabularies of young people, both general and media-specific. However, it is no longer necessary to view television to gain the benefit because these words and phrases will be passed on by people.

B. INTERESTS

Numerous anecdotes attest to the power of television to enhance the popularity of a book, an activity, or a subject. The interest in family origins aroused by the miniseries *Roots* is a fine example. However, the continuing day-to-day effects of viewing entertainment and news in this regard are extremely modest at best.

Himmelweit, Oppenheim, and Vince (1958) extensively examined this "interests" phenomenon among children and teenagers in Great Britain during a period when one would expect it to be at a maximum—the introduction of the medium. They found only scant evidence of influence. Some teenagers did seek out dramatized books, so that television could be said to have widened their experience. However, television's ostensible ability to stimulate participatory involvement among young people was largely nonexistent.

For example, they interviewed young persons at a museum before and after British Broadcasting Corporation (BBC) coverage of an exhibit. The number visiting was about the same in both time periods; only 10% of those visiting postcoverage had seen the program, and not all of them were there to see the exhibit.

When young persons from households with and without television were compared, the frequency of visiting museums and art galleries did not differ between the two groups. Neither did interest in visiting an exhibition, museum, or art gallery. Interest in an array of cultural activities also did not differ—going to a concert, opera, play, or ballet; discussing politics; reading books; and writing a play, poem, or story. Television availability similarly was unrelated to the liking or disliking of 20 different school subjects. Himmelweit and colleagues observe:

> Television stimulates interests, but only fleetingly. It is up to the adults around the child to maintain these interests and turn them into action: by rendering accessible the books that have been dramatized, by helping the child to find materials needed to make things suggested on television, by encouraging him to visit places (such as art galleries or exhibitions) that have been featured. (p.47)

We agree. The notion of television regularly and consistently stimulating new interests to any important degree is contrary to the physics of time, of which there is not enough to pursue more than a few interests. What television can and will achieve occasionally and what it does regularly are not the same.

C. Visual Skills

It has been hypothesized (Salomon, 1979) that television, because of its imagery and form features (such as pan shots and close-ups), increases the skills of young people at recalling, interpreting, and comprehending visual stimuli. The optimistic notion is that everyday viewing is producing generations that are more perceptually able and sensitive.

The evidence is consistent. Preschool children are unaffected (Hofmann & Flook, 1980; Salomon, 1979) except for video instruction at such simple tasks as serial ordering by size or height (Henderson & Rankin, 1986). Older children who see video examples of the relationships between a whole and its many parts (Salomon, 1979) or the way appearance changes as a function of perspective while the object remains the same (Rovet, 1983) become more proficient at such procedures. Even the viewing of entertaining educational programming, such as *Sesame Street,* to a small degree enhances visual task performance, such as ordering pictures logically or discerning an embedded figure (Salomon, 1979).

The video effects are most pronounced for thoroughly crafted, repetitive sequences designed to instruct. Performance on these visual tasks is generally enhanced by language ability, which may reflect superior labeling and categorization, and prior level of visual skills. Ironically and surprisingly, however, greater amounts of recent viewing may interfere with the exercise of these capabilities, for recent video viewing was helpful to the linguistically and visually less able but detrimental to the more able.

Our conclusion is that the contribution of everyday television viewing to enhanced visual skills is nonexistent. Our reasoning is that the entertainment predominantly viewed is not designed to be pedagogic and so lacks the repetition, focus, and order of the instructional examples that have proven effective. The variety of visual techniques employed is limited so that any effects occur very early and quickly and do not represent a gain over what eventually would be acquired from other sources, such as theater movies. And these very limited temporary gains are largely confined to those low in language ability and visual skills, whereas those more able on these dimensions may have the exercise of these superior skills actually disrupted by greater amounts of viewing.

D. Televised Interventions

The empirical literature evaluating the effectiveness of television programming intended to improve scholastic performance or otherwise alter cognition-related behavior is too extensive for a comprehensive review. However, we can readily summarize the main conclusions that such a review would reach.

We will discuss four types of programming: television specifically intended to increase knowledge while also being entertaining; televised courses analogous to those ordinarily taught in the classroom; television—other than product advertising and political campaigns—designed specifically to change attitudes, beliefs, and behavior; and educational programs for children.

The evidence is identical for television intended to increase knowledge and televised courses. This is not surprising because they are both instruction, only packaged in somewhat different formats. The data from about 4500 viewers and nonviewers of the CBS "National Citizenship Tests" (Alper & Leidy, 1970) and Chu and Schramm's (1967) analysis of many dozens of very early comparisons of televised courses with alternate modes of instruction are representative. Both can and do increase comprehension and factual knowledge of a subject—when given sufficient attention by a viewer. The significant caveat is that much of the time the latter condition will not be met. People tend to view with a mind set socialized by attending to undemanding entertainment and news and typically perceive television as comparatively easy to learn from. As a result, they frequently do not give televised instruction the attention they would give to an alternative source (Salomon, 1981a, 1981b, 1983a, 1983b; Salomon & Leigh, 1984).

Two well-studied examples of television designed to change attitudes, beliefs, and behavior are *Freestyle* and *The Great American Values Test*. *Freestyle* was a public television series of thirteen 30-minute episodes intended to change the beliefs and norms of preteens (ages 9–12) about gender roles, such as a girl doing auto repair (*Grease Monkey*) and a boy showing nurturing behavior (*Helping Hand*). *The Great American Values Test* was a 30-minute program designed to change attitudes in regard to the environment, gender equality, and relationships between Whites and Blacks that was broadcast in the evening simultaneously on all three network outlets in an eastern Washington city.

In the first instance (Johnston & Ettema, 1982), data from thousands of young viewers indicated that the programs had substantial effects on beliefs about what was appropriate for others but not on what the viewer might do, with effects largely confined to viewing accompanied by reinforcing classroom discussion. In the second instance (Ball-Rokeach, Rokeach, & Grube, 1984), data from about 2750 adults in the treatment site and a control site indicated that the program increased monetary contributions to direct mail appeals on behalf of the three themes and changed attitudes and beliefs in the intended direction.

The pattern for *Freestyle* is in accord with two principles of media influence. One is that knowledge and beliefs about others are more likely to be affected than is behavior—or behavioral intentions—on the part of the viewer. The other is that media effects are most likely to occur when their content is reinforced by more direct, personal channels. Although beliefs changed, the self remained obstinate and television was primarily influential when in concert with other influences.

Despite the monopoly of the three channels, only those in about one-fourth of treatment-site households saw any portion of *The Great American Values Test.* Nevertheless, contribution effects were strong enough that a statistically significant difference occurred when comparing all of those representing the control and treatment sites (including those in the latter who did not view the program). This comparison rules out viewing by those already more favorable toward the themes (i.e., self-selection) as an explanation for differences between the groups (a viable alternative if viewers only were compared with nonviewers).

We believe the most important conclusion to be reached with regard to *The Great American Values Test* is that the design of a program in accord with empirically supported psychological theory is more likely to achieve an intended purpose than one that relies on the conventions of television production emphasizing attention-getting and the attractiveness of participants. The program employed the principle that cognitions (expressed in this case by the behavior of contributing) change when they are placed in conflict with other, more firmly held cognitions (in this instance, labeled "values"). Change then occurs because it reduces the tension created as predicted by both Rokeach's (1968) theory of values and such formulations as Festinger's (1957) cognitive dissonance.

Sesame Street is not the only children's educational program that has been the subject of extensive research. However, this Children's Television Workshop (CTW) production is surely the most well-known, most widely distributed with foreign language versions all over the globe, and the most impressive patriarch of the genre with almost 30 years of awards and popularity. More important, the data reflect on most of the questions that might be raised about the genre.

The declared goal of the series was "to promote the intellectual and cultural growth of preschoolers, particularly disadvantaged preschoolers" (Cooney, 1968, as quoted in Cook et al., 1975, p.7); that is, children 2 to 5 in age. The focus on the disadvantaged was sounded repeatedly and widely before Congress, foundations, and the public. We will discuss four stages in the evolution of *Sesame Street:* the initial evaluative research; the revisionist assessment of that research; more recent evidence; and the present status of the series' achievements, costs, and claims to public support.

The initial evaluations were conducted by the Educational Testing Service (ETS) of Princeton, New Jersey, well known for the Scholastic Achievement Test (SAT) and Graduate Record Examination (GRE). Ball and Bogatz (1970; Bogatz & Ball, 1971) designed a series of field experiments that would compare viewers and nonviewers on such outcomes as symbol recognition (letters, numbers) and basic cognitive processes (classification, relations).

Ball and Bogatz interpreted the resulting data as recording high levels of success on both types of outcomes for both advantaged and disadvantaged children. However, fears that the novel program would go unwatched led to the use of home visitors. During the first 2 years of the series (1970 and 1971) they boosted the program to parents and children before the season began, and left balloons, buttons, and magazines promoting the series. During the first year, they visited weekly and during the second year, monthly. Substantial numbers of homes in the treatment condition received these visits—about two-thirds of homes during the first year and about half the second year. Meanwhile, *Sesame Street* proved so popular that nonviewers, not viewers, became the scarcity and the field experiments collapsed into comparing those with greater or lesser amounts of exposure, with many of the former the subject of home visitors.

Cook and colleagues (1975) later reanalyzed the same data. They concluded that although gains in achievement attributable to the *Sesame Street* experience were observable among all categories of children—"black and white children; urban, suburban, and rural children; three-, four-, and five-year-old children; and children of both sexes" (p. 152)—these differences were largely traceable to viewing under the condition of home visitor encouragement. Viewing by itself had little effect. They also concluded that learning was very modest in range and confined to recognition of letters and numbers rather than reasoning. Furthermore, Cook and colleagues argued that *Sesame Street* increased rather than decreased the achievement gap between advantaged and disadvantaged because children from advantaged homes gained more, and they raised the question of whether some other intervention might not be a better investment to address the lower achievement levels of disadvantaged children.

CTW was appalled; ETS was unhappy. It would be 3 years before the manuscript initially submitted to the sponsoring Sage Foundation in 1972 was published (Freeman, 1975). In the interim, there was a meticulous review by three of the most prominent national authorities on evaluation research, the sociologists James Coleman and Peter Rossi and the social psychologist Donald Campbell. In our opinion, the survival of critical scrutiny of this caliber justifies dismissal of the commentary by Ball and Bogatz (1975), "We have examined this work in great detail, and we reject its major conclusions" (p. 388). We concur with Cook and colleagues: effects of viewing the series were extremely modest and limited to recognition, and the size and breadth of effects ascribed to viewing by Ball and Bogatz were attributable to the influence of the home visitors.

The data analyzed by Cook and colleagues were confined to the introduction of the series. More recent data confirm and importantly extend these early findings (Huston, Wright, Rice, Kerkman, & Peters, 1990; Rice et al., 1990; Wright & Huston, 1995; Zill, 1994). The series remains popular. About 75% of preschoolers and 60% of those in kindergarten watch one or more times weekly. The viewing of children's educational programs by preschool-age children—and particularly *Sesame Street* because it accounts for about half of such viewing—is associated with increased language learning, increased school readiness, and better grades in high school many years later. These associations are very small in size, but are impressive because they remain after the influence of parental education, household socioeconomic status, and earlier language and cognitive abilities are statistically taken into account. We nevertheless are hesitant to infer causation because, except for the language acquisition, these seem like outcomes rather grand in kind to derive from viewing a television series and more likely represent differences in parenting of which regular viewing of *Sesame Street* or other educational programming is a reflection. However, we also think it possible that parental involvement in the regular viewing of such programming might have long-term benefits in socializing children toward more constructive use of mass media.

We conclude the following:

1. *Sesame Street* has a large regular audience of preschool age children. We estimate that it is viewed four or more times weekly by between 50 and 60% of children between the ages of 2 and 5 (we use regular viewing as our criterion rather than a cross section for one or more days a week because instructional benefits would be sharply diminished if viewing was sporadic, and we extrapolate from the calculations of Cook and colleagues to take into account the substantial intervening expansion in the reach of public television).

2. *Sesame Street* attracts fairly similar proportions of young viewers from households that are Black, White, Asian, and Hispanic and of differing socioeconomic status, but is noticeably more frequently viewed in Black households; in fact, the claim of public television that it reaches a substantial Black audience is largely dependent on the viewing of educational programming by Black children.

3. *Sesame Street* provides instruction for very young children that does not require intervention by an adult for some degree of effectiveness, but both exposure and effectiveness probably will be enhanced by adult encouragement to view and by some adult participation in verbal exchange with children about its contents.

4. *Sesame Street* and other educational programming for children merit public support because effectiveness is purchased at comparatively modest cost (Palmer, 1988)—between less than $2 and $6 per year per child (with the variation attributable to whether the target audience or those viewing regularly make up the denominator).

5. *Sesame Street* over the years has accounted for slightly more than half of the viewing of educational programming by children of preschool age, and the story the data tell is probably typical not only of children's educational programming but also of educational programming in general. Those who are advantaged socioeconomically or in mental ability will benefit more. This is attributable to greater access to additional resources (in this case, educational toys and games) and superior skills at media use. This is the knowledge gap phenomenon well documented in regard to public affairs in which those advantaged learn more from media coverage (Katz, 1989; Neuman et al., 1992; Tichenor, Donohue, & Olien, 1970), and in our view is an inevitable liability of using mass media to disseminate information. Instructional effects are small. We believe this is attributable largely to the great distance between clear and orderly presentation and effective attending. However, the modest cost per viewer often justifies the financial outlay, as exemplified by the estimates for children's educational programming.

II. ADDITIONAL RELATIONSHIPS

Expectations have been less favorable or more mixed and ambiguous for four additional areas. Three involve hypothesized effects: tolerance for schooling, fantasy play and daydreaming, and creativity. The fourth is a crucial mediating variable: mental ability.

A. Tolerance for Schooling

Television has been accused of encouraging a variety of modes of behavior in conflict with scholastic achievement—hyperactivity, reduced perseverance and attention span, and lowered impulse control (Halpern, 1975; Swerdlow, 1981; Winn, 1977). We concur with Hornik (1981) that although there is a variety of distinct outcomes, the evidence can be summarized under the blanket concept of an intolerance for the demands and pacing of school.

One set of studies examines preschool children (Anderson, Levin, & Lorch, 1977; Friedrich & Stein, 1973; Gadberry, 1980; Tower, Singer, Singer, & Biggs, 1979). The viewing of educational programming, such as *Sesame Street* and *Mr. Rogers' Neighborhood,* was consistently associated with more favorable scores on such measures. Pacing seemed not to matter, because there were no differences in outcomes when faster- and slower-paced versions of the same *Sesame Street* episode were compared. Content did matter, with violence associated with less favorable scores.

Another set largely examines school-age children (C. Anderson & McGuire, 1978; Desmond, Singer, & Singer, 1990; Salomon, 1979; J. L. Singer, Singer, Desmond, Hirsch, & Nicol, 1988; J. L. Singer, Singer, & Rapaczynski, 1984), although some longitudinal studies began when the children were of preschool age. The studies consistently find exposure to violence associated with less favorable scores on such measures. The adverse relationship appears to be enhanced when parents do not mediate viewing by discussing programs with children. However, in the case of violence parental mediation is generally ineffective because it is rare.

Our conclusion is that among children between the ages of 5 and 9 television viewing may interfere with acceding to the pace of schooling. Violence appears to be a key element in such adverse effects. Educational programming has favorable effects, with the one instance in which adverse effects were recorded (Salomon, 1979) involving 9-year-olds who viewed *Sesame Street,* a program designed for younger children that might understandably have made them restless and less ready to concentrate.

B. IMAGINATIVE PLAY AND DAYDREAMING

When the first author initially examined the evidence on the role of television in the cognitive behavior of children (Comstock, 1991a), he divided the research dealing in various ways with inventiveness into two categories, imaginativeness and creativity. In the first, data on imaginative play, daydreaming, and the degree of improvisation in response to stories were commingled. In the second, data were confined to the creating of whole stories and scores on the standard tests of creativity, Alternate Uses and Pattern Meanings. He concluded that in the case of imaginativeness, there was some shaping of responses and some facilitation of the quantity of responses, but that neither for imaginativeness nor creativity was there any evidence of any effects on such traits; that is, in some cases performance was affected but capability was not.

The work of Valkenburg and van der Voort (1994, 1995; van der Voort & Valkenburg, 1994) has convinced us that a three-way division is superior— fantasy play among young children, daydreaming, and creativity, with improvisation in regard to stories included among the latter. Our rationale is that both the activities encompassed and the degree of association with television viewing then become more homogeneous and thus more interpretable.

The evidence on fantasy play is extensive, with empirical data available from correlational studies (Lyle & Hoffman, 1972a, 1972b; D. G. Singer & Singer, 1981; J. L. Singer & Singer, 1981; J. L. Singer et al., 1984), quasi-experiments (Gadberry, 1980; Maccoby, 1951; Murray & Kippax, 1978; Schramm et al., 1961) and laboratory-type experiments (Anderson et al., 1977; Friedrich-Cofer et al., 1979; Greer et al., 1982; Huston-Stein et al., 1981; Noble, 1970, 1973; Potts, Huston, & Wright, 1986; Silvern & Williamson, 1987; Tower et al., 1979). There are also some qualitative descriptions based either on the observing of children (Alexander, Ryan, & Munoz, 1984; James & McCain, 1982; Reid & Frazer, 1980) or on memories of childhood play by those growing up with and without television (French & Penna, 1991). Almost all of those under scrutiny were between 3 and 7 in age with most between 3 and 5.

In our view, four major hypotheses have been offered:

- Television viewing decreases amount of fantasy play by displacing time that otherwise would be spent in play.
- Television viewing increases amount of fantasy play by supplying exciting new ideas.
- Television viewing shapes fantasy play by presenting examples of behavior that can be readily incorporated.
- Television viewing decreases fantasy play by mechanisms other than displacement, such as mental exhaustion, arousal, or anxiety and fear.

We find no support for significant time displacement. The data from the introduction of television, when there was some displacement, does not take into account later accommodations (Condry, 1989). The research records repeatedly that socially important and personally significant activities (such as moviegoing among teenagers) are least likely to be affected (Chapter 3) and the data are clear that among young children, free play well exceeds the amount of time spent viewing (Timmer, Eccles, & O'Brien, 1985). The opportunity for displacement, then, is very modest. We also find no support for the view that viewing increases fantasy play, although substantial amounts of viewing and playing can coexist (Mutz et al., 1993).

The apparent exception is children's educational programs designed to enhance imaginative activity. We do find repeated evidence that television shapes play. Thus, educational programs are especially effective when props and materials derived from the programs are provided. We were particularly impressed with the data of French and Penna (1991) in which those growing up with television recalled much more frequent superhero play as well as with the inventiveness of the investigators in using memories to measure the effects of a technological innovation. We do not find evidence that television viewing in general otherwise decreases play except for the viewing of violent programs. Repeatedly, the viewing of violent programs does so, but it is unclear what this should be attributed to—the rapid pacing, which could leave children somewhat exhausted for play; the arousal, which would interfere with play; or anxiety and fear, which would distract them from play.

As Valkenburg and van der Voort (1994) point out, fantasy play is important developmentally because it permits children to try on new roles and involves an inventiveness that conceivably might transfer to other contexts. So, too, does daydreaming. However, the first is particularly important for children when they are young and is voluntary and somewhat physical (sometimes very much so), whereas the latter is lifelong, not entirely voluntary, and entirely internal to the mind, so there is no reason to expect the two to behave the same in response to the same stimuli. As might be expected, the empirical literature rests on persons older than those in the case of fantasy play—largely young persons 7 and up in age and adults. This is not only because daydreaming is a lifelong activity but also because play can be observed, whereas the investigation of daydreams requires interviewing or the completion of questionnaires—techniques less likely to be reliable and valid with young children.

The empirical literature is not as extensive as for play, but there is a full range of methods and ages (Feshbach & Singer, 1971; Fraczek, 1986; Hart, 1972; Huesmann & Eron, 1986; McIlwraith, Jacobvitz, Kubey, & Alexander, 1991; McIlwraith & Josephson, 1985; McIlwraith & Schallow, 1982–83; Schallow & McIlwraith, 1986–87; Sheehan, 1987; Valkenburg & van der Voort, 1995; Valkenburg, Voojis, van der Voort, & Wiegman, 1992; Viemero & Paajanen, 1990). There have been the expected hypotheses:

- Television viewing decreases daydreaming by substituting for it.
- Television viewing increases daydreaming by stimulating thoughts and rumination.
- Television viewing shapes daydreaming by providing explicit subject matter.
- Unpleasant daydreams and thoughts increase television viewing as an escape from them.

We find no support for any diminution of daydreaming as a consequence of exposure to television. Neither do we find that television viewing in general promotes positive daydreaming or fantasy construction or that amount of exposure to any mass medium (movies, books, or compact discs and cassettes) promotes such fantasizing. However, we repeatedly find evidence of correspondences between types of daydreaming and what was seen on television. Viewing of science fiction is correlated with rumination about how things work. General drama and comedies and to a lesser degree music videos and entertainment features are correlated with pleasant fantasies. Children watching nonviolent children's programs are more likely to engage in a "positive-intense" (in the language of Valkenburg and van der Voort, 1995) daydreaming style. Violent dramatic programs encourage and nonviolent programs inhibit "aggressive-heroic" daydreaming. These data taken together clearly point to an influence of viewing on the mentalistic representations of daydreaming. This is not only because the positive correlations persist when other variables are taken into account, thus reducing the likelihood that they are artifactual, but also because in at least one instance (Valkenburg & van der Voort, 1995) changes in day-dreaming of about 780 third and fifth grade children over a 1-year period were documented as linked to the content of the television programs viewed in an earlier period. We can reject, then, the interpretation that the positive correlations (between what is viewed and the content of daydreams) are wholly explained by the viewing choices guided by preoccupations that also find representation in daydreams. Thus, the evidence is that television can both facilitate and inhibit the content of daydreaming.

The clearest correspondences have been between violent program viewing and heroic-aggressive daydreaming. For example, Viemero and Paajanen (1990) found in a large sample of 8- and 10-year-old Finnish children that boys and girls at both ages who viewed greater amounts of violent programs were more likely to fantasize about aggressive behavior and to replay in their minds violent scenes from the programs.

Finally, fantasies of guilt and failure predict purposeful use of television to dispel negative mood states and more frequent switching of channels. We interpret these outcomes as representing the search for distraction from the unpleasant state. Such fantasies do not predict exposure to specific content or amount viewed, which would be circumscribed by time available and the social circumstances of viewing. These data encourage the interpretation that television often serves as an escape from unpleasant daydreaming and thoughts and that the positive association observed in several instances between viewing and dysphoric mood states is explained by the use of the medium to avoid unpleasant thoughts.

Thus, both the shaping and escape hypotheses are supported. In sum, television does not interfere with the imaginative processes involved in daydreaming, but it does give shape to daydreams and serves as an escape when daydreams and thoughts are unpleasant.

C. CREATIVITY

The *Dictionary of Behavioral Science* (Wolman, 1989) defines creativity as "the ability to produce something new, such as a new idea, a new scientific system, a new solution to a problem, a piece of art, sculpture, painting, architecture, or a piece of film, drama, music, or ballet" (p. 79). Operationalization for the measurement of children's creativity has had the same emphases—the ability to generate new ideas, think about things in different ways, or elaborate to a greater degree in response to a stimulus or suggestion.

The hypothesis that has been advanced most often is that television viewing would decrease creativity. The twin grounds have been its concreteness and set pace, which presumably would inhibit inventiveness and rumination, and the conventionality of much of what it presents. Empirical data come from three sources: outcomes observed in the three-community British Columbia quasi-experiment (Williams, 1986); a series of experiments in which the retelling or construction of stories as a function of media exposure was examined (Greenfield & Beagle-Roos, 1988; Greenfield, Farrar, & Beagle-Roos, 1986; Kerns, 1981; Meline, 1976; Runco & Pedzek, 1984; Stern, 1973; Valkenburg & Beentjes, 1997; Vibbert & Meringoff, 1981; Watkins, 1988); and correlational studies comparing the measured creativity of those higher and lower in everyday viewing (Childs, 1979; Peterson, Peterson, & Carroll, 1987; J. L. Singer & Rapaczynski, 1984a; Williams, 1986; Zuckerman, Singer, & Singer, 1980).

T. M. Williams (1986) and colleagues in their three-community quasi-experiment used the two standard psychometric tasks to assess the creativity of those in the fourth and seventh grades. Alternative Uses asks for novel applications for such common objects as a chair, button, shoe, or car tire; Pattern Meaning seeks the discerning and naming of shapes in ambiguous drawings. The first is considered a measure of divergent thinking; the second is a measure of ideational fluency.

The arrival of television in Notel (the name given to the community without television) was accompanied by a decided decline in scores on the Alternatives Uses task. Comparing different samples of the same grades in the three communities before and after Notel had television (cross-sectional analysis), pupils in Notel initially scored much better than those in the two television communities. After television arrived, the scores for the three communities were much alike. Comparing scores for the same persons in the three communities before and after the arrival of television in Notel (longitudinal analysis), scores for the Notel sample decidedly decreased while those for the other two communities did not. The support from two distinct modes of analysis gives high credence to this outcome.

However, the obvious conclusion that the introduction of television reduced creativity is made less tenable by the failure of the Pattern Meanings task to produce interpretable differences. This is surely not because television compensatorily if paradoxically increased perceptual and visual skills because there is no evidence of such an effect.

The series of experiments fairly consistently indicates that completing or retelling a story experienced by television leads to less elaborate, original accounts than if the story were heard or read. In contrast, in one instance the assignment to create stories *for* television led to far more complex tales among those high in viewing than the assignment to create tales representing real life. Watkins (1988) asked about 80 young persons in the third, fifth, and eighth grades to write stories about real life and for television. In the early grades, real-life stories were more complex, but this difference decreased as amount of viewing increased. By the eighth grade, television stories were about three times more complex than real-life stories among those high in viewing. They were also longer, and higher on measures of affective tone and use of thoughts and emotions. Watkins observed that all the stories, but especially those for television, had elements typical of the medium.

The correlational data produce only a few negative associations between measures of creativity and amount of viewing, but particularly for measures close to the Williams measures—divergent thinking (Wade, 1971) and fluency (Peterson, Peterson, & Caroll, 1987). They also produce some negative correlations with viewing violent programs (J. L. Singer et al., 1984; Zuckerman et al., 1980).

We choose to rely exclusively on the correlational data from the Williams quasi-experiment. The measures are particularly good, the sample size is substantial (about 430), but more important, the sample has apparently exhibited a treatment effect on the Alternative Uses task that should be replicated in the correlational data if, in fact, the creativity of those who view more television is suppressed. The inferential key, for which we are indebted to the painstaking analyses of the original investigators (pp. 126–127), is the absence of a correlation between earlier creativity scores and later amounts of viewing. This eliminates self-selection as the explanation for any associations and is a vital property not possessed by any other set of correlational data. Whatever the outcome, the data can be interpreted as bearing on causality.

Now the evidence changes dramatically. Neither in Unitel (the community receiving only the Canadian Broadcasting Corporation channel) and Multitel (the community receiving the three American networks as well as the Canadian channel) before Notel received television nor in each of the three communities after its arrival were there any relationships between viewing and either creativity measure (Williams, 1986, Table 3.A7, p. 131). There was one exception, but it defies interpretation: When data for all three communities were combined, there appeared a marginal negative relationship for Pattern Meanings at the second measurement. When we then examine all four of their standard psychometric cognitive measures (Alternative Uses, Pattern Meaning, vocabulary, and block design), only for block design and only after Notel had received television was there a consistent negative association with viewing.

The absence of consistent negative correlations between viewing and the two creativity measures, Alternative Uses and Pattern Meanings, does not support a negative effect on creativity. In addition, these data further confirm that the failure of Pattern Meaning to replicate the Alternate Uses outcome can hardly be the result of a compensatory increase in perceptual or spatial skill because this is essentially what block design measures.

The results of the experiments in our view represent transient performance phenomena. Usually overlooked in their interpretation is that both those in the treatment and control or alternate media conditions have had lengthy histories of exposure to television, so that what is measured is not representative of a trait but a state, and performance would be reversed were the populations of these groups exchanged. Thus, they do not bear on creativity as a trait.

The evidence is that elaborateness and originality in completing or retelling a story are constrained when television is the source. The reason is the greater concreteness and specificity of television. In contrast, as a model for storytelling television encourages elaborateness and complexity because its narrative conventions exceed in these respects what young persons ordinarily perceive in everyday life (although as adults they are sure to remark that life is like a soap opera). If television did lower scores for divergent thinking, the correlational data from the same source indicate that greater or lesser viewing in the long term has no implication for creativity as a trait. Based on the lack of agreement between the two measures, the absence of correlations, and the clear limitation of the experiments to transient performance, we conclude that the evidence does not support the hypothesis that viewing diminishes creative capability.

D. MENTAL ABILITY

Schramm, Lyle, and Parker (1961), in their large-scale investigation of the effects on American children of the introduction of television—covering thousands of children and hundreds of parents and teachers—refer to mental ability as "one of the great building blocks (along with personal relationships and social norms, and of course, age and sex) that go into the structure of a child's television viewing patterns" (p. 79). They propose that television serves different functions that change with advancing age for children who are higher and lower in mental ability. In our view, their model has not been contradicted either by empirical inquiry or by common observation except for one amendment.

Brighter children typically were initially heavy viewers because brighter children make greater and more enthusiastic use of the opportunities offered them. Here is an example:

> In one school system we had the opportunity to study a group of fourth- and fifth-grade children who had been brought together because of their very high intelligence scores. . . . They were voracious readers. We rather expected that their broad intellectual curiosity and their wide reading would eat into their television time. But quite the contrary! Their television time was proportionately nearly as high as their

> reading time. They did *more* of everything—more television, more movies, more
> reading, more discussing, more investigating on their own. (p. 79)

Schramm, Lyle, and Parker recorded a marked change between the ages of about 10 and 13. Amount of viewing declined. This was the now well-documented decrease in television use (Chapter 3) that occurs as young people shift from the elementary grades toward high school. Also, the proportion of media time spent on television decreased, whereas the proportion spent on print increased. This occurred for young persons at every level of mental ability. However, for brighter children the change began earlier and was much more dramatic. When they did view television, they were more likely to view news and public affairs programming or more demanding entertainment. They also evaluated television in a more critical manner. Those lower in mental ability were more likely to remain heavy viewers. They were also less likely to use print, and when they did, they consumed less demanding content, such as comics and the then-popular pulp fiction.

In interpreting these changes, the authors apply the concepts of "reality" and "fantasy" to the function of media content. In our view, in this context reality denotes more than merely the portrayal of events and the expression of opinion. We construe it as referring to factual or fictional content that is intellectually stimulating, increases the range of experience as well as knowledge, and calls on cognitive skills (such as comprehension, interpretation, and insight)—content that contributes to maturation and the ability to cope. Thus, brighter young persons make better use of media. The authors comment:

> Both the high and low groups, in mental ability, are settling into adult patterns.
> The high group will use television less, and more selectively, and will turn to other
> media for much of its serious information needs. The low group will use television
> more, and printed media less. (pp. 46–47)

The number of young persons high in print use but low in television use increased markedly between the 6th and 10th grades, and such persons were more likely to value the norms of deferred gratification, self-betterment, and improving skills at coping. If mental ability were moderate or better, young persons with such norms were more likely to become serious users of print and more selective in television viewing, favoring reality content in both media to a greater degree. Among those high in mental ability and high in socioeconomic status, conflicts with parents or peers predicted greater television viewing, probably because these persons had substantial free time not yet devoted to the medium that could be diverted to it in stressful circumstances (E. E. Maccoby, 1954).

The Himmelweit and Swift (1976) data on several hundred British male teenagers covering 20 years confirm the long-term stability of media orientation. Television and print use and the emphases on reality and fantasy in later life varied in those same ways with mental ability and socioeconomic status essentially as they had earlier. Those high in earlier consumption of the then-dominant medium of undemanding content, theater movies, in later years were higher in television viewing.

Morgan and Gross (1982) conclude from a review of previous research that there has been a negative relationship between mental ability and amount of television consumed by young persons, although they offer no data that would contradict the model of Schramm and colleagues that before the ages of 10 to 13 children of high ability are often heavy viewers. In the analysis of their own data, representing more than 400 6th through 9th graders, they confirm a negative relationship, and find that it is largely independent of the inverse relationship between socioeconomic status and television viewing.

When T. M. Williams (1986) and colleagues in their three-community experiment pooled grades three and up and divided them into four groups on the basis of mental ability, there was an inverse, linear relationship between amount of television viewing and mental ability. However, this relationship was primarily attributable to Notel, where television was a novelty. Nevertheless, in Unitel and Multitel young persons high in mental ability used certain print media more, such as newspapers, magazines, and books, and read comics less.

The model of Schramm and colleagues thus requires the modest amendment that mental ability, although consistently identified to the present day as inversely associated with amount of viewing, is not quite as strong a predictor as it was in the early years of television. This is part of the historical pattern in which individual attributes such as socioeconomic status have declined somewhat as predictors of television use as segments of the population once comparatively low in amount of viewing more frequently spend time in the vicinity of an operating television set and are tabulated as viewing. Mental ability nevertheless remains forceful in predicting use of reality content, such as print and in the present environment, computer use, the Internet, and related electronic information sources and data banks.

III. VIEWING AND ACHIEVEMENT

We begin with the remarkably strong evidence on the relationship between viewing and scholastic performance. We then turn to data on use of the medium that provide a partial explanation.

A. THE RELATIONSHIP

The data are absolutely compelling because of the quality of measurement, the size and inclusiveness of the samples, and the consistency of the results. There are six major sources:

1. The 1980 California Assessment Program (CAP) data and successive follow-ups in 1982 and 1986.
2. The 1980 High School and Beyond (HSB) data collected by the National Center for Educational Statistics (Keith, Reimers, Fehrman, Pottebaum, & Aubey, 1986).
3. The 1983–1984 National Assessment of Educational Progress (NAEP) data collected by ETS (B. Anderson, Mead, & Sullivan, 1986).
4. The synthesis of data from eight state assessments (ESA), including that of California (S. Neuman, 1988).
5. A panel of HSB high school students from whom data were obtained when they were sophomores and seniors (Gaddy, 1986).
6. A nationally representative panel of children from the National Health Examination (NHE) surveys from whom data were obtained at two points in time about 4 years apart (Gortmaker et al., 1990).

We focus on the California data because of the extremely large number of cases, the representation of the greatest variety of achievement, and the opportunity to examine visually the relationships rather than being confined to summary statistics. The state-run CAP obtained data on mathematics, reading, and writing and television viewing for everyone present in the 6th and 12th grades on the day of testing. It was a census rather than a sampling. The number of participants for the 6th grade was 282,000; for the 12th grade it was 227,000. This represents 99% of enrollment. However, it is not sample size alone that promises meaningfulness. The sponsorship by a major state of a nationally visible endeavor ensures state-of-the-art reliability and validity (however far from perfection those may be).

For each of the three kinds of achievement there was a negative association between amount of television viewed and performance in both the 6th and 12th grades (Figure 7.1). The shape of the downward curves within grade levels is almost identical for mathematics, reading, and writing. Similarly, for each level of household socioeconomic status, there was a negative association for each of the three kinds of achievement as exemplified by the data on reading.

We mostly use data on reading as a proxy for achievement in general because there are no instances where the shape of curves differs appreciably by kind of achievement. Reading is also the category of achievement most widely represented throughout all the data and therefore is the preferred measure for comparison among sets of data, as well as the skill most pervasively drawn on throughout the curriculum.

FIGURE 7.1   Television viewing, achievement, and socioeconomic status—sixth grade. Adapted from "Survey of Sixth Grade School Achievement and Television Viewing Habits," California Assessment Program, 1980, Sacramento: California State Department of Education.

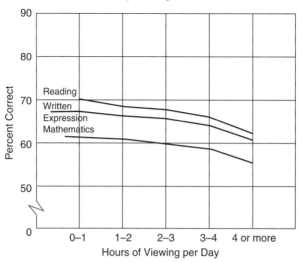

Achievement by Viewing—Three Basic Skills

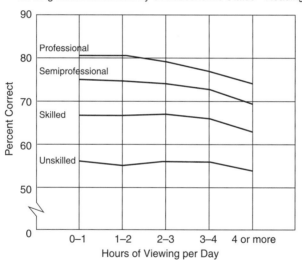

Viewing and Achievement by Socioeconomic Status—Reading

Number of students by socioeconomic status							
	Hours of television viewed per day						
Occupation of head of household	0–1	1–2	2–3	3–4	4 or more	Non-response	Total	Percent
Professional	15,731	11,176	7,022	3,787	4,976	337	43,029	15
Semiprofessional	15,634	12,927	9,449	5,812	9,631	495	53,948	19
Skilled	23,713	21,283	16,966	11,301	21,795	1,189	96,247	34
Unskilled	10,408	9,391	7,591	5,211	11,451	769	44,821	16
Nonresponse	11,505	9,866	7,266	4,627	9,481	1,173	43,918	16
Total	76,991	64,643	48,294	30,738	57,339	3,963	281,968	100
Percent	27	23	17	11	20	2		

There are five important qualifications:

1. Household socioeconomic status is positively associated with achievement, and this relationship is far stronger than the negative association between viewing and performance. This is readily seen by comparing average test scores between strata with those between different levels of viewing.
2. Socioeconomic status is a proxy for educational resources in the home (such as parental education and availability of books, newspapers, and magazines) and as socioeconomic status increases, the inverse association between viewing and achievement becomes more pronounced. This is observable in the differences in the slopes of the curves for the varying socioeconomic strata.
3. In the 12th grade, the inverse association between viewing and achievement is more pronounced than in the 6th grade.
4. Among the least advantaged, the inverse association is less pronounced and sometimes reversed. The former can be seen by comparing the shape of the curve for the lowest strata with those for higher strata; the latter occurs for those with limited English in the 1980 CAP data (Comstock, 1991a).
5. The proportions in the higher viewing categories are not trivial, with about 30% in both the 6th and 12th grades reporting viewing 3 or more hours daily (although, in accord with other data on audience behavior, teenagers view less than those younger).

The other data are wholly supportive. Keith and colleagues (1986) analyzed the achievement scores equally weighting mathematics and reading for more than 28,000 seniors in the HSB data. B. Anderson, Mead, and Sullivan (1986) collected NAEP data from a national sample of 70,000 in three grades on achievement, viewing, and related behavior. S. Neuman (1988) combined reading outcomes from eight statewide evaluations (California, Connecticut, Maine, Illinois, Michigan, Pennsylvania, Rhode Island, and Texas). Gaddy (1986) drew samples of 2400 to 5000 from the HSB data and focused on the reading, vocabulary, and mathematics performance of those who were sophomores in 1982 and seniors in 1984. Gortmaker et al. (1990) examined the reading, mathematics, and IQ scores of 1750 young persons over a 4-year interval, with data collection from 6- to 11-year-olds beginning in the mid-1960s.

Repeatedly, the CAP pattern recurs. The HSB sophomore panel parallels the CAP pattern at both the sophomore and senior levels for all measures of achievement and provides direct evidence that the inverse association becomes more pronounced in households with greater resources (Table 7.1): in this instance, number of books, having an encyclopedia, or subscribing

TABLE 7.1   Viewing and Achievement by Race, Gender, and Household
Educational Resources

Achievement measure	Correlation coefficients[a]					
	All students		Blacks		Females	
	Sophomore $N = 10{,}046$	Senior	Sophomore $N = 2365$	Senior	Sophomore $N = 4997$	Senior
Vocabulary	−.158	−.176	−.031	−.023	−.177	−.186
Reading	−.160	−.155	−.042	−.011	−.168	−.160
Math level 1	−.173	−.188	.008	−.011	−.202	−.196
Math level 2	−.157	−.169	−.021	−.030	−.159	−.176
Grades	−.128	−.127	−.032	.021	−.146	−.136
	High resource		Medium resource		Low resource	
	Sophomore $N = 2974$	Senior	Sophomore $N = 3960$	Senior	Sophomore $N = 3112$	Senior
Vocabulary	−.241	−.220	−.076	−.121	−.037	−.094
Reading	−.226	−.174	−.064	−.089	−.064	−.086
Math level 1	−.211	−.204	−.105	−.122	−.084	−.109
Math level 2	−.171	−.175	−.097	−.110	−.073	−.113
Grades	−.189	−.148	−.080	−.089	−.051	−.074

Sample size $(N) = 10{,}046$

[a] Smallest significant correlation (one-tailed alpha = .05, corrected for design effect) for all students
is .032; for Blacks, .047; for females, .032; for high-resource group, .042; for medium-resource
group, .036; and for low-resource group, .041. Calculated using Fishers r to Z transformation.
   Adapted from "Television's Impact on High School Achievement," by G. D. Gaddy, 1986, *Public
Opinion Quarterly, 50*(3), pp. 340–359.

to a newspaper. The NAEP data repeats the CAP pattern for socioeconomic
status, viewing, and reading at all three grades (Table 7.2). The HSB and
NAEP data also extend the pattern to Blacks and Hispanics. A CAP (1986)
follow-up documents that the phenomenon is curriculumwide. Scores for
science, history, and social science—as well as those for reading, writing, and
mathematics—were inversely associated with viewing in a census of about
285,000 8th graders.
   Fetler (1984) first introduced the possibility of curvilinearity in his analysis
of the reading, mathematics, and writing scores of a CAP follow-up sample of
about 10,000 6th graders. Potter (1987) later recorded a threshold of about
10 hours per week or fewer than 1.5 hours per day of viewing before a negative
association with a composite achievement score began among about 550 pupils
between the 8th and 12th grades in the Midwest. S. Neuman (1988) concluded

TABLE 7.2 Viewing and Reading Proficiency by Ethnicity and Household
Socioeconomic Status

	Hours of TV viewing per day		
	0–2	3–5	6 or more
		Reading scores	
		(based on 500-point exam)	
Ethnicity			
Grade 4			
White	232	228	213
Black	200	201	190
Hispanic	208	204	193
Grade 8			
White	274	268	253
Black	246	248	236
Hispanic	249	249	238
Grade 11			
White	301	291	275
Black	272	267	262
Hispanic	277	268	254
Socioeconomic status (parental education)			
Grade 4			
No high school diploma	201	207	195
High school graduate	220	220	206
Post-high school	237	231	210
Grade 8			
No high school diploma	247	252	236
High school graduate	262	259	246
Post-high school	279	271	255
Grade 11			
No high school diploma	274	272	260
High school graduate	287	279	268
Post-high school	305	295	279

Sample size (N) = 100,000

Adapted from "Television: What Do National Assessment Tests Tell Us?" by B. Anderson,
N. Mead, and S. Sullivan, 1986, Princeton, NJ: Educational Testing Service.

from her analysis of the huge ESA aggregation and the CAP data that there was
some curvilinearity.

However, neither the S. Neuman analyses nor Keith and colleagues in their
large HSB sample of seniors find curvilinearity at the high school level. Inspection of the massive 1980 CAP data indicates that nowhere is it substantial or
pronounced. Technically, there is slight curvilinearity in the CAP elementary
school data but it is minute. The rise in scores represents only a very small

portion of the curve before the curve begins a continual descent. Thus, curvilinearity has little significance except to indicate that a small amount of viewing in the earlier grades has no negative implications for scholastic performance.

Gaddy (1986) controlled for an extraordinary number of variables and then calculated the association between sophomore amount of viewing and senior achievement. An inverse association, paralleling the data we have examined, disappeared. However, such an analysis is not fully pertinent because any influence of television is confined to changes in achievement over the 2-year period, includes as controls some factors that may in some cases be the consequence of viewing, and ignores the level of viewing at the time of the decisive senior measurement. Our view is as follows:

- Changes in performance so late and over so short a period in the educational process would be minor at most.
- Controls for educational resources in the home (books, an encyclopedia, newspaper subscription) eliminate factors favorable for achievement whose availability may be foreclosed by high centrality of television in the household (Chapter 3) or heavy television use by a young person. The same can be said of controlling for earlier amount of reading, achievement, and vocabulary. These are all variables that to some degree may be affected by greater television exposure, so that controlling for them artificially reduces the likelihood of detecting a television effect.
- The data on the stability of viewing among young persons (Chapter 3) lead to the conclusion that correlations across 2 years in amount of viewing are insufficient to make sophomore viewing representative of senior viewing when the achievement data were collected.

Our interpretation is that variability in achievement was so constrained that negligible associations were inevitable. As a result, they are not informative in regard to the influence of viewing on scholastic performance. Fortunately, the Gaddy data permit us to test this interpretation. If we are correct, the associations of other variables with achievement should also be small, including variables that ordinarily are predictors of scholastic performance. As Gaddy comments:

> One logical basis for comparison is the set of estimates for other media activities, such as reading for pleasure or reading the front page of the newspaper, and "obvious" sources of academic effects such as high school program, private school attendance, and time spent on homework.

He continues:

> The estimated effect of TV (measured by betas averaged across the four achievement tests for the total sample) is not radically different in absolute value from the other

estimates: reading the newspaper (.001), private school attendance (.019), homework time (.021), reading for pleasure (.034), and being in an academic program
(.042). (p. 355)

Our interpretation survives the test.

Gortmaker and colleagues (1990) also controlled for an unusually large
number of variables in examining the relationship between viewing and scores
on the Wechsler Intelligence Scale for Children (WISC) and the Wide Range
Achievement Tests in Arithmetic (WRAT-A) and Reading (WRAT-R). As with
Gaddy, an initial inverse association again paralleling the data we have examined disappeared. Our judgment is that the very high reliabilities (.82,.70, and
.86, respectively) across the 4 or more years between points of data collection
essentially preclude any effect of an external variable when the variable first
entered as a control is the previous test score (Table 7.3)—in effect, a control
for the putative outcome. We are additionally skeptical of these data because
the authors found no differences by social strata, whereas the CAP (Figure 7.1)
and NAEP (Table 7.2) data clearly indicate that the achievement slopes for different strata differ.

We believe these data should be taken at face value. Gaddy and Gortmaker
both document that there is an initial inverse association between viewing and
their achievement measures. Each then demonstrates that these associations
diminish sharply when other variables are controlled. However, the controls
are so stringent that there is little likelihood of detecting a television effect. The
procedures are precise and accurate; the logic is amiss.

TABLE 7.3 Viewing, IQ, and Arithmetic and Reading Scores (IQ measured by Wechsler Intelligence
Scale for Children, WRAT-A measured by Wide Range Achievement Test in Arithmetic, WRAT-R
measured by Wide Range Achievement Test in Reading).

Variable	IQ	$p <$	WRAT-A	$p <$	WRAT-R	$p <$
(A) Current TV viewing	−2.23	.0001	−.97	.0001	−1.32	.0001
(B) Prior test score + (A)	−.51	.0006	−.25	.05	−.09	.30
(C) Season, region, population density + (B)	−.51	.0006	−.22	.08	−.10	.26
(D) All Other + (C)[a]	−.25	.10	−.04	.74	−.003	.98
Final R^2 (adjusted)	.69		.51		.75	

Sample size (N) = 1745
[a]All other variables include mother and father's education and age, income, number of children in family,
  child's birth order, race, and having conditions restricting activity.

Adapted from "The Impact of Television Viewing on Mental Aptitude and Achievement: A Longitudinal
Study," by S. L. Gortmaker, C. A. Salter, D. K. Walker, and W. H. Dietz, 1990, *Public Opinion Quarterly,* 54(4),
pp. 594–604.

B. Television Use

There is ample evidence that those who watch greater amounts of television disproportionately come from segments of the population less likely to perform well scholastically. We discuss this body of findings in terms of three topics: audience demographics, mental ability, and heavy vs light viewers.

Television viewing is inversely related to socioeconomic status. Socioeconomic status is positively and strongly related to scholastic performance as exemplified by the CAP data (Figure 7.1). The NAEP data (Table 7.2) in particular make clear the pivotal role of socioeconomic status in achievement. As one would expect from the absence among Black households of the marked inverse relationship between socioeconomic status and television use that exists for White households (Chapter 3), the inverse association between viewing and achievement is far less pronounced among Blacks than Whites, because Blacks would have a much higher proportion of households high in socioeconomic status among heavier viewing households. Nevertheless, at every level of viewing and in all three grades, achievement scores increase with socioeconomic status for both Blacks and Whites. Stressful social relationships also have a role. In households high in socioeconomic status where typically there is ample opportunity for young persons to increase the time they spend with television, conflicts with parents or peers predict greater viewing (Maccoby, 1954). In turn, such conflicts often will interfere with performance in school. We would expect, then, that because of the relationships between socioeconomic status, viewing, and achievement that average levels of achievement would be lower among those who view greater amounts of television. The inverse associations between viewing and achievement within strata seemingly support the view that socioeconomic status is not responsible for the overall negative relationship, but they do not fully eliminate the possibility because more subtle distinctions within strata may be at work.

The evidence of an inverse correlation between mental ability and viewing is pertinent because one-half to three-fourths of the variance in achievement scores typically is accounted for by mental ability (Fetler, 1984). The data point to the persistence of this relationship despite some diminution as a consequence of the greater use of television by all population groupings (Gortmaker et al., 1990; S. Neuman, 1991; Van Evra, 1998). More importantly for the present analysis, data from the same periods as the varied inverse associations between viewing and achievement clearly depict greater viewing by those of lower mental ability. We thus would expect that average levels of achievement would be lower among those who view greater amounts of television, and because young children who are very bright often view large amounts of television, we estimate stronger relationships among older children and teenagers.

Very heavy and very light viewers also differ in program preferences and other television-related behavior in ways that favor the expectation that those who view more on the average would perform less well scholastically. Our source is data on several thousand 6th graders in a CAP follow-up (1982; Fetler, 1984). Heavy viewers (above the 90th percentile) and light viewers (below the 10th percentile excluding those viewing no television) differed not only in socioeconomic status (lower for heavy viewers) and achievement (higher for light viewers), but also in viewing early in the day, late at night, and while doing homework (greater for heavy viewers) and in the watching of public television (greater for light viewers). For most programs, heavy viewers were more likely to have watched and among their 15 most-watched programs there was a much greater emphasis on light entertainment—in particular, situation comedies, prime-time soaps, and action-adventure. Heavy viewers conform to the pattern for unreflective ritualistic viewing. In contrast, the 15 most-watched programs of light viewers were largely informational in character (*60 Minutes, Jacques Cousteau*), with some comparatively thoughtful entertainment (*M*A*S*H*). Thus, light viewing by young persons is associated with more instrumental and information-oriented use that is unlikely to interfere with and might enhance scholastic performance, whereas heavy viewing reflects not only greater use but greater emphasis on less scholastically useful content.

These three bodies of data lead to two conclusions. The first is that a substantial portion of the inverse association between achievement and viewing is attributable to greater viewing by those from households of lower socioeconomic status, those who are less socially able to cope with their surroundings, and those of lower intellectual ability. The second is that amount of viewing, which in part is a function of the household centrality of television (Chapter 3), has implications for scholastic achievement because it is a predictor—particularly within White households—of the instrumentality or scholastic usefulness of media content consumed.

IV. INTERPRETATION

T. M. Williams (1986) and colleagues concluded that their three-community experiment identifies a negative effect on reading. We think there are too many instances in which either the introduction of television was associated with a rise in scores, scores uninterpretably increase in the two communities that had television, or the trend of scores in Notel parallel the trend in a community that had television to offer such a conclusion confidently (Comstock, 1991a). Gaddy (1986) and Gortmaker and colleagues (1990) conducted the two analyses of very large samples that report an initial inverse association between viewing and achievement that vanishes when a large variety of other variables are statistically controlled. In our judgment they use data too truncated to be convincing. The negative association between viewing and performance persists in several other sets of data when possibly confounding variables are taken into account (Comstock, 1991a), but the control variables are too few in our opinion to make a strong case for causal influence.

The alternative to direct evidence is to construct from the wide variety of relevant data the process by which an inverse association between television viewing and scholastic performance comes about. The criterion for validity then becomes our persuasiveness compared to alternative renderings.

We begin with two explanatory processes, interference and displacement. Then we identify three clusterings of data and present a mock path analysis that resolves the question of causality.

A. Interference

The interference hypothesis takes three forms. The first posits that television viewing cultivates skills that interfere with the processing of print (D. R. Anderson & Collins, 1988). The second holds that the pacing of much television suppresses impulse control and the ability to attend to the slower pace of schooling (J. L. Singer & Rapaczynski, 1984). The third predicts that television viewing in conjunction with scholastic tasks, such as reading and homework, lowers performance (Armstrong & Greenberg, 1990).

We find no evidence that attending to television stunts the ability to process text, whereas there is plenty of evidence that most of the time young viewers confronted with both will give precedence to visual stimuli (Comstock, 1991a). If there is an effect, it is short-lived because comprehension of text and television among young adults is positively correlated (Pezdek, Simon, Stoeckert, & Kiley, 1985). There is some evidence that violent portrayals—which are often fast-paced—suppress impulse control among very young children. There is little evidence that pace itself is a factor, but this would not explain inverse correlations between viewing and achievement at later ages. However, lower performance when scholastic tasks have been combined with viewing has been recorded in several instances. Fetler (1984), in a large CAP sample, found a very small but negative association between doing homework in front of the set and achievement—about one-fourth of that for viewing (negative) and one-seventh of that for a measure of amount of homework (positive). Armstrong and Greenberg (1990) compared academic task performance with and without the company of an operating television set, and found that those who completed the tasks in the company of the operating set scored lower in reading comprehension, spatial problem solving, and cognitive flexibility with the apparent explanation of interference with the exercise of cognitive skills because no differences in attention or physiological arousal were observed.

Koolstra and van der Voort (1996) examined relationships in a Dutch sample of more than a thousand 2nd and 4th graders between amount of viewing and mental effort invested while reading. Those who viewed greater amounts expended lower levels of effort, and statistical controls for mental ability and other pertinent variables favor attributing the outcome to the influence of viewing.

The CAP data (1980) record that in high school, very heavy viewers (5 or more hours a day) were also more likely to spend greater than average amounts of time reading and on homework. Similarly, over the 3 years of his study Morgan (1980) found that the correlation shifted from slightly negative to slightly positive between television viewing and reading for oneself. Our tentative interpretation is that those who view a great deal of television must either compensate for lower efficiency, possibly because they combine reading and homework with viewing, or they undertake undemanding ventures—easy tasks and superficial text—compatible with viewing at the same time. The large amounts of time spent with television among those who score high in viewing do not seem to permit other explanations.

Finally, Keith and colleagues (1986) in their sample of more than 28,000 seniors found that achievement was positively correlated with time spent on homework, and amount of time spent on homework was positively correlated with greater parental involvement with their children. For the average senior, television and homework did not compete for the same blocks of time because the amount of homework typically assigned was modest. Given the size and national representativeness of the sample and the more academically demanding character of high school compared to junior high and elementary school, we consider this convincing evidence that for the average child and teenager (who view an average amount of television) the two do not ordinarily compete for the same blocks of time. This proposition gains in credibility through the back door by the fact that at every level frequently in the United States no homework is assigned (Neuman, 1991).

B. DISPLACEMENT

The displacement hypothesis in its narrowest but probably most widely applied version holds that television viewing consumes time and attention that otherwise would be devoted to the acquisition of reading skills (Mutz et al., 1993; Williams, 1986). In a broader version, it extends the proposition to the other basic skills, mathematics and writing. More generally, the hypothesis holds that television displaces time that might be spent on more scholastically pertinent activities.

The key acquisition period for reading is specified by Chall (1983) as the first through third grades. In the first and second grades, alphabet mastery and matching of letters to spoken words occurs. The foundation for fluent reading is laid in the second and third grades, when reading is primarily the practicing of a skill. By the fourth grade, children begin to read for pleasure. Learning to read is often hard work for a child, whereas television viewing is comparatively undemanding. Children are certainly tempted to watch television instead of mastering reading, and those who succumb will be permanently impaired scholastically (Williams, 1986).

The question is whether such displacement occurs with any frequency. If so, we would logically expect it to occur for the two other basic skills. There is also the question of whether the maintenance and improvement, by practice, of the basic skills is deterred. Our attempt to resolve these questions led to a small propositional inventory:

1. Amount of time spent viewing television and reading among children are inversely associated (Heyns, 1976; Medrich et al., 1982). This inverse relationship becomes stronger the more stringent and demanding—in the sense of quantity or quality—the measure of reading (Comstock, 1991a; Koolstra & van der Voort, 1996). Thus, it may be obscured by a question that asks young people *whether* they read a newspaper, magazine, or book last week but will become apparent when they are queried about *how much time* they spent reading newspapers, magazines, or books yesterday or last week or *how many* or *how frequently* they read one or another last week or last month. The inverse association also is much more pronounced for reading than for participation in other activities, such as visiting a museum, taking music lessons, or engaging in hobbies and sports (Medrich et al., 1982). These activities only occasionally display minor negative associations with viewing. Negative associations with reading and with engaging in other activities become more frequent and pronounced when the independent variable is centrality of television. Furthermore, the occasional minor negative associations with amount of viewing for other activities were observable only in White households, whereas the more frequent and pronounced negative associations for reading and for other activities with household centrality of television are clear for both White and Black households (Medrich et al., 1982). These data mark values and norms as a greater culprit than time discplacement. Reading, then, is particularly at risk—both to amount of viewing and to values and norms that esteem television.

2. Television viewing does not displace activities that serve important functions for individuals that are not duplicated by watching television (Himmelweit et al., 1958; Schramm et al., 1961). The most prominent example is theater-

movie attendance by teenagers, which remains stable despite television viewing (Comstock, 1991a). Similarly, among those 9, 11, and 13 years of age, amount of time spent viewing is unrelated to time spent in sports or with friends (S. B. Neuman, 1988). Television, however, delivers many of the gratifications of reading.

3. The introduction of television displaced use of a variety of media (Robinson, 1972a, 1972b; Robinson & Converse, 1972; Szalai, 1972). Among the displaced were several types of reading, including the reading of books, magazines, fiction from public libraries, and comic books—the latter, of course, largely among children (Parker, 1960; Robinson, 1972a). Since then, the time allocated by adults to reading in general and newspapers in particular has declined whereas the time allocated to television has increased (Robinson & Godbey, 1997). The historical record, then, confirms the substitution of television for reading.

4. Reading achievement is inversely associated with amount of time spent viewing in both elementary and high school (B. Anderson, Mead, & Sullivan, 1986; CAP, 1980; Gaddy, 1986; Gortmaker et al., 1990; Keith et al., 1986; S. Neuman, 1988). Moreover, this relationship is robust and persistent except when other variables are controlled in a way that essentially precludes its appearance (as was the case with Gaddy, 1986, and Gortmaker et al., 1990). Morgan (1980) in a high-school sample of about 200 from whom data were obtained over 3 years found that reading comprehension scores of those higher and lower in mental ability converged as amount of television viewing increased. As one might expect, the narrowing was primarily attributable to the sharp decline in scores of those high and moderate in ability. Koolstra, van der Voort, and van der Kamp (1997) in their 1000-plus sample of Dutch elementary school children found reading comprehension skills negatively related to viewing even after controlling for IQ and socioeconomic status—two variables that predict greater use of television and thus might create an artifactual association between viewing and reading achievement. In another very thorough analysis, Morgan and Gross (1980) also found that the inverse association withstood controls for a wide range of variables, including mental ability, socioeconomic status, sex, grade, time spent on homework, and time spent reading for oneself—although in several other instances an inverse association was reduced to null by controlling for mental ability (S. Neuman, 1991). There is some support, then, for the interpretation that greater viewing is not only a correlate of but also contributes to lower reading achievement.

5. Time spent reading ordinarily increases between the second grade and high school. Although no increase was recorded in the huge (70,000) NAEP sample for self-estimates, we have much greater confidence in the meticulous data of Timmer and colleagues (1985) despite the comparatively small sample (about 400) because they used the more valid time-diary method that records

allocation of all time use (Robinson & Godbey, 1997). Thus, reading would be progressively more sensitive to competition from other activities.

6. Young people who view greater amounts of television are more likely to have a decidedly low opinion of book reading as an activity, are more likely to read comic books frequently (Koolstra & van der Voort, 1996), and are more likely to prefer media that resemble television in plot and content (Morgan, 1980). Television by its ease of use and modes of storytelling may discourage more demanding types of reading.

We believe the inverse relationships consistently recorded between viewing and our two major measures of reading, amount and achievement or comprehension, are somewhat suppressed in terms of representing the situation for most children by the high levels of viewing by very young children high in mental ability. The attractiveness of television as an alternative to reading makes displacement between the first and third grades almost a certainty for many who view a great deal. As a result, we extend the displacement of skill acquisition to mathematics and writing. We would expect these effects to occur only among those who well exceed the average in viewing (recalling the evidence of Keith and colleagues, 1986, that television and homework do not compete for the same blocks of time, which would exempt for the average child and teenager the reading done as part of school work), and so confidently if conservatively specify those at risk as the substantial 20% in the highest quintile whose viewing exceeds the average by more than 100%.

Television certainly takes up time after the acquisition period for basic skills that could be spent on reading and other scholastic pursuits. Viewing is nevertheless often selected by children and teenagers who probably would not read or otherwise engage in scholarly endeavors if they were not viewing. To expect otherwise, we would have to believe that such activities rank high among the preferences of the young. We thus see the practice that would maintain or improve basic skills as less subject to television than to the motives of viewers, and we suspect that mathematics and writing would suffer more than reading because they offer less in the way of intrinsic rewards. Unlike skill acquisition, the crux is not the lure of television but the way Americans dispose of unallocated time.

This pattern leads us to broaden the displacement hypothesis. Our reformulation is as follows:

> Television viewing is inversely related to achievement when it displaces intellectually and experientially richer stimuli. Viewing is positively related to achievement when the stimuli it supplies are intellectually and experientially richer than the available alternatives.

Highly suggestive data regarding the operation of displacement come from the CAP, NAEP, HSB panel and the early research of Schramm and colleagues (1961). In all four, collected at different times from different populations, an inverse relationship between viewing and achievement is clearest among those from whom the most would be expected: those of greater mental ability, from households of higher socioeconomic status, or with greater educational resources. In all four studies, the relationship is null, weak, or sometimes even positive among those from whom the least might be expected: those of lower mental ability, not fluent in English, from households lower in socioeconomic status, or with fewer educational resources.

Displacement, then, should be reconceptualized as having three distinct forms. One is the usurpation of time that might be devoted to basic skill acquisition. The second is the use of time for television that could but in all probability would not be spent on a scholastically constructive activity. The third is the socialization—in effect, training—by television that turns young people away from books and toward comic books and subject matter similar to television entertainment.

C. THREE CLUSTERS

We discern three clusters of data as follows:

1. *Self-selection.* Lower mental ability, conflicts with parents or peers, lower socioeconomic status, high household centrality of television, the perception that there is no other activity more necessary or rewarding—each of these predicts greater amounts of viewing. These five factors also reflect an individual trait, interpersonal relationships, a social attribute, a household norm, and personal values, respectively, that predict lower scholastic performance. Our conclusion is that a substantial portion of the negative association between amount of viewing and scholastic performance is attributable to self-selection, with those who for a variety of reasons would perform at a lower level watching greater amounts of television.

2. *Interference and Displacement.* The combining of homework, assigned reading, or reading outside of assignments with viewing results in a debased quality of experience. This is reflected in the modest but clearly negative correlations between achievement and homework in front of the set, in the experimental manipulation in which cognitive tasks were performed less well in the company of an operating television set, by lower degrees of concentration while reading among heavy viewers when other variables were held constant, and in the necessity of choosing undemanding, superficial material that can accommodate the monitoring of television at the same time.

Amount of time spent viewing and reading prior to the teenage years are inversely associated. This has often been masked by the use of weak criteria, such as "some" or "weekly" (for which almost everyone qualifies), and becomes consistently more pronounced as more quantitatively or qualitatively demanding measures are used (Comstock, 1991a; Koolstra & van der Voort, 1996). Among those who view large amounts of television between the first and third grades, television may displace acquisition of the basic skill of reading and, analogously, acquisition of the two other basic skills, mathematics and writing. Large amounts of viewing also may consume time that could be spent on maintenance and improvement of basic skills. Few, however, would opt to spend time on basic skills even if viewing were somehow constrained—the most likely replacement would be an activity similar in reward and effort, such as comic book reading.

3. *Pursuit of the Trivial, Triumph of the Banal.* To our surprise, we have concluded that the effects of television go well beyond interference and displacement. In our view, the data point convincingly and powerfully to the choices young people make among the media. Television not only disrupts and takes away from scholastically more constructive activities. It also leads toward activities that are less than optimally constructive. It functions not only as an antagonist; it acts as a counselor.

We will lay out our argument study by study. The findings array themselves in a linear progression of remarkable coherence, beginning with everyday reflections on television programming and ending with choices among media and beliefs about the worthiness of reading books. We use this tactic not because it makes our sources explicit but because it presents our case more strongly.

W. R. Neuman (1982) interviewed over 100 viewers while they were watching television, and found that their thoughts predominantly concerned the plot, presentation, and storytelling techniques rather than the social implications of what was portrayed. Viewers became involved with the manner and techniques of storytelling. The respondents were adults but there is no reason to think the same frame of mind does not apply equally to children and teenagers. When Watkins (1988) asked about 80 children and teenagers in the third, fifth, and eighth grades to write stories for television, the stories became progressively more complex and similar to television dramas, with those authored by children high in viewing in the eighth grade about three times more complex than stories written about real life. Morgan (1980; Morgan & Gross, 1980), in a sample of about 200 males and females from whom data were obtained over a 3-year period ending in high school, found not only a shift from a small negative to a small positive correlation between amount of viewing and reading but also a difference among heavy viewers favoring television-like reading matter:

> Heavy viewers are significantly more likely than light viewers to prefer stories about
> love and families, teenage stories, and true stories about stars. Light viewers . . .
> choose science fiction, mysteries, and general non-fiction. (p. 164)

Similarly, Koolstra and van der Voort (1996) found that between the second and fourth grades the correlation between reading comic books and amount of viewing shifted from negative to positive, those who viewed greater amounts of television came to invest less mental effort and concentration on reading and developed attitudes flagrantly and literally hostile to book reading as dull, boring, and unworthy. These latter data (Koolstra & van der Voort, 1996; Morgan, 1980; Morgan & Gross, 1980) make a strong case for the causal influence of viewing on use of print (and by implication, because they too are more demanding, all reality-based media that might contribute to the ability to cope with the problems, hazards, and challenges of life) because of the control for numerous other variables including mental ability. This is a crucially important confounding variable because lower ability predicts less use of print and less likelihood of instrumental media use—the very outcomes that can now be confidently ascribed to viewing.

Television promotes a particular way of storytelling. It socializes young viewers to prefer undemanding content. Young viewers come to express the values of television in their use of other media. Viewing not only interferes with and displaces scholastic endeavors but also shapes the motives and directs the preferences of the young toward the trivial and the banal.

We display what we construe to be the major elements in the relationships between viewing and scholastic performance in a mock path diagram (Figure 7.2). The single path analysis in the empirical literature (Keith et al., 1986) includes only seven variables, so we have drawn on the findings of other studies to expand it. (The weights represent our judgment of the direction and strength of the associations.)

Mental ability and household socioeconomic status are fundamental. Household environment (centrality of television, availability of print media, and parental involvement) is a substantial predictor of amount of television viewed. For Blacks as a group, centrality will be less significant. However, we would expect centrality to play the same role for many as it does for Whites, and primarily in the households of lower socioeconomic status that are disproportionately represented among Black households. Ability to read and other types of earlier achievement are major predictors of later achievement.

Our model accords somewhat greater influence to nontelevision factors. This is clear in tracing the routes from household socioeconomic status through mental ability and parental involvement. There is also a distinct causal contribution by television. This is most clear in the diminished motives and preferences for reading outside of assignments, homework without television, book reading,

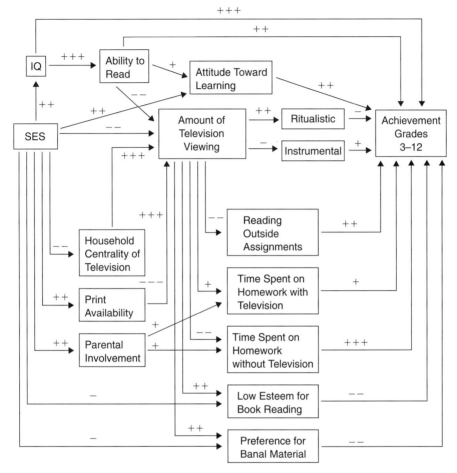

FIGURE 7.2 Path model—household variables, viewing, and scholastic performance. Adapted from *Television and the American child,* by G. Comstock, 1991a. San Diego, CA: Academic Press.

and more demanding content. However, we see instrumental viewing, which occurs almost exclusively among those who view lesser amounts of television, as contributing positively to achievement. Because of the uniformity of the data across ages and subject matter, we conclude that the model applies to scholastic performance in general.

More than 20 years ago Marie Winn argued in *The Plug-in Drug* (1977) that large amounts of television viewing interfered with learning to read, reduced the ability to concentrate while reading, and promoted the use of reading matter that could be scanned or read in brief segments with low involvement. Winn is one of the most cited names in communication, but almost universally as a strident voice to be corrected by the citing author(s). However, the evidence that has accumulated since *The Plug-in Drug* makes her essentially a visionary. She has become the indestructible straw woman as the data have reopened her Pandora's box.

Antisocial Behavior

Media violence has been a controversial issue throughout this century, with television the primary focus since its introduction in the late 1940s. Congress has held numerous hearings (by 1996, the count was at 28) regarding television violence (C. Cooper, 1996). Pulp fiction was a target early in the century, followed by the movies, as exemplified by the first empirical scientific inquiry into the effects of popular audiovisual media, the Payne Fund studies in the 1930s (Charters, 1933; Peterson & Thurstone, 1933). More recently, in the 1950s, comic books were the center of attention. Frederic Wertham, a New York psychiatrist, became a celebrity through such books as *Seduction of the Innocent* (1954) in which he argued that comics were an illustrated "school" for violence, crime, and terror perpetrated by young readers. As surveys of adolescent media use make clear (Comstock, 1991a; Lovibond, 1967), television drastically reduced the audience for comics and the readers of violent comics became viewers of violent television programming. Thus, television's contemporary preeminence in this regard is rooted in the behavior of young audiences.

However, there are a number of other reasons why television has drawn more attention than other media. Access by children and adolescents is difficult to control and often ignored by parents. Broadcast outlets, which account for a majority of programming that reaches the public, are required by the Federal Communications Act of 1934 to serve the "public interest, convenience, and necessity" and are open to regulation—if not censorship—by the Federal Communications Commission. Television has been a very violent medium since its beginnings (Head, 1954; Smythe, 1954) and it has become a major means of dissemination of its more violent competitor, theater movies (Cole, 1996, 1997). It has become a central element in our culture of violence—entertainment constructed of heinous and brave deeds, physical conflict, frightful wanderings and escapes, mischance and retribution, implosions and explosions, the cop, the serial killer, the deadly doll.

Our examination will cover four topics. They are the social context of public opinion and other media, the evidence of effects on aggressive and antisocial behavior, our criteria and schema for interpreting the evidence, and the broad implications of the data.

I. SOCIAL CONTEXT

The first congressional hearing devoted to television programming was held in the House in 1952. The topics were violence and sex. The committee concluded that some programming was offensive, portrayals of crime and violence were excessive, and self-regulation was preferable to government intervention, but that Congress had prerogatives despite the First Amendment because of the great potential for harm. This established the framework for numerous House and Senate hearings focusing on violence, and sometimes also sex, that would follow. These included very high profile hearings chaired by Senators Kefauver (1950s), Dodd (1960s), Pastore (1970s), and Simon (1990s).

Five federal fact-finding task forces have been concerned with media effects. The National Commission on the Causes and Prevention of Violence (1969), primarily concerned with rioting in urban Black communities, issued a compendium of research findings on the influence of media violence (Baker & Ball, 1969) and in its report specifically concluded that media violence contributed to antisocial behavior. The Commission on Obscenity and Pornography (1970) concluded that erotic media had no deleterious effects on antisocial behavior. The Surgeon General's Scientific Advisory Committee on Television and Social Behavior (1972), the sole inquiry primarily concerned with television violence, concluded that viewing violent programming increased the aggressive and antisocial behavior of some young viewers. The "Surgeon General's Update," a collection of commissioned papers (Pearl, Bouthilet, & Lazar, 1982b) and an overview by a committee of experts (Pearl, Bouthilet, & Lazar, 1982a) on the 10th anniversary of the report of the original committee, concluded that the evidence of the preceding decade strongly reinforced the initial conclusion. The Attorney General's Commission on Pornography (1986) concluded that media that portrayed females in a degrading manner or as the targets of violent assault, especially in a sexual context, increased aggressive and antisocial behavior on the part of males against females. Thus, four of the five endeavors concluded that violent media could be problematic in regard to the behavior of viewers, with one focused specifically on television entertainment.

A. PUBLIC OPINION

These institutional expressions of concern have had their counterpart in public opinion as measured by polls and surveys. The more prominent have been conducted by professional research organizations (Roper Starch, Gallup, Yankelovich, and others, often with media sponsorship) using national probability samples of about 1200 to 2000, so that outcomes can be said to accurately represent the American public.

Typically, about two-thirds of Americans have agreed (rather than disagreed or confessed to no opinion) with the statement that there is "too much violence" on television, although figures as low as 50% have been recorded (Comstock, 1988; Immerwahr & Doble, 1982; Rubens, 1981). Such proportions have been highly stable since the 1960s.

The proportion agreeing with the statement that television violence is harmful or encourages crime and delinquency typically has been about three-fourths of that endorsing the view that there is too much violence. If 66% agree there is too much violence, about 50% will agree it is harmful.

The pattern for "sex" on television—or, more accurately, the intimation, description, or designation of sexual activity, since graphic intercourse is not a part of entertainment on broadcast or most cable channels—has been similar, except that it typically scores a very few percentage points behind violence in regard to "too much" or harmfulness. Violence and sex compete, along with the number of commercials, as attributes of television with which the public says it is most dissatisfied (Bower, 1985).

The public is sensitive to the degree of attention given to television violence by the media. With the congressional and presidential pressure of the 1990s and consequent media attention, the proportion agreeing there is too much violence has increased to about 80% (Strasburger, 1995). Poll after poll in the mid-1990s has reported comparable results.

This suggests a scenario in which public anxiety has been reflected in the response of politicians and public institutions. However, a closer look at the evidence reveals a very different picture.

In the late 1970s and early 1980s, the Reverends Jerry Falwell and Daniel Wildmon attempted to organize viewer boycotts in protest of television sex and violence and had singled out 16 programs as particularly offensive. When a nationally representative sample was asked without any reference to violence to name things disliked about these programs, the average citing violence was under 5% (Rubens, 1981). During the same period, the percentage in comparable samples agreeing there was too much violence on television ranged from 50 to 66% (Comstock, 1991).

The phenomenon is repeated in very recently published data by Roper Starch (1995). When asked if they had seen something on television that offended them, only about 7% of a representative national sample cited a violent portrayal. This contrasts with the approximately 80% who during the same period endorsed the view that there is too much violence on television.

This is an example of a common circumstance (Comstock, 1989)—the radically different impressions about public views that may occur for "volunteered" opinions vs "elicited" responses. The former represent the free expression of views in response to a topic or subject area. The latter tabulate the selection of an option (agree, disagree, no opinion) in response to a preformulated stance. The more that volunteered opinions lag behind elicited responses in frequency, the less salient and deeply held is the opinion represented by the elicited responses, for the former represent viewpoints people are ready to articulate whereas the latter are merely multiple-choice endorsements.

The pattern has been repeatedly supported since World War II by the replies of the public when regularly asked by Gallup to name the most important problem facing the nation. Only a scant few have named media violence, even at times when the behavior of the media has been fairly high among the topics receiving attention in the news (Funkhouser, 1973a, 1973b).

Overall, the data led us to four conclusions:

1. Television violence, along with other media issues, is of very low salience to the public. It is not a topic where opinion is heartfelt or concern is of high priority.
2. The widely published survey data have exaggerated the degree of public concern because of the mode of collection. Similarly, the high percentages currently being recorded for elicited opinion decline to their former levels when media attention declines.
3. The notion that politicians and the federal task forces have responded to public anxiety is incorrect. The low salience attached by the public to media issues suggest they are of concern primarily to elites—those who work in the media and in public life. The rise in the proportion expressing dissatisfaction with television violence is a consequence of the attention of public figures and the media rather than the reverse.

4. When attacked about some genre of content, the best defense of the media is to direct attention toward specific offerings. Our example has been television violence, but we believe the principle holds broadly. The public is ready to endorse harsh views about a medium in general, but is far less prepared to do so in regard to explicitly identified examples.

B. Other Media

We now place violence in television entertainment in the context of violence in other media. We will examine the available data on Music Television (MTV), prerecorded videos, pay-per-view, and historical patterns.

1. Music Television

There have been a number of analyses of violence on MTV over the past decade (Baxter, DeReimer, Landini, Leslie, & Singletary, 1985; Caplan, 1985; Hansen & Hansen, 1990; Jones, 1997; Kalis & Neuendorf, 1989; Larson & Kubey, 1983; Makris, 1995; Sherman & Dominick, 1986). MTV also has been the target of "violence counts" by an advocacy group opposing violence in media, the National Coalition on Television Violence (NCTV) in 1983, 1984, and 1991 (Denisoff, 1988; Dunkley, 1993).

All analyses and counts concur that there has been considerable violence in music videos. However, many of the measures are increasingly less representative of the channel as news, comedy, commentary, and game shows by the mid-1990s constituted a majority of programming. What the data better represent are musical genres.

Nevertheless, there is no single formula for specifying amount of violence. All-MTV would produce a lower frequency than music-only MTV; concept videos would produce a higher frequency than all-music MTV; cues, symbols, and verbal violence would markedly increase the rate over that for physical violence; and frequency might give a different impression than elapsed time.

One of the most recent analyses is by Makris (1995). He defined a violent act as "a specific, manifest behavior . . . involving actual or potential harm to life or destruction of an object" based on a classification system developed at the American Broadcasting Company (ABC) (Wurtzel & Lometti, 1984). It is more conservative than the analyses of Gerbner and colleagues (Chapter 3) by ignoring accidents, acts of God, and threats without an implication of immediate harm; more conservative than many of the MTV analyses by omitting symbols, allusions, and nonharmful threats; and comparatively conservative by including both concept and performance videos.

There were an average of 1.5 violent acts per video. If we accept Makris'

TABLE 8.1   Violent Acts in MTV Videos
by Category

Category of violence	Total videos (includes repeats) (N = 125)	
	Percent of total	No. of acts
Weapons threats	10.9	21
Unarmed threats	7.2	14
Weapons assaults	24.4	47
Major assaults	14.5	28
Confinement	—	—
Minor assaults	12.4	24
Property assaults	30.6	59
Total	100	193

Adapted from "A Reexamination of Violent Content in MTV Music Videos: How Violent Are Videos?" by G. Makris, 1995, unpublished master's thesis, Syracuse University, Syracuse, NY.

estimate that videos average 2 to 6 minutes in length, the estimated rate per hour would range from 15 to 45, greater than the typical prime-time tallies of Gerbner and colleagues (Chapter 3). The analysis of types of violence (Table 8.1) identifies about half as very serious, involving major physical assaults, assaults with weapons, or threats accompanied by weapons. Violence was concentrated in a few videos, with about one-sixth of the sample producing almost 60% of the violent acts. The genres of music video where violence was most frequent were rap and hard rock/heavy metal. Similarly, Jones' (1997) analysis of over 200 videos found that rap videos contained more references to guns, drugs, alcohol, and gambling. The amount of elapsed time in the Makris sample devoted to violence, or duration, was startlingly brief: 2.7% of the 8.5 hours for total videos in the sample or an average of 6.5 seconds per video.

Our judgment is that the suspect (MTV) is guilty by measures of rate (because it exceeds the rate for prime-time television), and would be even more so had a more inclusive definition been employed or performance videos excluded. It also remains indictable on the basis of duration, because 6.5 seconds is sufficient to depict violent acts with attendant verve and glamor. More importantly, the violence was confined to a very few videos and was concentrated in two genres, so that when violence was depicted it usually well exceeded the average in the attention given to it. The data on the whole, then, support the view that MTV has been a particularly violent channel but they also make it clear that the violence has been largely confined to specific videos and certain genres.

2. Videos

The prerecorded video market provides a considerably wider perspective on Hollywood movies than current releases. It also represents a home alternative that has made possible greatly increased movie viewing by children and teenagers (Chapter 1), and provides—through indulgent older friends and indifferent video rental operators—an easy means for them to overcome the box office entry barriers of the age-restrictive codes of the Motion Picture Association of America (MPAA).

The most comprehensive analysis available is by Yang and Linz (1990). They sampled 30 titles each of then R-, X-, and XXX-rated videos (the first two being MPAA ratings, the third a video industry classification for erotica) from the general and adult inventories of a large, urban rental outlet and coded them for sexual, violent, sexually violent, and prosocial acts. An act was defined to include connected events across scenes so as not to inflate tallies for the usually more costly, general audience R-rated films with their many cuts and edits for cinematic impact. The results (Table 8.2) identify R-rated films as containing five or more times as many violent acts as the X- and XXX- categories (35% vs 7 and 5%, respectively), but only somewhat fewer sexually violent acts (3 versus

TABLE 8.2　Video Content by Rating

| | Frequency of acts | | | | | |
| | R-Rated | | X-Rated | | XXX-Rated | |
	N	%	N	%	N	%
Sexual	52	4.5	339	34.4	269	41.0
Violent	391	34.5	70	7.1	31	4.7
Sexually violent	37	3.2	48	4.8	31	4.7
Prosocial	123	10.8	21	2.1	20	3.0
Other	529	46.7	506	51.4	304	46.4
Total	1132	100.0	984	100.0	655	100.0

| | Number of videos | | | | | |
| | R-Rated | | X-Rated | | XXX-Rated | |
	N	%	N	%	N	%
Violence only	11	36.6	4	13.3	0	0.0
Sexual violence only	0	0.0	8	26.6	3	10.0
Violence and sexual violence	18	60.0	14	46.6	11	36.6
No violence or sexual violence	1	3.3	4	13.3	16	53.3
Total	30	100.0	30	100.0	30	100.0

Adapted from "Movie Ratings and the Content of Adult Videos: The Sex Violence Ratio," by N. Yang and D. Linz, 1990, *Journal of Communication, 40*(2), pp. 28–42.

5 and 5%, respectively). The X- and XXX-rated videos were overwhelming leaders in sexual acts, as were the R-rated in prosocial acts. Violence and sexual violence, although occurring jointly in about a third to a half of the XXX- and X-rated films, occurred jointly in fully 60% (a total of 18) of the R-rated films. The average duration for sexual violence for R-rated films was 1:03 (minutes and seconds); for X-rated, 4:10; and for XXX-rated, 3:44.

Our conclusion is that Hollywood films with sufficient sex or violence to earn a restricted rating (whatever the label may be at the time) are on the average very violent, are not without sexual violence, and often combine violence and sexual violence. Ironically, X-and XXX-rated films are comparatively low in violence. Our judgment that films with restricted ratings markedly exceed the violence in network prime-time television is supported by the recent large-scale analyses (Chapter 3) that indicate that premium movie channels and movies on television are the most violent of television offerings.

3. Pay-per-view

Pay-per-view could make hundreds and eventually thousands of motion picture and video titles available to viewers in their homes on demand. It could also remain in its present limited application (Deutschmann, 1994; Kaplan, 1992; Martin, 1994; Miller, 1995).

Most viewers are not so vigorous in their selectivity to use their VCRs to create a homogeneous or otherwise highly personalized intake of content (Chapter 1). The convenience of pay-per-view conceivably could somewhat overcome this inertia. The inventory could equal across several years the 450 movies released annually by Hollywood, about a third of which have violent themes. We nevertheless do not foresee large increases in movie viewing because of the constraint imposed by the time available for the greater attention usually given to movies than to ordinary television (Chapter 3), but we do think that for a few viewers, pay-per-view will produce what broadcast and cable do not so readily achieve even with a VCR—a subscription to violence (or any other genre).

4. Historical Patterns

One particular study spans several decades comparing prime-time television, theater movies, newspaper front pages, and family-magazine fiction (*Saturday Evening Post*). It represents the past, but remains highly informative—not only about the years of television's emergence, but also because it reveals surprising similarities and stability in the frequency of violence.

Clark and Blankenburg (1972) employed the featuring of a violent event as the criterion for categorizing a story or vehicle as violent, which made it possible to cover television and movies through plot synopses. The time periods are extremely long—17 to 42 years (for television and newspaper front pages respectively, the two extremes)—thus averages are highly reliable and trends are well represented. There are four important findings:

1. Amount of violence in the different media is very similar. Prime-time television (27.4% violent), popular magazine fiction (26.9%), and network news (26.3%) were almost identical, with movies averaging only somewhat higher (35.2%) and newspaper front pages only somewhat lower (17.6%).
2. Shifts from year to year are sometimes quite dramatic, but there is a danger of overinterpretation. For television and for two of the other three media, long-term trends were absent. This is essentially the same pattern that Gerbner and colleagues (Chapter 3) would record between the late 1960s and the mid-1990s—short-term oscillations with no dramatic long-term changes.
3. The sole secular trend observable was the upward if oscillating path for movies. Increases clearly predate the introduction of television, but the trend surely was furthered by Hollywood's attempts to attract young adults and teenagers to compensate for the reduced appeal of theater venues for family entertainment.
4. Media are sensitive to historical events that affect audience receptivity to real-life frequency of violence. In the tense international climate at the beginning of World War II the popular family magazine fiction avoided violence, whereas during the war newspaper front pages carried many more than the average number of stories concerned with violent events.

Our conclusion is that violence is a staple of mass media. We ascribe the year to year fluctuations to the competition for audiences and changing perceptions on the part of those who govern the media regarding the acceptability of violent content. Thus, Clark and Blankenburg (1972) found that violence peaked every 4 or 5 years, with the frequency of violent programs rising and falling with the average ratings for the genre the previous season. Thus, violence conforms to the season-to-season linkage observed earlier (Chapter 3) in which popularity of a genre predicts its future frequency in the schedule. Political and public pressure over violent entertainment usually provokes reductions in the frequency of the most violent acts, such as murder, and the number of principal characters participating in them. It also increases the renewal rate for nonviolent series, as Hamilton (1998) found when examining network behavior subsequent to congressional hearings on television violence. Movie but not magazine fiction or newspaper front page violence increased because that medium found it competitively useful in regard to the audience it could attract. Violence in television entertainment, then, is not particularly more frequent than in other media. What sets it apart is the extensive evidence in behalf of behavioral and other effects for television and film portrayals, the huge amount of time people and particularly children (even teenagers, who are the demographic segment with the lowest average viewing, are recorded as viewing many hours each week) spend with it, and the specialization of the medium in precisely the kinds of portrayals likely to figure in those effects.

II. EVIDENCE

The first two experiments demonstrating that exposure to violent portrayals can increase aggressiveness were published in 1963 in the *Journal of Abnormal and Social Psychology* (Bandura, Ross, & Ross, 1963a; Berkowitz & Rawlings, 1963). By 1990, a total of 217 separate studies, each examining a different set of empirical data addressing the question of television violence and antisocial behavior, had accumulated (Paik & Comstock, 1994).

We begin with laboratory-type experiments in which young children were the subjects. Next, we examine the same type of experiments in which the subjects were young adults of college age. We then explore sources that might confirm or disconfirm the generalizability of experimental findings for everyday life: field experiments and surveys.

A. EXPERIMENTS— CHILDREN

In their pioneer experiment, Bandura, Ross, and Ross (1963a) employed as a dependent variable the behavior of nursery school children in a playroom with a Bobo doll and other toys. There were four conditions: (a) no behavior involving the large, inflated rubber figure with a bulbous nose known as a Bobo doll; (b) a human male in ordinary attire verbally and physically attacking the Bobo doll; (c) a film sequence of the same attack; or (d) a film sequence of a female in a cat costume (the Cat Lady), such as might appear in children's entertainment, engaging in that same attack. To heighten the likelihood of aggressive behavior, the children were first mildly frustrated by being shown but denied the opportunity to play with an assortment of attractive toys.

Those children in all three treatment groups (b, c, and d) displayed more aggressive behavior toward the doll and with other toys than did those in the control condition. Nonimitative as well as imitative aggressive behavior was affected, although the effect was most prominent for imitative acts. The children exposed to the fantasy condition, the Cat Lady, exhibited less aggression than those seeing the live model, but definitely more than those in the control condition.

Bandura, Ross, and Ross (1963b) next manipulated the exposure of nursery school children to film sequences of two young adults. In one, Rocky takes Johnny's toys away and is rewarded. In the other, Johnny defends himself and Rocky is punished. The first increased imitation of Rocky's play with the toys and led to derogatory comments about Johnny as well as criticism of Rocky.

Later, Bandura (1965) followed film sequences in which an assault of a Bobo doll was either rewarded, punished, or without consequences by small rewards—fruit juice and a paste-on logo—for imitating what had been seen. Among children who saw the punished version imitation initially was at a much lower rate, and imitation by girls initially was much lower than by boys. When the reward was introduced, differences between conditions disappeared and the difference between boys and girls became barely discernible.

In the first experiment, behavior was a function of observation, modified somewhat by the degree to which what was observed seemed to represent reality. In the second, behavior was a function of efficacy; that is, perceived consequences. In fact, the children imitated Rocky despite criticizing him and were contemptuous of Johnny when he became a victim; bad behavior was no match for perceived success. The third exemplifies the underlying indifference of acquisition or learning of behavior to norms and rewards, whereas performance is heavily dependent on them. Girls (for whom aggressive acts would be less normative) and those who viewed punished models were initially less likely to perform the observed acts. However, they learned them and added them to their behavioral repertoires as demonstrated by the changes in behavior when a reward was specifically offered for imitating what had been seen. These are typical of the several dozen experiments by Bandura and others testing propositions derived from psychological theory (specifically, social cognition) regarding the influence of violent portrayals on young children. The conclusion that violent television and film portrayals cause aggressive and antisocial behavior among young children is strengthened by four additional sources:

1. *Experiments that introduce more naturalistic or ecologically valid elements.* Steuer, Applefield, and Smith (1971) and Josephson (1987) provide the most dramatic examples. In Steuer and colleagues' experiment, a small group of children who viewed violent children's programs became more aggressive on the playground than those comparable in pretreatment aggressiveness who viewed nonviolent programs. In Josephson's experiment, several hundred boys in grades two and three, in groups of six, watched either a violent or a nonviolent television program. Those who scored higher in prior "characteristic" aggressiveness who saw the violent program subsequently displayed greater aggression while playing floor hockey, and the effect was heightened by the presence of a cue from the program.

2. *Experiments with children in circumstances so violent that one would expect the effects of the media to be overshadowed.* Both Day and Ghandour (1984) and McHan (1985) found that Arab boys between the ages of 5 and 8 in

Beirut, Lebanon, became more aggressive after seeing televised portrayals in experiments similar to those conducted by Bandura and colleagues although their real-life circumstances included street fighting, sporadic explosions, and the threat of invasion.

3. *The three-community British Columbia experiment by T. M. Williams (1986) and colleagues.* Playground aggressiveness of children increased between the first and fourth grades in the treatment community after television was introduced, but not in the two control communities where television was already present.

4. *A series of studies by the Singers and their colleagues* (Desmond et al., 1985; D. G. Singer & J. L. Singer, 1980; J. L. Singer & D. G. Singer, 1981, 1987; J. L. Singer et al., 1984; J. L. Singer et al., 1988). Everyday aggression of children—for the most part, of preschool age—was greater when the everyday viewing of violent television entertainment was more frequent, with no evidence that this association was attributable to any of the many measured variables other than television.

Three of these four sets of supporting data have as a common strength the viewing of violent programs in an ordinary way (sources 1, 3, 4), coupled with the measurement of aggressive behavior within a paradigm that either encourages causal inference (sources 1, 3), or would permit the falsification of such a hypothesized relationship were another measured variable responsible (4). They demonstrate that the effects observed in the laboratory among young children occur in everyday life. The fourth (source 2) documents that this kind of influence is robust across environmental circumstances.

The experiments of Bandura and colleagues neatly approximate childhood experience—adults in charge, mild frustration involving toys, a little television, and an opportunity to act aggressively with little or no likelihood of punishment. Subjects at this age do not understand the concept of experimentation and thus could not practice guile, whereas play is the context of most childhood aggressiveness, and for that matter, of much adult aggression. Our view is that the applicability of these findings to the everyday behavior of young children is not open to challenge. We are reminded of an axiom: When real life approximates the circumstances of a laboratory-type experiment, challenges to generalizability to real life, or external validity (Cook & Campbell, 1979), are vanquished.

B. Experiments—Young Adults

In their pioneer experiment, Berkowitz and Rawlings (1963), had college-age subjects view the prize-fight sequence from the film *Champion* in which Kirk

Douglas is brutally beaten. The dependent measure was the competence ratings of the experimental assistant, with some hostility ensured by his insulting remarks during a bogus IQ test and some seriousness implied by the announcement that future employment would depend on the ratings. The crucial comparison was between those given two different synopses: the beating as justified or as unjustified.

Berkowitz and Rawlings designed their experiment to challenge Feshbach's (1961) interpretation of reduced hostility after exposure to a violent film sequence. He saw it as catharsis, a lowering—essentially, an expunging—of aggressive drive. Berkowitz and Rawlings argued that instead it represented heightened inhibition of aggressiveness attributable to attention drawn to such behavior by the violent stimulus. They hypothesized that ratings would be more negative in their justified condition on the grounds that it would lower inhibitions over retributive aggression. In contrast, a catharsis formulation would not distinguish between the two because the vicarious experience of violence was identical. The results supported Berkowitz and Rawlings. Inhibition instead of catharsis became the accepted explanation when media portrayals appear to reduce constraints against aggressive or antisocial behavior.

Berkowitz and Geen (1966, 1967) later manipulated the degree to which the experimental assistant was linked to the film. In one experiment, he was either "Bob" or "Kirk," the actor in the film. In another, he either was or was not described as an amateur boxer. Anger toward the assistant was aroused by his giving the subjects the maximum possible electrical shocks in a trial. Aggression was measured by the electric shocks delivered to the assistant when roles were reversed. Aggression was greater among those for whom the assistant was linked to the film.

Employing the same paradigm, Geen and Stonner (1972) and Berkowitz and Alioto (1973) manipulated the motives ascribed to the participants. In two instances, boxers were described as engaged either in a professional encounter or in a grudge match; in another, football teams were so distinguished. Subjects displayed greater aggressiveness when told the motive was malevolent.

Zillmann (1971), using the same paradigm employed by Berkowitz and colleagues (provocation, the experimental manipulation, an unavoidable minimum of aggressive behavior) showed college-age subjects either a violent film sequence, an erotic sequence, or a bland sequence. Electric shock delivery was greatest in the erotic condition, followed by that for the violent condition. Later, Zillmann, Johnson, and Hanrahan (1973) demonstrated that subsequent aggressiveness was greater when a violent sequence was unresolved than when it was concluded by a happy ending, presumably because the happy ending reduced the level of excitation.

The findings of Berkowitz and colleagues exemplify the dimensions of normativeness and pertinence. Normativeness of aggressive behavior (that is, that it is in the ordinary course of things) is strongly implied when portrayed events are described as merited retribution or the motive attributed to participants is malevolent. Pertinence represents the degree to which a portrayal is perceived by the viewer as applying to himself or herself, and may be heightened by something as broad as a link with real life in general or as specific as a connection with the circumstances of the viewer. In the instances cited, it was achieved by the match between the name or sport of the victim in the portrayal and that of the experimenter's assistant. The findings of Zillmann and colleagues demonstrate that increased excitement can heighten ongoing behavior.

Susceptibility of the subjects, of course, was heightened by the induced anger as it was by the toy deprivation in the Cat Lady experiment. That there sometimes may be subtle contingencies is apparent from Geen and Stonner's (1972) finding that the relationship between vengeful motive and greater aggressiveness occurred only among angered subjects. Among nonangered subjects, the "professional" condition evoked greater aggression. Our interpretation is that in the absence of anger, vengeful violence was dismissed as irrelevant.

These experiments also are typical of the several dozen experiments testing varied propositions derived from psychological theory (specifically, neoassociationism and excitation transfer). We cannot say that the inhibitory capacity of the media is not regularly exercised, because these portrayals are confined to those selected by the investigators. What we do conclude with certainty is that numerous types of portrayals hypothesized to increase aggressive and antisocial behavior on the basis of theory in fact do so among children as well as young adults within the confines of a laboratory setting. We also conclude, with equal certainty, that portrayals can lower as well as raise the likelihood of such behavior by increasing or decreasing the level of inhibition.

C. Field Experiments and Surveys

The challenges to external validity or generalizability to everyday life (Cook & Campbell, 1979) are serious. For young adults the laboratory departs from the everyday in the brevity of the television exposure, the absence of the possibility of retaliation, and the exclusion of competing and countervailing communications. Subjects also may deliver the routine behavior they perceive the experimenters as seeking (Anderson & Meyer, 1988; Rosenthal, 1966).

Field experiments seemingly would be the solution. They contrive to produce in naturalistic surroundings the factors on which causal inference in experimentation depend—the manipulation of experience and comparability among treatment and control groups. Unfortunately, these conditions are hard to achieve outside the laboratory.

The several field experiments involving teenagers or young adults (Feshbach

& Singer, 1971; Leyens & Camino, 1974; Leyens, Camino, Parke, & Berkowitz, 1975; Loye, Gorney, & Steele, 1977; Milgram & Shotland, 1973; Wells, 1973) are mixed in outcome, and the inferential ambiguities courted by the method are frequently apparent. We agree with Cook, Kendzierski, and Thomas (1983) that as a body of evidence they are difficult to interpret.

Our recourse is to seek evidence that reflects everyday events from a source without such problems. We are aware that a recent meta-analysis records a significant positive outcome for field experiments (Paik & Comstock, 1994), but we believe it prudent to rely on data of sounder methodological foundation because they are abundantly available. We refer to the surveys that began to influence conclusions about the effects of television and film violence when the first of the genre were published as part of the research sponsored by the Surgeon General's 1972 inquiry (Chaffee, 1972; Comstock, 1983; Comstock et al., 1978).

Each of the surveys attempts to measure exposure to television violence and aggressive or antisocial behavior as well as other variables that might enter into any relationship between the two. Most use questionnaires, some use interviews. Exposure typically is measured either by the degree of violence in favorite programs or by the frequency of watching violent programs ("actual exposure"). We divide the surveys into seven groups, based on date of data collection and similarities of method:

1. The large Maryland and national samples in the Surgeon General's inquiry (McIntyre & Teevan, 1972; Robinson & Bachman, 1972), with the former made up of about 2300 males and females from 13 high schools, and the latter a probability sample of about 1560 19-year-old males drawn from 87 high schools scattered across the country
2. The Wisconsin sample of about 600 high school boys and girls in the Surgeon General's inquiry (McLeod et al., 1972a, 1972b), whose data parallel a portion of that for the Maryland survey to make up a pooled Wisconsin-Maryland sample
3. Panel surveys in which data were obtained from the same samples at times as distant from one another as a decade (Lefkowitz, Eron, Walder, & Huesmann, 1977), as well as over briefer spans (Huesmann, Lagerspetz, & Eron, 1984), with the former, part of the Surgeon General's inquiry, involving several hundred upstate New York boys and girls who were in the third grade at the first measurement and in their late teens at the second measurement
4. Samples of about 3500 males and females in the 3rd through the 12th grade in a large southern metropolitan area (Thornton & Voigt, 1984) and of about 750 young persons ranging in age from preadolescence (about 11) to early adulthood (early 20s) in Manhattan (McCarthy, Langer, Gersten, Eisenberg, & Orzeck, 1975)

5. A survey of about 1600 London male teenagers (Belson, 1978)
6. A panel survey spanning $3\frac{1}{2}$ years in the lives of more than 2000 boys and girls and several hundred male teenagers in two American cities (Milavsky, Kessler, Stipp, & Rubens, 1982a, 1982b)
7. A set of panel surveys conducted in roughly parallel fashion spanning 3 years in the lives of boys and girls in six different countries: Australia, Finland, Israel, the Netherlands, Poland, and the United States (Huesmann et al., 1984; Huesmann & Eron, 1986; Wiegman, Kuttschreuter, & Baarda, 1986).

There is a discernible, consistent, and interpretable pattern with each of the seven adding progressively to the evidence. The numerous differences—in method and population—make the many commonalities in outcomes highly credible.

The Maryland (McIntyre & Teevan, 1972) and national (Robinson & Bachman, 1972) samples measured violence exposure by the content of four named favorites. The former found positive associations between violence-viewing scores for both boys and girls and both serious delinquency and less serious misbehavior. The latter found positive associations among the young adult males between violence viewing scores and both interpersonal aggression (but only among those earlier recorded as high in that respect) and serious delinquency (property damage and hurtful aggression).

The Wisconsin–Maryland sample (McLeod et al., 1972a, 1972b) documented a modest positive association for both boys and girls (the typical $r = .30$) between viewing violent programs and behaving aggressively. Exposure was measured by weighting frequency of self-reported viewing by a program violence score obtained from a viewer panel. Aggression was measured by ratings for interpersonal conflicts—fighting, name-calling, and the like—obtained from classmates. The data also indicated that, first, the relationship was not attributable to those more aggressive preferring violent entertainment because the correlation between preferences and behavior was much smaller than that between viewing and behavior. Second, a third variable such as poor school performance that might be associated with both greater viewing and greater aggressiveness was not responsible. Third, a causal, developmental sequence was a distinct possibility because of a correlation with much earlier viewing that was as large as that with contemporary viewing. (Decay of reliability of measurement as a consequence of the lengthier time span should result in a smaller correlation unless the association with earlier viewing in fact is larger.)

In their 10-year panel data Lefkowitz and colleagues (1977) found that earlier exposure of boys to television violence was more strongly associated with later teenage antisocial behavior than with concurrent antisocial behavior (although the latter correlation also was positive). These data increase the plausibility of a developmental sequence by the over-time association. They also increase the likelihood of a causal role for television by the resilience of the longitudinal association to the statistical elimination of any contribution by a major determinant of future antisocial behavior (Baron & Richardson, 1994)—prior aggression.

The southern urban (Thornton & Voight, 1984) and Manhattan samples (McCarthy et al., 1975) measured fairly serious levels of deviant behavior, with both equally divided between females and males, and with the genders pooled in the analyses rather than treated separately. Both also recorded positive associations between their measures of television violence exposure and antisocial behavior.

Thornton and Voigt (1984) drew probability samples from three large high schools, measuring antisocial behavior by a 27-item delinquency scale and exposure by the violence among four favorite programs and amount of television viewed. They recorded modest but statistically significant positive associations between the stated program preference measure and delinquency that were somewhat larger for the two most serious forms of delinquency—criminal damage to property and hurtful aggression using weapons. The two less serious categories of delinquency for which the significant positive correlations were somewhat smaller were minor theft and rebelliousness, exemplified by running away. Delinquency was negatively associated with amount of weekday viewing and unrelated to amount of weekend viewing, and there was no association between any of the television measures and drug- or alcohol-related delinquency. These two outcomes eliminate the possibility that the correlations are artifacts of the mode of measurement of either viewing or delinquency. They place the onus on the type of content viewed and its links with specific forms of delinquency—those representing antisocial behavior and not substance abuse. This pattern occurred after the control of 10 major variables, including demographics (age, sex, and socioeconomic status) and various "social control" variables, such as attachment to school and parents, engaging in constructive activities, commitment to conventional goals, and belief in the legal system. All of these social control variables were strongly and negatively associated with the four types of delinquency correlated with the television violence exposure measure. For two other social control variables, there were strong relationships for all the types of delinquency, including drug- and alcohol-related: delinquency of companions, positively related, and parental control over whereabouts, negatively related.

McCarthy and colleagues (1975) examined the 5-year follow-up of a larger probability sample of about 1050 young people ages 6–18 living between Houston and 125th Streets, with television violence exposure measured by the violence of four favorite programs weighted by total amount of viewing. Data were obtained from interviews with mothers. Two types of antisocial behavior, fighting and delinquency, were positively associated with the violence exposure measure. In contrast, scores for "desirable life experiences" (which would go up with the making of a new friend, an improvement in the feelings of parents, or getting along well with a teacher) and overall mental health were negatively associated with the television measure.

The Belson (1978) sample of about 1600 males 12 to 17 in age is not only large but remarkably is statistically representative of London boys of that age. Exposure and behavior data were collected in clinical interviews. Judges were employed not only to score viewed programs for violence, but also to score acts for seriousness. Scales include behavior that is unambiguously criminal and seriously harmful, such as attempted rape, attacking someone with a tire iron, and falsely reporting bomb plantings to the police. By sample and method, it is the most substantial survey to date.

Belson concluded the following:

> The evidence gathered through this investigation is very strongly supportive of the hypothesis that high exposure to television violence increases the degree to which boys engage in serious violence. Thus for serious violence by boys: (i) heavier viewers of television violence commit a great deal more serious violence than do lighter viewers of television violence who have been closely equated to the heavier viewers in terms of a wide array of empirically derived matching variables; (ii) the reverse form of this hypothesis is not supported by the evidence. (p. 15)

The data are more conservatively interpreted in terms of association (in contrast to causation) and the degree to which the pattern is suggestive as contrasted to it being compellingly indicative of a causal role for exposure to television violence. From this perspective, the major findings from the Belson survey are as follows:

- Male teenagers who had viewed a substantially greater quantity of violent television programs than those otherwise like them in measured attributes committed a markedly greater proportion—about 50%—of seriously harmful antisocial and criminal acts (Table 8.3). As with the Maryland and Wisconsin data, there was no justification for attributing this association entirely to the seeking out of violent entertainment by those rating high in antisocial behavior.
- Less serious categories of antisocial behavior also were positively correlated with violence viewing (Table 8.3). However, the reverse hypothesis that this represents the media behavior of those who engage in such acts could not be dismissed with as much confidence.
- Behavioral and cognitive variables were not symmetrical. There were no associations between violence viewing and beliefs and dispositions (that is, norms and values) favorable to aggression—attributing violence to human nature, willingness to engage in violence, thinking of violence as a way to solve problems, or being preoccupied with violence.

The panel survey by Milavsky et al. (1982a, 1982b) collected data in Fort Worth and Minneapolis from about 2400 boys and girls in the second through

TABLE 8.3   Antisocial Behavior and Exposure to Violent Television Among Teenage Males

| | Mean number of acts | | |
| | | | Percentage difference |
Level of behavior	Heavy viewers	Light viewers	Heavy–Light / Light
Original analysis			
Most serious acts only	7.48	5.02	49.0
All excluding most trivial	114.10	100.85	13.1
All including most trivial	294.10	265.03	11.0
Adjusted by seriousness			
Most serious	7.48	5.02	49.0
Moderately serious	106.62	95.83	11.2
All (most serious + most trivial)			
Least serious	180.00	164.18	9.6
All (most serious + moderately serious)			

Sample size $(N) = 1565$

Adapted from *Television Violence and the Adolescent Boy,* by W. A. Belson, 1978, Westmead, England: Saxon House, Teakfield.

sixth grades and about 800 male teenagers. Over $3\frac{1}{2}$ years, measures of television exposure and antisocial behavior were obtained repeatedly, resulting in 15 instances ("wave pairs") in which earlier viewing could be matched with later behavior. Attrition resulted in the number from whom data were collected at two times decreasing markedly as span of time increased; for example, among elementary school males with 3 months between measurements, $n = 497$; at 9 months, $n = 356$; at 2 years, $n = 211$; and at 3 years, $n = 112$. The major findings were as follows:

- At each point in time there were small positive statistically significant correlations between exposure to television violence and interpersonal aggression for both elementary school boys and girls and the teenage males.
- There was a pattern of positive correlations between earlier viewing and later behavior and especially so for the elementary school boys. In that case, all were positive and noticeably larger in size for the 5 of the 15 pairings representing the longest time spans (two years or more).
- Among 95 subgroups of elementary school boys formed on the basis of 43 social and personal attributes, a large majority of these wave-to-wave associations were positive, and 9% achieved statistical significance ($p < .05$); similar but less pronounced results occurred for the girls.

The wave-to-wave analyses encourage causal attribution when the association is positive and statistically significant because all other influences are eliminated, but the model used by the authors is very conservative (Cook et al.,

1983) because it eliminates any influences of earlier violence viewing. Even so, the two significant positive associations among the elementary school boys reported by the investigators are at the border of the criterion of three positive associations advanced by them for inferring causation (a step they argue is necessary because the large number of coefficients invites significance for one or more as the result of sampling variability, and the lack of complete independence could result in any anomaly making a multiple appearance—although they are silent on the possibility that an anomaly could work equally well against meeting the criterion).

In our view, two secondary analyses are crucial to interpretation of these data. Cook and colleagues (1983) identify patterns that point toward an effect of viewing on behavior. Kang (1990) performed adroit statistical manipulations that produce significant positive associations well in excess of the authors' original criterion.

Cook and colleagues (1983) arrayed the data by time span, with three important outcomes. First, the increasing degree of association with lengthening of span appears to hold generally for both boys and girls, except for spans of middling length. Second, the possibility that the strongest pattern, the positive associations for elementary school males, is an artifact of socioeconomic status (an interpretation proffered by Milavsky and colleagues) is eliminated by the outcomes for middle class girls (about 70% of the entire female sample), which display the same trend as do the males. Third, they isolated what they judged to be the data of highest quality for the teenage male sample and found (a) for personal aggression, nonnegative coefficients that increase with the span of time between waves; (b) for teacher aggression, nonnegative coefficients unrelated in size to the time spanned; (c) for property aggression, inconsistent results; and (d) for delinquency aggression, nonnegative coefficients that increase with the span of time between waves. Thus, in three of four instances there were nonnegative (if not significant) associations and in two of the four the same pattern of increasing size with time span.

Kang (1990) applied a banal correction for heteroscedasticity (uneven clustering of the data), and the frequency of significant positive associations among the elementary school males increased from two to five (out of a possible 15). He then employed exploratory data analysis (Tukey, 1977) to examine the influence of outliers and found that when a very few extreme cases were eliminated (an average of six per wave pairing) the number of significant, positive associations increased to eight.

This second outcome identifies an important substantive phenomenon: the real-life relationship between violence viewing and antisocial behavior in any large sample may be somewhat disguised by what McGuire (1986) has called "wimps," who watch a lot of television but engage in no antisocial behavior and "street fighting men," who are so occupied with antisocial behavior they have no time for television.

Kang further found that with the additional coefficients the pattern of increasing size with longer time lags became pronounced, with five of the eight significant representing the longest time lags. In contrast, a test of the reverse hypothesis (that greater aggressiveness predicts higher levels of violence viewing) produced only four significant coefficients with three clustered among the shortest time spans. The Kang analysis, then, points to an increasing effect of television violence on aggressiveness as children grow up, and primarily short-term effects of aggression on violence viewing—so that the aggressiveness of viewers is not a convincing explanation for associations between the two.

We believe the data of Milavsky and colleagues add importantly to those of earlier surveys. They do so by confirming repeatedly that those who view larger amounts of violence engage in greater amounts of antisocial behavior. These data make it unambiguously clear that television's violent entertainment is pervasively popular among and attuned to young persons of both genders who commit greater numbers of such acts. They point to causation, whether one limits inspection to the borderline frequency of positive, significant wave-to-wave associations and the 9% significance rate among the 95 subgroups (about twice what could reasonably be attributed to sampling variability or "chance") presented by the original investigators or includes the reanalyses of Cook and colleagues and Kang. In two respects, they are also suggestive of a developmental sequence. First, there is the clustering of the largest coefficients among the longest time spans in the original male elementary school sample. Second, there is the pattern of increasing coefficient size with lengthening time spans in both elementary and teenage samples in the reanalyses by Cook and colleagues. It is inferentially far more important that of those longest-span coefficients in the original, complete sample most (four out of five) are large enough to attain significance were the number of respondents not reduced by attrition than that they do not do so, a conclusion that follows from the statistical axiom that the best estimate of an unknown figure (provided there are no biases) is that appearing in the available empirical data. We also agree with Cook and colleagues that it is less likely that the somewhat discontinuous time-span pattern they present is a coincidence than that some unknown factor or factors distorted data for a middle wave.

Kang discovered that most of his newly uncovered significant associations involved a single cohort. This raises the possibility of some important, unidentified necessary condition or conditions but only somewhat limits the inferential sweep of the Kang analysis (because we would expect these same circumstances to apply to numerous other groups of young persons) and does not affect the conclusions we offer.

Finally, the six-country data roughly parallel the similar, earlier U.S. surveys by Lefkowitz and colleagues. Some group and cultural distinctions appear; not all investigators are in accord in interpretation. As we observed earlier, the relationship between violence viewing and antisocial or aggressive behavior apparently is robust enough to occur under a variety of social and cultural conditions.

We have spent a great deal of time on these surveys because we consider them to be crucial evidence. In our view, the major outcomes are as follows:

1. Small positive synchronous (same-time) correlations between an ambiguous measure of exposure (number of violent programs among favorites) and both interpersonal aggression and delinquency. Modest positive synchronous correlations between a measure of exposure with greater apparent validity (frequency of viewing weighted by program violence) and interpersonal aggression. The meta-analysis of Paik and Comstock (1994) found very similar behavior effect sizes for actual exposure, favorite programs, and total viewing. However, when such measures can be compared in the same set of data the first is clearly more strongly associated with behavior (Chaffee, 1972). This has inferential importance because it reduces the case for attributing the association between exposure and behavior to the preferences of the persons high in aggressiveness—in which case preference should have the stronger association with behavior.

2. These are modest over-time (wave-to-wave) positive correlations (in the data of Milavsky and colleagues) between the same apparently more valid measure of earlier exposure and later interpersonal aggression, and positive correlations of greater magnitude for longer time spans.

3. There is no compelling demonstration that any of these associations are explained wholly by one or more variables that do not include a causal contribution by television.

4. Positive associations occur for both males and females. However, they have been recorded somewhat more frequently among males.

5. The measure of antisocial behavior most convincingly associated with violence viewing has been interpersonal aggression, as it has been examined the most frequently and correlations have been repeatedly positive, both synchronously and over time. Nevertheless, in the six instances in which measured behavior clearly exceeded the threshold of the seriously harmful, the associations with a measure of exposure to television violence have been uniformly positive (Belson, 1978; Cook et al., 1983; McCarthy et al., 1975; McIntyre & Teevan, 1972; Robinson & Bachman, 1972; Thornton & Voigt, 1984).

In sum, there are positive correlations between the violence in four favorite programs and interpersonal aggression and delinquency cross-sectionally (that is, when viewing and behavior are recorded at the same time). There are also positive correlations between actual exposure and both interpersonal aggression and delinquency cross-sectionally. Longer time spans produce correlations of greater magnitude. When data for four favorites and actual exposure are examined from the same sample, correlations are much stronger for actual exposure. The data for delinquency and serious harmful behavior parallel that for interpersonal aggression, although they are not as plentiful. The longitudinal (over time) data parallel that for the cross-sectional data. These outcomes in conjunction with the experimental findings that demonstrate causation within the experimental setting make a strong case for a contribution by television to a wide range of aggressive and antisocial behavior.

III. INTERPRETATION

Our conclusions depend on the conformity of the survey data to the outcomes of the experiments. They indicate that the relationships required if there is an everyday effect in fact occur, both widely and consistently. We draw further on a group of meta-analyses that make it clear that the studies to which we have chosen to give attention are representative of a larger depository of data. Then we acknowledge some studies that are pertinent to the topic of television violence but unnecessary to our inferential paradigm. Finally, we subject the evidence to a half dozen additional considerations, including a possible artifact, that help identify the likely social impact of television violence.

A. META-ANALYSES

Five quantitative aggregations of findings provide incontestable documentation that empirically there is a positive association between exposure to television violence and antisocial behavior. However, the aggregations vary considerably in their focus.

Andison (1977) tabulated the outcomes of 67 experiments and surveys and found that a majority, regardless of method or age of subjects and respondents, reported a positive association between violence viewing and antisocial behavior. Hearold later (1986) analyzed 168 studies and found substantial positive associations for laboratory-type experiments and surveys but not for field experiments. Wood, Wong, and Chachere (1991) examined 23 experiments in and out of laboratories that employed a measure of "unconstrained interpersonal aggression" among children and adolescents, such as playground fights, and found that scores were increased by exposure to television violence. Allen, D'Alessio, and Brezgel (1995) examined 33 laboratory-type experiments in which the independent variable was erotica and the dependent variable was aggression, and found that portrayals classified as violent erotica produced the highest levels of aggression.

Paik and Comstock (1994), in a recent and thorough effort, collected 217 studies, with 82 that appeared after the last large-scale assessment (Hearold). These 217 generated 1142 instances in which a relationship between television viewing and antisocial behavior was recorded. They used two relatively new techniques for meta-analysis (Mullen, 1989): tests of statistical significance and "fail-safe" numbers representing the additional outcomes recording a null relationship necessary to reduce an observed association to null.

Outcomes were positive for laboratory experiments, field experiments, time series, and surveys. All were statistically significant, and fail-safe numbers ranged from the extremely large to the extraordinary (444,350 for laboratory experiments, 507,701 for surveys, 2.4 million for all observations combined). Effects were similar for males and females when the bias of more males appearing in laboratory-type experiments (which registered effects sizes that were among the largest) was taken into account.

Effects were positive and significant for the three categories used to classify antisocial behavior: simulated aggression, interpersonal aggression, and illegal and seriously harmful activities (Table 8.4). For the first two, statistical significance was achieved and fail-safe numbers were substantial to huge. Among the third, the degree of association was very small for violence against a person but larger for grand theft and burglary. However, all categories of illegal and seriously harmful activities achieved statistical significance, and violence against a person registered a reputable fail-safe number of 2978. One of the strongest associations was recorded between violent erotica and aggression. Effects held up robustly when two study attributes were taken into account—methodological quality and ecological validity.

The meta-analyses powerfully establish as an empirical fact a positive association between violence viewing and antisocial and aggressive behavior. Whether one examines laboratory experiments or surveys, simulated aggression, minor aggression, illegal and seriously harmful activities, or a narrow category of everyday interaction such as unconstrained interpersonal conflict, the pattern is the same.

B. OTHER STUDIES

There are a number of studies representing everyday behavior on which we choose not to draw explicitly. The reasons are that they are methodologically problematic and are unnecessary to our paradigm.

Messner (1986) used A. C. Nielsen Company estimates of the audience size for violent programs and found negative associations within 281 Standard Metropolitan Statistical Areas (SMSAs) with four types of crime: homicide, rape, robbery, and aggravated assault. Our interpretation is that there is not sufficient variation in the independent variable for it to be a meaningful measure of differences in individual exposure, which is the datum required for examining effects of television violence.

TABLE 8.4 Meta-Analysis Effect Sizes by Types of Agressive Behavior

Effect sizes	N	r	r^2	Fail-safe N
	Simulated aggressive behavior			
All observations combined	587	.33	.11	484237
Experimental designs	432	.38	.14	207502
Surveys	155	.17	.03	57586
Intensity of using aggressive machines/self-report of aggressive behavior				
All observations	515	.31	.10	345134
Experimental designs	402	.36	.13	169588
Surveys	113	.15	.21	30729
Plays with aggressive toys				
Experimental designs	7	.52	.28	38
Unclassified simulated aggressive behavior				
All observations	65	.40	.16	10270
Experimental designs	23	.64	.41	1345
Surveys	42	.24	.06	4140
	Minor aggressive behavior			
All observations combined	406	.31	.10	348814
Experimental designs	249	.39	.16	107479
Surveys	212	.20	.04	133356
Physical violence against an object				
Experimental designs	104	.52	.27	26905
Verbal aggression				
All observations	86	.27	.07	10603
Experimental designs	77	.26	.07	6300
Surveys	12	.27	.08	544
Physical violence against a person (nonillegal behavior)				
All observations	271	.23	.05	181165
Experimental designs	71	.32	.10	7896
Surveys	200	.20	.04	113162
	Illegal and seriously harmful activities			
All observations combined	94	.17	.03	26729
Experimental designs	51	.19	.04	2793
Surveys	43	.15	.02	11417
Burglary				
All observations	13	.28	.08	4169
Experimental designs	8	.19	.04	126
Surveys	5	.42	.18	2816
Grand theft				
All observations	23	.28	.08	1627
Experimental designs	11	.36	.13	212
Surveys	12	.20	.04	646
Violence against a person (homicide, suicide, stabbing, etc.)				
All observations	58	.10	.01	2978
Experimental designs	32	.13	.02	687
Surveys	26	.06	.004	774

Adapted from "The Effects of Television Violence on Antisocial Behavior: A Meta-Analysis," by H. Paik and G. Comstock, 1994, *Communication Research, 21*(4), pp. 516–546.

However, we do agree with two of his arguments. Young persons are likely to be socialized to act criminally by association with peers, and such persons are more likely to be on the streets or in other locales where crime is possible than viewing television, whereas greater amounts of television viewing may suppress the convergence in time and space of potential offenders, plausible victims, and the absence of guardians. These are the street-fighting men and wimps Kang extracted from his data.

Then there are the time series in which media coverage or portrayal is employed as an independent variable for various subsequent social statistics (Bollen & Phillips, 1982; Gould & Shaffer, 1986; Phillips, 1983, 1986; Phillips & Cartensen, 1986; Phillips & Hensley, 1984). Among the reported outcomes are the following: teenage suicides rose after the topic received attention in television news and drama, suicide rates increased after coverage of prominent suicides, and homicide rates rose after the televising of championship boxing matches among males of the same race as the losing fighter. Baron and Reiss (1985) offer a sweeping rejection of the validity of such time series with a demonstration that random dates can produce a replication. Kessler, Downey, Milavsky, and Stipp (1988) analyzed some of the same data with only partially different results. However, Mark, Sanna, and Shotland (1992) subjected the 1983 data of Phillips to every statistical manipulation they could think of to support their opinion that the prize fight–homicide relationship was artifactual, and failed to do so; their subhead, "This Study Makes Me Want to Kill" (p. 116) expresses their frustration.

A dramatic example is the cross-cultural time series by Centerwall (1989) in which the introduction of television is followed in numerous countries by a substantial and sustained increase in homicides. The inferential problem is that the analysis essentially exhausts the data so that replication is not possible.

Heath, Kruttschnitt, and Ward (1986) found that young male prison inmates who recalled both parental abuse and viewing greater amounts of violent programs as teenagers were more likely to have committed violent offenses. The developmental sequence is plausible, but it is hard to give full weight to a media recall measure extending as much as a decade into the past.

We do not wholly reject these studies. We simply choose not to adjudicate the methodological issues they raise because their evidence is concretely and logically unnecessary to our paradigm, which rests on the validation of the findings produced by the one research design that permits unambiguous causal inference—the experiment—and by survey data representing everyday life.

C. IMPACT

The next step is to specify the social impact of the influence of television violence on antisocial behavior. We begin with the data that point to a developmental pattern. We then turn to an alternative explanation that could impugn our interpretation as artifactual—the reverse hypothesis—and a potential necessary condition—aggressive predisposition. Finally, we examine the role of gender, the seriousness of affected behavior, and the size of effects.

1. Developmental Pattern

The Maryland-Wisconsin sample (McLeod et al., 1972a, 1972b) initially suggested a developmental sequence in which early viewing affects later behavior. Four subsequent sets of data, however, provide much more significant evidence in its behalf. Two are the 10-year panel by Lefkowitz and colleagues (1977) and the $3\frac{1}{2}$-year panel by Milavsky and colleagues (1982b). Both strongly support a developmental sequence by the robustness and size of their positive associations over long periods of time. In the first instance, the decade-long over-time correlation for boys exceeds that for aggression at the time of first measurement, and remains as strong when prior aggression is statistically eliminated as an influence—*prima facie* suggestive of causal influence. In the second, the five largest of the eight coefficients significant after the adjustments of Kang (1990) occupy the longest time spans of 2 to 3 years.

The contribution of television to the development of the trait of aggressiveness is further strongly supported by the data of Huesmann, Eron, Lefkowitz, and Walder (1984) and Huesmann, Eron, Dubow, and Seebauer (summarized in Eron and Huesmann, 1987) which spectacularly add one and two decades, respectively, to the original panel of Lefkowitz and colleagues. Twenty and 30 as well as 10 years after the third-grade period of initial measurement, those higher earlier in the viewing of violence scored as more aggressive.

Eron and Huesmann (1987) attempt to place these findings in perspective:

> It is not claimed that the specific programs these adults watched when they were 8 years old still had a direct effect on their behavior. However, the continued viewing of these programs probably contributed to the development of certain attitudes and norms of behavior and taught these youngsters ways of solving interpersonal problems which remained with them over the years. (p. 196)

As we will soon explain, we believe the data identify a different underlying mechanism. We do agree that one would not expect much lasting influence from exposure to a specific, individual program (although in a few instances a particularly powerful portrayal might be recalled years later and be relied on as a guide to behavior) but we would point out that it is precisely exposure to specific categories of programs that the data say makes a difference in later behavior.

The Milavsky data pinpoint the developmental effect as primarily occurring before the teenage years because the increases in magnitude of association over the $3\frac{1}{2}$ years was greater for the elementary school sample than for the teenage male one. The Milavsky data also encourage the view that early plus continuing high exposure is a factor because the associations for the longer time spans are considerably larger when there is no control for earlier exposure to television violence (Tables 6.1 and 6.2, pp. 126–127; Tables 8.14 and 8.15, pp. 239–240).

2. Reverse Hypothesis

The commonsense challenge to interpreting the positive correlations between amount of everyday viewing of violent entertainment and aggressive or antisocial behavior as identifying a causal contribution by television is the reverse hypothesis—that the associations represent the preferences for violent entertainment of those who behave in an aggressive or antisocial manner. In fact, the data do not give much support to this alternative view.

Atkin, Greenberg, Korzenny, and McDermott (1979) found among about 225 4th, 6th, and 8th graders that a propensity to act aggressively, measured by the pooled replies of mothers and their children about what the child would do in hypothetical situations, predicted violent program consumption 1 year later. Huesmann (1982) and Huesmann and Eron (1986) concluded from the analysis of several sets of data that there was some reciprocity, with violence viewing influencing behavior and behavior motivating greater violence viewing. Bryant (1989), drawing on Bryant, Comisky, and Zillmann (1981), presents evidence that more aggressive males derive greater pleasure from portrayals of sports violence, especially when the violence and injury is inflicted on a target they dislike. This certainly confirms that at least under some circumstances more aggressive persons may be motivated to view violent acts. However, in his re-analyses of the data of Milavsky and colleagues Kang (1990) presents dazzlingly convincing evidence that the role of aggressive and antisocial behavior in explaining the associations is slight, and particularly for those that occur over longer spans of time.

Kang found only one instance (out of a possible 15, the total number of wave pairs) of mutual prediction, the criterion for reciprocity (Granger, 1969). There were only four instances in which aggression predicted later viewing of violence, whereas there were eight in which violence viewing predicted later aggression. Furthermore, the fewer associations for behavior-to-viewing were concentrated among the shorter time spans of 9 months whereas five of the eight for viewing-to-behavior occupied the longest time spans for 2 years or more. These data are wholly inconsistent with a strong explanatory role for aggressive behavior, give little support to reciprocity, document that any contribution by behavior is confined to the short term, and make it clear that for longer time spans behavior-to-viewing does not constitute an alternative explanation. They are particularly convincing because they not only validly represent viewing and behavior but also incorporate an important foundation for causal inference that is missing from much of the survey data—time order. That is, these linkages do not represent associations at a point in time but rather predictions of a later state by a circumstance occurring earlier.

Belson (1978) similarly concluded after a painstaking analysis that among his sample of delinquents high in violence viewing who committed the most serious offenses that the data were not consistent with a behavior-to-viewing hypothesis. McCarthy and colleagues (1975) in their Manhattan sample found no correlation between fighting and delinquency and a stated preference for violent programs. Menzies in two separate studies (1971, 1973) found no relationship between the violence committed by the criminally incarcerated and the choosing of violent entertainment. Chaffee (1972) in his analysis of data from the surveys sponsored by the Surgeon General's inquiry concluded that any contribution to viewing by behavior was minor compared to the contribution to behavior by viewing (primarily because the correlation in the same sample between actual viewing and behavior was much greater than between four favorites and behavior). Our conclusion is that there may be some contribution to viewing by behavior, but that it is less certain or strong than a contribution to behavior by viewing, and cannot be considered a viable alternative explanation for the positive associations between the two.

3. Predisposition

Predisposition is an issue distinct from that of the reverse hypothesis in which prior aggression would nurture a taste for violent entertainment (and thereby explain the recorded associations between exposure to violent television entertainment and higher levels of aggressive or antisocial behavior). The issue here is whether those who are more aggressive or antisocial in behavior are more susceptible to the influence of violent television entertainment on those kinds of behavior.

There is ample evidence that predisposition, represented either by attributes that are correlates of or actual higher levels of initial antisocial behavior, identifies those who are very likely to be affected by violent portrayals. For example, the male teenagers who scored higher in viewing violence in the Belson (1978) sample were statistically matched in other characteristics with those scoring lower, so the implication is clear that except for the viewing these other boys were equally predisposed toward delinquency—and, in fact, did perform such acts at a substantial although lower rate (Table 8.3) than those who viewed more violence. Robinson and Bachman (1972) found in their national sample of 19-year-old males that interpersonal aggression was correlated with violence viewing only among those earlier scoring higher in interpersonal aggression. Josephson (1987) found that only those high in initial aggressiveness increased their aggressive behavior as a consequence of exposure to a violent portrayal in a naturalistic experiment with 400 second- and third-grade boys playing floor hockey. Celozzi, Kazelskis, and Gutsch (1981) found that measures of hostility were greater after exposure to a violent 10-minute hockey film among those scoring higher for the trait of aggressiveness. Paik (1991) in her meta-analysis found that effects of television violence were greater among those scoring higher on one or another measure of aggressive predisposition.

Certainly, the portrayal of successful violence administered to a disliked recipient whose punishment can be ethically justified would be particularly likely to influence those who are highly aggressive. Such stimuli not only will evoke aggressive thoughts and identify a target whose punishment will provide satisfaction, but also such a viewer will possess a superior repertoire of aggressive acts. However, lower inhibitions and greater aggressive skills often will be associated with diminished media influence because these very individuals may be as aggressive as prudence or self-preservation will permit. In some respects, the less aggressive will be equally or even more susceptible to media influence. The disinhibition of internal restraints and the linking of aggression with environmentally present cues will affect those both higher and lower in initial aggression and the enhancement of aggressive skills will be greatest for persons comparatively lacking in them—those lower in initial aggressiveness. Finally, the high rate of positive outcomes for experiments implies that predisposition is not essential for effects unless the concept is stripped of any meaningful distinctiveness. Our conclusion is that predisposition is not a necessary condition for effects.

4. Gender

Although the early experimental literature appeared to indicate that males were more susceptible to influence than females (Comstock et al., 1978) and two of the most prominent surveys (Lefkowitz et al., 1977; Milavsky et al., 1982b) record somewhat stronger patterns of association among males than among females, the meta-analysis of Paik and Comstock (1994) makes it clear that measured effects are quite similar, with the best measure of actual effects, the survey, almost identical (Table 2, p. 528). Our conclusion is that males and females are affected about equally with the similarity in scores on the same scales particularly convincing given the inclination of males and females to differ in the expression of aggression, with the former typically more direct and the latter typically more indirect (Bjorkqvist, 1994).

The experimental record in fact supports such an expectation. Gender of model and viewer interact (Bandura, 1965, 1973; Bandura et al., 1963a, 1963b; Berkowitz & Rawlings, 1963). Among boys, males are more effective as models. Among girls, males and females are about equally effective. The least effective pairing is the female model and the male subject. Status, which would favor the male, and appropriateness of behavior, which in the case of aggression would also favor the male (behavior perceived as inappropriate is likely to lower re-gard for the perpetrator, and thus decrease the likelihood of emulation by an observer) take precedence over the demonstrated effectiveness of similarity be-tween model and viewer. Male models, plentiful in entertainment as violence perpetrators, are thus not without influence on females. The influence of vio-lent entertainment on females would also be enhanced by social changes: the increasing number of aggressive female models in entertainment and the in-creasing degree to which behavior once considered the province of males is perceived as unisexual.

5. Seriousness

The interpersonal aggression that has been measured most often represents be-havior that would be unpleasant, unwelcome, disruptive, and often painful and sometimes injurious to victims and sometimes painful and injurious to perpe-trators. That is clearly denoted by the "fighting," "hitting," and "name-calling" that are part of the typical interpersonal aggression scale.

In the Belson (1978) data, the most convincing outcome was among delin-quents for seriously harmful and criminal acts. These included, "I twisted a boy's arm until he yelled with pain," "I broke into a house and smashed every-thing I could find," and "I threw the cat into the fire." None qualifies as benign.

The meta-analysis of Paik and Comstock (1994) recorded similar effect sizes for simulated and interpersonal aggression and smaller effect sizes that progres-sively declined with the seriousness of illegal and seriously harmful activities. However, the three instances of data of good quality that permit direct com-parisons among acts varying in seriousness do not encourage a conclusion of sharply declining television influence as seriousness increases. Thornton and Voigt (1984) found slightly stronger relationships with more serious forms of delinquency, even when other variables were controlled. Within the teenage sample of Milavsky and colleagues (1982a, 1982b), the size of the association for interpersonal aggression was only somewhat greater than for the more se-rious teacher and delinquency measures. Belson (1978), of course, found the largest proportional and inferentially most convincing difference for the most serious offenses.

Our wary interpretation is that some categories of illegal and seriously harmful acts are affected to a degree not much different than is interpersonal aggression but that probably the most harmful acts are affected to a much smaller degree. We base the former on the within-study comparisons and the inclusion in interpersonal aggression of acts that are or could escalate into ille-gal or seriously harmful behavior. We base the latter on the small effect size in the meta-analysis for violence against persons and our belief that in those in-stances social taboos and possible sanctions would constrain media effects.

6. Effect Size

There are three ways to address size of effect: draw on a compelling documentation of everyday outcomes; derive an estimate from the meta-analyses, which average results across studies; or examine and select among the recorded associations from the surveys.

The most compelling documentation is offered by a group led by the methodologist Thomas Cook (Hennigan et al., 1982). These investigators took advantage of the natural experiment unintendedly produced by the FCC's freeze on television station licensing in the late 1940s to conduct an interrupted time-series with switching replications in which the role of the treatment and control sites reverses over time (Cook & Campbell, 1979). They compared crime trends for early (prefreeze) and late (postfreeze) adoption sites for two semi-independent pools of data—cities and states.

There were four types of statistics: violent crime, larceny theft, auto theft, and burglary. The authors draw on the legal code for a definition of larceny theft:

> The unlawful taking, carrying, leading, or riding away of property from the possession or constructive possession of another. Thefts of bicycles, automobile accessories, shoplifting, pocket-picking, or any stealing of property or article which is not taken by force and violence or by fraud. Excluded embezzlement, "con" games, forgery, worthless checks, etc. (p. 465)

Burglary is distinguished from larceny by breaking and entering.

The results are striking (Figure 8.1). There were no significant shifts for violent crimes or burglary. There were two for auto theft, both for the prefreeze sites. For larceny theft, all four—prefreeze cities, prefreeze states, postfreeze cities, and postfreeze states—showed significant shifts.

Multiple replications and the variety of sites eliminate the possibility that the outcomes represent some peculiar set of circumstances unrelated to television, and the use of reported crimes stifles the complaint that the dependent measures are a mere proxy for real life behavior. Thus, the results for larceny are convincing evidence of a real-life television effect on antisocial behavior.

The authors attribute the larceny outcomes to relative deprivation induced by the increased exposure to consumer goods in television commercials and programs, and reject emulation as an explanation because there was no increase in violent crime although violence was plentiful on television (Chapter 3). We think that relative deprivation and emulation at a level where likelihood of apprehension and the severity of sanctions would be minimal are equally plausible. We also speculate that the greater proximity to World War II (with its gasoline rationing and bans on civilian auto production that would make joy-riding more exciting) explains the two positive outcomes for auto theft, which the authors decline to interpret because of the lack of full replication.

Increases in larceny theft ranged from 5.5 to 18%. Our conservative (and

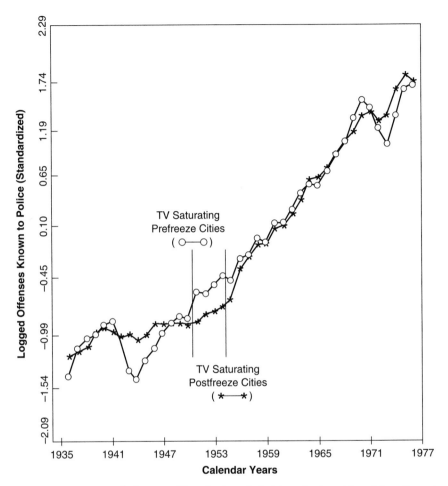

FIGURE 8.1   Larceny theft rates and introduction of television: city data. Adapted from "Impact of the Introduction of Television on Crime in the United States: Empirical Findings and Theoretical Implications," by K. M. Hennigan, L. Heath, J. D. Wharton, M. L. Del Rosario, T. D. Cook, and B. J. Calder, 1982, *Journal of Personality and Social Psychology, 42*(3), pp. 461–467.

arbitrary) approach is to accept the smallest estimate as the lower limit and take the average of the remaining three as the upper limit. This leads to a range of 5.5 to 15.1%, with a midpoint of 10.3%.

In our view these data identify a continuing effect of television on minor crime. Our reasoning is that both the experimental and survey findings point to differences in exposure to violent portrayals as sufficient for behavioral effects and the kind of portrayals posited by either explanation (displaying well-being or antisocial acts) remain plentiful. However, the effect sizes recorded at that time might have been somewhat greater than they are today because of the sudden increase in public exposure to such portrayals.

As part of her meta-analysis, Hearold (1986) constructed curves representing those in the control and treatment conditions. The area under a curve accurately represents the quantity of cases as well as their distribution. When the two curves are placed side by side, they lead to an estimated effect size of about 10% because that is the proportion the treatment curve shifts in the direction of heightened aggressive and antisocial behavior as a consequence of the higher mean for the treatment group. The more recent Paik and Comstock (1994) meta-analysis leads to similar estimates of overall control and treatment differences.

When the first author collated 22 separate estimates of effect size from the surveys (Comstock, 1991a; Table 6.4, pp. 268–273), several approximated these 10% estimates. On the whole, however, the estimates were somewhat smaller. The range for variance explained for the 22 was between 4 and 10%. The positive association between earlier violence viewing and later interpersonal aggression over the 10-year span of the Lefkowitz et al. (1977) panel is in the upper portion of this range.

Our conclusion is that the size of effect for the most measured and most common type of antisocial behavior, interpersonal aggression, is modest but far from minute—between 4 and 10% of the variation in scores. We estimate from the Paik and Comstock meta-analysis that the effect size for the most serious acts is smaller than for interpersonal aggression. The large Belson estimate of a 50% increase in seriously harmful behavior does not convince us otherwise because it derives only from the very small group of serious delinquents high in violence viewing and would decrease to well within our proposed range were it converted to a rate for all young males.

There nevertheless are two reasons to suspect that the measures of association are underestimates. Unreliability of components drives any estimate of association below its true level, and surely there can be no disagreement that the measures of exposure and behavior have a degree of unreliability. Television also is near ubiquitous, so those "low" in exposure have had a substantial degree, and associations are depressed when the range of possible scores is truncated. By Cohen's (1988) carefully calculated criteria, the effect sizes for interpersonal aggression barely achieve his medium category and those for the most serious offenses fall into his small category. Our conclusion, then, is that size of the effect is moderate to small in magnitude but socially substantial.

IV. BEYOND ANTISOCIAL BEHAVIOR

Three bodies of psychological theory lead to the expectation that those exposed to violence in television or film entertainment are more likely to behave in an aggressive or antisocial manner. They are social cognition (Bandura, 1986), an elaboration of social learning theory (Bandura, 1973); neoassociationism (Berkowitz, 1984, 1990), an extension of disinhibition and cue theory; and excitation transfer (Zillmann, 1971, 1982; Tannenbaum & Zillmann, 1975), often called arousal theory. These theories apply to behavior in general, thereby implicating television as affecting a wide range of behavior. Our interpretation now moves beyond aggressive and antisocial behavior to a broader realm.

A. THREE THEORIES

Social cognition emphasizes the meaning individuals ascribe to the observed behavior of others. Observation is fundamental, but interpretation is decisive. The capability of performing an act is enhanced by observing its performance by another person. Unfamiliar acts become learned; familiar acts are refined. Observation of the setting and consequences affect the appropriateness and efficacy attributed to an act. Acquisition, which governs the content and skill of an individual's behavioral repertoire, is ongoing. Observation is paramount, but its effectiveness will vary with degree of attention and amount of retention, which are a function of the attractiveness and perceived utility of the behavior in question. Performance, the display of behavior, in contrast is instrumental. People will emulate only what is perceived as appropriate and effective. Aggressive and antisocial acts may be learned from television and film, and so too will their suitability and likely effectiveness.

Neoassociationism focuses on the role of words and symbols in affecting internal states. Words and symbols call forth related, similar mental images. Such images are semantically linked and retrieval is essentially autonomic. Their character and quantity are a function of prior experience and observation, including television viewing. There are two consequences in regard to aggressive and antisocial behavior. Television, by affecting the images evoked, may alter inhibitions. Images reflecting justified aggression, for example, will lower inhibitions over retribution. Television also may affect whether such behavior is linked to an environmental cue. Aggressive and antisocial acts may be inhibited or disinhibited by violent portrayals, depending on the depicted motives and consequences, and their likelihood may be increased or decreased by the linkages to environmental stimuli such as individuals and groups, objects and weapons, or physical settings suggested by portrayals.

Excitation transfer assigns a major place to the physiological arousal that may be induced by an exciting occurrence. It holds that such excitation may transfer to subsequent behavior. Violent as well as otherwise stimulating television portrayals may have the capacity to induce such arousal. Ongoing behavior will be heightened in intensity. Probable behavior will become more likely. Aggressive and antisocial acts, when likely, may be further encouraged by violent as well as other stimulating television portrayals.

We now draw further from the data to examine how effects occur. We then turn to effects of television violence other than aggressive or antisocial behavior. Finally, we present principles that apply broadly to the influence of media on behavior.

B. How Effects Occur

The second inferential role of the laboratory-type experiments, which test hypotheses derived from the theories, is to catalogue conditions on which effects are contingent. (The first, of course, was to establish causation.) These conditions include the following:

1. Reward or lack of punishment for the portrayed perpetrator (Bandura, 1965; Bandura et al., 1963b; Rosekrans & Hartup, 1967)
2. Portrayal of violence as justified (Berkowitz & Rawlings, 1963; Meyer, 1973)
3. Cues in the portrayal likely to be encountered in real life, such as a name, attribute, or object (Berkowitz & Geen, 1966, 1967; Donnerstein & Berkowitz, 1981; Geen & Berkowitz, 1967)
4. Portrayal of the perpetrator as similar to the viewer (Rosekrans, 1967)
5. Involvement with the portrayed aggressor, such as imagining oneself in his or her place (Turner & Berkowitz, 1972)
6. Depiction of behavior ambiguous as to intent—such as violent sports—as motivated by the desire to inflict harm or injury (Berkowitz & Alioto, 1973; Geen & Stonner, 1972)
7. Violence portrayed so that its consequences are not disturbing, such as violence without pain or suffering on the part of the victim, sorrow among friends and lovers, or remorse by the perpetrator (Berkowitz & Rawlings, 1963)
8. Violence that is presented realistically or ostensibly represents real events (Atkin, 1983; Bandura et al., 1963a; Feshbach, 1972; Geen & Rakosky, 1973; Hapkiewicz & Stone, 1974)
9. The portrayal of hypermasculinity on the part of those who commit violence, and especially among viewers scoring high in hypermasculinity themselves (Scharrer, 1998)
10. Portrayed violence that is not the subject of critical or disparaging commentary (Lefcourt, Barnes, Parke, & Schwartz, 1966)
11. Portrayals of violence whose commission pleases the viewer (Ekman et al., 1972; Slife & Rychlak, 1982)
12. Portrayals in which the violence is not interrupted by humor (Lieberman Research, 1975)
13. Portrayed abuse that includes physical aggression instead of or in addition to verbal abuse (Lieberman Research, 1975)

14. Portrayals, violent or otherwise, that leave the viewer in a state of unresolved excitement (Zillmann, 1971; Zillmann et al., 1973)

15. Viewers who are in a state of anger or provocation before seeing a violent portrayal (Berkowitz & Geen, 1966; Caprara et al., 1987; Donnerstein & Berkowitz, 1981; Geen, 1968; Thomas, 1982)

16. Viewers who are in a state of frustration after viewing a violent portrayal, whether from an extraneous source or as a consequence of
viewing the portrayal (Geen, 1968; Geen & Berkowitz, 1967; Worchel,
Hardy, & Hurley, 1976)

Each of these contingencies increases the likelihood that a portrayal will increase aggressive or antisocial behavior. They represent four dimensions: three
are perceived attributes of the portrayed behavior and the fourth is an internal
state of the viewer open to influence by media as well as by other factors:

Efficacy (reward or lack of punishment)
Normativeness (justified, consequenceless, intentionally hurtful, physical
violence; hypermasculine portrayals; absence of criticism)
Pertinence (cues from real life, similarity of perpetrator to viewer, involve-
ment with the perpetrator, absence of humorous violence)
Susceptibility (pleasure; motive, anger, frustration; hypermasculinity).

The violent erotica experiments with college-age males as subjects (Donnerstein & Barrett, 1978; Donnerstein & Berkowitz, 1981; Donnerstein & Hallam,
1978; Donnerstein, Linz, & Penrod, 1987) exemplify the operation of these
dimensions. Aggressive responses directed at a female were heightened by the
portrayal of physical aggression against a female by a male, the portrayal of
forcible rape when the real-life female has angered the subject, and the portrayal of the eventual enjoyment of forcible rape by the victim. From the perspective of our formulation, these respectively represent the manipulation of
normativeness, pertinence, and efficacy.

The operation of the four dimensions depends on a variety of factors associated with the presentation, the viewer, and the circumstances. For example, violent cartoons have been implicated in the aggression of young children and parental mediation, which might have a mitigating effect, is at its
minimum during children's programming. Comprehension of adverse consequences, which seemingly would increase with age, should be an inhibiting
factor but effect sizes in the meta-analyses (Hearold, 1986; Paik & Comstock,
1994) at first decline with age then increase for young adults—the group most
likely to engage in seriously harmful behavior. Certainly, much in popular
entertainment belittles adverse consequences—daring crime, team violence,
ruthlessness. The power of justified aggression (Berkowitz & Rawlings, 1963;
Hearold, 1986) provides no comfort over the frequent dramas with retributive
and vigilante themes. The same must be said of the harassment and victimiza-

tion of women, given the role of cues (Berkowitz & Geen, 1966, 1967; Geen & Berkowitz, 1967), particularly when there is an erotic undertone given the demonstrated facilitation of aggression against women by portrayals in which males abuse females in a sexual context (Donnerstein, 1980; Donnerstein & Barrett, 1978; Donnerstein & Berkowitz, 1981; Donnerstein & Hallam, 1978; Donnerstein & Malamuth, 1984; Malamuth, Feshbach, & Jaffee, 1977). There is also the ascendancy of immediate over delayed consequences. Television and film dramas supply numerous instances of aggressive and antisocial behavior that are rewarding in the short term. Viewers can easily recast the plot so that the mistake, the miscue, the accident, the flaw that brought ruin was not inevitable.

Generalizability of the experimental findings has been challenged on the grounds that unusual provocation or frustration approaches a necessary condition. However, Hearold's meta-analysis (1986) documents that effects occur in the absence of frustration or provocation, although they are typically greater when such a state is present. Furthermore, the provocations and frustrations are the peccadilloes encountered daily—rudeness, small pain, and minor deprivation. Thus, provocation or frustration enhance effects but they neither have been out of the ordinary nor are effects dependent on them.

The evidence points to three distinct broad dynamics by which television and film violence contribute to antisocial and aggressive behavior. We label them Type D, Type R, and Type C.

Type D. Developmental Sequence   Immediate effects in childhood may be tokens of lasting influence because aggressiveness, once established, is a fairly enduring trait. The contribution of the media in this respect occurs before adolescence (Eron & Huesmann, 1987) but it is not possible to specify an age when the process begins because children as young as 14 and 24 months imitate what they see on the screen (Meltzoff, 1988), whereas the many experiments of Bandura and colleagues demonstrate effects among children between the ages of 5 and 6.

Type R. Repetitive Exposure   By presenting repetitive, somewhat redundant portrayals of aggression, retributive justice, and violence, the media increase the number and variety of antisocial acts in the repertoire of an individual, increase the number of environmental cues that make such behavior pertinent, and increase the mental content related to antisocial behavior. Perceptions and expectations become crude scripts and scenarios for behavior.

Type C. Compelling Portrayals   Singular, nonredundant arousing depictions may invite emulation. Such portrayals usually will be distinct from what has been experienced in real life or through the media, although sometimes the novelty may reside in the level of arousal. Publicity, sometimes based on incidents attributed to these vehicles, will further the readiness of viewers for emotional involvement.

Types D, R, and C encompass early effects that contribute to traits, continuing effects of banal and repetitive portrayals, and the effects of unusual and compelling stimuli. They thus include cumulative effects rooted in childhood as well as effects of violence exposure at all ages, a topic we will return to shortly in regard to effects on those beyond young adulthood.

In our judgment, the data give strong support to the three theories. Laboratory-type experiments consistently produce hypothesized outcomes and the surveys extend validity to the generalizability of the findings to everyday life. However, excitation transfer as a product of television viewing has comparatively limited applicability. The arousal it postulates is of short duration and would occur only among viewers particularly excited by a portrayal, who often would be the very young or comparatively naive. For example, the meta-analysis of Hearold (1986) confirms the latter by recording that the magnitude of physiological arousal instigated by portrayals is inversely associated with age. The experiment of Thomas (1982), in which college-age subjects became more aggressive after seeing a 15-minute highly violent condensation of a *Mannix* episode but had a lowered pulse rate while aggressing, further makes a case for processes that operate in the absence of physiological arousal. Like provocation or frustration, which mediate it, arousal is a facilitating but not a necessary factor.

Social cognition and neoassociationism have much broader implications and both lead to the same predictions. We can neither find nor invent an outcome that one but not the other could be said to explain. It would be impossible to identify from which of the two the following contingencies derive without a citation:

> The ideas the observers have at the time they were exposed to the communication, their interpretations as to whether the witnessed actions are appropriate, profitable, or morally justified, the nature of the available targets, and whether the depicted incident is real or fictional. (Berkowitz, 1984, p. 410)

Both concur that television influences behavior through internalized sequences of behavior and associated thoughts retrieved in response to cues. This view received impressive support from the Belson data, when exposure to violent programs failed to predict antisocial attitudes, approval of violence, hostile personality traits, willingness to commit violence, or social contagion (in this instance, engaging in aggressive and antisocial acts while in the company of other boys). The first four represent the direct, explicit measurement of norms and values, and the latter represents the role of the norms and values implied by the behavior of others with whom a person keeps company. None, then, were the means by which television influenced behavior. Thus, norms and values do not have the central place ascribed to them by Eron and Huesmann (1987). Our interpretation is also reinforced by Belson's finding that the types of acts influenced in his data by greater television violence exposure were not premeditated acts or acts that would have a built-in deterrent, such as picking a fight that might be lost—acts that would involve calculation—but acts that were "spontaneous, unplanned and unskilled in character . . ." (Belson, p. 523). If norms and values were central, we would expect the influence to extend to other types of aggressive and antisocial acts as well. The most plausible alternative is that influence occurred through cognitions and images retrieved in response to environmental cues.

Neither social cognition nor neoassociationism requires that a portrayal be perceived as antisocial or aggressive. The less social stigma, the more likely portrayed behavior will be taken as a guide; the dimension of normativeness clearly posits that not attaching a label with negative valence enhances the likelihood that behavior will be engaged in. Neither demands much in the way of cognitive skills. This is evident from the autonomic aspects of neoassociationism and effects among young children predicted by social cognition. Both would predict that greater cognitive skills would deter effects (because of enhanced ability to discriminate between portrayals and real life and infer undesirable consequences), but the consistent positive outcomes for teenagers and those of college age in both laboratory-type experiments and surveys simply testifies to the power of the medium.

The two theoretical frameworks do differ in the responsible mechanisms. Social cognition emphasizes learning processes—acquisition and performance—and neoassociationism emphasizes the storing and retrieval of thoughts and images. The former focuses on the content of beliefs and perceptions whereas the latter focuses on their autonomic linking. Both encompass articulatable and conscious as well as less readily verbalizable components of thought. Both incorporate increased levels of excitation as a motivating factor.

Reeves, Lang, Thorson, and Rothschild (1989) propose that affect governs mode of processing, and thereby the applicability of social cognition and neoassociationism. Violent portrayals perceived positively would be processed primarily by the verbal left hemisphere (so as to be savored and reflected upon); social cognition would apply. Violent portrayals that arouse negative emotions would be processed by the nonverbal right hemisphere (because they would be so distasteful); neoassociationism would apply.

Certainly for a particular set of circumstances, one or the other may be more appropriate or parsimonious. Josephson (1987) justifiably chose neoassociationism for the enhancement of aggression by the real-life presentation of a cue from a just-viewed violent portrayal.

The Belson data strongly suggest that one underlying mechanism is not changes in norms and values but rather the incorporation and enhanced accessibility in the behavioral repertoires of viewers of generic modes of behavior.

This conclusion derives clearly from the failure of Belson to find *any* positive correlations between norms and values and aggressive and antisocial behavior. This held true both for norms and values when measured directly as beliefs and attitudes and for the norms implied by the company of other boys when they are committing aggressive and antisocial acts. This incorporation and enhanced accessibility—greater acceptance of a mode of behavior, in general terms—is dependent on the portrayal of the behavior as efficacious, pertinent, or normative, and its expression in behavior is further enhanced when the viewer is in a susceptible state. These are the clear implications of the experimental findings. Thus, the crux of television's behavioral influence resides in the elaboration and codification by the viewer of the portrayed behavior—which benefits from the pictorial might of the medium—and not in changes in beliefs and dispositions.

In our view, this places norms and values often as competitors with and not coconspirators of observation as an influence on behavior. This lowers the predictive power of norms and values in regard to behavior, and makes observation in the case of the media—and particularly television and films—sometimes a source of quite surprising and occasionally shocking behavior.

This interpretation leads us to posit two routes to behavioral influence in accord with the two theories of social cognition and neoassociationism. The first rests on the appeal of specific acts after reflection. The second rests on the retrieval of stored acts without much reflection. Efficacy, pertinence, and normativeness are determinative in both instances. We thus see the airline bomb threats following the televising of the movie *Doomsday Flight* discussed by Bandura (1986) as falling into two categories—calculated plotting (those who followed through with extortion attempts, sometimes successfully) and spontaneous outbursts (those who only telephoned threats).

C. OTHER EFFECTS

Aggression and antisocial behavior are not the only hypothesized effects of television violence for which there is empirical support. Three others are desensitization, fearfulness, and pessimism.

The UC-Santa Barbara analyses of violence in television entertainment are of particular interest because the categories were derived from the empirical documentation of effects. This is a strategy advocated more than 15 years ago by the first author (Comstock, 1982) on the grounds that if concern motivates measurement then measurement should conform to what is empirically known about the bases for concern—effects.

We have added pessimism to the three outcomes examined by the UC-Santa Barbara group (Table 8.5) and revised their interpretation of humor. The outcomes are complementary to antisocial behavior; that is, the pessimistic, desensitized, and fearful will be more expectant of antisocial behavior, less likely to

TABLE 8.5   Relationships Between Four Outcomes of Television Violence and Selected Portrayals

Portrayals	Outcomes			
	Antisocial behavior	Fearfulness	Desensitization	Pessimism
Attractive perpetrator	Δ			
Attractive victim		Δ		Δ
Justified violence	Δ			
Unjustified violence	▼	Δ		Δ
Conventional weapons	Δ			Δ
Extensive/graphic violence	Δ	Δ	Δ	Δ
Realistic violence	Δ	Δ		Δ
Rewards	Δ	Δ		Δ
Punishment for perpetrator	▼	▼		▼
Pain/harm cues	▼			Δ
Aggressive/insulting humor	Δ		Δ	Δ
Humorous elements	▼			▼

Δ = Likely to increase the outcome.

▼ = Likely to decrease the outcome.

Adapted from *National Television Violence Study, Vol. 1,* 1997, Santa Barbara, CA: Mediascope; and *National Television Violence Study, Vol. 2,* 1997, Santa Barbara, CA: The Regents of the University of California.

intervene when it occurs, and more likely to think that forceful opposition is necessary for survival.

Our addition of pessimism is based on the consistent dichotomy in the survey literature for doleful opinions and perceptions, which in our schema encompass the mean-world syndrome of Gerbner and colleagues (Gerbner et al., 1986; Signorielli, 1990) and expressions of fear about personal safety (Comstock, 1982; Hughes, 1980; Tyler, 1978, 1980, 1984; Tyler & Cook, 1984). The former clearly increase with greater television exposure; the latter, equally clearly, do not. Television influences the conception people have of the world but not how safe they believe they are, which in our view is largely a function of the ability to avoid dangerous circumstances.

Our retention of fearfulness is based on a wholly different conceptualization—fright in response to a portrayal. This is a phenomenon most common among but hardly confined to children. Cantor (1991, 1994a, 1994b) has pioneered in the examination of this topic. The principal findings are that fear on the part of children is a common reaction to portrayals; children enjoy fearful responses if they are not drawn out or overwhelming, and do not lead to anxious rumination; what is logically or concretely more threatening is not necessarily more frightening to children; young children are particularly frightened by horrendous occurrences however improbable (a man involuntarily transformed into a spider) whereas older ones are more disturbed by the debilitating implications of possible events (such as war); benign experiences with possibly threatening entities, such as spiders or dogs, may reduce fearful responses; and negative responses to televised violence are heightened for children experiencing anxiety over real-life experiences with violence (Bruce, 1996).

Desensitization or lowered responsiveness to violent stimuli as a consequence of violence viewing has been recorded often (Cline, Croft, & Courrier, 1973; Comstock, 1991a; Donnerstein, Linz, & Penrod, 1987; Drabman & Thomas, 1974; Linz, Donnerstein, & Adams, 1989; Thomas, Horton, Lippencott, & Drabman, 1977) but there is a crucial qualification. The stimuli employed in the research invariably have been televised portrayals. Nurses and therapists may be desensitized to real-life trauma they will treat by pedagogically progressive media depictions of injured or dying patients. Similarly, portrayals of progressively close involvement with frightening stimuli can reduce fearful reactions in real life (Bandura, 1969, 1997; Bandura, Blanchard, & Ritter, 1969). However, ordinary viewing lacks several key factors: the explicit progression in the severity of the stimulus; the match of what is portrayed with real-life stimuli; and the desire of the viewer to achieve the end state. Thus, what the evidence points to is not lowered responsiveness to violence but depictions of violence in the media, and this desensitization to media violence further identifies excitation transfer as having a limited role because it would seldom be a factor among those who view large amounts of violence while amount of violence viewing itself is a consistent and pervasive positive correlate of aggressive and antisocial behavior.

This is not a trivial type of influence. Mass media are the means by which much that is important but conceivably repugnant comes to attention. Depictions that might evoke sorrow and pity or anger now court indifference. It is no accident that media figure in the mobilization of national populations for the pursuit of war by portraying the enemy as a justified target. This is the process of dehumanization or marginalization that makes the suffering of others acceptable (Bandura, 1986).

The UC-Santa Barbara group construe humor as facilitating aggressive acts either by trivializing them or making them seem attractive. They draw on the evidence that aggressive or insulting humor encourages like behavior toward those that are its target. We agree, and we include increases for humor of this type. However, we also think that other types of humorous elements may detract from the pertinence attributed to an act by impugning its significance. Empirically, we draw on the ABC-sponsored experiments of Lieberman Research (1975), whose data on this point have considerable credence because all their other outcomes paralleled those already recorded in the empirical literature. Thus, we include decreases for such humorous elements.

D. GENERAL PRINCIPLES

The theories and dimensions that figure in the effects of television violence on aggressive and antisocial behavior apply to all categories of behavior and all media. This has become a commonplace in the social and behavioral sciences—the conformity of broad ranges of behavior to the same few general principles (Bandura, 1997). The result is a general psychology of the behavioral influence of media.

We base this conclusion on three bodies of evidence. The first is the symmetry in the meta-analytic data on the effects of antisocial and prosocial television portrayals (Comstock, 1991a; Hearold, 1986). Exposure to prosocial portrayals has been associated with lower levels of aggressive or antisocial behavior and higher levels of prosocial behavior. Exposure to antisocial portrayals has been associated with higher levels of aggressive or antisocial behavior and lower levels of prosocial behavior. Although most of the data describe the link between the viewing of violent portrayals and aggressive and antisocial behavior, there are enough data on these other linkages to give a clear picture of this striking symmetry. Despite the obviously great disparities between them, the two categories of behavior behave essentially alike. The second is the success of the health belief model (Becker, 1974), which is derived from social learning theory, the precursor of social cognition. It is accurate conceptual genealogy to recognize that large-scale federally sponsored programs employing media (among other means) to change the health behavior of the public have their theoretical roots in the responses of children to the thumping of Bobo dolls (Comstock, 1983) and thereby testify to the wide applicability of the underlying theory. For example, in the multicommunity Stanford health experiments (Farquar et al., 1977, 1990), the dimension of susceptibility is represented by the greater effectiveness of the media appeals among those aware that they were at greater risk of cardiac disease. Our third source is the extensive literature on the modification of behavior—phobias, fears, anxieties—by the calculated use of media portrayals to make the stimuli involved less arousing and the viewer more confident in reacting to them (Bandura, 1969, 1986, 1997; Comstock et al., 1978). Such outcomes are limited in their applicability to ordinary viewing, but they further document that television can influence a wide variety of behavior.

We have emphasized psychological dynamics because most of the research has been conducted within that framework and the most prominent questions have centered on television's influence on individual behavior (in fact, two meta-analyses, Hearold, 1986, and Paik and Comstock, 1994, record that about half the empirical studies come from the discipline of psychology and about one-fourth from the field of communications, with the remainder from a miscellany of sources). However, a sociological interpretation also is demanded by the available data.

Amount of viewing is greater in households lower in socioeconomic status, in Black households, and in households high in the centrality of television, our term for norms and practices that encourage heavy television consumption. Young persons in these households are also likely to be high in the viewing of violent entertainment (Thornton & Voigt, 1984). Viewing also is likely to be greater for young persons in a stressful situation (Chapter 3), and violence viewing is likely to be greater among those scoring low on scales reflecting mental health and desirable life experiences, such as recently making a friend or getting along with a teacher (McCarthy et al., 1975).

Parenting, as would be expected, also plays a role. Parental attention to the whereabouts of their children is a negative predictor of delinquency (Thornton & Voigt, 1984). On the other hand, parents may actually endorse the importance of violent portrayals by their own attention, and only infrequently make critical comments about such portrayals that might mitigate their influence. The communicatory atmosphere established by parents enters, with an emphasis on free exchange of ideas a positive correlate of instrumental television use and a negative correlate of the viewing of entertainment and violence, particularly when it is joined by an emphasis on social harmony (Chaffee, McLeod, & Atkin, 1971; McLeod, Atkin, & Chaffee, 1972b).

The household most resistant to the influence of television on the aggressive and antisocial behavior of the young is of middle to higher socioeconomic status, endorses norms and engages in practices that do not particularly encourage television viewing (and thus where other media would be more likely to be at hand), has a parent or parents who become involved with and pay attention to the activities of their sons and daughters, and is one where topics and issues are freely discussed. It is an atmosphere of varied and constructive media use, parental care, and reasoned discipline. The household least resistant to such influence is of lower socioeconomic status, household centrality of television is high and it is the primary mass medium in use, parents pay only token attention to the activities of their children, and there is little discussion of topics and issues: consequently, there is a great deal of consumption of violent television entertainment and little that would mitigate its influence.

From a psychological perspective, these social factors are eminently plausible as conditions that would moderate or enhance the influence of television. The pernicious element is the sociological role of this mass medium in cultivating conflict with other young persons as well as adults and occasionally the law, thereby subverting the life changes of those facing the greatest challenges: the poor, the Black, and those disadvantaged in psychological resilience and desirable social experiences.

The data and our analysis somewhat beg the issue of effects on adults by being confined to persons ranging in age from nursery school through college age. We believe the data clearly point to effects on adults, but by way of the process by which aggressive traits develop. We also think that greater amounts of violence viewing during adulthood increase the likelihood of aggressive and antisocial behavior but in a somewhat circumscribed way.

Our reasoning is that adults would not be fully immune either from the observation of acts with some appeal for approximate emulation or the instigation of thoughts and images that would make aggressive and antisocial responses more available—the two major means by which television affects behavior of the kind under scrutiny. This lack of immunity is implied by the positive outcomes for young adults (in regard to an association between exposure to television violence and aggressive or antisocial behavior) in the experiments and the surveys. It is also apparent in the data on the increase in larceny theft that accompanied the introduction of television (Hennigan et al., 1982) where age has a role only in that substantial numbers of such crimes are perpetrated by youthful offenders, and the adaptive adjustment of criminal behavior in response to information and portrayals in the media (Bandura, 1986).

However, we think the role of television would be circumscribed among those beyond young adulthood for several reasons: the greater familiarity with the plots and portrayals of the medium, which would make it less important as a source of novel behavior; the stability of well-developed traits that would exemplify greater maturity; the fewer opportunities—represented by places and companions—for the expression of aggressive and antisocial behavior; and the lack of appeal at an older age of the spontaneous acts documented by Belson (1978) as particularly likely to be influenced by television compared to calculated and motivated acts (where television's influence would be confined to the few with some appeal for emulation). As for the kind of effect on adults we would expect to be quite common, we offer as a concrete example the likely increase in the use of aggressive language, such as *whack him*, that would follow from extensive exposure to such films as *Goodfellas* and *Casino*.

We conclude not only that the Surgeon General's Advisory Committee on Television and Social Behavior (1972) was correct in arguing that television violence increases aggressiveness. We also conclude that the data now take us beyond that point—to the opportunity for influence on an enduring trait, on illegal and seriously harmful behavior, on other categories of behavior, and on the social functioning of the young and particularly those facing the great challenges. Television has been at the forefront of concern and interest among the media because of its ubiquity, the high levels of use, its great popularity among children (and substantial although lower use by teenagers), and explicitness and full dimensionality of portrayals, all of which make it particularly effective at the kinds of influence in which social cognition and neoassociationism traffic. It is unmatched in these respects. However, the crucial explanatory factors do not reside in the surface characteristics of the different media, but rather in how effectively in a given circumstance the conditions on which effects depend are achieved—efficacy, normativeness, pertinence, and susceptibility.

REFERENCES

Abernethy, A. M. (1990). Television exposure: Programs vs. advertising. *Journal of Current Issues and Research in Advertising, 13*(1/2), 61–77.

Abernethy, A. M. (1992). The information context of newspaper advertising. *Journal of Current Issues and Research in Advertising, 14*(1), 63–68.

Abernethy, A. M., & Butler, D. D. (1992). Advertising information: Services versus products. *Journal of Retailing, 68*(4), 398–419.

Abramowitz, A. I. (1996). Bill and Al's excellent adventure: Forecasting the 1996 presidential election. *American Politics Quarterly, 24*(4), 434–442.

Adams, W. C. (1978). Local public affairs content of TV news. *Journalism Quarterly, 55*(4), 690–695.

Adams, W. C. (1986). Whose lives count? TV coverage of natural disasters. *Journal of Communication, 36*(2), 113–122.

Adams, W. J. (1998). Scheduling practices based on audience flow: What are the effects on new program success? *Journalism and Mass Communication Quarterly, 74*(4), 839–858.

Adler, R. P., Lesser, G. S., Meringoff, L. K., Robertson, T. S., Rossiter, J. R., & Ward, S. (1980). *The effect of television advertising on children: Review and recommendations.* Lexington, MA: Lexington Books.

Ajzen, I., & Fishbein, M. (1980). *Understanding attitudes and predicting social behavior.* Englewood Cliffs, NJ: Prentice Hall.

Albarran, A. B., & Umphrey, D. (1993). An examination of television motivations and program preferences by Hispanics, blacks, and whites. *Journal of Broadcasting and Electronic Media, 37*(1), 95–103.

Albiniak, P., & McConnell, C. (1998). Broadcasters cry "foul" over V-chip sets. *Broadcasting and Cable, 128*(31), 14–15.

Alden, D. L., & Hoyer, W. D. (1993). An examination of cognitive factors related to humorousness in television advertising. *Journal of Advertising, 22*(2), 29–37.

Alexander, A., Ryan, M., & Munoz, P. (1984). Creating a learning context: Investigations on the interactions of siblings during television viewing. *Critical Studies in Mass Communication, 1,* 345–364.

Allen, C. L. (1965). Photographing the TV audience. *Journal of Advertising Research, 5,* 2–8.

Allen, M., D'Alessio, D., & Brezgel, K. (1995). A meta-analysis summarizing the effects of pornography II: Aggression after exposure. *Human Communication Research, 22*(2), 258–283.

Almond, G. A., & Verba, S. (1989a). *The civic culture.* Newbury Park, CA: Sage.

Almond, G. A., & Verba, S. (1989b). *The civic culture revisited.* Newbury Park, CA: Sage.

Alper, W. S., & Leidy, T. R. (1970). The impact of information transmission through television. *Public Opinion Quarterly, 33*(2), 556–562.

Altemeyer, B. (1998). The other "authoritarian personality." In Zanna, M. P. (Ed.), *Advances in experimental social psychology* (Vol. 30, pp. 47–92). San Diego: Academic Press.

Altheide, D. M. (1976). *Creating reality: How TV news distorts events.* Beverly Hills, CA: Sage.

Alwitt, L. F., Benet, S. B., & Pitts, R. E. (1993, May/June). Temporal aspects of TV commercials influence viewers' online evaluations. *Journal of Advertising Research,* 9–21.

Alwitt, L. F., & Prabhaker, P. R. (1992, September/October). Functional and belief dimensions of attitudes to television advertising: Implications for copytesting. *Journal of Advertising Research,* 30–42.

Alwitt, L. F., & Prabhaker, P. R. (1994, November/December). Identifying who likes television advertising: Not by demographics alone. *Journal of Advertising Research,* 17–29.

Ambady, N., & Rosenthal, R. (1992). Thin slices of expressive behavior as predictors of interpersonal consequences: A meta-analysis. *Psychological Bulletin, 111*(92), 256–274.

Andersen, R. E., Crespo, C. J., Bartlett, S. J., Cheskin, L. J., & Pratt, M. (1998). Relationship of physical activity and television watching with body weight and level of fatness among children. *Journal of the American Medical Association, 279*(12), 938–942.

Anderson, B., Mead, N., & Sullivan, S. (1986). *Television: What do National Assessment Tests tell us?* Princeton, NJ: Educational Testing Service.

Anderson, C., & McGuire, T. (1978). The effect of TV viewing on the educational performance of thirteen elementary school children. *Alberta Journal of Educational Research, 24,* 156–163.

Anderson, D. R., & Collins, P. A. (1988). *The impact on children's education: Television's influence on cognitive development.* Washington, DC: U.S. Department of Education.

Anderson, D. R., Collins, P. A., Schmitt, K. L., & Jacobvitz, R. S. (1996). Stressful life events and television viewing. *Communication Research, 23*(3), 243–260.

Anderson, D. R., Levin, S., & Lorch, E. (1977). The effects of TV program pacing on the behavior of preschool children. *AV Communication Review, 25*(2), 159–166.

Anderson, D. R., Lorch, E. P., Field, D. E., Collins, P. A., & Nathan, J. G. (1986). Television viewing at home: Age trends in visual attention and time with TV. *Child Development, 57*(4), 1024–1033.

Anderson, J. A., & Meyer, T. P. (1988). *Mediated communication: A social action perspective.* Newbury Park, CA: Sage.

Andison, F. S. (1977). TV violence and viewer aggression: A cumulation of study results. *Public Opinion Quarterly, 41*(3), 314–331.

Ansolabehere, S., & Iyengar, S. (1994). Riding the wave and claiming ownership over issues: The joint effects of advertising and news coverage in campaigns. *Public Opinion Quarterly, 58*(3), 335–357.

Argenta, D. M., Stoneman, Z., & Brody, G. H. (1986). The effects of three different television programs on young children's peer interactions and toy play. *Journal of Applied Developmental Psychology, 7*(4), 355–371.

Armstrong, G. B., & Greenberg, B. S. (1990). Background television as an inhibitor of cognitive processing. *Human Communication Research, 16*(3), 355–386.

Atkin, C., Hocking, J., & McDermott, S. (1977). Home state viewer response and secondary media coverage. In Kraus, S. (Ed.), *The great debates: Carter vs. Ford, 1976* (pp. 429–436). Bloomington: Indiana University Press.

Atkin, C., Neuendorf, K., & McDermott, S. (1983). The role of alcohol advertising in excessive and hazardous drinking. *Journal of Drug Education, 13*(4), 313–325.

Atkin, C. K. (1972). Anticipated communication and mass media information-seeking. *Public Opinion Quarterly, 36*(2), 188–199.

Atkin, C. K. (1977). Effects of campaign advertising and newscasts on children. *Journalism Quarterly, 54*(3), 503–508.

Atkin, C. K. (1978). Observations of parent-child interaction in supermarket decision-making. *Journal of Marketing, 42*(4), 41–45.

Atkin, C. K. (1981). Political socialization. In D. Nimmo & K. Sanders (Eds.), *Handbook of political communication.* Beverly Hills, CA: Sage.

Atkin, C. K. (1983). Effects of realistic TV violence vs. fictional violence on aggression. *Journalism Quarterly, 60*(4), 615–621.

Atkin, C. K., Greenberg, B. S., Korzenny, F., & McDermott, S. (1979). Selective exposure to televised violence. *Journal of Broadcasting, 23*(1), 5–13.

Atkin, C. K., Hocking, J., & Block, M. (1984). Teenage drinking: Does advertising make a difference? *Journal of Communication, 34*(2), 157–167.

Atkin, D. (1991). The evolution of television series addressing single women, 1966–1990. *Journal of Broadcasting and Electronic Media, 35*(4), 517–523.

Atkin, D., Moorman, J., & Lin, C. A. (1991). Ready for prime time: Network series devoted to working women in the 1980s. *Sex Roles, 25*(11/12), 677–685.

Atwater, T. (1989). News format in network evening news coverage of the TWA hijacking. *Journal of Broadcasting and Electronic Media, 33*(3), 293–304.

Atwater, T., & Green, N. F. (1988). News sources in network coverage of international terrorism. *Journalism Quarterly, 65*(4), 967–971.

Atwater, T., Salwen, M. B., & Anderson, R. B. (1985). Media agenda-setting with environmental issues. *Journalism Quarterly, 62*(2), 393–397.

Austin, E. W., & Johnson, K. K. (1997). Immediate and delayed effects of media literacy training on third graders' decision making for alcohol. *Health Communication, 9*(4), 323–349.

Axford, B., Madgwick, P., & Turner, J. (1992). Image management, stunts, and dirty tricks: The marketing of political brands in television campaigns. *Media, Culture, and Society, 14*(4), 637–651.

Babrow, A. S., & Swanson, D. L. (1988). Disentangling antecedents of audience exposure levels: Extending expectancy-value analyses of gratifications sought from television news. *Communication Monographs, 55*(1), 1–21.

Bailey, G. A., & Lichty, L. W. (1972). Rough justice on a Saigon street: A gatekeeper study of NBC's Tet execution film. *Journalism Quarterly, 49*(2), 221–229, 238.

Baker, R. K., & Ball, S. J. (Eds.). (1969). *Violence and the media. A staff report to the National Commission on the Causes and Prevention of Violence.* Washington, DC: U.S. Government Printing Office.

Baldwin, T. F., Barrett, M., & Bates, B. (1992). Uses and values for news on cable television. *Journal of Broadcasting and Electronic Media, 36*(2), 225–233.

Baldwin, T. F., & Lewis, C. (1972). Violence in television: The industry looks at itself. In G. A. Comstock & E. A. Rubinstein (Eds.), *Television and social behavior, Media content and control* (Vol. 1). Washington, DC: U.S. Government Printing Office.

Ball, S., & Bogatz, G. A. (1970). *The first year of "Sesame Street": An evaluation.* Princeton, NJ: Educational Testing Service.

Ball, S., & Bogatz, G. A. (1975). Some thoughts on this secondary evaluation. In T. D. Cook, H. Appleton, R. F. Conner, A. Shaffer, G. Tamkin, & S. J. Weber, *"Sesame Street" revisited* (pp. 387–403). New York: Russell Sage.

Ball-Rokeach, S. J., Rokeach, M., & Grube, J. W. (1984). *The great American values test.* New York: Free Press.

Ballard-Campbell, M. (1983). *Children's understanding of television advertising: Behavioral assessment of three developmental skills.* Unpublished doctoral dissertation, University of California, Los Angeles.

Bandura, A. (1965). Influence of model's reinforcement contingencies on the acquisition of imitative responses. *Journal of Personality and Social Psychology, 1*(6), 589–595.

Bandura, A. (1969). *Principles of behavior modification.* New York: Holt, Rinehart and Winston.

Bandura, A. (1973). *Aggression: A social learning analysis.* Englewood Cliffs, NJ: Prentice Hall.

Bandura, A. (1986). *Social foundations of thought and action: A social cognitive theory.* Englewood Cliffs, NJ: Prentice Hall.

Bandura, A. (1997). *Self-efficacy: The exercise of control.* New York: Freeman.

Bandura, A., Blanchard, E. B., & Ritter, B. (1969). Relative efficacy of desensitization and modeling approaches for inducing behavioral, affective, and attitudinal changes. *Journal of Personality and Social Psychology, 13*(3), 173–199.

Bandura, A., Ross, D., & Ross, S. A. (1963a). Imitation of film-mediated aggressive models. *Journal of Abnormal and Social Psychology, 66*(1), 3–11.

Bandura, A., Ross, D., & Ross, S. A. (1963b). Vicarious reinforcement and imitative learning. *Journal of Abnormal and Social Psychology, 67*(6), 601–607.

Barlow, T., & Wogalter, M. S. (1993). Alcoholic beverage warnings in magazine and television advertisements. *Journal of Consumer Research, 20*(1), 147–156.

Barnes, J. H., Jr., & Dotson, M. J. (1990). An exploratory investigation into the nature of offensive television advertising. *Journal of Advertising, 19*(3), 61–69.

Barnett, S. (1997). New media, old problems: New technology and the political process. *European Journal of Communication, 12*(2), 193–218.

Barnouw, E. (1978). *The sponsor: Notes on a modern potentate.* New York: Oxford University Press.

Baron, J. N., & Reiss, P. C. (1985). Same time, next year: Aggregate analyses of the mass media and violent behavior. *American Sociological Review, 50*(3), 347–363.

Baron, R. A., & Richardson, D. R. (1994). *Human aggression* (2nd ed.). New York: Plenum.

Bartels, L. M. (1993). Messages received: The political impact of media exposure. *American Political Science Review, 87*(2), 267–285.

Barwise, T. P. (1986, August/September). Repeat viewing of prime-time TV series. *Journal of Advertising Research, 26,* 9–14.

Barwise, T. P., & Ehrenberg, A. S. C. (1987). The liking and viewing of regular TV series. *Journal of Consumer Research, 14*(1), 63–70.

Barwise, T. P., & Ehrenberg, A. S. C. (1988). *Television and its audience.* Newbury Park, CA: Sage.

Barwise, T. P., Ehrenberg, A. S. C., & Goodhardt, G. J. (1982). Glued to the box? Patterns of TV repeat viewing. *Journal of Communication, 32*(4), 22–29.

Batra, R., & Ray, M. L. (1985). How advertising works at contact. In Alwitt, L. F., & Mitchell, A. W. (Eds.), *Psychological processes and advertising effects* (pp. 13–43). Hillsdale, NJ: Erlbaum.

Bauer, R. A. (1971). The obstinate audience: The influence process from the point of view of social communication. In W. Schramm and D. F. Roberts (Eds.), *The process and effects of mass communication* (Rev. ed, pp. 326–346). Urbana: University of Illinois Press.

Baxter, R. S., DeReimer, C., Landini, A., Leslie, L., & Singletary, M. W. (1985). A content analysis of music videos. *Journal of Broadcasting and Electronic Media, 29*(3), 333–340.

Bechtel, R. B., Achelpohl, C., & Akers, R. (1972). Correlates between observed behavior and questionnaire responses on television viewing. In E. A. Rubinstein, G. A. Comstock, and J. P. Murray (Eds.), *Television and social behavior. Television in day-to-day life: Patterns of use* (Vol. 4). Washington, DC: U.S. Government Printing Office.

Becker, G. S., & Murphy, K. M. (1993, November). A simple theory of advertising as good or bad. *The Quarterly Journal of Economics,* 941–964.

Becker, L. B., Weaver, D. H., Graber, D. A., & McCombs, M. E. (1979). Influence on public agendas. In S. Kraus (Ed.), *The great debates: Carter vs. Ford, 1976* (pp. 418–428). Bloomington: Indiana University Press.

Becker, M. H. (Ed.). (1974). The health belief model and personal health behavior. *Health Education Monographs, 2*(4).

Becker, S. L., Pepper, R., Wenner, L. A., & Kim, J. K. (1979). Information flow and the shaping of meanings. In S. Kraus (Ed.), *The great debates: Carter vs. Ford, 1976* (pp. 384–397). Bloomington: Indiana University Press.

Bédy, Z. (1996). *Couch potatoes and the indifferent electorate: Television viewing, voting, and responsible citizenship.* Unpublished doctoral dissertation. Syracuse University, Syracuse, NY.

Bellamy, R. V., McDonald, D. G., & Walker, J. R. (1990). The spin-off as television program form and strategy. *Journal of Broadcasting and Electronic Media, 34*(3), 283–297.

Bellotti, F. X. (1975, July). Petition before the F.C.C. of the Attorneys General of Massachusetts, Alaska, Colorado, Delaware, Hawaii, Illinois, Maryland, Nebraska, New Hampshire, North Carolina, Maine, Pennsylvania, Rhode Island, and Wyoming to promulgate a rule restricting the advertising of over-the-counter drugs. Washington, DC: U.S. House of Representatives.

Belson, W. A. (1959). Effects of television on the interests and initiative of adult viewers in Greater London. *British Journal of Psychology, 50,* 145–158.

Belson, W. A. (1978). *Television violence and the adolescent boy.* Westmead, England: Saxon House, Teakfield.

Bennett, C. (1997). Assessing the impact of ad watches on the strategic decision-making process: A comparative analysis of ad watches in the 1992 and 1996 presidential elections. *American Behavioral Scientist, 40*(8), 1161–1182.

Benton, M., & Frazier, J. (1976). The agenda-setting function of the mass media at three levels of "information holding." *Communication Research, 3,* 261–274.

Benze, J. G., & Declercq, E. R. (1985). Content of television political spot ads for female candidates. *Journalism Quarterly, 62*(2), 278–283, 288.

Berelson, B. R., Lazarsfeld, P. F., & McPhee, W. N. (1954). *Voting.* Chicago: University of Chicago Press.

Berkowitz, D. (1991). Assessing forces in the selection of local television news. *Journal of Broadcasting and Electronic Media, 35*(2), 245–251.

Berkowitz, D., & Adams, D. B. (1990). Information subsidy and agenda-building in local television news. *Journalism Quarterly, 67*(4), 723–731.

Berkowitz, L. (1984). Some effects of thoughts on anti- and prosocial influences of media events: A cognitive-neoassociationistic analysis. *Psychological Bulletin, 95*(3), 410–427.

Berkowitz, L. (1990). On the formation and regulation of anger and aggression: A cognitive-neoassociationistic analysis. *American Psychologist, 45*(4), 494–503.

Berkowitz, L., & Alioto, J. T. (1973). The meaning of an observed event as a determinant of aggressive consequences. *Journal of Personality and Social Psychology, 28*(2), 206–217.

Berkowitz, L., & Geen, R. G. (1966). Film violence and the cue properties of available targets. *Journal of Personality and Social Psychology, 3*(5), 525–530.

Berkowitz, L., & Geen, R. G. (1967). Stimulus qualities of the target of aggression: A further study. *Journal of Personality and Social Psychology, 5*(3), 364-368.

Berkowitz, L., & Rawlings, E. (1963). Effects of film violence on inhibitions against subsequent aggression. *Journal of Abnormal and Social Psychology, 66*(3), 405–412.

Bernstein, J. M., Lacy, S., Cassara, C., & Lau, T. (1990). Geographic coverage by local television news. *Journalism Quarterly, 67*(4), 663–671.

Bettie, J. (1995). *Roseanne* and the changing face of working-class iconography. *Social Text, 14*(4), 125–149.

Beville, H. M., Jr. (1988). *Audience ratings: Radio, television, cable* (Rev. ed.). Hillsdale, NJ: Erlbaum.

Biel, A. L., & Bridgwater, C. A. (1990, June/July). Attributes of likable television commercials. *Journal of Advertising Research,* 38–44.

Bielby, W. T., & Bielby, D. D. (1994). "All hits are flukes": Institutionalized decision making and the rhetoric of network prime-time program development. *American Journal of Sociology, 99*(5), 1287–1313.

Biocca, F., David, P., Dion, A., Goodson, S., Lashley, M., & Tan, H. I. (1992). The effect of commercials on memory and perceived importance of television news. *Mass Communication Review (MCR), 12,* 14–20.

Bjorkqvist, K. (1994). Sex differences in physical, verbal and indirect aggression: A review of recent research. *Sex Roles, 30*(3/4), 177-188.

Blair, M. H., & Rosenberg, K. E. (1994). Convergent findings increase our understanding of how advertising works. *Journal of Advertising Research, 34*(3), 35–45.

Blood, R. W. (1989). Public agendas and media agendas: Some news that may matter. *Media Information Australia, 52*(1), 7–15.

Blosser, B. J., & Roberts, D. F. (1985). Age differences in children's perceptions of message intent: Responses to TV news, commercials, educational spots, and public service announcements. *Communication Research, 12*(4), 455–484.

Blum, R. A., & Lindheim, R. D. (1987). *Primetime: Network television programming.* Stoneham, MA: Focal Press.

Blumler, J. G., & Spicer, C. M. (1990). Prospects for creativity in the new television marketplace: Evidence from program-makers. *Journal of Communication, 40*(4), 78–101.

Boddy, W. (1990). *Fifties television: The industry and its critics.* Urbana: University of Illinois Press.

Bogart, L. (1972a). Negro and white media exposure: New evidence. *Journalism Quarterly, 49*(1), 15–21.

Bogart, L. (1972b). *The age of television* (3rd ed.). New York: Ungar.

Bogart, L. (1989). *Press and public* (Rev. ed.). Hillsdale, NJ: Erlbaum.

Bogart, L., & Lehman, C. (1983, February). The case of the 30-second commercial. *Journal of Advertising Research, 23,* 11–19.

Bogatz, G. A., & Ball, S. (1971). *The second year of "Sesame Street": A continuing evaluation, Vols. 1 and 2.* Princeton, NJ: Educational Testing Service.

Bollen, K. A., & Phillips, D. P. (1982). Imitative suicides: A national study of the effects of television news stories. *American Sociological Review, 47*(6), 802–809.

Bowen, L. (1994). Time of voting decision and use of political advertising: The Slade Gorton–Brock Adams senatorial campaign. *Journalism Quarterly, 71*(3), 665–675.

Bower, R. (1973). *Television and the public.* New York: Holt, Rinehart, and Winston.

Bower, R. (1985). *The changing television audience in America.* New York: Columbia University Press.

Bowler, S., Donovan, T., & Snipp, J. (1993). Local sources of information and voter choice in state elections: Microlevel foundations of the "friends and neighbors" effect. *American Politics Quarterly, 21*(4), 473–489.

Boyd, H. H. (1996). *Images of the news media, attention to the news and civic participation.* Paper presented at the annual meeting of the International Communication Association, Chicago, IL.

Breed, W. (1955). Newspaper "opinion leaders" and processes of standardization. *Journalism Quarterly, 35*(3), 277–284, 328.

Breed, W. (1960). Social control in the newsroom: A functional analysis. In W. Schramm (Ed.), *Mass communications* (pp. 178–194). Urbana: University of Illinois Press. (Reprinted from *Social Forces, 33,* 1955, 326–335.)

Breed, W., & DeFoe, J. R. (1981). The portrayal of the drinking process on prime-time television. *Journal of Communication, 31*(1), 58–67.

Bretl, D. J., & Cantor, J. (1988). The portrayal of men and women in U.S. television commercials: A recent content analysis and trends over 15 years. *Sex Roles, 18*(9/10), 595–609.

Brinson, S. L. (1992). The use and opposition of rape myths in prime-time television dramas. *Sex Roles, 27*(7/8), 359-375.

Bristor, J. M., Lee, R. G., & Hunt, M. R. (1995). Race and ideology: African-American images in television advertising. *Journal of Public Policy and Marketing, 14*(1), 48–59.

Broach, V. C., Page, T. J., Jr., & Wilson, R. D. (1995). Television programming and its influence on viewers' perceptions of commercials: The role of program arousal and pleasantness. *Journal of Advertising, 24*(4), 45–54.

Broholm, J. (1985). SNG research. *RTNDA Communicator,* 26–27.

Bromley, R. V., & Bowles, D. (1995). Impact of Internet on use of traditional news media. *Newspaper Research Journal, 16*(2), 14–27.

Brosius, H. B. (1989). Influence of presentation features and news content on learning from television news. *Journal of Broadcasting and Electronic Media, 33*(1), 1–14.

Brosius, H. B. (1991). Format effects on comprehension of television news. *Journalism Quarterly, 68*(3), 396–401.

Brosius, H. B. (1993). The effects of emotional pictures in television news. *Communication Research, 20*(1), 105–124.

Brosius, H. B., & Kepplinger, H. M. (1990). The agenda-setting function of television news. *Communication Research, 17*(2), 183–211.

Brown, J. D., Bybee, C. R., Weardon, S. T., & Murdock, D. (1987). Invisible power: Newspaper news sources and the limits of diversity. *Journalism Quarterly, 64*(1), 45–54.

Brown, L. (1971). *Television: The business behind the box.* New York: Harcourt, Brace, Jovanovich.

Brown, L. (1977). *The New York Times encyclopedia of television.* New York: Times Books.

Brown, T. J., & Rothschild, M. L. (1993). Reassessing the impact of television advertising clutter. *Journal of Consumer Research, 20*(1), 138–146.

Browning, G. (1994, February 26). Push-button violence. *The National Journal, 26*(9), 458.

Bruce, L. R. (1996). *The victimization and "re-victimization" of American children: An examination of the relationship between traumatic exposure to real-life violence and the emotional outcomes associated with television violence.* Paper presented at the annual meeting of the International Communication Association, Chicago, IL.

Bruner, G. C., II. (1990). Music, mood, and marketing. *Journal of Marketing, 54*(4), 94–104.

Bryant, J. (1989). Viewers' enjoyment of televised sports violence. In L. A. Wenner (Ed.), *Media, sports, and society* (pp. 270–289). Newbury Park, CA: Sage.

Bryant, J., Comisky, P., & Zillmann, D. (1981). The appeal of rough-and-tumble play in televised professional football. *Communication Quarterly, 29*(4), 256–262.

Bryant, J., & Zillmann, D. (1984). Using television to alleviate boredom and stress: Selective exposure as a function of induced excitational states. *Journal of Broadcasting, 28*(1), 1–20.

Bryce, W. J., & Yalch, R. F. (1993). Hearing versus seeing: A comparison of consumer learning of spoken and pictorial information in television advertising. *Journal of Current Issues and Research in Advertising, 15*(1), 1–20.

Burriss, L. L. (1989a). Changes in presidential press conferences. *Journalism Quarterly, 66*(2), 468-470.

Burriss, L. L. (1989b). How anchors, reporters, and newsmakers affect recall and evaluation of stories. *Journalism Quarterly, 66*(2), 514–532.

Bush, A. J., Hair, J. F., Jr., & Bush, R. P. (1983). A content analysis of animation in television advertising. *Journal of Advertising, 12*(4), 20–41.

Butter, E. J., Popovich, P. M., Stackhouse, R. H., & Garner, R. K. (1981). Discrimination of television programs and commercials by preschool children. *Journal of Advertising Research, 21*(2), 53–56.

Cacioppo, J. T., & Petty, R. E. (1985). Central and peripheral routes to persuasion: The role of message repetition. In L. F. Alwitt & A. A. Mitchell (Eds.), *Psychological processes and advertising effects: Theory, research and application* (pp. 91–111). Hillsdale, NJ: Erlbaum.

Cairns, E., Hunter, D., & Herring, L. (1980). Young children's awareness of violence in Northern Ireland: The influence of Northern Irish television in Scotland and Northern Ireland. *British Journal of Social and Clinical Psychology, 19*(1), 3–6.

Calfee, J. E., & Ringold, D. J. (1994). The 70% majority: Enduring consumer beliefs about advertising. *Journal of Public Policy and Marketing, 13*(2), 228–238.

California Assessment Program. (1980). *Student achievement in California schools. 1979–80 annual report.* Sacramento: California State Department of Education.

California Assessment Program. (1982). *Survey of sixth grade school achievement and television viewing habits.* Sacramento: California State Department of Education.

California Assessment Program. (1986). *Annual report, 1985–1986.* Sacramento: California State Department of Education.

Callcott, M. F., & Lee, W. N. (1994). A content analysis of animation and animated spokes-characters in television commercials. *Journal of Advertising, 23*(4), 1–12.

Cameron, G. T., & Blount, D. (1996). VNRs and airchecks: A content analysis of the use of video news releases in television newscasts. *Journalism and Mass Communication Quarterly, 73*(4), 890–904.

Cameron, G. T., Schleuder, J., & Thorson, E. (1991). The role of news teasers in processing television news and commercials. *Communication Research, 18*(5), 667–684.

Campbell, A., Gurin, G., & Miller, W. E. (1954). *The voter decides.* Evanston, IL: Row, Peterson.

Campbell, J. E. (1996). Polls and votes: The trial-heat presidential election forecasting model, certainty, and political campaigns. *American Politics Quarterly, 24*(4), 408–433.

Campbell, J. E., Cherry, L., & Wink, K. (1992). The convention bump. *American Politics Quarterly, 20*(3), 287–307.

Campbell, K., Wiggins, E. L., & Duhe, S. F. (1997). *Still knowing their place: African Americans in Southeast TV newscasts.* Paper presented at the annual meeting of the Association for Education in Journalism and Mass Communication, Chicago, IL.

Campbell, R., & Reeves, J. L. (1989). Covering the homeless: The Joyce Brown story. *Critical Studies in Mass Communication, 6*(1), 21–42.

Canary, D. J., & Spitzberg, B. H. (1993). Loneliness and media gratification. *Communication Research, 20*(6), 800–821.

Cantor, J. (1991). Fright responses to mass media productions. In J. Bryant & D. Zillmann (Eds.), *Responding to the screen: Reception and reaction processes* (pp. 169–197). Hillsdale, NJ: Erlbaum.

Cantor, J. (1994a). Confronting children's fright responses to mass media. In D. Zillmann, J. Bryant, & A. C. Huston (Eds.), *Media, children, and the family: Social scientific, psychodynamic, and clinical perspectives* (pp. 139–150). Hillsdale, NJ: Erlbaum.

Cantor, J. (1994b). Fright reactions to mass media. In J. Bryant and D. Zillmann (Eds.), *Media effects: Advances in theory and research* (pp. 213–246). Hillsdale, NJ: Erlbaum.

Cantor, M. G. (1991). The American family on television: From Molly Goldberg to Bill Cosby. *Journal of Comparative Family Studies, 22*(2), 205–216.

Cantril, H. (1940). *The invasion from Mars: A study of the psychology of panic.* Princeton, NJ: Princeton University Press.

Caplan, R. E. (1985). Violent program content in music videos. *Journalism Quarterly, 62*(1), 144–147.

Cappella, J. N., & Jamieson, K. H. (1994). Broadcast adwatch effects: A field experiment. *Communication Research, 21*(3), 342–365.

Cappella, J. N., & Jamieson, K. H. (1997). *Spiral of cynicism: The press and the public good.* New York: Oxford University Press.

Caprara, G. V., D'Imperio, G., Gentilomo, A., Mammucari, A., Renzi, P., & Travaglia, G. (1987). The intrusive commercial: Influence of aggressive TV commercials on aggression. *European Journal of Social Psychology, 17*(1), 23–31.

Carey, J. (1989). Public broadcasting and federal policy. In P. R. Newberg (Ed.), *New directions in telecommunications policy. Regulatory policy: Telephony and mass media* (Vol. 1, pp. 192–221). Durham, NC: Duke University Press.

Carroll, R. L. (1988). Changes in the news: Trends in network news production. *Journalism Quarterly, 65*(4), 940–945.

Carroll, R. L., & Tuggle, C. A. (1997). The world outside: Local TV news treatment of imported news. *Journalism and Mass Communication Quarterly, 74*(1), 123–133.

Carroll, R. L., & Tuggle, C. A., McCollum, J. F., Mitrook, M. A., Arlington, K. J., & Hoerner, J. M., Jr. (1997). Consonance in local television news program content: An examination of intermarket diversity. *Journal of Broadcasting and Electronic Media, 41*(1), 132–144.

Carter, R. F. (1962). Some effects of the debates. In S. Kraus (Ed.), *The great debates: Kennedy vs. Nixon, 1960* (pp. 253–270). Bloomington: Indiana University Press.

Carter, R. F., & Greenberg, B. S. (1965). Newspapers or television: Which do you believe? *Journalism Quarterly, 42*(1), 29–34.

Cassata, M., & Irwin, B. J. (1997). Young by day: The older person on daytime serial drama. Al-Deen, H. S. N. (Ed.), *Cross-cultural communication and aging in the United States.* Mahwah, NJ: Erlbaum.

Celozzi, M. J., II, Kazelskis, R., & Gutsch, K. U. (1981). The relationship between viewing televised violence in ice hockey and subsequent levels of personal aggression. *Journal of Sport Behavior, 4*(4), 157–162.

Centerwall, B. S. (1989). Exposure to television as a cause of violence. In G. Comstock (Ed.), *Public communication and behavior* (Vol. 2, pp. 1–58). New York: Academic Press.

Chaffee, S. H. (1972). Television and adolescent aggressiveness (overview). In G. A. Comstock & E. A. Rubinstein (Eds.), *Television and social behavior. Television and adolescent aggressiveness* (Vol. 3, pp. 1–34). Washington, DC: U.S. Government Printing Office.

Chaffee, S. H., & Frank, S. (1996). How Americans get political information: Print versus broadcast news. *Annals of the American Academy of Political and Social Science, 546*, 48–58.

Chaffee, S. H., & McLeod, J. M. (1973). Individual vs. social predictors of information-seeking. *Journalism Quarterly, 50*(2), 237–245.

Chaffee, S. H., McLeod, J. M., & Wackman, D. B. (1973). Family communication patterns and adolescent political participation. In J. Dennis (Ed.), *Socialization to politics: A reader* (pp. 349–364). New York: Wiley.

Chaffee, S. H., Moon, Y., & McDevitt, M. (1996). *Immediate and delayed effects of an intervention in political socialization: A disequilibration-restabilization model.* Paper presented at the annual meeting of the International Communication Association, Chicago, IL.

Chaffee, S. H., Ward, L. S., & Tipton, L. P. (1970). Mass communication and political socialization. *Journalism Quarterly, 47*(4), 647-659, 666.

Chaffee, S. H., Zhao, X., & Leshner, G. (1994). Political knowledge and the campaign media of 1992. *Communication Research, 22*(3), 305–324.

Chall, J. S. (1983). *Stages of reading development.* New York: McGraw Hill.

Chan, S. (1997). Effects of attention to campaign coverage on political trust. *International Journal of Public Opinion Research, 9*(3), 286–296.

Chang, T. K., Shoemaker, P. J., & Brendlinger, N. (1987). Determinants of international news coverage in the U.S. media. *Communication Research, 14*(3), 396–414.

Charters, W. W. (1933). *Motion pictures and youth: A summary.* New York: Macmillan.

Chen, A. C. (1989). Televised international news in five countries: Thoroughness, insularity, and agenda capacity. *International Communications Bulletin (ICB), 24*(1–2), 4–8.

Chester, E. W. (1969). *Radio, television, and American politics.* New York: Sheed and Ward.

Chi, H. H., Thorson, E., & Coyle, J. (1995). *An application of the intensity-affect model using commercial-to-program involvement ratios to predict ad memory.* Paper presented at the annual meeting of the American Academy of Advertising, Norfolk, VA.

Childs, J. H. (1979). *Television viewing, achievement, IQ and creativity.* Unpublished doctoral dissertation, Brigham Young University, Provo, UT.

Chirco, A. P. (1990). *An examination of stepwise regression models of adolescent alcohol and marijuana use with special attention to the television exposure—teen drinking issue.* Unpublished doctoral dissertation, Syracuse University, Syracuse, NY.

Chow, S., Rose, R. L., & Clarke, D. G. (1992). Sequence: Structural equations estimation of new copy effectiveness. *Journal of Advertising Research, 32*(4), 60–72.

Christ, W. G., Thorson, E., & Caywood, C. (1994). Do attitudes toward political advertising affect information processing of televised political commercials? *Journal of Broadcasting and Electronic Media, 38*(3), 251–270.

Chu, G. C., & Schramm, W. (1967). *Learning from television: What the research says.* Stanford, CA: Institute for Communication Research, Stanford University.

Clark, D. G., & Blankenburg, W. S. (1972). Trends in violent content in selected mass media. In G. Comstock & E. Rubinstein (Eds.), *Television and social behavior: Media content and control* (Vol. 1, pp. 188–243). Washington, DC: U.S. Government Printing Office.

Clarke, P., & Fredin, E. (1978). Newspapers, television and political reasoning. *Public Opinion Quarterly, 42*(2), 143–160.

Clayman, S. E. (1995). Defining moments, presidential debates, and the dynamics of quotability. *Journal of Communication, 45*(3), 118–146.

Clifford, B. R., Gunter, B., & McAleer, J. L. (1997). Children's memory and comprehension of two science programmes. *Journal of Educational Media, 23*(1), 25–50.

Cline, V. B., Croft, R. G., & Courrier, S. (1973). Desensitization of children to television violence. *Journal of Personality and Social Psychology, 27*(3), 360–365.

Cobb-Walgren, C. J. (1990). The changing commercial climate. *Current Issues and Research in Advertising, 13*(1/2), 343–368.

Cohen, A. A., Levy, M. R., & Golden, K. (1988). Children's uses and gratifications of home VCRs: Evolution or revolution. *Communication Research, 15*(6), 772–780.

Cohen, B. (1963). *The press and foreign policy.* Princeton, NJ: Princeton University Press.

Cohen, E. E. (1988). *Children's television commercialization survey.* Washington, DC: National Association of Broadcasters.

Cohen, J., & Davis, R. G. (1991). Third person effects and the differential impact in negative political advertising. *Journalism Quarterly, 68*(4), 680–688.

Cole, J. (1995). *The UCLA television violence monitoring report, 1995.* Los Angeles, CA: UCLA Center for Communication Policy.

Cole, J. (1996). *The UCLA television violence monitoring report, 1996.* Los Angeles, CA: UCLA Center for Communication Policy.

Cole, J. (1997). *The UCLA television violence report, 1997.* Los Angeles, CA: UCLA Center for Communication Policy.

Comstock, G. (1982). Violence in television content: An overview. In D. Pearl, L. Bouthilet, & J. Lazar (Eds.), *Television and behavior: Ten years of scientific inquiry and implications for the eighties. Technical reviews* (Vol. 2, pp. 334–348). Washington, DC: U.S. Government Printing Office.

Comstock, G. (1983). Media influences on aggression. In A. Goldstein (Ed.), *Prevention and control of aggression* (pp. 241–272). Elmsford, NY: Pergamon.

Comstock, G. (1988). Today's audiences, tomorrow's media. In S. Oskamp (Ed.), *Applied social psychology annual* (Vol. 8, pp. 324–345). Newbury Park, CA: Sage.

Comstock, G. (1989). *The evolution of American television.* Newbury Park, CA: Sage.

Comstock, G. (1991a). *Television and the American child.* San Diego, CA: Academic Press.

Comstock, G. (1991b). *Television in America.* (2nd ed.), Newbury Park, CA: Sage.

Comstock, G., Chaffee, S., Katzman, N., McCombs, M., & Roberts, D. (1978). *Television and human behavior.* New York: Columbia University Press.

Comstock, J., & Strzyzewski, K. (1990). Interpersonal interaction on television: Family conflict and jealousy on primetime. *Journal of Broadcasting and Electronic Media, 34*(3), 263–282.

Condry, J. (1989). *The psychology of television.* Hillsdale, NJ: Erlbaum.

Condry, J., & Scheibe, C. (1989). Nonprogram content of television: Mechanisms of persuasion. In J. Condry, *The psychology of television* (pp. 173–232). Hillsdale, NJ: Erlbaum.

Cook, T. D., Appleton, H., Conner, R. F., Shaffer, A., Tamkin, G., & Weber, S. J. (1975). *"Sesame Street" revisited.* New York: Russell Sage.

Cook, T. D., & Campbell, D. T. (1979). *Quasi-experimentation: Design and analysis issues for field settings*. Chicago: Houghton Mifflin.

Cook, T. D., Kendzierski, D. A., & Thomas, S. A. (1983). The implicit assumptions of television research: An analysis of the 1982 NIMH report on television and behavior. *Public Opinion Quarterly, 47*(2), 161–201.

Cooper, C. A. (1996). *Violence on television, congressional inquiry, public criticism and industry response, a policy analysis*. Lanham, MD: University Press of America.

Cooper, R. (1996). The status and future of audience duplication research: An assessment of ratings-based theories of audience behavior. *Journal of Broadcasting and Electronic Media, 40*(1), 96–111.

Cotter, P. R., & Stovall, J. R. (1994). Is one as good as another? The relative influence of preelection surveys on voter behavior. *Newspaper Research Journal, 15*(4), 13–19.

Cranston, P. (1960). Political convention broadcasts: Their history and influence. *Journalism Quarterly, 37*(2), 186–194.

Crask, M. R., & Laskey, H. A. (1990). A positioning-based decision model for selecting advertising messages. *Journal of Advertising Research, 30*(4), 32–38.

Cronin, J. J., & Menelly, N. E. (1992). Discrimination vs. avoidance: "Zipping" of television commercials. *Journal of Advertising, 21*(2), 1–7.

Csapo-Sweet, R. M. (1997). *Sesame Street*, English vocabulary and word usage of Hungarian ESL students. *European Journal of Communication Research, 22*(2), 175–190.

Cundy, D. T. (1989). Televised political editorials and the low-involvement viewer. *Social Science Quarterly, 70*(4), 911–922.

Cundy, D. T. (1994). Televised news, trait inferences, and support for political figures. *Journal of Broadcasting and Electronic Media, 38*(1), 49–63.

Daddario, G. (1994). Chilly scenes of the 1992 Winter Games: The mass media and the marginalization of female athletes. *Sociology of Sport Journal, 11*(3), 275–288.

Davie, W. R., & Lee, J. S. (1993). Television news technology: Do more sources mean less diversity? *Journal of Broadcasting and Electronic Media, 37*(4), 453–464.

Davies, M. M. (1996). *Fake, fact and fantasy*. Mahwah, NJ: Erlbaum.

Davis, D. K. (1979). Influence on vote decisions. In S. Kraus (Ed.), *The great debates: Carter vs. Ford, 1976* (pp. 331–347). Bloomington: Indiana University Press.

Day, R. C., & Ghandour, M. (1984). The effect of television-mediated aggression and real-life aggression on the behavior of Lebanese children. *Journal of Experimental Child Psychology, 38*(1), 7–18.

Dayan, D., & Katz, E. (1992). *Media events*. Cambridge, MA: Harvard University Press.

Dearing, J. W., & Rogers, E. M. (1996). *Agenda-setting*. Thousand Oaks, CA: Sage.

Denisoff, R. S. (1988). *Inside MTV*. New Brunswick, NJ: Transaction Books.

Dennis, J. (1986). Preadult learning of political independence. *Communication Research, 13*(3), 401–433.

Dennis, J., & Chaffee, S. (1977). Impact of the debates upon partisan, image and issue voting. In S. Kraus (Ed.), *The great debates: Carter vs. Ford, 1976*. Bloomington: Indiana University Press.

Dennis, J., Chaffee, S. H., & Choe, S. Y. (1979). Impact on partisan, image, and issue voting. In S. Kraus (Ed.), *The great debates: Carter vs. Ford, 1976* (pp. 314–330). Bloomington: Indiana University Press.

Desmond, R. J., Singer, J. L., & Singer, D. G. (1990). Family mediation: Parental communication patterns and the influences of television on children. In J. Bryant (Ed.), *Television and the American family* (pp. 293–310). Hillsdale, NJ: Erlbaum.

Desmond, R. J., Singer, J. L., Singer, D. G., Calam, R., & Colimore, K. (1985). Family mediation patterns and television viewing: Young children's use and grasp of the medium. *Human Communication Research, 11*(4), 461–480.

Deutschman, A. (1994, February 7). Scramble on the information highway. *Fortune, 129,* 129–131.

Devlin, L. P. (1989). Contrasts in presidential campaign commercials of 1988. *American Behavioral Scientist, 32*(4), 389–414.

Devlin, L. P. (1993). Contrasts in presidential campaign commercials of 1992. *American Behavioral Scientist, 37*(2), 272–290.

Devlin, L. P. (1997). Contrasts in presidential campaign commercials of 1996. *American Behavioral Scientist, 40*(8), 1058–1084.

Devries, W., & Tarrance, L., Jr. (1972). *The ticket-splitter: A new force in American politics.* Grand Rapids, MI: Eerdmans.

Dickson, G. (1998, July 20). Counting down to DTV. *Broadcasting and Cable, 128*(30), 22–23.

Diener, B. J. (1993). The frequency and context of alcohol and tobacco cues in daytime soap opera programs: Fall 1986 and fall 1991. *Journal of Public Policy and Marketing, 12*(2), 252–257.

Dietz, W. H. (1990). You are what you eat—what you eat is what you are. *Journal of Adolescent Health Care, 11*(1), 76–81.

Dilawari, S. R., Stewart, R., & Flournoy, D. (1991). Development news on CNN "World Report." *Gazette, 47*(2), 121–137.

Dobrow, J. R. (1990). *Social and cultural aspects of VCR use.* Hillsdale, NJ: Erlbaum.

Dominick, J. R. (1973). Crime and law enforcement in the mass media. In C. Winick (Ed.), *Deviance and the mass media* (pp. 105–131). Beverly Hills, CA: Sage.

Domke, D., Fan, D. P., Fibison, M., Shah, D. V., Smith, S. S., & Watts, M. D.(1997). New media, candidates and issues, and public opinion in the 1996 presidential campaign. *Journalism and Mass Communication Quarterly, 74*(4), 718–737.

Donnerstein, E. (1980). Pornography and violence against women: Experimental studies. In F. Wright, D. Bahn, & R. W. Reiber (Eds.), *Annals of the New York Academy of Sciences: Forensic psychology and psychiatry* (Vol. 347, pp. 277–288). New York: New York Academy of Sciences.

Donnerstein, E., & Barrett, G. (1978). The effects of erotic stimuli on male aggression against women. *Journal of Personality and Social Psychology, 36*(2), 180–188.

Donnerstein, E., & Berkowitz, L. (1981). Victim reactions in aggressive erotic films as a factor in violence against women. *Journal of Personality and Social Psychology, 36*(11), 1270–1277.

Donnerstein, E., & Hallam, J. (1978). The facilitating effects of erotica on aggression against women. *Journal of Personality and Social Psychology, 36*(11), 1270–1277.

Donnerstein, E., Linz, D., & Penrod, S. (1987). *The question of pornography: Research findings and policy implications.* New York: Free Press.

Donnerstein, E., & Malamuth, N. (Eds.). (1984). *Pornography and sexual aggression.* New York: Academic Press.

Dorr, A., & Kunkel, D. (1990). Children and the media environment: Change and constancy amid change. *Communication Research, 17*(1), 5–25.

Douglas, W. (1996). The fall from grace? The modern family on television. *Communication Research, 23*(6), 675–702.

Douglas, W., & Olson, B. M. (1996). Subversion of the American family? An examination of children and parents in television families. *Communication Research, 23*(1), 73–99.

Downs, A. (1957). *An economic theory of democracy.* New York: Harper.

Drabman, R. S., & Thomas, M. H. (1974). Does media violence increase children's tolerance of real-life aggression? *Developmental Psychology, 10*(3), 418–421.

Drew, D., & Grimes, T. (1987). Audio-visual redundancy and TV news recall. *Communication Research, 14*(4), 452–461.

Drew, D., & Reese, S. (1984). Children's learning from a television newscast. *Journalism Quarterly, 61*(1), 83–88.

Drew, D. G., & Weaver, D. (1991). Voter learning in the 1988 presidential election: Did the debates and the media matter? *Journalism Quarterly, 68*(1/2), 155–164.

Dubow, J. S. (1994). Point of view: Recall revisited, recall redux. *Journal of Advertising Research, 34*(3), 92–106.

Ducey, R., Krugman, D., & Eckrich, D. (1983). Predicting market segments in the cable industry: The basic and pay subscribers. *Journal of Broadcasting, 27*(2), 155–161.

Dunkley, C. (1993, March 3). A night in purgatory—television. [On-line]. *Financial Times,* sec. A., 17.

Dupagne, M. (1994). Testing the relative constancy of mass media expenditures in the United Kingdom. *Journal of Media Economics, 7*(3), 1–14.

Dupagne, M. (1997). Effect of three communication technologies on mass media spending in Belgium. *Journal of Communication, 47*(4), 54–68.

Eastman, S. T., Neal-Lumsford, J., & Riggs, K. E. (1995). Coping with grazing: Prime-time strategies for accelerated program transitions. *Journal of Broadcasting and Electronic Media, 39*(1), 92–108.

Eastman, S. T., & Newton, G. D. (1995). Delineating grazing: Observations of remote control use. *Journal of Communication, 45*(1), 77–95.

Eastman, S. T., Newton, G. D., Riggs, K. E., & Neal-Lumsford, J. (1997). Accelerating the flow: A transition effect in programming theory? *Journal of Broadcasting and Electronic Media, 41*(2), 265–283.

Eastman, S. T., & Otteson, J. L. (1994). Promotion increases ratings, doesn't it? The impact of program promotion in the 1992 Olympics. *Journal of Broadcasting and Electronic Media, 38*(3), 307–322.

Eaton, B. C. (1997). Prime-time stereotyping on the new television networks. *Journalism and Mass Communication Quarterly, 74*(4), 859–872.

Ehrenberg, A. S. C., Goodhardt, G. J., & Barwise, T. P. (1990). Double jeopardy revisited. *Journal of Marketing, 54*(3), 82–91.

Ehrenberg, A. S. C., & Wakshlag, J. (1987). Repeat-viewing with people meters. *Journal of Advertising Research, 27*(1), 9–13.

Ekman, P., Liebert, R. M., Friesen, W. V., Harrison, R., Zlachtin, C., Malstrom, E. J., & Baron, R. A. (1972). Facial expressions of emotion while watching televised violence as predictors of subsequent aggression. In G. A. Comstock, E. A. Rubinstein, & J. P. Murray (Eds.), *Television and social behavior. Television's effects: Further explorations* (Vol. 5, pp. 22–58). Washington, DC: U.S. Government Printing Office.

Elliott, W. R., & Sothirajah, J. (1993). Post-debate analysis and media reliance: Influences on candidate image and voting probabilities. *Journalism Quarterly, 70*(2), 321–335.

Elliott, W. R., & Wickert, D. A. (1993). *Campaign media use, candidate image, and voting probabilities: Three models of influence.* Paper presented at the annual meeting of the Midwest Association for Public Opinion Research, Chicago, IL.

Englis, B. G., Solomon, M. R., & Ashmore, R. D. (1994). Beauty before the eyes of beholders: The cultural encoding of beauty types in magazine advertising and music television. *Journal of Advertising, 23*(2), 49–64.

Entman, R. M. (1991). Framing U.S. coverage of international news: Contrasts in narratives of the KAL and Iran Air incidents. *Journal of Communication, 41*(4), 6–27.

Entman, R. M. (1992). Blacks in the news: Television, modern racism and cultural change. *Journalism Quarterly, 69*(2), 329–340.

Entman, R. M. (1994). Representation and reality in the portrayal of blacks on network television news. *Journalism Quarterly, 71*(3), 509–520.

Entman, R. M. (1996). *Manufacturing discord: Media in the affirmative action debate.* Paper presented at the annual meeting of the International Communication Association, Chicago, IL.

Epstein, E. J. (1973). *News from nowhere: Television and the news.* New York: Random House.

Eron, L. D., & Huesmann, L. R. (1987). Television as a source of maltreatment of children. *School Psychology Review, 16*(2), 195–202.

Estep, R., & MacDonald, P. T. (1983). How prime-time crime evolved on TV, 1976–1981. *Journalism Quarterly, 60*(2), 293–300.

Eyal, C. (1980). *Time frame in agenda-setting research: A study of the conceptual and methodological factors affecting the time frame context of the agenda-setting process.* Unpublished doctoral dissertation, Syracuse University, Syracuse, NY.

Faber, R. J., Tims, A. R., & Schmitt, K. G. (1993). Negative political advertising and voting intent: The role of involvement and alternative information sources. *Journal of Advertising, 22*(4), 67–76.

Fair, J. E., & Astroff, R. J. Constructing race and violence: U.S. news coverage and the signifying practices of apartheid. *Journal of Communication, 41*(4), 58–74.

Fallows, J. (1992). *Breaking the news.* New York: Vintage Books.

Farquar, J. W., Fortmann, S. P., Flora, J. A., Taylor, C. B., Haskell, W. L., Williams, P.T., Maccoby, N., & Wood, P. D. (1990). Effects of communitywide education on cardiovascular disease risk factors: The Stanford Five-City Project. *Journal of the American Medical Association, 264*(3), 359–365.

Farquar, J. W., Maccoby, N., Wood, P. D., Alexander, J. K., Breitrose, H., Brown, B. W., Jr., Haskell, W. L., McAlister, A. L., Meyer, A. J., Nash, J. D., & Stern, M. P. (1977). Community education for cardiovascular health. *Lancet, 1,* 1192–1195.

Ferguson, D. A. (1994). Measurement of mundane TV behaviors: Remote control device flipping frequency. *Journal of Broadcasting and Electronic Media, 38*(1), 35–47.

Ferguson, D. A., & Perse, E. M. (1993). Media and audience influences on channel repertoire. *Journal of Broadcasting and Electronic Media, 37*(1), 31–47.

Ferri, A. J. (1988). Perceived career barriers of men and women television news anchors. *Journalism Quarterly, 65*(3), 661–667.

Feshbach, S. (1961). The stimulating versus cathartic effects of a vicarious aggressive activity. *Journal of Abnormal and Social Psychology, 63*(2), 381–385.

Feshbach, S. (1972). Reality and fantasy in filmed violence. In J. P. Murray, E. A. Rubinstein, & G. A. Comstock (Eds.), *Television and social behavior: Television and social learning* (Vol. 2, pp. 318–345). Washington, DC: U.S. Government Printing Office.

Feshbach, S., & Singer, R. D. (1971). *Television and aggression: An experimental field study.* San Francisco: Jossey-Bass.

Festinger, L. (1954). A theory of social comparison processes. *Human Relations, 7,* 117–140.

Festinger, L. (1957). *A theory of cognitive dissonance.* Evanston, IL: Row and Peterson.

Fetler, M. (1984). Television viewing and school achievement. *Journal of Communication, 34*(2), 104–118.

Findhal, O. (1981). The effect of visual illustrations upon perception and retention of news programmes. *Communications, 7,* 151–167.

Fishman, M. (1980). *Manufacturing the news.* Austin: University of Texas Press.

Fishman, M. (1998). Ratings and reality: The persistence of the reality crime genre. In M. Fishman & G. Cavender (Eds.), *Entertaining crime* (pp. 59–75). New York: Aldine de Gruyter.

Fiske, S., & Taylor, S. (1984). *Social cognition.* Reading, MA: Addison-Wesley.

Flanders, L. (1997). *Real majority, media minority: The cost of sidelining women in reporting.* Monroe, ME: Common Courage Press.

Foote, C. F., Jr. (1993, March 30). *Newsroom minorities top 10 percent, ASNE 1993 survey shows.* News release from the American Society of Newspaper Editors, Reston, VA.

Foote, J. S. (1995). Standpoint: The structure and marketing of global television news. *Journal of Broadcasting and Electronic Media, 39*(1), 127.

Foote, J. S., & Saunders, A. C. (1991). Graphic forms in network television news. *Journalism Quarterly, 67*(3), 501–507.

Ford, J. B., & LaTour, M. S. (1993, September/October). Differing reactions to female role portrayals in advertising. *Journal of Advertising Research,* 43–52.

Fox, J. R., & Goble, C. (1997). *Hype versus substance in campaign coverage: Are the television networks cleaning up their act?* Paper presented at the annual meeting of the Association for Education in Journalism and Mass Communication, Chicago, IL.

Fraczek, A. (1986). Socio-cultural environment, television viewing, and the development of aggression among children in Poland. In L. R. Huesmann & L. D. Eron (Eds.), *Television and the aggressive child: A cross-national comparison* (pp. 119–159). Hillsdale, NJ: Erlbaum.

Frank, R. E., & Greenberg, M. G. (1980). *The public's use of television.* Newbury Park, CA: Sage.

Freedman, J. L. (1984). Effect of television violence on aggressiveness. *Psychological Bulletin, 96*(2), 227–246.

Freedom Forum. (1997). *The Freedom Forum 1997 annual report.* Washington, DC: Freedom Forum.

Freeman, H. E. (1975). Traditional sex role development and amount of time spent watching television. *Developmental Psychology, 11*(1), 109.

French, J., & Penna, S. (1991). Children's hero play of the 20th century: Changes resulting from television's influence. *Child Study Journal, 21*(2), 79–94.

Friedenberg, R. V. (1997). Patterns and trends in national political debates: 1960–1996. In Friedenberg, R. V. (Ed.), *Rhetorical studies of national political debates—1996.* Westport, CT: Greenwood Press.

Friedman, S. M., Gorney, C. M., & Egolf, B. P. (1987). Reporting on radiation: A content analysis of Chernobyl coverage. *Journal of Communication, 37*(3), 58–79.

Friedrich, L., & Stein, A. H. (1973). Aggressive and prosocial television programs and the natural behavior of preschool children. *Monographs of the Society for Research in Child Development 38* (4, Serial No. 151).

Friedrich-Cofer, L. K., Huston-Stein, A., McBride Kipnis, D., Susman, E. J., & Clewett, A. S. (1979). Environmental enhancement of prosocial television content: Effects on interpersonal behavior, imaginative play, and self-regulation in a natural setting. *Developmental Psychology, 15*(4), 637–646.

Fuchs, D. A. (1966). Election day radio-television and Western voting. *Public Opinion Quarterly, 30*(2), 226–236.

Funk, J. (1993a). Reevaluating the impact of video games. *Clinical Pediatrics, 32*(1), 86–90.

Funk, J. (1993b). Video games. In V. Strasburger & G. Comstock (Eds.), Adolescent medicine, state of the art reviews. *Adolescents and the Media, 4*(3), 589–598.

Funkhouser, G. R. (1973a). The issues of the sixties: An exploratory study in the dynamics of public opinion. *Public Opinion Quarterly, 37*(1), 62–75.

Funkhouser, G. R. (1973b). Trends in media coverage of the issues of the sixties. *Journalism Quarterly, 50*(3), 533–538.

Furnham, A. F., & Gunter, B. (1985). Sex, presentation mode and memory for violent and non-violent news. *Journal of Educational Television, 11*(2), 99–105.

Gadberry, S. (1980). Effects of restricting first graders' TV viewing on leisure time use, IQ change, and cognitive style. *Journal of Applied Developmental Psychology, 1*(1), 161–176.

Gaddy, G. D. (1986). Television's impact on high school achievement. *Public Opinion Quarterly, 50*(3), 340–359.

Gaddy, G. D., & Tanjong, E. (1986). Earthquake coverage by the Western press. *Journal of Communication, 36*(2), 105–112.

Galician, M. L. (1986). Perceptions of good news and bad news on television. *Journalism Quarterly, 63*(3), 611–616.

Galician, M. L., & Pasternack, S. (1987). Balancing good news and bad news: An ethical obligation? *Journal of Mass Media Ethics, 2*(2), 82–92.

Galician, M. L., & Vestre, N. D. (1987). Effects of "good news" and "bad news" on newscast image and community image. *Journalism Quarterly, 64*(2/3), 399–405.

Galst, J. P., & White, M. A. (1976). The unhealthy persuader: The reinforcing value of television and children's purchase attempts at the supermarket. *Child Development, 47*(4), 1089–1096.

Galtung, J. (1989). U.S. political discourse and U.S. media. *Gazette, 43*(4), 195–204.

Gans, H. J. (1979). *Deciding what's news: A study of CBS Evening News, NBC Nightly News, Newsweek, and Time.* New York: Pantheon Books.

Ganzert, C., & Flournoy, D. M. (1992). The Weekly "World Report" on CNN: An analysis. *Journalism Quarterly, 69*(1), 188–194.

Garramone, G. M. (1984). Voter responses to negative political ads. *Journalism Quarterly, 61*(2), 250–259.

Garramone, G. M., & Atkin, C. K. (1986). Mass communication and political socialization: Specifying the effects. *Public Opinion Quarterly, 50*(1), 76–86.

Garramone, G. M., Atkin, C. K., Pinkleton, B. E., & Cole, R. T. (1990). Effects of negative political advertising on the political process. *Journal of Broadcasting and Electronic Media, 34*(3), 299–311.

Gawiser, S. R., & Witt, A. (1994). *A journalist's guide to public opinion polls.* Westport, CT: Praeger.

Gaziano, C. (1988). How credible is the credibility crisis? *Journalism Quarterly, 65*(2), 267–278.

Geen, R. G. (1968). Effects of frustration, attack, and prior training in aggressiveness upon aggressive behavior. *Journal of Personality and Social Psychology, 9*(4), 316–321.

Geen, R. G., & Berkowitz, L. (1967). Some conditions facilitating the occurrence of aggression after the observation of violence. *Journal of Personality, 35,* 666–676.

Geen, R. G., & Rakosky, J. (1973). Interpretations of observed violence and their effects on GSR. *Journal of Experimental Research in Personality, 6*(4), 289–292.

Geen, R. G., & Stonner, D. (1972). Context effects in observed violence. *Journal of Personality and Social Psychology, 25*(2), 145–150.

Geis, M. L. (1982). *The language of advertising.* New York: Academic Press.

Gentner, D. (1975). Evidence for the psychological reality of semantic components: The verbs of possession. In D. Norman & D. Rumelhart (Eds.), *Explorations in cognition* (pp. 211–246). San Francisco: Freeman.

Gerbner, G. (1972). Violence in television drama: Trends and symbolic functions. In G. A. Comstock and E. A. Rubinstein (Eds.), *Television and social behavior: Media content and control* (Vol. 1). Washington, DC: U.S. Government Printing Office.

Gerbner, G., Gross, L., Morgan, M., & Signorielli, N. (1980). The "mainstreaming" of America. *Journal of Communication, 30*(3), 10–29.

Gerbner, G., Gross, L., Morgan, M., & Signorielli, N. (1984). Political correlates of television viewing. *Public Opinion Quarterly, 48*(1B), 283–300.

Gerbner, G., Gross, L., Signorielli, N., & Morgan, M. (1986). *Television's mean world: Violence profile no. 14–15.* Unpublished manuscript, The Annenberg School of Communication, The University of Pennsylvania, Philadelphia.

Gerbner, G., Morgan, M., & Signorielli, N. (1994). *Television violence profile no. 16.* Unpublished manuscript, The Annenberg School of Communication, University of Pennsylvania, Philadelphia.

Ghanem, S. (1997). Filling in the tapestry: The second level of agenda-setting. In M. McCombs, D. L. Shaw, & D. Weaver (Eds.), *Communication and democracy: Exploring the intellectual frontiers in agenda-setting theory* (pp. 3–14). Mahwah, NJ: Erlbaum.

Gibbons, J., Anderson, D. R., Smith, R., Field, D. E., & Fischer, C. (1986). Young children's recall and reconstruction of audio and audiovisual narratives. *Child Development, 57*(4), 1014–1028.

Gilly, M. C. (1988, April). Sex roles in advertising: A comparison of television advertisements in Australia, Mexico, and the United States. *Journal of Marketing, 52,* 75–85.

Gilmore, R. F., & Secunda, E. (1993). Zipped TV commercials boost prior learning. *Journal of Advertising Research, 32*(4), 28–38.

Gitlin, T. (1980). *The whole world is watching: Mass media in the making and unmaking of the new left.* Berkeley: University of California Press.

Glascock, J. (1993). Effect of cable television on advertiser and consumer spending on mass media, 1978–1990. *Journalism Quarterly, 70*(3), 509–517.

Glynn, C. J., Hayes, A. F., & Shanahan, J. (1997). Perceived support for one's opinions and willingness to speak out: A meta-analysis of survey studies on the "spiral of silence." *Public Opinion Quarterly, 61*(3), 452–463.

Glynn, C. J., & McLeod, J. M. (1992). Public opinion, communication processes, and voting decisions. In M. Burgoon (Ed.), *Communication Yearbook 6* (pp. 759–774). Beverly Hills, CA: Sage.

Goldberg, M. E., Gorn, G. J., & Gibson, W. (1978). TV messages for snacks and breakfast foods: Do they influence children's preferences? *Journal of Consumer Research, 5*(2), 73–81.

Goldenberg, E. N., & Traugott, M. W. (1987). Mass media in U.S. congressional elections. *Legislative Studies Quarterly, 12*(3), 317–339.

Goldenberg, E. N., Traugott, M. W., & Baumgartner, F. R. (1986). Preemptive and reactive spending in US House races. *Political Behavior, 8*(1), 3–20.

Goodhardt, G. J., & Ehrenberg, A. S. C. (1969). Duplication of viewing between and within channels. *Journal of Marketing Research, 6,* 169–178.

Goodhardt, G. J., Ehrenberg, A. S. C., & Collins, M. A. (1987). *The television audience: Patterns of viewing* (2nd ed.). Westmead, England: Gower.

Gorn, G. J. (1982, Winter). The effects of music in advertising on choice behavior: A classical conditioning approach. *Journal of Marketing, 46,* 94–101.

Gorn, G. J., & Goldberg, M. E. (1982). Behavioral evidence of the effects of televised food messages on children. *Journal of Consumer Research, 9,* 200–205.

Gorney, C. (1992). Numbers versus pictures: Did network television sensationalize Chernobyl coverage? *Journalism Quarterly, 69*(2), 455–465.

Gortmaker, S. L., Salter, C. A., Walker, D. K., & Dietz, W. H. (1990). The impact of television viewing on mental aptitude and achievement: A longitudinal study. *Public Opinion Quarterly, 54*(4), 594–604.

Gottschalk, M. (1992). Operation desert cloud: The media and the Gulf War. *World Policy Journal, 9*(3), 449–486.

Gould, M. S., & Shaffer, D. (1986). The impact of suicide in television movies: Evidence of imitation. *New England Journal of Medicine, 315*(11), 690–694.

Gozenbach, W. J., Arant, M. D., & Stevenson, R. L. (1992). The world of U.S. network television news: Eighteen years of international and foreign news coverage. *Gazette, 50*(1), 53–72.

Grabe, M. E. (1996). Tabloid and traditional television news magazine crime stories: Crime lessons and reaffirmation of social class distinctions. *Journalism and Mass Communication Quarterly, 73*(4), 926–946.

Graber, D. A. (1971). The press as opinion resource during the 1968 presidential campaign. *Public Opinion Quarterly, 35*(2), 168–182.

Graber, D. A. (1987). Framing election news broadcasts: News content and its impact on the 1984 presidential election. *Social Science Quarterly, 68*(3), 552–568.

Graber, D. A. (1988). *Processing the news* (2nd ed.). New York: Longman.

Graber, D. (1989a). *Mass media and American politics* (3rd ed.). Washington, DC: Congressional Quarterly.

Graber, D. (1989b). Flashlight coverage: State news on national broadcasts. *American Politics Quarterly, 17*(3), 277–290.

Graber, D. A. (1990). Seeing is remembering: How visuals contribute to learning from television news. *Journal of Communication, 40*(3), 134–155.

Graber, D. A. (1996). Say it with pictures. *Annals of the American Academy of Political and Social Science, 546,* 85–96.

Graber, D. A., with Downey, L. (1996). *Making sense of televised international news: Can citizens meet the challenge?* Paper presented at the annual meeting of the International Communication Association, Chicago, IL.

Granger, C. W. (1969). Investigating causal relations by econometric models and cross-spectral methods. *Econometrica, 37,* 424–438.

Greenberg, B. S. (1980). *Life on Television.* Norwood, NJ: Ablex.

Greenberg, B. S., Abelman, R., & Neuendorf, K. (1981). Sex on the soap operas: Afternoon delight. *Journal of Communication, 31*(3), 83–89.

Greenberg, B. S., & Collette, L. (1997). The changing faces on TV: A demographic analysis of network television's new seasons, 1966–1992. *Journal of Broadcasting and Electronic Media, 41*(1), 1–13.

Greenberg, B. S., & Heeter, C. (1987). VCRs and young people. *American Behavioral Scientist, 30*(5), 509–521.

Greenberg, M. R., Sachsman, D. B., Sandman, P. M., & Salomone, K. L. (1989). Risk, drama and geography in coverage of environmental risk by network TV. *Journalism Quarterly, 66*(2), 267–276.

Greenfield, P., & Beagles-Roos, J. (1988). Television versus radio: The cognitive impact on different socio-economic and ethnic groups. *Journal of Communication, 38*(2), 71–92.

Greenfield, P., Farrar, D., & Beagles-Roos, J. (1986). Is the medium the message? An experimental comparison of the effects of radio and television on imagination. *Journal of Applied Developmental Psychology, 7*(3), 201–218.

Greer, D., Potts, R., Wright, J., & Huston, A. C. (1982). The effects of television commercial form and commercial placement on children's social behavior and attention. *Child Development, 53*(3), 611–619.

Gregg, R. B. (1994). Rhetorical strategies for a culture of war: Abortion in the 1992 campaign. *Communication Quarterly, 42*(3), 229–243.

Grimes, T. (1990). Encoding television news messages into memory. *Journalism Quarterly, 67*(4), 757–766.

Grimes, T. (1991). Mild auditory-visual dissonance in television news may exceed viewer attentional capacity. *Human Communication Research, 18*(2), 268–298.

Gronbeck, B. E. (1992). Negative narrative in 1988 presidential campaign ads. *Quarterly Journal of Speech, 78*(3), 333–346.

Gunter, B. (1987). *Poor reception: Misunderstanding and forgetting broadcast news.* Hillsdale, NJ: Erlbaum.

Gurevitch, M., & Levy, M. (1986). Information and meaning: Audience explanations of social issues. In J. Robinson & M. Levy (Eds.), *The main source: Learning from television news* (pp. 159–175). Newbury Park, CA: Sage.

Hacker, K. L., Coste, T. G., Kamm, D. F., & Bybee, C. R. (1991). Oppositional readings of network television news: Viewer deconstruction. *Discourse & Society, 2*(2), 183–202.

Haefner, M. J., & Comstock, J. (1990). Compliance gaining on prime time family programs. *Southern Communication Journal, 55*(4), 402–420.

Hajjar, W. J. (1997). The image of aging in television commercials: An update for the 1990s. In H. S. N. Al-Deen (Ed.), *Cross-cultural communication and aging in the United States*. Mahwah, NJ: Erlbaum.

Halbert, C., & Latimer, M. (1994). "Battling" gendered language: An analysis of the language used by sports commentators in a televised coed tennis competition. *Sociology of Sport Journal, 11*(3), 298–308.

Haley, R. I., Staffaroni, J., & Fox, A. (1994). The missing measures of copy testing. *Journal of Advertising Research, 34*(3), 46–60.

Hallin, D. C. (1992). Soundbite news: Television coverage of elections, 1968–1988. *Journal of Communication, 42*(2), 5–24.

Halpern, D. H. (1996). *Media marginalization of political parties and candidates: The focus on fringe issues and the lack of consistent coverage in both print and broadcast.* Paper presented at the annual meeting of the International Communication Association, Chicago, IL.

Halpern, W. (1975). Turned-on toddlers. *Journal of Communication, 25*(4), 66–70.

Hamilton, J. T. (1998). *Channeling violence.* Princeton, NJ: Princeton University Press.

Hansen, C. H., & Hansen, R. D. (1990). The influence of sex and violence on the appeal of rock music videos. *Communication Research, 17*(2), 212–234.

Hansen, C. H., & Krygowski, W. (1994). Arousal-augmented priming effects: Rock music videos and sex object schemas. *Communication Research, 21*(1), 24–47.

Hapkiewicz,W. G., & Stone, R. D. (1974). The effects of realistic versus imaginary aggressive models on children's interpersonal play. *Child Study Journal, 4*(2), 47–58.

Harmon, M. D. (1989). Mr. Gates goes electronic: The what and why questions in local television news. *Journalism Quarterly, 66*(4), 888–893.

Harris, R. J. (1994). *A cognitive psychology of mass communication* (2nd ed.). Hillsdale, NJ: Erlbaum.

Harrington, D. E. (1989). Economic news on television: The determinants of coverage. *Public Opinion Quarterly, 53*(1), 17–40.

Harrison, L., & Williams, T. M. (1986). Television and cognitive development. In T. M. Williams (Ed.), *The impact of television: A natural experiment in three communities* (pp. 87–142). New York: Academic Press.

Harrison, T. M., Stephen, T. B., Husson, W., & Fehr, B. J. (1991). Images versus issues in the 1984 presidential election: Differences between men and women. *Human Communication Research, 18*(2), 209–227.

Hart, L. R. (1972). *Immediate effects of exposure to filmed cartoon aggression on boys.* Unpublished doctoral dissertation, Emory University, Atlanta, GA.

Harwood, J. (1997). Viewing age: Lifespan identity and television viewing choices. *Journal of Broadcasting and Electronic Media, 41*(2), 203–213.

Haugtvedt, C. P., Schumann, D. W., Schneier, W. L., & Warren, W. L. (1994). Advertising repetition and variation strategies: Implications for understanding attitude strength. *Journal of Consumer Research, 21*(1), 176–189.

Havick, J. (1997). Determinants of national media attention. *Journal of Communication, 47*(2), 97–111.

Head, S. W. (1954). Content analysis of television drama programs. *Quarterly Journal of Film, Radio and Television, 9*(2), 175–194.

Headen, R. S., Klompmaker, J. E., & Teel, J. E. (1979). Predicting network TV viewing patterns. *Journal of Advertising Research, 19*(4), 49–54.

Hearold, S. (1986). A synthesis of 1043 effects of television on social behavior. In G. Comstock (Ed.), *Public communication and behavior* (Vol. 1, pp. 65–133). New York: Academic Press.

Heath, L., Kruttschnitt, C., & Ward, D. (1986). Television and violent criminal behavior: Beyond the Bobo doll. *Violence and Victims, 1*(3), 177–190.

Heeter, C., & Greenberg, B. S. (1988). *Cable-viewing.* Norwood, NJ: Ablex.

Heintz, K. E., Delwiche, A., Lisosky, J., & Shively, A. (1996). *The reflection on the screen: Television's image of children.* Paper presented at the annual meeting of the International Communication Association, Chicago, IL.

Henderson, R. W., & Rankin, R. J. (1986). Preschoolers' viewing of instructional television. *Journal of Educational Psychology, 78*(1), 44–51.

Hennigan, K. M., Heath, L., Wharton, J. D., Del Rosario, M. L., Cook, T. D., & Calder, B. J. (1982). Impact of the introduction of television on crime in the United States: Empirical findings and theoretical implications. *Journal of Personality and Social Psychology, 42*(3), 461–477.

Hernson, P. S. (1995). *Congressional elections: Campaigning at home and in Washington, D.C.* Washington, DC: Congressional Quarterly.

Hess, S. (1986). *The ultimate insiders: U.S. Senators and the national media.* Washington, DC: Brookings Institute.

Hester, A. (1978). Five years of foreign news on U.S. television evening newscasts. *Gazette, 24*(1), 88–95.

Heuer, F., & Reisberg, D. (1990). Vivid memories of emotional events: The accuracy of remembered minutiae. *Memory and Cognition, 18*(5), 494–506.

Heyns, B. (1976). *Television: Exposure and the effects of schooling.* Washington, DC: National Institute of Education.

Hickey, N. (1972, April 8). What America thinks of TV's political coverage. *TV Guide,* 6–11.

Hiebert, R. E. (Ed.). (1971). *Political image merchants: Strategy in new politics.* Washington, DC: Acropolis.

Himmelweit, H. T., Oppenheim, A. N., & Vince, P. (1958). *Television and the child.* London: Oxford University Press.

Himmelweit, H. T., & Swift, B. (1976). Continuities and discontinuities in media usage and taste: A longitudinal study. *Journal of Social Issues, 32*(4), 133–156.

Hitchon, J. C., & Chang, C. (1995). Effects of gender schematic processing on the reception of political commercials for men and women candidates. *Communication Research, 22*(4), 430–458.

Hitchon, J., Chang, C., & Harris, R. (1997). Should women emote? Perceptual bias and opinion change in response to political ads for candidates of different genders. *Political Communication, 14*(1), 49–69.

Hitchon, J., Duckler, P., & Thorson, E. (1994). Effects of ambiguity and complexity on consumer response to music video commercials. *Journal of Broadcasting and Electronic Media, 38*(3), 289–306.

Hoffman, D. L., & Batra, R. (1991, August/September). Viewer response to programs: Dimensionality and concurrent behavior. *Journal of Advertising Research,* 46–56.

Hofman, R. J., & Flook, M. A. (1980). An experimental investigation of the role of television in facilitating shape recognition. *Journal of Genetic Psychology, 136,* 305–306.

Hofstetter, C. R. (1976). *Bias in the news.* Columbus: Ohio State University Press.

Holbrook, T. M. (1994). The behavioral consequences of vice-presidential debates: Does the undercard have any punch? *American Politics Quarterly, 22*(4), 469–482.

Holbrook, T. M. (1996). *Do campaigns matter?* Thousand Oaks, CA: Sage.

Hollander, B. A. (1993). Candidate discrimination and attention to the news. *Mass Communication Review, 20*(1/2), 76–85.

Hollander, N. (1971). Adolescents and the war: The sources of socialization. *Journalism Quarterly, 58*(3), 472–479.

Hopkins, N. M., & Mullis, A. K. (1985). Family perceptions of television viewing habits. *Family Relations, 34*(2), 177–181.

Hornik, R. (1981). Out-of-school television and schooling: Hypotheses and methods. *Review of Educational Research, 51*(2), 193–214.

Housel, T. (1984). Understanding and recall of TV news. *Journalism Quarterly, 61*(3), 505–508, 741.

Hovland, C. I., Lumsdaine, A. A., & Sheffield, F. D. (1949). *Experiments in mass communication.* Princeton, NJ: Princeton University Press.

Hoy, M. G., & Stankey, M. J. (1993). Structural characteristics of televised advertising disclosures: A comparison with the FTC clear and conspicuous standard. *Journal of Advertising, 22*(2), 47–58.

Huesmann, L. R. (1982). Television violence and aggressive behavior. In D. Pearl, L. Bouthilet, & J. Lazar (Eds.), *Television and behavior: Ten years of scientific inquiry and implications for the eighties. Technical reviews* (Vol. 2, pp. 126–137). Washington, DC: U.S. Government Printing Office.

Huesmann, L. R. (1984). Ally or enemy? A review of Milavsky et al. *Contemporary Psychology, 29*(4), 283–285.

Huesmann, L. R., & Eron, L. D. (Eds.). (1986). *Television and the aggressive child: A cross-national comparison.* Hillsdale, NJ: Erlbaum.

Huesmann, L. R., Eron, L. D., Lefkowitz, M. M., & Walder, L. O. (1984). The stability of aggression over time and generations. *Developmental Psychology, 20*(6), 1120–1134.

Huesmann, L. R., Lagerspetz, K., & Eron, L. D. (1984). Intervening variables in the TV violence-aggression relation: Evidence from two countries. *Developmental Psychology, 20*(5), 746–775.

Hughes, C. D. (1992). Realtime response measures redefine advertising wearout. *Journal of Advertising Research, 32*(3), 61–77.

Hughes, M. (1980). The fruits of cultivation analysis: A reexamination of the effects of television watching on fear of victimization, alienation, and the approval of violence. *Public Opinion Quarterly, 44*(3), 287–302.

Hunt, M. (1997). *How science takes stock.* New York: Russell Sage.

Huston, A., & Wright, J. C. (1989). The forms of television and the child viewer. In G. Comstock (Ed.), *Public communication and behavior* (Vol. 2, pp. 103–159). New York: Academic Press.

Huston, A., & Wright, J. C., Rice, M. L., Kerkman, D., & St. Peters, M. (1990). Development of television viewing patterns in early childhood: A longitudinal investigation. *Developmental Psychology, 26*(3), 409–420.

Huston-Stein, A., Fox, S., Greer, D., Watkins, B. A., & Whitaker, J. (1981). The effects of TV action and violence on children's social behavior. *Journal of Genetic Psychology, 138,* 183–191.

Immerwahr, J., & Doble, J. (1982). Public attitudes toward freedom of the press. *Public Opinion Quarterly, 46*(2), 177–194.

Israel, H., & Robinson, J. P. (1972). Demographic characteristics of viewers of television violence and news programs. In E. A. Rubinstein, G. A. Comstock, and J. P. Murray (Eds.), *Television and social behavior. Television in day-to-day life: Patterns of use* (Vol. 4, pp. 87–128). Washington, DC: U.S. Government Printing Office.

Iyengar, S. (1987). Television news and citizens' explanations of national affairs. *American Politics Science Review, 81*(3), 815–832.

Iyengar, S. (1991). *Is anyone responsible? How television frames political issues.* Chicago: University of Chicago Press.

Iyengar, S., & Kinder, D. R. (1987a). More than meets the eye: TV news, priming, and public evaluations of the President. In G. A. Comstock (Ed.), *Public Communication and Behavior* (Vol. 1, pp. 135–171). San Diego, CA: Academic Press.

Iyengar, S., & Kinder, D. R. (1987b). *News that matters.* Chicago: University of Chicago Press.

Iyengar, S., Peters, M. D., & Kinder, D. R. (1982). Experimental demonstrations of the "not-so-minimal" consequences of television news programs. *American Political Science Review, 76,* 848–858.

Iyengar, S., & Simon, A. (1993). News coverage of the Gulf crisis and public opinion: A study of agenda-setting, priming, and framing. *Communication Research, 20*(3), 265–383.

Jacobs, R. (1995). Exploring the determinants of cable television subscriber satisfaction. *Journal of Broadcasting and Electronic Media, 39*(2), 262–274.

James, N. C., & McCain, T. A. (1982). Television games preschool children play: Patterns, themes, and uses. *Journal of Broadcasting, 26*(4), 783–800.

Jamieson, K. H. (1986). The evolution of political advertising in America. In L. L. Kaid, D. Nimmo, & K. R. Sanders (Eds.), *New Perspectives in Political Advertising.* Carbondale, IL: SIU Press.

Jamieson, K. H. (1992). *Packaging the presidency* (2nd ed.). New York: Oxford University Press.

Jennings, M. K., & Niemi, R. G. (1968). The transmission of political values from parent to child. *American Political Science Review, 62,* 443–467.

Jensen, K. B. (1994). Reception as flow: The "new television viewer" revisited. *Cultural Studies, 8*(2), 293–305.

Johnson, E. (1984). Credibility of black and white newscasters to a black audience. *Journal of Broadcasting, 28*(3), 365–368.

Johnson, K. A. (1991). Objective news and other myths: The poisoning of young black minds. *Journal of Negro Education, 60*(3), 328–341.

Johnson, R. L., & Cobb-Walgren, C. J. (1994). Aging and the problem of television clutter. *Journal of Advertising Research, 34*(4), 54–62.

Johnson, T. J. (1993). Filling out the racing form: How the media covered the horse race in the 1988 primaries. *Journalism Quarterly, 70*(2), 300–310.

Johnson, T. J., Boudreau, T., & Glowaki, C. (1996). Turning the spotlight inward: How five leading news organizations covered the media in the 1992 presidential election. *Journalism and Mass Communication Quarterly, 73*(3), 657–671.

Johnson-Cartee, K. S., & Copeland, G. (1989). Southern voters' reaction to negative political advertisements in the 1986 election. *Journalism Quarterly, 66*(4), 888–893.

Johnston, A., & White, A. B. (1994). Communication styles and female candidates: A study of the political advertising during the 1986 Senate elections. *Journalism Quarterly, 71*(2), 321–329.

Johnston, D. D. (1989). Image and issues political information: Message content or interpretation? *Journalism Quarterly, 66*(2), 277–284.

Johnston, J., & Ettema, J. S. (1982). *Positive images: Breaking stereotypes with children's television.* Newbury Park, CA: Sage.

Jones, J. P. (1989). *Does it pay to advertise? Cases illustrating successful brand advertising.* Lexington, MA: Lexington Books.

Jones, K. (1997). Are rap videos more violent? Style differences and the presence of sex and violence in the age of MTV. *Howard Journal of Communications, 8*(4), 343–356.

Jordan, D. L., & Page, B. I. (1992). Shaping foreign policy opinions. *Journal of Conflict Resolution, 36*(2), 227–241.

Josephson, W. L. (1987). Television violence and children's aggression: Testing the priming, social script, and disinhibition predictions. *Journal of Personality and Social Psychology, 53*(5), 882–890.

Just, M., Crigler, A., & Wallach, L. (1990). Thirty seconds or thirty minutes: What viewers can learn from spot advertisements and candidate debates. *Journal of Communication, 40*(3), 120–133.

Kahn, K. F. (1993). Gender differences in campaign messages: The political advertisements of men and women candidates for the U.S. Senate. *Political Research Quarterly, 46*(3), 481–502.

Kaid, L. L. (1997). Effects of the television spots on images of Dole and Clinton. *American Behavioral Scientist, 40*(8), 1085–1094.

Kaid, L. L., Chanslor, M., & Hovind, M. (1992). The influence of program and commercial type on political advertising effectiveness. *Journal of Broadcasting and Electronic Media, 36*(2), 303–320.

Kaid, L. L., Downs, V. C., & Ragan, S. (1990). Political argumentation and violations of audience expectations: An analysis of the Bush–Rather encounter. *Journal of Broadcasting and Electronic Media, 34*(1), 1–15.

Kaid, L. L., Gobetz, R., Garner, J., Leland, C., & Scott, D. (1993). Television news and presidential campaigns: The legitimization of televised political advertising. *Social Science Quarterly, 74*(2), 274–285.

Kaid, L. L., Leland, C. M., & Whitney, S. (1992). The impact of televised political advertisements: Evoking viewer response in the 1988 presidential campaign. *Southern Communication Journal, 57*(4), 285–295.

Kalis, P., & Neuendorf, K. A. (1989). Aggressive cue prominence and gender participation in MTV. *Journalism Quarterly, 66*(1), 148–154, 229.

Kalisch, P. A., & Kalisch, B. J. (1984). Sex-role stereotyping of nurses and physicians on prime-time television: A dichotomy of occupational portrayals. *Sex Roles, 10*(7/8), 533–553.

Kamber, V. (1993). Television big winner of '92 election, '93 presidency. *Public Relations Quarterly, 38*(2), 26.

Kamins, M. A., Marks, L. J., & Skinner, D. (1991). Television commercial evaluation in the context of program induced mood: Congruency versus consistency effects. *Journal of Advertising, 20*(2), 1–14.

Kang, N. (1990). *A critique and secondary analysis of the NBC study on television and aggression.* Unpublished doctoral dissertation, Syracuse University, Syracuse, NY.

Kaplan, D. (1989). Milestones in racial politics. *Congressional Quarterly,* 4–5A.

Kaplan, R. (1992, June). Video on demand. *American Demographics,* 38–44.

Katz, E. (1988). On conceptualizing media effects: Another look. In S. Oskamp (Ed.), *Applied social psychology annual: Television as a social issue* (Vol. 8, pp. 361–374). Newbury Park, CA: Sage.

Katz, E. (1989). Mass media effects. In E. Barnouw (Ed.), *International encyclopedia of communication, Vol. 2* (pp. 492–497). New York: Oxford University Press.

Katz, E., Adonni, H., & Parness, P. (1977). Remembering the news: What pictures add to recall. *Journalism Quarterly, 54*(2), 231–239.

Katz, E., & Feldman, J. J. (1962). The debates in the light of research: A survey of surveys. In S. Kraus (Ed.), *The great debates: Kennedy vs. Nixon, 1960* (pp. 173–223). Bloomington: Indiana University Press.

Katz, J., & Aspden, P. (1997). Motivations for and barriers to Internet usage: Results of a national public opinion survey. *Internet Research, 7*(3), 170–188.

Katz, K. L. (1985). *Television news coverage of incumbents and challengers in Senate elections.* Unpublished manuscript. In Goldenberg, E. N. & Traugott, M. W. (1987). Mass media in U.S. Congressional elections. *Legislative Studies Quarterly, 12*(3), 317–339.

Katzman, N. (1972). Television soap operas: What's been going on anyway? *Public Opinion Quarterly, 36*(2), 200–212.

Keenan, K. (1986). Polls in network newscasts in the 1984 presidential race. *Journalism Quarterly, 63*(3), 616–618.

Keenan, K. (1995). *Television news coverage of advertising: An exploratory census of content.* Paper presented at the annual meeting of the American Academy of Advertising, Norfolk, VA.

Keith, T. Z., Reimers, T. M., Fehrmann, P. G., Pottebaum, S. M., & Aubey, L. W. (1986). Parental involvement, homework, and TV time: Direct and indirect effects on high school achievement. *Journal of Educational Psychology, 78*(5), 373–380.

Kellaris, J. J., & Cox, A. D. (1987). The effects of background music in advertising: A replication and extension. In M. R. Solomon et al. (Eds.), *AMA Educators' Conference Proceedings* (p. 283). Chicago: American Marketing Association.

Kellaris, J. J., & Cox, A. D. (1989, June). The effects of background music in advertising: A reassessment. *Journal of Consumer Research, 16,* 113–118.

Keller, E. B., & Fay, W. B. (1996). How many are really on the electronic super highway? An analysis of the effects of survey methodologies. *Journal of Advertising Research, 36*(6), RC2–RC8.

Kendall, K. E. (1993). Public speaking in the presidential primaries through media eyes. *American Behavioral Scientist, 37*(2), 240–251.

Kendall, K. E. (1997). Presidential debates through media eyes. *American Behavioral Scientist, 40*(8), 1193–1207.

Kennamer, J. D. (1987). How media use during campaign affects the intent to vote. *Journalism Quarterly, 64*(2/3), 291–300.

Kennamer, J. D. (1990). Comparing predictions of the likelihood of voting in a primary and general election. *Journalism Quarterly, 67*(4), 777–784.

Kenny, J. F. (1985). *The family as a mediator of television use and the cultivation phenomenon among college students.* Unpublished doctoral dissertation, Syracuse University, Syracuse, NY.

Kent, R. J. (1993). Competitive versus noncompetitive clutter in television advertising. *Journal of Advertising Research, 33*(2), 40–46.

Kent, R. J., & Allen, C. T. (1993). Does competitive clutter in television advertising "interfere" with recall and recognition of brand names and ad claims? *Marketing Letters, 4*(2), 175–184.

Kern, M. (1989). *Thirty-second politics: Political advertising in the eighties.* New York: Praeger.

Kern, M., & Just, M. (1995). The focus groups method, political advertising, campaign news, and the construction of candidate images. *Political Communication, 12*(2), 127–145.

Kerns, T. Y. (1981). Television: A bisensory bombardment that stifles children's creativity. *Phi Delta Kappan, 62,* 456–457.

Kessler, R. C., Downey, G., Milavsky, J. R., & Stipp, H. (1988). Clustering of teenage suicides after television news stories about suicides: A reconsideration. *American Journal of Psychiatry, 145*(11), 1379–1383.

Key, W. B. (1972). *Subliminal seduction: Ad media's manipulation of a not-so-innocent America.* New York: Signet.

Key, W. B. (1976). *Media sexploitation.* New York: Signet.

Key, W. B. (1980). *The clam-plate orgy and other techniques for manipulating your behavior.* New York: Signet.

Key, W. B. (1989). *Age of manipulation: The con in confidence and the sin in sincere.* New York: Signet.

Kinder, D. R., & Sears, D. O. (1985). Public opinion and political action. In G. Lindzey & E. Aronson (Eds.), *Handbook of social psychology* (3rd ed., pp. 659–741). New York: Random House.

King, P. (1997). The press, candidate images, and voter perceptions. In M. McCombs, D. L. Shaw, & D. Weaver (Eds.), *Communication and democracy: Exploring the intellectual frontiers in agenda-setting theory* (pp. 29–40). Mahwah, NJ: Erlbaum.

Kitagawa, Y., Salwen, M. B., & Driscoll, P. D. (1994). International news on Japanese and American network television: Regionalism and conflict. *Gazette, 54*(1), 87–93.

Kitzinger, J., & Reilly, J. (1997). The rise and fall of risk reporting: Media coverage of human genetics research, "false memory syndrome," and "mad cow disease." *European Journal of Communication, 12*(3), 319–350.

Klapper, J. T. (1960). *The effects of mass communication.* New York: Free Press.

Kohn, P. M., & Smart, R. G. (1984). The impact of television advertising on alcohol consumption: An experiment. *Journal of Studies on Alcohol, 45*(4), 295–301.

Kohn, P. M., & Smart, R. G. (1987). Wine, women, suspiciousness, and advertising. *Journal of Studies on Alcohol, 48*(3), 161–166.

Kohut, A. (1995). *Technology in the American household.* Washington, DC: Times-Mirror Center for the People and the Press.

Kolbe, R. H., & Muehling, D. D. (1992). A content analysis of the "fine print" in television advertising. *Journal of Current Issues and Research in Advertising, 14*(2), 47–61.

Koolstra, C. M., & van der Voort, T. H. A. (1996). Longitudinal effects of television on children's leisure-time reading. A test of three explanatory models. *Human Communication Research, 23*(1), 4–35.

Koolstra, C. M., van der Voort, T. H. A., & van der Kamp, L. J. T. (1997). Television's impact on children's reading comprehension and decoding skills: A 3-year panel study. *Reading Research Quarterly, 32*(2), 128–152.

Kotch, J. B., Coulter, M., & Lipsitz, A. (1986). Does drinking influence children's attitudes toward alcohol? *Addictive Behaviors, 11*(1), 67–70.

Kraus, S. (Ed.) (1962). *The great debates: Kennedy vs. Nixon, 1960.* Bloomington: Indiana University Press.

Kraus, S. (Ed.) (1979). *The great debates: Carter vs. Ford, 1976.* Bloomington: Indiana University Press.

Kraus, S. (1988). *Televised presidential debates and public policy.* Hillsdale, NJ: Erlbaum.

Kraus, S. (1996). Winners of the first 1960 televised presidential debate between Kennedy and Nixon. *Journal of Communication, 46*(4), 78–96.

Kraus, S., & Davis, D. (1976). *The effects of mass communication on political behavior.* University Park: Pennsylvania State University Press.

Krippendorf, K. (1980). *Content analysis: An introduction to its methodology.* Newbury Park, CA: Sage.

Krugman, H. E. (1965). The impact of television advertising: Learning without involvement. *Public Opinion Quarterly, 29*(3), 349–356.

Krugman, H. E. (1971). Brain wave measures of media involvement. *Journal of Advertising Research, 11*(1), 3–9.

Kubey, R. W., & Csikszentmihalyi, M. (1990). *Television and the quality of life. How viewing shapes everyday experience.* Hillsdale, NJ: Erlbaum.

Kubey, R. W., & Larson, R. (1990). The use and experience of the new video media among children and young adolescents. *Communication Research, 17*(1), 107–130.

Kubey, R., Shifflet, M., Weerakkody, N., & Ukeiley, S. (1995). Demographic diversity on cable: Have the new cable channels made a difference in the representation of gender, race, and age? *Journal of Broadcasting and Electronic Media, 39*(4), 459–471.

Kuklinski, J. H., & Sigelman, L. (1992). When objectivity is not objective: Network television news coverage of U.S. senators and the "paradox of objectivity." *Journal of Politics, 54*(3), 810–833.

Kunkel, D. (1988). From a raised eyebrow to a turned back: The F.C.C. and children's product-related programming. *Journal of Communication, 38*(4), 90–108.

Kunkel, D., Farinola, W. J. M., Cope, K. M., Donnerstein, E., Biely, E., & Zwarun, L. (1998). *Rating the TV ratings: One year out.* Menlo Park, CA: Henry J. Kaiser Family Foundation.

Kuse, A. R. (1997). The measurement of advertising effectiveness: Empirical learning and application. In W. D. Wells (Ed.), *Measuring advertising effectiveness* (pp. 301–322). Mahwah, NJ: Erlbaum.

Lacy, S., Atwater, T., & Powers, A. (1988). Use of satellite technology in local television news. *Journalism Quarterly, 65*(4), 925–929.

Lake, C. C. (1989, November 20). Racial sensitivity in polling. *The Polling Report, 5*(22), Washington, DC: The Polling Report, Inc.

Lang, G. E., & Lang, K. (1983). *The battle for public opinion: The president, the press and the polls during Watergate.* New York: Columbia University Press.

Lang, K. (1968). *Politics and television*. Chicago: Quadrangle Books.

Lang, K., & Lang, G. E. (1953). The unique perspective of television and its effects: A pilot study. *American Sociological Review, 18*, 3–12.

Lanoue, D. J. (1991). The "turning point": Viewers' reactions to the second 1988 presidential debate. *American Politics Quarterly, 19*(1), 80–95.

Larson, M. S. (1989). Interaction between siblings in primetime television families. *Journal of Broadcasting and Electronic Media, 33*(3), 305–315.

Larson, M. S. (1993). Family communication on prime-time television. *Journal of Broadcasting and Electronic Media, 37*(3), 349–357.

Larson, R., & Kubey, R. (1983). Television and music: Contrasting media in adolescent life. *Youth and Society, 15*(1), 13–31.

Larson, S. G. (1991). Television's mixed messages: Sexual content on *All My Children*. *Communication Quarterly, 39*(2), 156–163.

Lavidge, R. J., & Steiner, G. A. (1961). A model for predictive measurements of advertising effectiveness. *Journal of Marketing, 25*, 59–62.

Lavrakas, P. J., Holley, J. K., & Miller, P. V. (1991). Public reactions to polling news during the 1988 presidential election campaign. In P. J. Lavrakas & J. K. Holley (Eds.), *Polling and presidential election coverage* (pp. 151–183). London: Sage.

Lazarsfeld, P. F., Berelson, B., & Gaudet, H. (1948). *The people's choice*. New York: Columbia University Press.

Lazarsfeld, P. F., & Merton, R. K. (1971). Mass communication, popular taste, and organized social action. In W. Schramm & D. F. Roberts (Eds.), *The process and effects of mass communication* (Rev. ed.). Urbana: University of Illinois Press.

Leather, P., McKechnie, S., & Amirkhanian, M. (1994). The importance of likeability as a measure of television advertising effectiveness. *International Journal of Advertising, 13*(3), 265–280.

Lee, B., & Lee, R. S. (1995, November/December). How and why people watch TV: Implications for the future of interactive television. *Journal of Advertising Research*, 9–18.

Lefcourt, H. M., Barnes, K., Parke, R., & Schwartz, F. (1966). Anticipated social censure and aggression-conflict as mediators of response to aggression induction. *Journal of Social Psychology, 70*(2), 251–263.

Lefkowitz, M. M., Eron, L. D., Walder, L. O., & Huesmann, L. R. (1977). *Growing up to be violent: A longitudinal study of the development of aggression*. Elmsford, NY: Pergamon.

Lemert, J. B. (1974). Content duplication by the networks in competing evening newscasts. *Journalism Quarterly, 51*(2), 238–244.

Lemert, J. B. (1993). Do televised presidential debates help inform voters? *Journal of Broadcasting and Electronic Media, 37*(1), 83–94.

Lemish, D., & Rice, M. L. (1986). Television as a talking picture book: A prop for language acquisition. *Journal of Child Language, 13*(2), 251–274.

Levin, S. R., Petros, T. V., & Petrella, F. W. (1982). Preschoolers' awareness of television advertising. *Child Development, 53*(4), 933–937.

Levy, M. R. (1978). The audience experience with television news. *Journalism Monographs, 55*.

Levy, M. R. (1989). Why VCRs aren't pop-up toasters: Issues in home video research. In M. R. Levy (Ed.), *The VCR age* (pp. 9–18). Newbury Park, CA: Sage.

Levy, M. R., & Fink, E. L. (1984). Home video recorders and the transience of television broadcasts. *Journal of Communication, 34*(2), 56–71.

Levy, M. R., & Windahl, S. (1984). Audience activity and gratifications: A conceptual clarification and exploration. *Communication Research, 11*(1), 51–78.

Leyens, J. P., & Camino, L. (1974). The effects of repeated exposure to film violence on aggressiveness and social structure. In J. DeWit & W. P. Hartup (Eds.), *Determinants and origins of aggressive behavior.* The Hague, Netherlands: Mouton.

Leyens, J. P., Camino, L., Parke, R. D., & Berkowitz, L. (1975). Effects of movie violence on aggression in a field setting as a function of group dominance and cohesion. *Journal of Personality and Social Psychology, 32*(2), 346–360.

Lichter, S. R., Rothman, S., & Lichter, L. S. (1986). *The media elite.* Bethesda, MD: Adler and Adler.

Lichty, L. W. (1982). Video vs. print. *Wilson Quarterly, 6*(5), 49–57.

Lichty, L. W. (1989). Television in America: Success story. In P. S. Cook, D. Gomery, & L. W. Lichty (Eds.), *American media* (pp. 159–176). Washington, DC: Wilson Center Press.

Lieberman Research. (1975). *Children's reactions to violent material on television* (Report to the American Broadcasting Company). New York: Author.

Liebert, D. E., Sprafkin, J. N., Liebert, R. M., & Rubinstein, E. A. (1977). Effects of television commercial disclaimers on the production expectations of children. *Journal of Communication, 27*(1), 118–124.

Liebler, C. M., & Bendix, J. (1996). Old-growth forests on network news: News sources and the framing of an environmental controversy. *Journalism and Mass Communication Quarterly, 73*(1), 53–65.

Liebler, C. M., & Smith, S. J. (1997). Tracking gender differences: A comparative analysis of network correspondents and their sources. *Journal of Broadcasting and Electronic Media, 41*(1), 58–68.

Lin, C. A. (1990). Audience activity and VCR use. In J. R. Dobrow (Ed.), *Social and cultural aspects of VCR use* (pp. 75–92). Hillsdale, NJ: Erlbaum.

Lin, C. A. (1992). Audience selectivity of local television newscasts. *Journalism Quarterly, 69*(2), 373–382.

Lin, C. A. (1993). Exploring the role of VCR use in the emerging home entertainment culture. *Journalism Quarterly, 70*(4), 833–842.

Lin, C. A. (1995). Network prime-time programming strategies in the 1980s. *Journal of Broadcasting and Electronic Media, 39*(4), 482–495.

Lin, C. A. (1997). Beefcake versus cheesecake in the 1990s: Sexist portrayals of both genders in television commercials. *Howard Journal of Communication, 8*(3), 237–249.

Lin, C. A., & Jeffres, L. W. (1998). Factors influencing the adoption of multimedia cable technology. *Journalism Quarterly, 75*(2), 341–352.

Lindstrom, P. B. (1997). The Internet: Nielsen's longitudinal research on behavioral changes in the use of this counterintuitive medium. *Journal of Media Economics, 10*(2), 35–40.

Linz, D., Donnerstein, E., & Adams, S. M. (1989). Physiological desensitization and judgments about female victims of violence. *Human Communication Research, 15*(4), 509–522.

Lipman, J. (1989, July 20). Jordan McGrath drops the name of the game that made its fame. *Wall Street Journal.*

Lipset, S., & Schneider, W. (1983). *The confidence gap: Business, labor, and government in the public mind.* New York: Free Press.

Litman, B. R., & Kohl, L. S. (1992). Network rerun viewing in the age of new programming services. *Journalism Quarterly, 69*(2), 383–391.

Loeghlin, J. C., & Nichols, R. C. (1976). *Heredity, environment, and personality.* Austin: University of Texas Press.

Longman, K. A. (1997). If not effective frequency, then what? *Journal of Advertising Research, 37*(4), 44–50.

LoSciuto, L. A. (1972). A national inventory of television viewing behavior. In E. A. Rubinstein, G. A. Comstock, and J. P. Murray (Eds.), *Television and social behavior. Television in day-to-day life: Patterns of use* (Vol. 4, pp. 33–86). Washington, DC: U.S. Government Printing Office.

Lovdal, L. T. (1989). Sex role messages in television commercials: An update. *Sex Roles, 21*(11/12), 715–724.

Lovibond, S. H. (1967). The effect of media stressing crime and violence upon children's attitudes. *Social Problems, 15*(1), 91–100.

Lowden, A. B., Andersen, P. A., Dozier, D. M., & Lauzen, M. M. (1994). Media use in the primary election: A secondary medium model. *Communication Research, 21*(30), 366–379.

Lowry, B. (1996, October 9). Debate attracts a third of potential TV audience; Television: Viewership is down considerably from '92, but closer to level of '88. *Los Angeles Times,* Part F, p. 2.

Lowry, D. T. (1971). Gresham's Law and network TV news selection. *Journal of Broadcasting, 25*(4), 397–408.

Lowry, D. T., Bridges, J. A., & Barefield, P. A. (1990). Effects of television "instant analysis and querulous criticism" following the first Bush-Dukakis debate. *Journalism Quarterly, 67*(4), 814–825.

Lowry, D. T., & Shidler, J. A. (1993). Prime time TV portrayals of sex, "safe sex" and AIDS: A longitudinal analysis. *Journalism Quarterly, 70*(3), 628–637.

Lowry, D. T., & Shidler, J. A. (1995). The sound bites, the biters and the bitten: An analysis of network TV news bias in campaign '92. *Journalism and Mass Communication Quarterly, 72*(1), 33–44.

Lowry, D. T., & Towles, D. E. (1989). Prime time TV portrayals of sex, contraception and venereal diseases. *Journalism Quarterly, 66*(2), 347–352.

Loye, D., Gorney, R., & Steele, G. (1977). Effects of television: An experimental field study. *Journal of Communication, 27*(3), 206–216.

Lucas, W. A., & Adams, W. C. (1977). *The undecided voter and political communication in the 1976 presidential election.* Paper presented at the annual meeting of the Southwestern Political Science Association, Dallas, TX.

Lucas, W. A., & Adams, W. C. (1978). Talking TV and voter indecision. *Journal of Communication, 28*(4), 120–131.

Lyle, J., & Hoffman, H. R. (1972a). Children's use of television and other media. In E. A. Rubinstein, G. A. Comstock, and J. P. Murray (Eds.), *Television and social behavior. Television in day-to-day life: Patterns of use* (vol. 4, pp. 257–273). Washington, DC: U.S. Government Printing Office.

Lyle, J., & Hoffman, H. R. (1972b). Explorations in patterns of television viewing by preschool-age children. In E. A. Rubinstein, G. A. Comstock, and J. P. Murray (Eds.),

Television and social behavior. Television in day-to-day life: Patterns of use. (Vol. 4, pp. 257–273). Washington, DC: U.S. Government Printing Office.

Maccoby, E. E. (1951). Television: Its impact on school children. *Public Opinion Quarterly, 15*(3), 421–444.

Maccoby, E. E. (1954). Why do children watch television? *Public Opinion Quarterly, 18*(3), 239–244.

Maccoby, E. E., & Wilson, W. C. (1957). Identification and observational learning from films. *Journal of Abnormal and Social Psychology, 55,* 76–87.

Maccoby, E. E., Wilson, W. C., & Burton, R. V. (1958). Differential movie-viewing behavior of male and female viewers. *Journal of Personality, 26,* 259–267.

MacBeth, T. M. (1996). *Tuning in to young viewers: Social science perspectives on television.* Thousand Oaks, CA: Sage.

MacInnis, D. J., & Stayman, D. M. (1993). Focal and emotional integration: Constructs, measures, and preliminary evidence. *Journal of Advertising, 22*(4), 51–66.

MacLachlan, J., & Logan, M. (1993, March/April). Camera shot length in TV commercials and their memorability and persuasiveness. *Journal of Advertising Research,* 57–61.

Makris, G. (1995). *A reexamination of violent content in MTV music videos: How violent are videos?* Unpublished master's thesis, Syracuse University, Syracuse, NY.

Malamuth, N. M., Feshbach, S., & Jaffe, T. (1977). Sexual arousal and aggression: Recent experiments and theoretical issues. *Journal of Social Issues, 33*(2), 110–133.

Manno, H. (1997). Affect and persuasion: The influence of pleasantness and arousal on attitude formation and message elaboration. *Psychology and Marketing, 14*(4), 315–335.

Mark, M. M., Sanna, L. J., & Shotland, R. L. (1992). Time series methods in applied social research. In F. B. Bryant et al. (Eds.), *Methodological issues in applied social psychology* (pp. 111–134). New York: Plenum Press.

Martin, M. C. (1997). Children's understanding of the intent of advertising: A meta-analysis. *Journal of Public Policy and Marketing, 16*(2), 205–216.

Martin, P. (1994, May 2). The consumer market for interactive services: Observing past trends and current demographics. *Telephony, 226,* 126–128, 130.

Martinelli, K., & Chaffee, S. H. (1995). Measuring new-voter learning via three channels of political information. *Journalism and Mass Communication Quarterly, 72*(1), 18–32.

Massey, K. K., & Baran, S. J. (1990). VCRs and people's control of their leisure time. In J. R. Dobrow (Ed.), *Social and cultural aspects of VCR use* (pp. 93–106). Hillsdale, NJ: Erlbaum.

Mayerle, J., & Rarick, D. (1989). The image of education in primetime network television series 1948–1988. *Journal of Broadcasting and Electronic Media, 33*(2), 139–157.

McCarthy, E. D., Langner, T. S., Gersten, J. C., Eisenberg, J. G., & Orzeck, L. (1975). Violence and behavioral disorders. *Journal of Communication, 25*(4), 71–85.

McCarthy, J. D., McPhail, C., & Smith, J. (1996). Images of protest: Dimensions of selection bias in media coverage of Washington demonstrations, 1982 and 1991. *American Sociological Review, 61*(3), 478–499.

McCombs, M. E. (1968). Negro use of television and newspapers for political information, 1952–1964. *Journal of Broadcasting, 12*(3), 261–266.

McCombs, M. E. (1972). Mass media in the marketplace. *Journalism Monographs, 24.*

McCombs, M. E. (1976). Agenda-setting research: A bibliographic essay. *Political Communication Review, 1*(1), 1–17.

McCombs, M. E. (1981). The agenda-setting approach. In D. Nimmo & K. Sanders (Eds.), *Handbook of political communication* (pp. 121–140). Beverly Hills, CA: Sage.

McCombs, M. E. (1992). Explorers and surveyors: Expanding strategies for agenda-setting research. *Journalism Quarterly, 69*(4), 813–824.

McCombs, M. E., & Eyal, C. H. (1980). Spending on mass media. *Journal of Communication, 30*(1), 153–158.

McCombs, M. E., & Shaw, D. L. (1972). The agenda-setting function of mass media. *Public Opinion Quarterly, 36*(2), 176–185.

McCombs, M. E., & Shaw, D. L. (1993). The evolution of agenda-setting research: Twenty-five years in the marketplace of ideas. *Journal of Communication, 43*(2), 58–67.

McCombs, M. E., & Zhu, J. (1995). Capacity, diversity, and volatility of the public agenda: Trends from 1965 to 1994. *Public Opinion Quarterly, 59* (4), 495–535.

McConnell, C., & Albiniak, P. (1998, Apr. 6). NAB's public service tally: Will it pay the rent? *Broadcasting and Cable, 128*(14), 70–80.

McDonald, D. G. (1990). Media orientation and television news viewing. *Journalism Quarterly, 67*(1), 11–20.

McDonald, D. G., & Reese, S. D. (1987). Television news and audience selectivity. *Journalism Quarterly, 64*(4), 763–768.

McDonald, D. G., & Schechter, R. (1988). Audience role in the evolution of fictional television content. *Journal of Broadcasting and Electronic Media, 32*(1), 61–71.

McGuire, W. J. (1986). The myth of massive media impact: Savagings and salvagings. In G. Comstock (Ed.), *Public communication and behavior* (Vol. 1, pp. 173–257). New York: Academic Press.

McHan, E. J. (1985). Imitation of aggression by Lebanese children. *Journal of Social Psychology, 125*(5), 613–617.

McIlwraith, R. D., Jacobvitz, R. S., Kubey, R., & Alexander, A. (1991). Television addiction: Theories and data behind the ubiquitous metaphor. *American Behavioral Scientist, 35*(2), 104–121.

McIlwraith, R. D., & Josephson, W. L. (1985). Movies, books, music, and adult fantasy life. *Journal of Communication, 35*(2), 167–179.

McIlwraith, R. D., & Schallow, J. (1982–83). Television viewing and styles of children's fantasy. *Imagination, Cognition and Personality, 2*(4), 323–331.

McIntyre, J. J., & Teevan, J. J., Jr. (1972). Television violence and deviant behavior. In G. A. Comstock & E. A. Rubinstein (Eds.), *Television and social behavior: Television and adolescent aggressiveness* (Vol. 3, pp. 383–435). Washington, DC: U.S. Government Printing Office.

McLeod, J. M., Atkin, C. K., & Chaffee, S. H. (1972a). Adolescents, parents, and television use: Adolescent self-report measures from Maryland and Wisconsin samples. In G. A. Comstock & E. A. Rubinstein (Eds.), *Television and social behavior: Television and adolescent aggressiveness* (Vol. 3, pp. 173–238). Washington, DC: U.S. Government Printing Office.

McLeod, J. M., Atkin, C. K., & Chaffee, S. H. (1972b). Adolescents, parents, and television use: Self-report and other-report measures from the Wisconsin sample. In G. A. Comstock & E. A. Rubinstein (Eds.), *Television and social behavior: Television and adolescent aggressiveness* (Vol. 3, pp. 239–313). Washington, DC: U.S. Government Printing Office.

McLeod, J. M., & Becker, L. B. (1974). Testing the validity of gratification measures through political effects analysis. In J. G. Blumler and E. Katz (Eds.), *The uses of mass communications: Current perspectives on gratifications research* (pp. 137–164). Beverly Hills, CA: Sage.

McLeod, J. M., Durall, J. A., Ziemke, D. A., & Bybee, C. R. (1979). Reactions of young and older voters: Expanding the context of effects. In S. Kraus (Ed.), *The great debates: Carter vs. Ford, 1976* (pp. 348–367). Bloomington: Indiana University Press.

McLeod, J. M., Guo, Z., Daily, K., Steele, C., Huang, H., Horowitz, E., & Chen, H. (1993). *The impact of traditional and non-traditional forms of political communication in the 1992 US presidential election.* Paper presented at the annual meeting of the Midwest Association for Public Opinion Research, Chicago, IL.

McLeod, J. M., Sotirovic, M., Eveland, W. P., Jr., Guo, Z., Horowitz, E. M., Moy, P., & Daily, K. (1996). *Let the punishment fit the (perceptions of) crime: Effects of local television news on evaluations of crime policy proposals.* Paper presented at the annual meeting of the International Communication Association, Chicago, IL.

McLeod, J. M., Ward, S., & Tancill, K. (1965). Alienation and uses of the mass media. *Public Opinion Quarterly, 29*(4), 583–594.

McManus, J. H. (1992). What kind of commodity is news? *Communication Research, 19*(6), 787–805.

Meadowcroft, J. M. (1986). Family communication patterns and political development: The child's role. *Communication Research, 13*(4), 603–624.

Medrich, E. A., Roizen, J., Rubin, V., & Buckley, S. (1982). *The serious business of growing up: A study of children's lives outside of school.* Los Angeles: University of California Press.

Meline, C. W. (1976). Does the medium matter? *Journal of Communication, 26*(3), 81–89.

Meltzoff, A. N. (1988). Imitation of televised models by infants. *Child Development, 59*(5), 1221–1229.

Mendelsohn, H. A. (1966). Election day broadcasts and terminal voting decisions. *Public Opinion Quarterly, 30*(2), 212–225.

Mendelsohn, H. A., & Crespi, I. (1970). *Polls, television and the new politics.* San Francisco: Chandler.

Mendelsohn, H. A., & O'Keefe, G. J. (1976). *The people choose a president: Influences on voter decision-making.* New York: Praeger.

Menzies, E. S. (1971). *Preferences in television content among violent prisoners.* Unpublished master's thesis, Florida State University, Tallahassee, FL.

Menzies, E. S. (1973). *The effects of repeated exposure to televised violence upon attitudes towards violence among youthful offenders.* Unpublished doctoral dissertation, Florida State University, Tallahassee, FL.

Meringoff, L. K. (1980). The effects of children's television food advertising. In R. P. Adler, G. S. Lesser, L. K. Meringoff, T. S. Robertson, J. R. Rossiter, & S. Ward (Eds.), *The effects of television advertising on children: Review and recommendations* (pp. 123–152). Lexington, MA: Lexington Books.

Meringoff, L. K., Vibbert, M. M., Char, C. A., Ferme, D. E., Banker, G. S., & Gardner, H. (1983). How is children's learning from television distinctive? Exploiting the medium methodologically. In J. Bryant & D. R. Anderson (Eds.), *Children's understanding of television: Research on attention and comprehension* (pp. 151–179). New York: Academic Press.

Merton, R. K. (1996). Sociological ambivalence. In P. Sztompka (Ed.), *Robert K. Merton. On social structure and science* (pp. 123–131). Chicago: University of Chicago Press.

Messner, M. A., Duncan, M. C., & Jensen, K. (1993). Separating the men from the girls: The gendered language of televised sports. *Gender and Society, 7*(1), 124–137.

Messner, S. F. (1986). Television violence and violent crime: An aggregate analysis. *Social Problems, 33*(3), 218–235.

Meyer, T. P. (1973). Children's perceptions of favorite television characters as behavioral models. *Educational Broadcasting Review, 7*(1), 25–33.

Milavsky, J. R. (1992). How good is the A. C. Nielsen people-meter system? A review of the report by the committee on nationwide television audience measurement. *Public Opinion Quarterly, 56*(1), 102–115.

Milavsky, J. R., Kessler, R., Stipp, H. H., & Rubens, W. S. (1982a). Television and aggression: Results of a panel study. In D. Pearl, L. Bouthilet, & J. Lazar (Eds.), *Television and social behavior: Ten years of scientific progress and implications for the eighties. Technical reviews* (Vol. 2, pp. 138–157). Washington, DC: U.S. Government Printing Office.

Milavsky, J. R., Kessler, R., Stipp, H. H., & Rubens, W. S. (1982b). *Television and aggression: A panel study.* New York: Academic Press.

Milavsky, J. R., Pekowsky, B., & Stipp, H. (1975). TV drug advertising and proprietary and illicit drug use among teenage boys. *Public Opinion Quarterly, 39*(4), 457–481.

Milgram, S., & Shotland, R. L. (1973). *Television and antisocial behavior: A field experiment.* New York: Academic Press.

Miller, R. E., & Wanta, W. (1996). Race as a variable in agenda setting. *Journalism and Mass Communication Quarterly, 73*(4), 913–925.

Miller, T. E. (1995, April). New markets for information? *American Demographics, 17*(4), 46–54.

Mills, K. (1993). The media and the year of the woman. *Media Studies Journal, 7*(1–2), 18–31.

Minow, N. N. (1978). Address by Newton N. Minow to the National Association of Broadcasters, Washington, DC. In F. Kahn (Ed.), *Documents of American broadcasting* (3rd ed., pp. 281–291). Englewood Cliffs, NJ: Prentice Hall.

Mittal, B. (1994, January/February). Public assessment of TV advertising: Faint praise and harsh criticism. *Journal of Advertising Research*, 35–53.

Morello, J. T. (1988a). Argument and visual structuring in the 1984 Mondale–Reagan debates: The medium's influence on the perception of clash. *Western Journal of Speech Communication, 52*(4), 277–290.

Morello, J. T. (1988b). Visual structuring of the 1976 and 1984 nationally televised presidential debates. *Central States Speech Journal, 39*(3/4), 233–243.

Morgan, M. (1980). Television viewing and reading: Does more equal better? *Journal of Communication, 30*(1), 159–165.

Morgan, M., Alexander, A., Shanahan, J., & Harris, C. (1990). Adolescents, VCRs, and the family environment. *Communication Research, 17*(1), 83–106.

Morgan, M., & Gross, L. (1980). Television viewing, IQ, and academic achievement. *Journal of Broadcasting, 24*(2), 117–133.

Morgan, M., & Gross, L. (1982). Television and educational achievement and aspiration. In D. Pearl, L. Bouthilet, & J. Lazar (Eds.), *Television and behavior: Ten years of scientific progress and implications for the eighties. Technical reviews* (Vol. 2, pp. 78–90). Washington, DC: U.S. Government Printing Office.

Moriarty, S. E., & Everett, S. L. (1994). Commercial breaks: A viewing behavior study. *Journalism Quarterly, 71*(2), 346–355.

Morris, D., & Gamache, M. E. (1994). *Handbook of campaign spending: Money in the 1992 congressional races.* Washington, DC: Congressional Quarterly.

Muehling, D. D., & McCann, M. (1993). Attitude toward the ad: A review. *Journal of Current Issues and Research in Advertising, 15*(2), 25–58.

Mueller, A., & Kamerer, D. (1995). Reader preference for electronic newspapers. *Newspaper Research Journal, 16*(3), 2–13.

Mughan, A. (1995). Media markets and candidate awareness in House elections, 1978–1990. *Political Communication, 12*(3), 305–325.

Mullen, B. (1989). *Advanced basic meta-analysis.* Hillsdale, NJ: Erlbaum.

Mullen, B., & Johnson, C. (1990). *The psychology of consumer behavior.* Hillsdale, NJ: Erlbaum.

Mundorf, N., Zillmann, D., & Drew, D. (1991). Effects of disturbing televised events on the acquisition of information from subsequently presented commercials. *Journal of Advertising, 20*(1), 46–53.

Mundorf, N., Drew, D., Zillmann, D., & Weaver, J. (1990). Effects of disturbing news on recall of subsequently presented news. *Communication Research, 17*(5), 601–615.

Murray, J. P., & Kippax, S. (1978). Children's social behavior in three towns with differing television experience. *Journal of Communication, 28*(4), 19–29.

Mutz, D. C., Roberts, D. F., & van Vuuren, D. P. (1993). Reconsidering the displacement hypothesis. Television's influence on children's time use. *Communication Research, 20*(1), 51–75.

National Television Violence Study. (1996a). *National Television Violence Study: Executive summary, 1994–95.* Studio City, CA: Mediascope.

National Television Violence Study. (1996b). *National Television Violence Study: Scientific papers, 1994–95.* Studio City, CA: Mediascope.

National Television Violence Study. (1997a). *National Television Violence Study: Executive summary* (Vol. II). Santa Barbara: Center for Communication and Social Policy, University of California.

National Television Violence Study. (1997b). *National Television Violence Study* (Vol. II). Santa Barbara: Center for Communication and Social Policy, University of California.

National Television Violence Study. (1998a). *National Television Violence Study: Executive summary* (Vol. III). Santa Barbara: Center for Communication and Social Policy, University of California.

National Television Violence Study. (1998b). *National Television Violence Study* (Vol. III). Santa Barbara: Center for Communication and Social Policy, University of California.

Neuman, R. (1976). Patterns of recall among television news viewers. *Public Opinion Quarterly, 40*(1), 115–123.

Neuman, S. B. (1988). The displacement effect: Assessing the relation between television viewing and reading performance. *Reading Research Quarterly, 23*(4), 414–440.

Neuman, S. B. (1991). *Literacy in the television age.* Norwood, NJ: Ablex.

Neuman, W. R. (1982). Television and American culture: The mass medium and the pluralistic audience. *Public Opinion Quarterly, 46*(4), 471–487.

Neuman, W. R. (1986). *The paradox of mass politics.* Cambridge, MA: Harvard University Press.

Neuman, W. R. (1990). The threshold of public attention. *Public Opinion Quarterly, 54*(2), 159–176.

Neuman, W. R. (1991). *The future of the mass audience.* Cambridge, England: Cambridge University Press.

Neuman, W. R., Just, M., & Crigler, A. (1992). *Common knowledge: News and the construction of political meaning.* Chicago: University of Chicago Press.

Newhagen, J. E. (1994a). The relationship between censorship and the emotional and critical tone of television news coverage of the Persian Gulf War. *Journalism Quarterly, 71*(1), 32–42.

Newhagen, J. E. (1994b). Self-efficacy and call-in political television show use. *Communication Research, 21*(3), 366–379.

Newhagen, J. E. (1998). TV news images that induce anger, fear, and disgust: Effects on approach-avoidance and memory. *Journal of Broadcasting and Electronic Media, 42*(2), 265–276.

Newhagen, J. E., Cordes, J. W., & Levy, M. R. (1995). Nightly@nbc.com: Audience scope and the perception of interactivity in viewer mail on the Internet. *Journal of Communication, 45*(3), 164–175.

Newhagen, J. E., & Nass, C. (1989). Differential criteria for evaluating credibility of newspaper and television news. *Journalism Quarterly, 66*(2), 277–284.

Newhagen, J. E., & Reeves, B. (1991). Emotion and memory responses for negative political advertising: A study of television commercials used in the 1988 presidential election. In F. Biocca (Ed.), *Television and political advertising: Psychological processes* (Vol. 1, pp. 197–220). Hillsdale, NJ: Erlbaum.

Newhagen, J. E., & Reeves, B. (1992). The evening's bad news: Effects of compelling negative television news images on memory. *Journal of Communication, 42*(2), 25–41.

Newman, B. I. (1993). *The marketing of the president.* Thousand Oaks, CA: Sage.

Nie, N. H., Verba, S., & Petrocik, J. R. (1976). *The changing American voter.* Cambridge, MA: Harvard University Press.

Nielsen Media Research. (1993). *Report on television, 1992–1993.* New York: Author.

Nielsen Media Research. (1998). *1998 report on television.* New York: Author.

Nimmo, D. (1970). *The political persuaders.* Englewood Cliffs, NJ: Prentice Hall.

Nimmo, D. (1989). Episodes, incidents, and eruptions: Nightly network television coverage of candidates 1988. *American Broadcasting Society, 32*(4), 415–424.

Noble, G. (1970). Film-mediated aggressive and creative play. *British Journal of Social and Clinical Psychology, 9*(1), 1–7.

Noble, G. (1973). Effects of different forms of filmed aggression on children's constructive and destructive play. *Journal of Personality and Social Psychology, 26*(1), 54–59.

Noelle-Neumann, E. (1984). *The spiral of silence—Our social skin.* Chicago: University of Chicago Press.

Nog, G. Y., & Grant, A. E. (1997). Media functionality and the principle of relative constancy: An explanation of the VCR aberration. *Journal of Media Economics, 10*(3), 17–31.

Nugent, G. C. (1982). Pictures, audio, and print: Symbolic representation and effect on learning. *Educational Communication and Technology Journal, 30*(3), 163–174.

O'Callaghan, J., & Dukes, J. O. (1992). Media coverage of the Supreme Court's caseload. *Journalism Quarterly, 69*(1), 195–203.

Ogilvy, D., & Raphaelson, J. (1982, July/August). Research on advertising techniques that work—and don't work. *Harvard Business Review, 60,* 14.

O'Keefe, G. J., & Mendelsohn, H. (1979). Media influences and their anticipation. In S. Kraus (Ed.), *The great debates: Carter vs. Ford, 1976* (pp. 405–417). Bloomington: Indiana University Press.

Oliver, M. B. (1994). Portrayals of crime, race, and aggression in "reality-based" police shows: A content analysis. *Journal of Broadcasting and Electronic Media, 38*(2), 179–192.

Olson, B. (1994). Sex and the soaps: A comparative content analysis of health issues. *Journalism Quarterly, 71*(4), 840–850.

O'Neal, E. C., & Taylor, S. L. (1989). Status of the provoker, opportunity to retaliate, and interest in video violence. *Aggressive Behavior, 15*(2), 171–180.

Ostroff, D. H., & Sandell, K. L. (1989). Campaign coverage by local television news in Columbus, Ohio 1978–1986. *Journalism Quarterly, 66*(1), 114–120.

Owen, B. M., Beebe, J. H., & Manning, W. G. (1974). *Television economics.* Lexington, MA: Lexington Books.

Owen, D., & Dennis, J. (1992). Sex differences in politicization: The influence of mass media. *Women and Politics, 12*(4), 19–42.

Page, B., & Shapiro, R. (1992). *The rational public: Fifty years of trends in American policy preferences.* Chicago: University of Chicago Press.

Paget, K. F., Kritt, D., & Bergemann, L. (1984). Understanding strategic interactions in television commercials: A developmental study. *Journal of Applied Developmental Psychology, 5*(2), 145–161.

Paik, H. (1991). *The effects of television violence on aggressive behavior: A meta-analysis.* Unpublished doctoral dissertation, Syracuse University, Syracuse, NY.

Paik, H., & Comstock, G. (1994). The effects of television violence on antisocial behavior: A meta-analysis. *Communication Research, 21*(4), 516–546.

Paletz, D. L., & Guthrie, K. K. (1987). The three faces of Ronald Reagan. *Journal of Communication, 37*(4), 7–23.

Palmer, E. L. (1988). *Television and America's children.* New York: Oxford University Press.

Palmer, E. L., & McDowell, C. N. (1979). The program/commercial separators in children's television programming. *Journal of Communication, 29*(3), 197–201.

Palmgreen, P., Wenner, L. A., & Rayburn, J. D., III. (1981). Gratification discrepancies and news program choice. *Communication Research, 8*(4), 451–478.

Pan, Z., & Kosicki, G. M. (1997). Priming and media impact on the evaluations of the president's performance. *Communication Research, 24*(1), 3–30.

Parker, E. B. (1960). *The functions of television for children.* Unpublished doctoral dissertation, Stanford University, Palo Alto, CA.

Patterson, O., III. (1984). An analysis of television coverage of the Vietnam War. *Journal of Broadcasting, 28*(4), 397–404.

Patterson, T. E. (1980). *The mass media election: How Americans choose their president.* New York: Praeger.

Patterson, T. E. (1993). *Out of order.* New York: Random House.

Patterson, T. E. (1996). Bad news, bad governance. *Annals of the American Academy of Political and Social Science, 546,* 97–108.

Patterson, T. E., & McClure, R. D. (1976). *The unseeing eye: The myth of television power in national elections.* New York: Putnam.

Patzer, G. L. (1991, August/September). Multiple dimensions of performance for 30-second and 15-second commercials. *Journal of Advertising Research,* 18–25.

Pearl, D., Bouthilet, L., & Lazar, J. (Eds.). (1982a). *Television and behavior: Ten years of scientific progress and implications for the eighties. Summary report* (Vol. 1). Washington, DC: U.S. Government Printing Office.

Pearl, D., Bouthilet, L., & Lazar, J. (Eds.). (1982b). *Television and behavior: Ten years of scientific progress and implications for the eighties. Technical reviews* (Vol. 2). Washington, DC: U.S. Government Printing Office.

Pechmann, C., & Stewart, D. W. (1988). Advertising repetition: A critical review of wear-in and wear-out. *Current Issues and Research in Advertising, 11*(1/2), 285–329.

Peer, L., & Chestnut, B. (1995). Deciphering media independence: The Gulf War debate in television and newspaper news. *Political Communication, 12*(1), 81–95.

The people's choice, Nov. 3–9. (1997, November 17). *Broadcasting and Cable, 127* (47), 56.

The people's choice, Jan. 5–11. (1998, January 26). *Broadcasting and Cable, 128*(4), 37.

The people's choice, Jan. 26–Feb. 1. (1998, February 9). *Broadcasting and Cable, 128* (6), 34.

The people's choice, Oct. 5–11. (1998, October 19). *Broadcasting and Cable, 128* (43), 57.

Percy, L., & Rossiter, J. R. (1992). Advertising stimulus effects: A review. *Journal of Current Issues and Research in Advertising, 14*(1), 75–90.

Perloff, R. M. (1989). Ego-involvement and the third person effect of televised news coverage. *Communication Research, 16*(2), 236–262.

Perloff, R., Wartella, E., & Becker, L. (1982). Increasing learning from TV news. *Journalism Quarterly, 59*(1), 83–86.

Perry, S. D. (1997). Using humorous programs as a vehicle for humorous commercials. *Journal of Communication, 47*(1), 20–39.

Perse, E. M. (1990a). Audience selectivity and involvement in the newer media environment. *Communication Research, 17*(5), 675–697.

Perse, E. M. (1990b). Media involvement and local news effects. *Journal of Broadcasting and Electronic Media, 34*(1), 17–36.

Perse, E. M., & Ferguson, D. A. (1993). The impact of newer television technologies on television satisfaction. *Journalism Quarterly, 70*(4), 843–853.

Perse, E. M., Pavitt, C., & Burggraf, C. (1990). Implicit theories of marriage and evaluations of marriage on television. *Human Communication Research, 16*(3), 387–408.

Peterson, C. C., Peterson, J. L., & Carroll, J. (1987). Television viewing and imaginative problem solving during preadolescence. *Journal of Genetic Psychology, 147*(1), 61–67.

Peterson, R. C., & Thurstone, L. L. (1933). *Motion pictures and the social attitudes of children.* New York: Macmillan.

Petty, R. E., & Cacioppo, J. T. (1980). Effects of issue involvement on attitude in an advertising context (pp. 75–79). In J. G. Gorn & M. E. Goldberg (Eds.), *Proceedings of the Division 23 Program, 88th Annual American Psychological Association Meeting,* Montreal, Quebec, Canada.

Petty, R. E., & Cacioppo, J. T. (1981). *Attitudes and persuasion: Classic and contemporary approaches.* Dubuque, IA: Brown.

Petty, R. E., & Cacioppo, J. T. (1986). The elaboration likelihood model of persuasion. In L. Berkowitz (Ed.), *Advances in experimental social psychology, Vol. 19* (pp. 123–205). New York: Academic Press.

Petty, R. E., & Cacioppo, J. T. (1990). Involvement and persuasion: Tradition vs. integration. *Psychological Bulletin, 107*(3), 367–374.

Pezdek, K., Simon, S., Stoeckert, J., & Kiley, J. (1985). *Individual differences in television comprehension.* Paper presented at the annual meeting of the Psychonomic Society, Boston, MA.

Pfau, M., & Burgoon, M. (1988). Inoculation in political campaign communication. *Human Communication Research, 15*(1), 91–111.

Pfau, M., & Burgoon, M. (1989). The efficacy of issue and character attack message strategies in political campaign communication. *Communication Reports, 2*(2), 53–61.

Pfau, M., Diedrich, T., Larson, K. M., & Van Winkle, K. M. (1993). Relational and competence perception of presidential candidates during primary election campaigns. *Journal of Broadcasting and Electronic Media, 37*(3), 275–292.

Pfau, M., & Eveland, W. P., Jr. (1996). *The influence of traditional and non-traditional news media in the initial phase of a presidential election campaign on voters' perceptions of candidates during the initial and final phases of the campaign.* Paper presented at the annual meeting of the International Communication Association, Chicago, IL.

Pfau, M., & Kang, J. G. (1991). The impact of relational messages on candidate influence in televised debates. *Communication Studies, 42*(2), 114–128.

Pfau, M., & Kenski, H. C. (1990). *Attack politics: Strategy and defense.* New York: Praeger.

Pfau, M., & Louden, A. (1994). Effectiveness of adwatch formats in deflecting political attack ads. *Communication Research, 21*(3), 325–341.

Pfau, M., Tusing, K. J., Koerner, A. F., Lee, W., Godbold, L. C., Penaloza, L. J., Yang, V. S., & Hong, Y. (1997). Enriching the inoculation construct: The role of critical components in the process of resistance. *Human Communication Research, 24*(2), 187–215.

Phalen, P. F. (1996). *Information and markets and the market for information: A study of the market for television audiences.* Unpublished doctoral dissertation, Northwestern University, Evanston, IL.

Phillips, D. P. (1983). The impact of mass media violence on U.S. homicides. *American Sociological Review, 48,* 560–568.

Phillips, D. P. (1986). The found experiment: A new technique for assessing the impact to mass media violence on real-world aggressive behavior. In G. Comstock (Ed.), *Public communication and behavior* (Vol. 1, pp. 260–307). New York: Academic Press.

Phillips, D. P., & Carstensen, L. L. (1986). Clustering of teenage suicides after television news stories about suicide. *New England Journal of Medicine, 315*(11), 685–689.

Phillips, D. P., & Hensley, J. E. (1984). When violence is rewarded or punished. *Journal of Communication, 34*(3), 101–116.

Pieters, R. G. M., & Bijmolt, T. H. A. (1997). Consumer memory for television advertising: A field study of duration, serial position, and competition effects. *Journal of Consumer Research, 23*(4), 362–372.

Pinkleton, B. (1997). The effects of negative comparative political advertising on candidate evaluations and advertising evaluations: An exploration. *Journal of Advertising,* 26(1), 19–29.

Pinkleton, B. E., Austin, E. W., & Fortman, K. K. J. (1998). Relationships of media use and political disaffection to political efficacy and voting behavior. *Journal of Broadcasting and Electronic Media,* 42(1), 34–49.

Plomin, R., Corley, R., DeFries, J. C., & Fulker, D. W. (1990). Individual differences in television viewing in early childhood: Nature as well as nurture. *Psychological Science,* 6(1), 371–377.

Plomin, R., & DeFries, J. C. (1985). *Origins of individual differences in infancy: The Colorado Adoption Project.* New York: Academic Press.

Poiesz, T. B. C., & Robben, H. S. J. (1994). Individual reactions to advertising: Theoretical and methodological developments. *International Journal of Advertising,* 13, 25–33.

Polling the nations. [CD-ROM]. (1997). Bethesda, MD: ORS.

Pope, K. (1998, April 3). TV plans to use new digital capacity to improve picture, not add channels. *Wall Street Journal.*

Pope, K., & Robichaux, M. (1997, September 12). Waiting for HDTV? Don't go dumping your old set just yet. *Wall Street Journal.*

Popkin, S. L. (1997). Voter learning in the 1992 presidential campaign. In S. Iyengar & R. Reeves (Eds.), *Do the media govern?* Thousand Oaks, CA: Sage.

Potter, W. J. (1987). Does television viewing hinder academic achievement among adolescents? *Human Communication Research,* 14(1), 27–46.

Potter, W. J. (1988). Three strategies for elaborating the cultivation hypothesis. *Journalism Quarterly,* 65(4), 930–939.

Potter, W. J., & Vaughan, M. (1997). Anti-social behavior in television entertainment: Trends and profiles. *Communication Research Reports,* 14(1), 116–124.

Potter, W. J., Vaughan, M. W., Warren, R., Howley, K., Land, A., & Hagemeyer, J. C. (1995). How real is the portrayal of aggression in television entertainment programming? *Journal of Broadcasting and Electronic Media,* 39(4), 496–516.

Potter, W. J., & Ware, W. (1987a). Traits of perpetrators and receivers of antisocial and prosocial acts on television. *Journalism Quarterly,* 21(3), 382–391.

Potter, W. J., & Ware, W. (1987b). An analysis of the contexts of antisocial acts on prime-time television. *Communication Research,* 14(6), 664–686.

Potts, R., Huston, A. C., & Wright, J. C. (1986). The effects of television form and violent content on boys' attention and social behavior. *Journal of Experimental Child Psychology,* 41(1), 1–17.

Potts, R., & Sanchez, D. (1994). Television viewing and depression: No news is good news. *Journal of Broadcasting and Electronic Media,* 38(1), 79–90.

Powell, F. C., & Wanzenried, J. W. (1993). Perceptions of Bush, Clinton, and Perot in relation to frequency of presidential debate viewing. *Perceptual and Motor Skills,* 77(4), 35–41.

Prescott, C. A., Johnson, R. C., & McArdle, J. J. (1991). Genetic contributions to television viewing. *Psychological Science,* 2(6), 430–431.

Price, J. H., Merrill, E. A., & Clause, M. E. (1992). The depiction of guns on prime time television. *Journal of School Health,* 62(1), 15–18.

Procter, D. E., Aden, R. C., & Japp, P. (1988). Gender/issue interaction in political identity making: Nebraska's woman vs. woman gubernatorial campaign. *Central States Speech Journal, 39*(3/4), 190–203.

Procter, D. E., Schenck-Hamlin, W. J., & Haase, K. A. (1994). Exploring the role of gender in the development of negative political advertisements. *Women and Politics, 14*(2), 1–22.

Provenzo, E. F., Jr. (1991). *Video kids: Making sense of Nintendo.* Cambridge, MA: Harvard University Press.

Putnam, R. (1995, December). Tuning in, tuning out: The strange disappearance of social capital in America. *P.S.*

Rakow, L. F., & Kranich, K. (1991). Women as sign in television news. *Journal of Communication, 4*(1), 8–23.

Randall, D. M. (1987). The portrayal of corporate crime in network television newscasts. *Journalism Quarterly, 64*(1), 150–153.

Randall, D., & DeFillippi, R. (1987). Media coverage of corporate malfeasance in the oil industry. *Social Science Journal, 24*(1), 31–42.

Randall, D. M., Lee-Sammons, L., & Hagner, P. R. (1988). Common versus elite crime coverage in network news. *Social Science Quarterly, 69*(4), 910–929.

Ratzan, S. C. (1989). The real agenda setters: Pollsters in the 1988 presidential campaign. *American Broadcasting Society, 32*(4), 451–463.

Real, M. R. (1996). *Exploring media culture: A guide.* Thousand Oaks, CA: Sage.

Reece, B. B., Vanden Bergh, B. G., & Li, H. (1994). What makes a slogan memorable and who remembers it. *Journal of Current Issues and Research in Advertising, 16*(2), 41–55.

Reese, S. D. (1984). Visual-verbal redundancy effects on television news learning. *Journal of Broadcasting, 28*(1), 79–87.

Reese, S. D., & Buckalew, B. (1995). The militarism of local television: The routine framing of the Persian Gulf War. *Critical Studies in Mass Communication, 12*(1), 40–59.

Reese, S. D., Daly, J. A., & Hardy, A. P. (1987). Economic news on network television. *Journalism Quarterly, 64*(1), 137–144.

Reese, S. D., Grant, A., & Danielian, L. (1994). The structure of news sources on television: A network analysis of "CBS News," "Nightline," "MacNeil/Lehrer," and "This Week with David Brinkley." *Journal of Communication, 44*(2), 84–107.

Reeves, B., Lang, A., Thorson, E., & Rothschild, M. (1989). Emotional television series and hemispheric specialization. *Human Communication Research, 15*(4), 493–507.

Reid, L. N., & Frazer, C. F. (1980). Children's use of television commercials to initiate social interaction in family viewing situations. *Journal of Broadcasting, 24*(2), 149–158.

Reitzes, K. A., & White, M. A. (1982). Children's expectations for television entertainment vs. television news events. *Journal of Applied Communication Research, 10*, 168–173.

Rhee, J. W. (1997). Strategy and issue frames in election campaign coverage: A social cognitive account of framing effects. *Journal of Communication, 47*(3), 26–48.

Rhee, J. W., & Cappella, J. N. (1997). The role of political sophistication in learning from news: Measuring schema development. *Communication Research, 24*(3), 197–233.

Rice, M. L. (1983). The role of television in language acquisition. *Developmental Review, 3*(2), 211–224.

Rice, M. L. (1984). The world of children's television. *Journal of Broadcasting, 28*(4), 445–461.

Rice, M. L., Huston, A. C., Truglio, R., & Wright, J. C. (1990). Words from "Sesame Street": Learning vocabulary while viewing. *Developmental Psychology, 26*(3), 421–428.

Rice, M. L., & Woodsmall, L. (1988). Lessons from television: Children's word learning when viewing. *Child Development, 59*(2), 420–429.

Riffe, D., Place, P. C., & Mayo, C. M. (1993). Game time, soap time and prime time TV ads: Treatment of women in Sunday football and rest-of-week advertising. *Journalism Quarterly, 70*(2), 437–446.

Roberts, M., Anderson, R., & McCombs, M. (1994). 1990 Texas gubernatorial campaign influence of issues and images. *Mass Communication Review, 21*(1/2), 20–35.

Roberts, S. V. (1995, Nov. 6). Near-death experience. *US News and World Report,* 28–38.

Robertson, T. S., Rossiter, J. R., & Gleason, T. C. (1979). *Televised medicine advertising and children.* New York: Praeger.

Robinson, J., Keegan, C., Karth, M., Triplett, T., & Holland, J. (1985). *Arts participation in America.* College Park, MD: Survey Research Center, University of Maryland.

Robinson, J. P. (1971). The audience for national TV news programs. *Public Opinion Quarterly, 35*(3), 403–405.

Robinson, J. P. (1972a). Toward defining the functions of television. In E. A. Rubinstein et al. (Eds.), *Television and social behavior. Television in everyday life: Patterns of use* (Vol. 4, pp. 568–603). Washington, DC: U.S. Government Printing Office.

Robinson, J. P. (1972b). Television's impact on everyday life: Some cross-national evidence. In E. A. Rubinstein et al. (Eds.), *Television and social behavior. Television in everyday life: Patterns of use.* (Vol. 4, pp. 410–431), Washington, DC: U.S. Government Printing Office.

Robinson, J. P. (1977). *How Americans use time: A social-psychological analysis of everyday behavior.* New York: Praeger.

Robinson, J. P. (1979). The polls. In S. Kraus (Ed.), *The great debates: Carter vs. Ford, 1976* (pp. 262–268). Bloomington: Indiana University Press.

Robinson, J. P. (1990). Television's effects on families' use of time. In J. Bryant (Ed.), *Television and the American family* (pp. 195–210). Hillsdale, NJ: Erlbaum.

Robinson, J. P., & Bachman, J. G. (1972). Television viewing habits and aggression. In G. A. Comstock & E. A. Rubinstein (Eds.), *Television and social behavior: Television and adolescent aggressiveness.* (Vol. 3, pp. 372–382). Washington, DC: U.S. Government Printing Office.

Robinson, J. P., Chivian, E., & Tudge, J. (1989). News media use and adolescents' attitudes about nuclear issues: An American-Soviet comparison. *Journal of Communication, 39*(2), 105–113.

Robinson, J. P., & Converse, P. E. (1972). The impact of television on mass media usages: A cross-national comparison. In A. Szalai (Ed.), *The use of time: Daily activities of urban and suburban populations in twelve countries* (pp. 197–212). The Hague, Netherlands: Mouton.

Robinson, J. P., & Godbey, G. (1997). *Time for life: The surprising ways Americans use their time.* University Park: Pennsylvania State University Press.

Robinson, J. P., & Levy, M. R. (1986a). *The main source: Learning from television news.* Newbury Park, CA: Sage.

Robinson, J. P., & Levy, M. R. (1986b). Interpersonal communication and news comprehension. *Public Opinion Quarterly, 50*(2), 160–175.

Robinson, M. J., & Sheehan, M. A. (1983). *Over the wire and on TV: CBS and UPI in campaign '80.* New York: Russell Sage.

Roddy, B. L., & Garramone, G. M. (1988). Appeals and strategies of negative political advertising. *Journal of Broadcasting and Electronic Media, 32*(4), 415–427.

Rodin, J. (1985). The application of social psychology. In G. Lindzey & E. Aronson (Eds.), *Handbook of social psychology* (3rd ed., pp. 805–881). New York: Random House.

Rogers, E. M. (1995). *Diffusion of innovations* (4th ed.). New York: Free Press.

Rogers, E. M., & Chang, S. (1991). Media coverage of technology issues: Ethiopian drought of 1984, AIDS, Challenger and Chernobyl. In L. Wilkens & P. Patterson (Eds.), *Risky business: Communicating issues of science, risk and public policy* (pp. 75–96). New York: Greenwood.

Rogers, E. M., Dearing, J. W., & Bregman, D. (1993). The anatomy of agenda-setting research. *Journal of Communication, 43*(2), 68–84.

Rogers, M., & Seiler, C. A. (1994, March/April). The answer is no: A national survey of advertising industry practitioners and their clients about whether they use subliminal advertising. *Journal of Advertising Research, 36*–45.

Rogers, M., & Smith, K. H. (1993, March/April). Public perceptions of subliminal advertising: Why practitioners shouldn't ignore this issue. *Journal of Advertising Research, 33*, 10–18.

Rojecki, A. (1996). *The deadly embrace: News constructions of Black-Jewish antagonism.* Paper presented at the annual meeting of the International Communication Association, Chicago, IL.

Rokeach, M. (1968). *Beliefs, attitudes and values.* San Francisco: Jossey-Bass.

Rokeach, M. (1979). *Understanding human values.* New York: Free Press.

Rolandelli, D. R. (1989). Children and television: The visual superiority effect reconsidered. *Journal of Broadcasting and Electronic Media, 33*(1), 69–81.

Roper. (1973). *What people think of television and other mass media, 1959–1972.* New York: Television Information Office.

Roper. (1975). *Trends in public attitudes toward television and other mass media, 1959–1972.* New York: Television Information Office.

Roper Starch. (1995). *America's watching: Public attitudes toward television.* New York: Roper Starch Worldwide.

Rosekrans, M. A., & Hartup, W. W. (1967). Imitative influences of consistent and inconsistent response consequences to a model on aggressive behavior in children. *Journal of Personality and Social Psychology, 7*(4), 429–434.

Rosenstein, A. W., & Grant, A. E. (1997). Reconceptualizing the role of habit: A new model of television audience activity. *Journal of Broadcasting and Electronic Media, 41*(3), 324–344.

Rosenthal, R. (1966). *Experimenter effects in behavioral research.* New York: Appleton-Century-Crofts.

Ross, M. H. (1992). Television news and candidate fortunes in presidential nominations campaigns: The case of 1984. *American Politics Quarterly, 20*(1), 69–98.

Ross, R. P., Campbell, T., Wright, J. C., Huston, A. C., Rice, M. L., & Turk, P. (1984).

When celebrities talk, children listen: An experimental analysis of children's responses to TV ads with celebrity endorsement. *Journal of Applied Developmental Psychology, 5*(4), 185–202.

Rossiter, J. R., & Robertson, T. S. (1974). Children's TV commercials: Testing the defenses. *Journal of Communication, 24*(4), 137–144.

Rotfeld, H. J., Abernethy, A. M., & Parsons, P. R. (1990). Self-regulation and television advertising. *Journal of Advertising, 19*(4), 18–26.

Rothenbuhler, E. W. (1988). The living room celebration of the Olympic games. *Journal of Communication, 38*(4), 61–81.

Rothschild, N., Thorson, E., Reeves, B., Hirsch, J. E., & Goldstein, R. (1986). EEG activity and the processing of television commercials. *Communication Research, 13*(2), 182–220.

Rovet, J. (1983). The education of spatial transformations. In D. R. Olson & E. Bialystok (Eds.), *Spatial cognition: The structures and development of mental representations of spatial relations* (pp. 164–181). Hillsdale, NJ: Erlbaum.

Rubens, W. S. (1981). Sex and violence on television. *Journal of Advertising Research, 21*(6), 13–20.

Rubin, A. M. (1983). Television uses and gratifications: The interactions of viewing patterns and motivations. *Journal of Broadcasting, 27*(1), 37–51.

Rubin, A. M. (1984). Ritualized and instrumental television viewing. *Journal of Communication, 34*(3), 67–77.

Rubin, B. (1967). *Political television.* Belmont, CA: Wadsworth.

Rubin, R. S. (1972). *An exploratory investigation of children's responses to commercial content of television advertising in relation to their stages of cognitive development.* Unpublished doctoral dissertation, University of Massachusetts, Amherst, MA.

Rudd, R., & Fish, M. J. (1989). Depth of issue coverage in television news: Campaign '84. *Journal of Broadcasting and Electronic Media, 33*(2), 197–202.

Runco, M., & Pezdek, K. (1984). The effect of television and radio on children's creativity. *Human Communication Research, 11*(1), 109–120.

Russo, F. D. (1971). A study of bias in TV coverage of the Vietnam War: 1969 and 1970. *Public Opinion Quarterly, 35*(4), 539–43.

Rutherford, P. (1995). *The new icons?: The art of television advertising.* Toronto, Canada: University of Toronto Press.

Rychtarik, R. G., Fairbank, J. A., Allen, C. M., Foy, D. W., & Drabman, R. S. (1983). Alcohol use in television programming: Effects on children's behavior. *Addictive Behaviors, 8*(1), 19–22.

Ryu, J. S. (1982). Public affairs and sensationalism in local TV news programs. *Journalism Quarterly, 59*(1), 74–79.

Salomon, G. (1979). *Interaction of media, cognition and learning.* San Francisco: Jossey-Bass.

Salomon, G. (1981a). *Communication and education: Social and psychological interactions.* Newbury Park, CA: Sage.

Salomon, G. (1981b). Introducing AIME: The assessment of children's mental involvement with television. In H. Kelly & H. Gardner (Eds.), *New directions for child development: Viewing children through television* (No. 13, pp. 89–102). San Francisco: Jossey-Bass.

Salomon, G. (1983a). Beyond the formats of television: The effects of student preconceptions on the experience of televiewing. In M. Meyer (Ed.), *Children and the formal features of television*. Munich, Germany: K. G. Saur.

Salomon, G. (1983b). Television watching and mental effort: A social psychological view. In J. Bryant & D. R. Anderson (Eds.), *Children's understanding of television: Research on attention and comprehension* (pp. 181–198). New York: Academic Press.

Salomon, G. (1984). Television is "easy" and print is "tough": The differential investment of mental effort in learning as a function of perceptions and attributions. *Journal of Educational Psychology, 76*(4), 647–658.

Salomon, G., & Leigh, T. (1984). Predispositions about learning from print and television. *Journal of Communication, 34*(2), 119–135.

Sapolsky, B. S., & Tabarlet, J. O. (1991). Sex in primetime television: 1979 versus 1989. *Journal of Broadcasting and Electronic Media, 35*(4), 505–516.

Schallow, J. R., & McIlwraith, R. D. (1986–87). Is television viewing really bad for your imagination?: Content and process of TV viewing and imaginal styles. *Imagination, Cognition and Personality, 6*(1), 25–42.

Scharrer, E. (1998). *Men, muscles, and machismo: The relationship between exposure to television violence and antisocial outcomes in the presence of hypermasculinity.* Unpublished doctoral dissertation, Syracuse University, Syracuse, NY.

Schneider, F. P. (1985). *The substance and structure of network television news: An analysis of content features, format features, and formal features.* Unpublished doctoral dissertation, Syracuse University, Syracuse, NY.

Schoenbach, K. (1991). Agenda-setting effects of print and television in West Germany. In D. L. Protess & M. E. McCombs (Eds.), *Agenda-setting: Readings on media, public opinion, and policymaking* (pp. 127–129). Hillsdale, NJ: Erlbaum.

Schor, J. (1991). *The overworked American.* New York: Basic Books.

Schram, S. F. (1991). The post-modern presidency and the grammar of electronic engineering. *Critical Studies in Mass Communication, 8*(2), 210–216.

Schramm, W., Lyle, J., & Parker, E. B. (1961). *Television in the lives of our children.* Stanford, CA: Stanford University Press.

Schudson, M. (1992). *Watergate in American memory: How we remember, forget, and reconstruct the past.* New York: Basic Books.

Scott, D. K., & Gobetz, R. H. (1992). Hard news/soft news content of the national broadcast networks, 1972–1987. *Journalism Quarterly, 69*(2), 406–412.

Scott, R. K., & Goff, D. H. (1988). How excitation from prior programming affects television news recall. *Journalism Quarterly, 65*(3), 615–620.

Sears, D. O., & Chaffee, S. H. (1979). Uses and effects of the 1976 debates: An overview of empirical studies. In S. Kraus (Ed.), *The great debates: Carter vs. Ford, 1976.* Bloomington: Indiana University Press.

Seidman, S. A. (1992). An investigation of sex-role stereotyping in music videos. *Journal of Broadcasting and Electronic Media, 36*(2), 209–216.

Selnow, G. W. (1986). Solving problems on prime-time television. *Journal of Communication, 36*(2), 63–72.

Selnow, G., & Bettinghaus, E. (1982). Television exposure and language development. *Journal of Broadcasting, 26*(1), 469–479.

Semetko, H. A., Blumler, J. G., Gurevitch, M., & Weaver, D. H. (1991). *The formation of campaign agendas: A comparative analysis of party and media roles in recent American and British elections.* Hillsdale, NJ: Erlbaum.

Sharbutt, J. (1988, October 8). Second debate comes in second. *Los Angeles Times,* Part 6, p. 8.

Shaw, D., & Martin, S. (1992). The function of mass media agenda-setting. *Journalism Quarterly, 69*(4), 902–920.

Sheckels, T. F., Jr. (1994). Mikulski vs. Chavez for the Senate from Maryland in 1986 and the "rules" for attack politics. *Communication Quarterly, 42*(3), 311–326.

Sheehan, P. W. (1987). Coping with exposure to aggression: The path from research to practice. *Australian Psychologist, 22*(3), 291–311.

Shelley, M. C., II, & Hwang, H. D. (1991). The mass media and public opinion polls in the 1988 presidential election: Trends, accuracy, consistency, and events. *American Politics Quarterly, 19*(1), 59–79.

Sherman, B. L., & Dominick, J. R. (1986). Violence and sex in music videos: TV and rock'n'roll. *Journal of Communication, 36*(1), 79–93.

Shields, S. A., & MacDowell, K. A. (1987). "Appropriate" emotion in politics: Judgments of a televised debate. *Journal of Communication, 37*(2), 78–89.

Shoemaker, P. J., Chang, T. K., & Brendlinger, N. (1987). Deviance as a predictor of newsworthiness: Coverage of international events in the U.S. media. In M. McLaughlin (Ed.), *Communication yearbook 10* (pp. 348–365). Newbury Park, CA: Sage.

Shoemaker, P. J., Danielian, L., & Brendlinger, N. (1991). Deviant acts, risky business, and U.S. interests: The newsworthiness of world events. *Journalism Quarterly, 68*(4), 781–795.

Shyles, L. (1984). The relationships of images, issues and presentational methods in televised spot advertisements for 1980's American presidential primaries. *Journal of Broadcasting, 28*(4), 405–421.

Sidney, S., Sternfeld, B., Haskell, W. L., Jacobs, D. R., Chesney, M. A., & Hulley, S. B. (1998). Television viewing and cardiovascular risk factors in young adults: The CARDIA study. *Annals of Epidemiology, 6*(2), 154–159.

Sigelman, L., & Bullock, D. (1991). Candidates, issues, horse races, and hoopla: Presidential campaign coverage, 1888–1988. *American Politics Quarterly, 19*(1), 5–32.

Signorielli, N. (1989). Television and conceptions about sex roles: Maintaining conventionality and the status quo. *Sex Roles, 21*(5/6), 341–360.

Signorielli, N. (1990). Television's mean and dangerous world: A continuation of the cultural indicators perspective. In N. Signorielli & M. Morgan (Eds.), *Cultivation analysis: New directions in media effects research* (pp. 85–106). Newbury Park, CA: Sage.

Signorielli, N., Gross, L., & Morgan, M. (1982). Violence in television programs: Ten years later. In D. Pearl, L. Bouthilet, & J. Lazar (Eds.), *Television and behavior: Ten years of scientific progress and implications for the eighties. Technical reviews* (Vol. 2, pp. 158–173). Washington, DC: U.S. Government Printing Office.

Signorielli, N., McLeod, D., & Healy, E. (1994). Gender stereotypes in MTV commercials: The beat goes on. *Journal of Broadcasting and Electronic Media, 38*(1), 91–101.

Silvern, S. B., & Williamson, P. A. (1987). The effects of video game play on young children's aggression, fantasy, and prosocial behavior. *Journal of Applied Developmental Psychology, 8*(4), 453–462.

Simon, A. F. (1997). Television news and international earthquake relief. *Journal of Communication, 47*(3), 82–95.

Simon, D. M., & Ostrom, C. W., Jr. (1989). The impact of televised speeches and foreign travel on presidential approval. *Public Opinion Quarterly, 53*(1), 58–82.

Simon, J. (1996). Media use and voter turnout in a presidential election. *Newspaper Research Journal, 17*(1/2), 25–34.

Simon, J., & Merrill, B. D. (1997). The next generation of news consumers: Children's news media choices in an election campaign. *Political Communication, 14*(3), 307–321.

Simons, H. W., & Leibowitz, K. (1979). Shifts in candidate images. In S. Kraus (Ed.), *The great debates: Carter vs. Ford, 1976* (pp. 398–404). Bloomington: Indiana University Press.

Sims, J. B. (1989). VCR viewing patterns: An electronic and passive investigation. *Journal of Advertising Research, 29*(2), 11–17.

Singer, B. D. (1972). Violence, protest and war in television news: The US and Canada compared. *Public Opinion Quarterly, 34*(4), 611–616.

Singer, D. G., & Singer, J. L. (1980). Television viewing and aggressive behavior in preschool children: A field study. *Annals of the New York Academy of Sciences, 347,* 289–303.

Singer, E., & Endreny, P. M. (1987). Reporting hazards: Their benefits and costs. *Journal of Communication, 37*(3), 10–26.

Singer, E., Endreny, P., & Glassman, M. B. (1991). Media coverage of disasters: Effect of geographic location. *Journalism Quarterly, 68*(1/2), 48–58.

Singer, J. L., & Singer, D. G. (1981) *Television, imagination, and aggression: A study of preschoolers.* Hillsdale, NJ: Erlbaum.

Singer, J. L., & Singer, D. G. (1987). Some hazards of growing up in a television environment: Children's aggression and restlessness. In S. Oskamp (Ed.), *Television as a social issue. Applied psychology manual* (Vol. 8, pp. 172–188). Newbury Park, CA: Sage.

Singer, J. L., Singer, D. G., Desmond, R., Hirsch, R., & Nicol, A. (1988). Family mediation and children's cognition, aggression, and comprehension of television: A longitudinal study. *Journal of Applied Developmental Psychology, 9*(3), 329–347.

Singer, J. L., Singer, D. G., & Rapaczynski, W. S. (1984). Family patterns and television viewing as predictors of children's beliefs and aggression. *Journal of Communication, 34*(2), 73–89.

Singh, S. N., Mishra, S., Bendapudi, N., & Linville, D. (1994). Enhancing memory of television commercials through message spacing. *Journal of Marketing Research, 31*(3), 384–392.

Skill, T., & Robinson, J. D. (1994). Four decades of families on television: A demographic profile, 1950–1989. *Journal of Broadcasting and Electronic Media, 38*(4), 449–464.

Skill, T., & Wallace, S. (1990). Family interactions on primetime television: A descriptive analysis of assertive power interactions. *Journal of Broadcasting and Electronic Media, 34*(3), 243–262.

Skinner, M., & Mullen, B. (1991). Facial asymmetry in emotional expression: A meta-analysis of research. *British Journal of Social Psychology, 30*(2), 113.

Slater, M. D., Rouner, D., Domenech-Rodriguez, M., Beavais, F., Murphy, K., & Van Leuven, J. K. (1997). Adolescent responses to TV beer ads and sports content/context: Gender and ethnic differences. *Journalism and Mass Communication Quarterly,* 74(1), 108–122.

Slattery, K. L., & Hakanen, E. A. (1994). Sensationalism versus public affairs content of local TV news: Pennsylvania revisited. *Journal of Broadcasting and Electronic Media,* 38(2), 205–216.

Slattery, K., & Tiedge, J. T. (1992). The effect of labeling staged video on the credibility of TV news stories. *Journal of Broadcasting and Electronic Media,* 36(2), 279–286.

Slife, B. D., & Rychiak, J. F. (1982). Role of affective assessment in modeling behavior. *Journal of Personality and Social Psychology,* 43(4), 861–868.

Smith, C. (1988). Profile of local television reporters and photographers. *Journalism Quarterly,* 65(2), 181–185.

Smith, C. (1989). News critics, newsworkers, and local television news. *Journalism Quarterly,* 66(1), 341–346.

Smith, K. A., & Ferguson, D. A. (1990). Voter partisan orientations and use of political television. *Journalism Quarterly,* 67(4), 864–874.

Smith, L. D., & Golden, J. L. (1988). Electronic storytelling in electoral politics: An anecdotal analysis of television advertising in the Helms-Hunt Senate race. *Southern Speech Communication Journal,* 53(3), 244–258.

Smith, S. A., & Roden, C. D. (1988). CBS, *The New York Times,* and reconstructed political reality. *Southern Speech Communication Journal,* 53(2), 140–158.

Smith, T. J., Lichter, S. R., Harris, L., & Associates. (1997). *What the people want from the press.* Washington, DC: Center for Media and Public Affairs.

Smoller, F. (1988). Presidents and their critics: The structure of television news coverage. *Congress and The Presidency,* 15(1), 75–89.

Smythe, D. W. (1954). Reality as presented by television. *Public Opinion Quarterly,* 18(2), 143–156.

Sniderman, P. M. (1972). *A question of loyalty.* Berkeley: University of California Press.

Solomon, M. R., & Greenberg, L. (1993). Setting the stage: Collective selection in the stylistic context of commercials. *Journal of Advertising,* 22(1), 11–21.

Sommers-Flanagan, R., Sommers-Flanagan, J., & Davis, B. (1993). What's happening on music television? A gender role content analysis. *Sex Roles,* 28(11/12), 745–753.

Son, J., & McCombs, M. E. (1993). A look at the constancy principle under changing market conditions. *Journal of Media Economics,* 6(2), 23–36.

Soong, R. (1988). The statistical reliability of people meter ratings. *Journal of Advertising Research,* 28(1), 50–56.

Speck, P. S., & Elliott, M. T. (1997). Predictors of advertising avoidance in print and broadcast media. *Journal of Advertising,* 26(3), 61–76.

Spencer, J. W., Seydlitz, R., Laska, S., & Triche, E. (1992). The different influences of newspaper and television news reports of a natural hazard on response behavior. *Communication Research,* 19(3), 299–325.

Sprafkin, J. N., & Liebert, R. M. (1978). Sex-typing and children's preferences. In G. Tuchman, A. K. Daniels, & J. Benet (Eds.), *Hearth and home: Images of women in the mass media* (pp. 288–339). New York: Oxford University Press.

Squire, P. (1988). Who gets national news coverage in the U.S. Senate? *American Politics Quarterly,* 16(2), 139–156.

Sreberny-Mohammadi, A. (1984). The "World of the News" study: Results of international co-operation. *Journal of Communication, 34*(1), 121–133.

Stamm, K., Johnson, M., & Martin, B. (1997). Differences among newspapers, television, and radio in their contribution to knowledge of the Contract with America. *Journalism and Mass Communication Quarterly, 74*(4), 687–702.

Stayman, D. M., Aaker, D. A., & Bruzzone, D. E. (1989). The incidence of commercial types broadcast in prime time: 1976–1986. *Journal of Advertising Research, 29*(3), 26–33.

Steele, C. A., & Barnhurst, K. G. (1996). The journalism of opinion: Network news coverage of U.S. presidential campaigns, 1968–1988. *Critical Studies in Mass Communication, 13*(3), 187–209.

Steiner, G. A. (1963). *The people look at television.* New York: Knopf.

Stempel, G. H., III. (1988). Topic and story choice of five network newscasts. *Journalism Quarterly, 65*(3), 750–752.

Stephens, M., & Edison, N. G. (1982). News media coverage of issues during the accident at Three Mile Island. *Journalism Quarterly, 59*(2), 199–204, 259.

Stern, S. L. (1973). *Television and creativity: The effect of viewing certain categories of commercial television broadcasting on the divergent thinking abilities of intellectual gifted elementary students.* Unpublished doctoral dissertation, University of Southern California.

Stern, B. L., & Resnik, A. J. (1991, June/July). Information content in television advertising: A replication and extension. *Journal of Advertising Research,* 36–46.

Steuer, F. B., Applefield, J. M., & Smith, R. (1971). Televised aggression and interpersonal aggression of preschool children. *Journal of Experimental Child Psychology, 11,* 442–447.

Stevenson, R. L., Eisinger, R. A., Feinberg, B. M., & Kotok, A. B. (1973). Untwisting the news twisters: A replication of Efron's study. *Journalism Quarterly, 50*(2), 211–219.

Stewart, D. W., Farmer, K. M., & Stannard, C. I. (1990, August/September). Music as a recognition cue in advertising-tracking studies. *Journal of Advertising Research,* 39–48.

Stewart, D. W., & Furse, D. H. (1986). *Effective television advertising: A study of 1000 commercials.* Lexington, MA: Lexington Books.

Stewart, D. W., & Koslow, S. (1989). Executional factors and advertising effectiveness: A replication. *Journal of Advertising, 18*(3), 21–32.

Stipp, H. (1992). Crisis in advertising. *Marketing Research, 4*(1), 39–46.

Stone, G. C., & Grusin, E. (1984). Network TV as the bad news bearer. *Journalism Quarterly, 61*(3), 517–523, 592.

Stone, G., Hartung, B., & Jensen, D. (1987). Local television news and the good-bad dyad. *Journalism Quarterly, 64*(1), 37–44.

Stone, V. (1995). *Minorities and women in television news.* (On-line). http://www.missouri.edu/~jourvs/gtvminw.html

Stone, V. A. (1988). Trends in the status of minorities and women in broadcast news. *Journalism Quarterly, 65*(2), 288–293.

Strand, P. J., Dozier, D. M., Hofstetter, C. R., & Ledingham, J. D. (1983). Campaign messages, media usage, and types of voters. *Public Relations Review, 9*(4), 53–63.

Strasburger, V. C. (1995). *Adolescents and the media: Medical and psychological impact.* Newbury Park, CA: Sage.

Strickland, D. E. (1983). Advertising exposure, alcohol consumption and misuse of alcohol. In M. Grant, M. Plant, & A. Williams (Eds.), *Economics and alcohol: Consumption and controls* (pp. 201–222). New York: Gardner Press.

Stutts, M. A., & Hunnicutt, G. G. (1987). Can young children understand disclaimers in television commercials? *Journal of Advertising, 16*(1), 41–46.

Sullivan, D. G., & Masters, R. D. (1988). "Happy Warriors": Leaders' facial displays, viewers emotions, and political support. *American Journal of Political Science, 32*(2), 345–368.

Swerdlow, J. (1981). What is television doing to real people? *Today's Education, 70*(1), 50–57.

Synodinos, N. E. (1988). Subliminal stimulation: What does the public think about it? *Current Issues and Research in Advertising, 11*(1/2), 157–187.

Szalai, A. (Ed.). (1972). *The use of time: Daily activities of urban and suburban populations in twelve countries.* The Hague, Netherlands: Mouton.

Sztompka, P. (1996). Introduction. In P. Sztompka (Ed.), *Robert K. Merton: On Social Structure and Science* (pp. 1–20). Chicago: University of Chicago Press.

Takeshita, T. (1997). Exploring the media's roles in defining reality: From issue-agenda setting to attribute-agenda setting. In M. McCombs, D. L. Shaw, & D. Weaver (Eds.), *Communication and democracy: Exploring the intellectual frontiers in agenda-setting theory* (pp. 15–27). Mahwah, NJ: Erlbaum.

Tannenbaum, P. H., & Kostrich, L. J. (1983). *Turned-on TV/Turned-off voters.* Beverly Hills, CA: Sage.

Tannenbaum, P. H., & Zillmann, D. (1975). Emotional arousal in the facilitation of aggression through communication. In L. Berkowitz (Ed.), *Advances in experimental social psychology* (Vol. 8, pp. 149–192). New York: Academic Press.

Television Bureau of Advertising. (1997). *Trends in television.* New York: Author.

Tellis, G. J. (1997). Effective frequency: One exposure or three factors? *Journal of Advertising Research, 37*(4), 75–80.

Thayer, F., & Pasternack, S. (1992). Testing viewer perception of a foreign television-news source: Attitudes toward direct vs. translator presentation. *International Communication Bulletin, 27*(1/2), 32–35.

Thomas, G. P., & Soldow, G. F. (1988). Nonverbal behavior in television advertising: How forceful is a forceful actor? *Current Issues and Research in Advertising, 11*(1/2), 75–88.

Thomas, M. H. (1982). Physiological arousal, exposure to a relatively lengthy aggressive film, and aggressive behavior. *Journal of Research in Personality, 16*(1), 72–81.

Thomas, M. H., Horton, R. W., Lippencott, E. C., & Drabman, R. S. (1977). Desensitization to portrayals of real-life aggression as a function of exposure to television violence. *Journal of Personality and Social Psychology, 35*, 450–458.

Thornton, W, & Voigt, L. (1984). Television and delinquency. *Youth and Society, 15*(4), 445–468.

Thorson, E., Christ, W. G., & Caywood, C. (1991). Effects of issues-image strategies, attack and support appeals, music, and visual content in political commercials. *Journal of Broadcasting and Electronic Media, 35*(4), 465–486.

Tichenor, P. J., Donohue, C. A., & Olien, C. N. (1970). Mass media flow and differential growth of knowledge. *Public Opinion Quarterly, 34*(2), 159–170.

Tiemens, R. K., Sillars, M. O., Alexander, D. C., & Werling, D. (1988). Television coverage of Jesse Jackson's speech to the 1984 democratic national convention. *Journal of Broadcasting and Electronic Media, 32*(1), 1–22.

Timmer, S. G., Eccles, J., & O'Brien, K. (1985). How children use time. In F. T. Juster & F. P. Stafford (Eds.), *Time, goods, and well-being* (pp. 353–382). Ann Arbor: Institute for Social Research, University of Michigan.

Tinkham, S. F., & Weaver-Lariscy, R. A. (1990). Advertising message strategy in U.S. congressional campaigns: Its impact on election outcome. *Journal of Current Issues and Research in Advertising, 13*(1/2), 207–226.

Tinkham, S. F., & Weaver-Lariscy, R. A. (1993). A diagnostic approach to assessing the impact of negative political television commercials. *Journal of Broadcasting and Electronic Media, 37*(4), 377–400.

Tinkham, S. F., & Weaver-Lariscy, R. A. (1994). Ethical judgments of political television commercials as predictors of attitude toward the ad. *Journal of Advertising, 23*(3), 43–57.

Tinkham, S. F., & Weaver-Lariscy, R. A. (1995). Incumbency and its perceived advantage: A comparison of 1982 and 1990 congressional advertising strategies. *Political Communication, 12*(3), 291–304.

Tinkham, S. F., & Weaver-Lariscy, R. A. (1996). *The role of research in political campaigns: US Congressional races, 1982, 1990.* Paper presented at the annual meeting of the International Communication Association, Chicago, IL.

Tolley, H., Jr. (1973). *Children and war: Political socialization to international conflict.* New York: Teachers College Press, Columbia University.

Tower, R., Singer, D., Singer, J., & Biggs, A. (1979). Differential effects of television programming on preschoolers' cognition, imagination and social play. *American Journal of Orthopsychiatry, 49*(2), 265–281.

Trent, J. S., & Sabourin, T. (1993). Sex still counts: Women's use of televised advertising during the decade of the '80s. *Journal of Applied Communication Research, 21*(1), 21–40.

Trumbo, C. (1995). Longitudinal modeling of public issues: An application of the agenda-setting process to global warming. *Journalism Monographs, 57.*

Tuchman, G. (1973). Making news by doing work: Routinizing the unexpected. *American Journal of Sociology, 79*(1), 110–131.

Tuchman, G. (1978). *Making news: A study in the construction of reality.* New York: Free Press.

Tuchman, S., & Coffin, T. E. (1971). The influence of election night television broadcasts in a close election. *Public Opinion Quarterly, 35*(3), 315–326.

Tucker, L. A. (1985). Television's role regarding alcohol use among teenagers. *Adolescence, 20*(79), 593–598.

Tucker, L. A. (1986). The relationship of television viewing to physical fitness and obesity. *Adolescence, 21*(84), 797–806.

Tucker, L. A. (1987). Television, teenagers, and health. *Journal of Youth and Adolescence, 16*(5), 415–425.

Tukey, J. W. (1977). *Exploratory data analysis.* Reading, MA: Addison-Wesley.

Turner, C. W., & Berkowitz, L. (1972). Identification with film aggressor (covert role taking) and reactions to film violence. *Journal of Personality and Social Psychology, 21*(2), 256–264.

Turow, J. (1989). *Playing doctor: Television, storytelling, and medical power.* New York: Oxford University Press.

Tyler, T. R. (1978). *Drawing inferences from experiences: The effect of crime victimization experiences upon crime-related attitudes and behaviors.* Unpublished doctoral dissertation, University of California, Los Angeles, CA.

Tyler, T. R. (1980). The impact of directly and indirectly experienced events. The origin of crime-related judgments and behaviors. *Journal of Personality and Social Psychology, 39*(1), 13–28.

Tyler, T. R. (1984). Assessing the risk of crime victimization: The integration of personal victimization experience and socially-transmitted information. *Journal of Social Issues, 40*(1), 27–38.

Tyler, T. R., & Cook, F. L. (1984). The mass media and judgments of risk: Distinguishing impact on personal and societal level judgments. *Journal of Personality and Social Psychology, 47*(4), 693–708.

Tyndall, A. (1998). What goes on the networks? The O.J. Simpson trial dominated recent coverage of the courts. *Media Studies Journal* (1), 54–59.

U.S. Bureau of the Census. (1997). *Statistical Abstract of the United States: 1997* (117th ed.). Washington, DC: Author.

Valkenburg, P. M., & Beentjies, W. J. (1997). Children's creative imagination in response to radio and television stories. *Journal of Communication, 47*(2), 21–38.

Valkenburg, P. M., & van der Voort, T. H. A. (1994). Influence of TV on daydreaming and creative imagination: A review of research. *Psychological Bulletin, 116*(2), 316–339.

Valkenburg, P. M., & van der Voort, T. H. A. (1995). The influence of television on children's daydreaming styles: A one-year panel study. *Communication Research, 22*(3), 267–287.

Valkenburg, P. M., Voojis, M. W., van der Voort, T. H. A., & Wiegman, O. (1992). The influence of television on children's fantasy styles: A secondary analysis. *Imagination, Cognition and Personality, 12,* 55–67.

Vallone, R., Ross, L., & Lepper, M. (1985). The hostile media phenomenon: Biased perception and perceptions of media bias in coverage of the Beirut massacre. *Journal of Personality and Social Psychology, 49*(3), 577–585.

Vande Berg, L. R., & Streckfuss, D. (1992). Prime-time television's portrayal of women and the world of work: A demographic profile. *Journal of Broadcasting and Electronic Media, 36*(2), 195–208.

van der Voort, T. H. A., & Valkenburg, P. M. (1994). Television's impact on fantasy play: A review of research. *Developmental Review, 14*(1), 27–51.

Van Evra, J. (1998). *Television and child development* (2nd ed). Mahwah, NJ: Erlbaum.

Vibbert, M. M., & Meringoff, L. K. (1981). *Children's production and application of story imagery: A cross-medium investigation.* Cambridge, MA; Harvard University Press.

Viemero, V., & Paajanen, S. (1992). The role of fantasies and dreams in the TV viewing–aggression relationship. *Aggressive Behavior, 18*(2), 109–116.

Vincent, R. C. (1989). Clio's consciousness raised? Portrayal of women in rock videos, reexamined. *Journalism Quarterly, 66*(1), 155–160.

Vincent, R. C., & Basil, M. D. (1997). College students' news gratifications, media use, and current events knowledge. *Journal of Broadcasting and Electronic Media, 41*(3), 380–392.

Vincent, R. C., Davis, D. K., & Boruszkowski, L. A. (1987). Sexism on MTV: The portrayal of women in rock videos. *Journalism Quarterly, 64*(4), 750–755, 941.

Wade, S. E. (1971). Adolescents, creativity, and media: An exploratory study. *American Behavioral Scientist, 14*(3), 341–351.

Wadsworth, A. J., Patterson, P., Kaid, L. L., Cullers, G., Malcomb, D., & Lamirand, L. (1987). "Masculine" vs. "feminine" strategies in political advertisements: Implications for female candidates. *Journal of Applied Communication Research, 15*(1/2), 77–94.

Wafai, M. (1989). Senators' television visibility and political legitimacy. *Journalism Quarterly, 66*(2), 323–331.

Wakshlag, J. J., Agostino, D. E., Terry, H. A., Driscoll, P., & Ramsey, B. (1983). Television news viewing and network affiliation changes. *Journal of Broadcasting, 27*(1), 53–68.

Walker, D., & Dubitsky, T. M. (1994). Why liking matters. *Journal of Advertising Research, 34*(3), 9–18.

Walker, J. R., & Bellamy, R. V. (Eds.). (1993). *The remote control in the new age of television.* Westport, CT: Praeger.

Wallack, L., Grube, J. W., Madden, P. A., & Breed, W. (1990). Portrayals of alcohol on prime-time television. *Journal of Studies on Alcohol, 51*(5), 428–437.

Walters, L. M., & Hornig, S. (1993). Faces in the news: Network television news coverage of Hurricane Hugo and the Loma Prieta earthquake. *Journal of Broadcasting and Electronic Media, 37*(2), 219–232.

Wanta, W. (1992). The influence of the president on the news media and public agendas. *Mass Communication Review, 19*(1/2), 14–21.

Wanta, W. (1997a). *The public and the national agenda: How people learn about important issues.* Mahwah, NJ: Erlbaum.

Wanta, W. (1997b). The messenger and the message: Differences across news media. In M. McCombs, D. L. Shaw, & D. Weaver (Eds.), *Communication and democracy: Exploring the intellectual frontiers in agenda-setting theory* (pp. 137–151). Mahwah, NJ: Erlbaum.

Wanta, W., & Foote, J. (1994). The president-news media relationship: A time series analysis of agenda setting. *Journal of Broadcasting and Electronic Media, 38*(4), 437–448.

Wanta, W., & Hu, Y. W. (1994). The effects of credibility, reliance, and exposure on media agenda-setting: A path analysis. *Journalism Quarterly, 71*(1), 99–109.

Wanta, W. Lemert, J. B., & Lee, T. (1997). *Consequences of negative political advertising exposure.* Paper presented at the annual meeting of the Association for Education in Journalism and Mass Communication, Chicago, IL.

Wartella, E., Heintz, K. E., Aidman, A. J., & Mazzarella, S. R. (1990). Television and beyond: Children's video media in one community. *Communication Research, 17*(1), 45–64.

Waterman, D. (1986). The failure of cultural programming on cable TV: An economic interpretation. *Journal of Communication, 36*(3), 92–108.

Watkins, B. (1988). Children's representations of television and real-life stories. *Communication Research, 15*(2), 159–184.

Weaver, D. H. (1977). Political issues and voter need for orientation. In D. L. Shaw & M. E. McCombs (Eds.), *The emergence of American political issues: The agenda-setting function of the press* (pp. 107–119). St. Paul, MN: West.

Weaver, D. H. (1984). Media agenda-setting and public opinion: Is there a link? In R. N. Bostrom (Ed.), *Communication yearbook 8* (pp. 680–691). Beverly Hills, CA: Sage.

Weaver, D. H. (1996). What voters learn from media. *Annals of the American Academy of Political and Social Science, 546,* 34–47.

Weaver, D., & Drew, D. (1995). Voter learning in the 1992 presidential election: Did the "nontraditional" media and debates matter? *Journalism and Mass Communication Quarterly, 72*(1), 7–17.

Weaver, D., Graber, D., McCombs, M., & Eyal, C. (1981). *Media agenda-setting in a presidential election: Issues, images and interest.* New York: Praeger.

Weaver, D. H., & Wilhoit, G. C. (1986). *The American journalist: A portrait of US newspeople and their work.* Bloomington: Indiana University Press.

Weaver, D. H., & Wilhoit, G. C. (1992, November 12). *The American journalist in the 1900s.* Preliminary report released at the Freedom Forum World Center, Arlington, VA.

Weaver, J. B., Porter, C. J., & Evans, M. E. (1984). Patterns of foreign news coverage on U.S. network TV: A 10-year analysis. *Journalism Quarterly, 61*(2), 356–363.

Weaver-Lariscy, R. A., & Tinkham, S. F. (1991). News coverage, endorsements and personal campaigning: The influence of non-paid activities in Congressional elections. *Journalism Quarterly, 68*(3), 432–444.

Webster, J. G., & Lichty, L. W. (1991). *Ratings analysis.* Hillsdale, NJ: Erlbaum.

Webster, J. G., & Newton, G. D. (1988). Structural determinants of the television news audience. *Journal of Broadcasting and Electronic Media, 32*(4), 381–389.

Webster, J. G., & Phalen, P. F. (1997). *The mass audience: Rediscovering the dominant model.* Mahwah, NJ: Erlbaum.

Wei, R. (1993). Earthquake prediction: Did the news media make a difference? *Mass Communication Review, 20*(1/2), 111–121.

Weimann, G., & Brosius, H. B. (1991). The newsworthiness of international terrorism. *Communication Research, 18*(3), 333–354.

Weir, W. (1984, October 15). Another look at subliminal "facts." *Advertising Age.*

Weiss, A. J., & Wilson, B. J. (1996). Emotional portrayals in family television series that are popular among children. *Journal of Broadcasting and Electronic Media, 40*(1), 1–29.

Weiss, W. (1969). Effects of the mass media of communication. In G. Lindzey & E. Aronson (Eds.), *The handbook of social psychology. Applied Social Psychology* (2nd ed.) (Vol. 5, pp. 77–195). Reading, MA: Addison-Wesley.

Wells, W. D. (1973). *Television and aggression: Replication of an experimental field study.* Unpublished manuscript, Graduate School of Business, University of Chicago, Chicago, IL.

Wertham, F. (1954). *Seduction of the innocent.* New York: Rinehart.

West, D. M. (1991). Television and presidential popularity in America. *British Journal of Political Science, 21*(2), 199–214.

West, D. M., Kern, M., Alger, D., & Goggin, J. M. (1995). Ad buys in presidential campaigns: The strategies of electoral appeal. *Political Communication, 12*(3), 275–290.

White, D. M. (1940). The "gate-keeper": A case study in the selection of news. *Journalism Quarterly, 27*(4), 383–390.

Wiegman, O., Kuttschreuter, M., & Baarda, B. (1986). *Television viewing related to aggressive and prosocial behavior.* Enschede, Netherlands: Stitchting voor Orderzoek can het Onderwijs, Foundation for Educational Research in the Netherlands (SVO) and Department of Psychology, Technical University of Enschede (THT).

Wilhoit, G. C., & Sherrill, K. S. (1968). Wire service visibility of US Senators. *Journalism Quarterly, 45*(1), 42–48.

Williams, F., Phillips, A., & Lum, P. (1985). Gratifications associated with new communication technologies. In K. Rosengren, L. Wenner, & P. Palmgren (Eds.), *Media gratifications research: Current perspectives* (pp. 241–254). Beverly Hills, CA: Sage.

Williams, T. M. (Ed.). (1986). *The impact of television: A natural experiment in three communities.* New York: Praeger.

Williams, W., Jr., Shapiro, M., & Cutbirth, C. (1983). The impact of campaign agendas on perceptions of issues in the 1980 campaign. *Journalism Quarterly, 60*(2), 226–231.

Willnat, L. (1997). Agenda setting and priming: Conceptual links and differences. In M. McCombs, D. L. Shaw, & D. Weaver (Eds.), *Communication and democracy: Exploring the intellectual frontiers in agenda-setting theory* (pp. 51–66). Mahwah, NJ: Erlbaum.

Wilson, C. E. (1974). The effect of medium on loss of information. *Journalism Quarterly, 51*(1), 111–115.

Windahl, S., Hojerback, I., & Hedinsson, E. (1986). Adolescents without television: A study in media deprivation. *Journal of Broadcasting and Electronic Media, 30*(1), 47–63.

Winick, C. (1988). The functions of television: Life without the big box. In S. Oskamp (Ed.), *Television as a social issue* (pp. 217–237). Newbury Park, CA: Sage.

Winn, M. (1977). *The plug-in drug.* New York: Viking Press.

Winston, B. (1986). *Misunderstanding media.* Cambridge, MA: Harvard University Press.

Winter, J. P., & Eyal, C. H. (1981). Agenda-setting for the civil rights issue. *Public Opinion Quarterly, 45*(3), 376–383.

Wolman, B. B. (1989). *Dictionary of behavioral science* (2nd ed.). New York: Academic Press.

Wonsek, P. L. (1992). College basketball on television: A study of racism in the media. *Media, Culture and Society, 14*(3), 449–461.

Wood, W., Wong, F., & Chachere, J. (1991). Effects of media violence on viewers' aggression in unconstrained social interaction. *Psychological Bulletin, 109*(3), 371–383.

Wood, W. C., & O'Hare, S. L. (1991). Paying for the video revolution: Consumer spending on the mass media. *Journal of Communication, 41*(1), 24–30.

Worchel, S., Hardy, T. W., & Hurley, R. (1976). The effects of commercial interruption of violent and nonviolent films on viewers' subsequent aggressiveness. *Journal of Experimental Psychology, 12*(2), 220–232.

Wright, C. R. (1960). Functional analysis and mass communication. *Public Opinion Quarterly, 24*(4), 605–620.

Wright, J. C., & Huston, A. C. (1995). *Effects of educational TV viewing of lower income preschoolers on academic skills, school readiness, and school adjustment one to three years later.* Technical report. Lawrence: University of Kansas.

Wulfemeyer, K. T. (1983). The interests and preferences of audience for local television news. *Journalism Quarterly, 60*(2), 323–328.

Wurtzel, A., & Lometti, G. (1984). Determining the acceptability of violent program content at ABC. *Journal of Broadcasting, 28*(1), 89–97.

Xiaoming, H. (1994). Television viewing among American adults in the 1990s. *Journal of Broadcasting and Electronic Media, 38*(3), 353–360.

Yang, N., & Linz, D. (1990). Movie ratings and the content of adult videos: The sex violence ratio. *Journal of Communication, 40*(2), 28–42.

Young, C. E., & Robinson, M. (1989). Video rhythms and recall. *Journal of Advertising Research, 29*(3), 22–25.

Young, C. E., & Robinson, M. (1992, March/April). Visual connectedness and persuasion. *Journal of Advertising Research,* 51–59.

Zanot, E. J. Pincus, J. D., & Lamp, E. J. (1983). Public perceptions of subliminal advertising. *Journal of Advertising, 12*(1), 39–45.

Zhao, X., & Bleske, G. L. (1995). Measurement effects in comparing voter learning from television news and campaign advertisements. *Journalism and Mass Communication Quarterly, 72*(1), 72–83.

Zhao, X., & Chaffee, S. H. (1995). Campaign advertisements versus television news as sources of political issue information. *Public Opinion Quarterly, 59*(1), 41–65.

Zhao, X., Shen, F., & Blake, K. (1995). *Position of TV advertisement in a natural pod—a preliminary analysis of concepts, measurements and effects.* Paper presented at the annual meeting of the American Academy of Advertising, Norfolk, VA.

Zhu, J., Milavsky, J. R., & Biswas, R. (1994). Do televised debates affect image perception more than issue knowledge? A study of the first 1992 presidential debate. *Human Communication Research, 20*(3), 302–333.

Zhu, J. H., & Boroson, W. (1997). Susceptibility to agenda setting: A cross-sectional and longitudinal analysis of individual differences. In M. McCombs, D. L. Shaw, & D. Weaver (Eds.), *Communication and democracy: Exploring the intellectual frontiers in agenda-setting theory* (pp. 69–83). Mahwah, NJ: Erlbaum.

Ziegler, D., & White, A. (1990). Women and minorities on network television news: An examination of correspondents and news makers. *Journal of Broadcasting and Electronic Media, 34*(2), 215–223.

Zill, N., Davies, E., & Daly, M. (1994). *Viewing of Sesame Street by preschool children in the United States and its relationship to school readiness.* Report prepared for Children's Television Workshop: Westat, Inc., Rockville, MD.

Zill, N., & Robinson, J. (1994). Name that tune. *American Demographics, 16*(8), 22–27.

Zillmann, D. (1971). Excitation transfer in communication-mediated aggressive behavior. *Journal of Experimental Social Psychology, 7*(4), 419–434.

Zillmann, D. (1982). Television viewing and arousal. In D. Pearl, L. Bouthilet, & J. Lazar (Eds.), *Television and behavior: Ten years of scientific inquiry and implications for the eighties. Technical reviews* (Vol. 2, pp. 53–67). Washington, DC: U.S. Government Printing Office.

Zillmann, D. (1988). Mood management: Using entertainment to full advantage. In L. Donohew, H. E. Sypher, & E. T. Higgins (Eds.), *Communication, social cognition, and affect* (pp. 147–171). Hillsdale, NJ: Erlbaum.

Zillmann, D. (1993). Mental control of angry aggression. In D. M. Wegner & J. W. Pennebaker (Eds.), *Handbook of mental control* (pp. 370–392). Englewood Cliffs, NJ: Prentice Hall.

Zillmann, D., & Bryant, J. (1985). Affect, mood, and emotion as determinants of selective media exposure. In D. Zillmann & J. Bryant (Eds.), *Selective exposure to communication* (pp. 157–190). Hillsdale, NJ: Erlbaum.

Zillmann, D., Hezel, R. T., & Medoff, N. J.(1980). The effect of affective states on selective exposure to televised entertainment fare. *Journal of Applied Social Psychology, 10*(4), 323–339.

Zillmann, D., Johnson, R. C., & Hanrahan, J. (1973). Pacifying effect of a happy ending of communications involving aggression. *Psychological Reports, 32*(3), 967–970.

Zuckerman, D. M., Singer, D. G., & Singer, J. L. (1980). Television viewing, children's reading, and related classroom behavior. *Journal of Communication, 30*(1), 166–174.

Zuckerman, P., & Gianinno, L. (1981). Measuring children's responses to television advertising. In J. Esserman (Ed.), *Television advertising and children: Issues, research and findings* (pp. 83–93). New York: Child Research Service.

Zufryden, F. S., Pedrick, J. H., & Sankaralingam, A. (1993). Zapping and its impact on brand purchase behavior. Special issue: The growing importance of media research. *Journal of Advertising Research, 33*(1), 58–66.

AUTHOR INDEX

The complete reference can be found on the page number(s) listed in *italics*.

SUBJECT INDEX

viewing (*continued*)
  by race/ethnicity, 80
  surveillance, 81–82
  TV newscasts, 143–144
  over life span, 91, 106
  paradox of indifference in, 61
  ritualistic vs. instrumental, 75–77
    division of time between, 90–91
  and scholastic achievement, 245–253
    by household educational resources, race, and
      gender, 249
  seasonal variations, 91
  time allocation to, 95
    consistency in, 85
    news coverage, 136
    and social interaction, 97
    vs. other recreational activities, 97–101, 99
  vs. monitoring, 84
violence
  audience for, 70–71
  and behavior in general, 298
    contingencies of effects, 300
    desensitization, 305, 307
    fearfulness, 306
    pessimism, 305–306
    theories, 299–300
  as catharsis, 277
  criteria for, 65
  depictions of, overall industry averages, 70
  in erotica, experiments, 301
  and impulse control, 255
  in mass media, historical patterns, 272–274
  media exposure, association with antisocial be-
    havior, 282
    among teenage males, 283
    correlations, 286
    dynamics, 302
    real-life relationship, 284–285
  on Music Television (MTV), 269–270
    by category, 270

portrayal of, and outcomes, 306
preference for entertainment with, and aggressive behavior, 292–293
susceptibility to influence of, 293–294
  gender differences, 294–295
  and household characteristics, 309
  vs. preference for violent entertainment, 293–
    294
trends
  in portrayal of, 62
  in programming, 64–71, 66
  on videos, 271–272
    by category, 271
voter behavior
  and exit polls, 177–178
  influence of political advertising, 168–169
  media influence on, 145–146, 212–213
    classic studies, 216
voting studies, pretelevision, 145

W
Warner Brothers Network, 15
Wechsler Intelligence Scale for Children, 228
Wertham, Frederic, 265
White, David Manning, 115
Wildmon, Daniel, 268
Winn, Marie, 263
World News (CNN), 126

Y
youth
  commercial viewing by, influence on alcohol
    and drug use, 56–58
  male, antisocial behavior and TV violence expo-
    sure, 283
  media exposure and political knowledge, 221
  suicides among, and media coverage, 290
  television news viewing, 219, 220–221
  in TV news audience, 136–137

DATE DUE